CANADIAN
ROCKIES
ACCESS GUIDE

CANADIAN
ROCKIES
ACCESS GUIDE

JOHN DODD

GAIL HELGASON

LONE
PINE

The Publisher: Lone Pine Publishing

10145 – 81 Ave.	202A, 1110 Seymour St.	1901 Raymond Ave. SW, Suite C
Edmonton, AB T6E 1W9	Vancouver, BC V6B 3N3	Renton, WA 98055
Canada	Canada	USA

Lone Pine Publishing web site:
http://www.lonepinepublishing.com

Canadian Cataloguing in Publication Data
Dodd, John, (date)
    The Canadian Rockies access guide

    Includes bibliographical references and index.
    ISBN 1-55105-176-1

    1. Trails—Rocky Mountains, Canadian (B.C. and Alta.)—
Guidebooks.* 2. Hiking—Rocky Mountains, Canadian (B.C.
and Alta.)—Guidebooks.* 3. Rocky Mountains, Canadian (B.C.
and Alta.)—Guidebooks.* I. Helgason, Gail (date) II. Title.
FC219.H45 1998   917.1104'4   C98-910347-1
F1090.H45 1998

Senior Editor: Nancy Foulds
Project Editor: Lee Craig
Technical Review: Parks Canada
Production Manager: David Dodge
Layout and Production: Michelle Bynoe
Book and Cover Design: Michelle Bynoe
Cover Photographs: Daryl Benson, Leslie and Mark Degner
Cartography: Volker Bodegom
Illustrations: Gary Ross, Ted Nordhagen, Horst Krause
Separations and Film: Elite Lithographers, Edmonton, Alberta, Canada

Photography: The photos in this book were taken by Leslie and Mark Degner, except for the following:
Courtesy of Banff/Lake Louise Tourism Bureau: 26, 28, 30, 34, 38, 49, 55, 57, 81, 345, 351, 365, 370, 381
Gail Helgason and John Dodd: 40, 66, 72, 86, 93, 95, 98, 105, 110, 115, 118, 124, 159, 180, 183, 185, 198, 269, 275, 281, 283, 285, 286, 287, 291, 293, 295, 297, 299, 316, 317, 328, 330, 334, 340, 346, 349, 351, 355, 357, 361, 378, 383, 400
The remaining photos were supplied courtesy of the following organizations and individuals: Banff Springs Hotel: 75; Don Beers: 242, 289; Brewster Transportation and Tours: 194; Canadian Rocky Mountain Resorts: 385; David Dodge: 145, 329, 343, 359; B. Falvey: 36, 151; Jasper Tourism and Commerce: 21, 190, 193, 196, 231; Jasper Park Lodge: 200, 203, 384; Hugh Lecky: 206, 267; Harvey Locke: 88, 106, 147, 176; The Lodge at Kananaskis: 271, 272, 276; Parks Canada: 314, 320, 322; Rocky Mountain Railtours: 14; White Mountain Adventures: 97, 101, 377; Yoho Burgess Shale Foundation: 168.

The publisher gratefully acknowledges the support of the Department of Canadian Heritage.

PC: P4

Acknowledgements

Many thanks to Parks Canada staff for providing information and checking this manuscript: Don Gorrie in Banff National Park, Jim Suttill and Wes Bradford in Jasper National Park, Pam Clark in Kootenay and Yoho national parks, Janice Smith at Waterton Lakes National Park and Ruth Oltmann at Kananaskis Country. Thanks as well to the Banff-Lake Louise Tourism Bureau, Jasper Tourism and Commerce and many others who provided insights, suggestions and photos. The authors especially appreciate the fine photography by Mark and Leslie Degner and the dedication of the Lone Pine team: Volker Bodegom, who produced the maps; designer Michelle Bynoe; project editor Lee Craig, production manager David Dodge, senior editor Nancy Foulds and publisher Shane Kennedy.

Contents

Lk Louise
or Sunshine
Grizzly LK
ELK ISLAND NP
16 KM

List of maps and legend . . .8 & 9
Introduction 11

Chapter 1: Banff National Park 23

Outdoor Adventures 28
Indoor and Rainy-Day Guide .40
Be Sensible about Bears 58

Banff: Townsite
1. Cave and Basin Marsh Trail 60
2. Discovery Trail 62
3. Sundance Canyon 65
4. Fenland Nature Trail 66
5. Vermilion Lakes 68
6. Sulphur Mountain Vista Trail 71
7. Tunnel Mountain 73
8. Tunnel Mountain Drive . .75
9. Banff to the Hoodoos 77
10. Central Park East 80
11. Central Park West 81
12. Bow Falls Trail 82
13. Spray River Loop 84

Banff: North of Townsite
14. Bankhead Historical Loop 86
15. Upper Bankhead 88
16. Stewart Canyon 89
17. Stoney Squaw Lookout . .91
18. Cascade Amphitheatre . . .92
19. Cory Pass 94
20. Rock Isle Lake 96
21. Bourgeau Lake 98
22. Johnston Canyon 100
23. Silverton Falls 102
24. Castle Mountain Lookout 104
25. Boom Lake Trail 106
26. Vista Lake 107
27. Taylor Lake Trail 109

Banff: Lake Louise
28. Moraine Lake Viewpoint 110
29. Moraine Lake Shoreline .111

30. Consolation Lakes 113
31. Eiffel Lake 114
32. Larch Valley 116
33. Sentinel Pass and
    Paradise Valley 118
34. Lakeshore Trail 120
35. Plain of Six Glaciers ...123
36. Fairview Mountain
    Lookout 125
37. Saddle Pass 127
38. Lake Agnes 129

39. Big Beehive Loop 131
40. Little Beehive 134
Banff: Icefields
41. Dolomite Pass 135
42. Bow Lake Trail 136
43. Peyto Lake Viewpoint ..138
44. Mistaya Canyon 141
45. Panther Falls and Bridal
    Veil Falls 143
46. Nigel Pass 145
47. Parker Ridge 146

Chapter 2: Kootenay National Park **149**

Outdoor Adventures/Indoor and
Rainy-Day Guide 150
48. Fireweed Trail 156

49. Stanley Glacier 158
50. Marble Canyon 160
51. Paint Pots 162

Chapter 3: Yoho National Park **165**

Outdoor Adventures/Indoor and
Rainy-Day Guide 167
52. Takakkaw Falls 172
53. Yoho Valley and Iceline ..174
54. Emerald Lake Circuit ...177

55. Hamilton Lake 178
56. Lake O'Hara Circuit ...180
57. Lake McArthur 182
58. Lake Oesa 185
59. Wapta Falls 186

Chapter 4: Jasper National Park **189**

Outdoor Adventures 192
Indoor and Rainy-Day Guide 202
Jasper Icefields
60. Wilcox Pass 208
61. Athabasca Glacier 211
62. Stanley Falls 214
63. Lower Sunwapta Falls ...216
64. Athabasca Falls 218
65. Horseshoe Lake 220
66. Wabasso Lake 221
67. Valley of the Five Lakes .223
68. Path of the Angel Glacier
    Trail 224
69. Angel Glacier–Cavell
    Meadows Loop 226
70. Tramway to Whistlers
    Summit 229

Jasper: Townsite
71. Old Fort Point Trail ...232
72. Lac Beauvert Loop 234
73. Along the Athabasca
    River 1 236
74. Along the Athabasca
    River 2 237
75. Along the Athabasca
    River 3 238
76. Lake Annette Loop 239
77. Lake Edith Loop 242
78. Overlander Trail 244
79. Jasper–Pyramid Lake Trail 247
80. Patricia Lake Loop 250
Jasper: East of Townsite
81. Maligne Canyon Loop ..253
82. Maligne Canyon to Sixth
    Bridge 255

6

83. Summit Lakes 257
84. Maligne Lakeside Loop   .259
85. Opal Hills Loop 262

86. Bald Hills 264
87. Miette Hot Springs Trail .266
88. Sulphur Summit 268

Chapter 5: Kananaskis Country 271

Outdoor Adventures 273
Indoor and Rainy-Day Guide 277
89. Ptarmigan Cirque 282
90. Mt. Indefatigable 284
91. 1982 Cdn. Mt. Everest
    Expedition Trail   ____286
92. Upper Kananaskis Lake   .287

93. Black Prince Cirque   . . .288
94. Many Springs 290
95. Grotto Canyon 292
96. Grassi Lakes 294
97. Chester Lake 297
98. Burstall Pass 299

Chapter 6: Waterton Lakes National Park 301

Outdoor Adventures 304
Indoor and Rainy-Day Guide 309
99. Lower Bertha Falls   . .314
100. Bear's Hump 316
101. Summit Lake–Carthew
     Summit 317

102. Rowe Lakes 319
103. Crandell Campground
     to Lake Crandell 321
104. Crypt Lake Trail 322
105. Red Rock Canyon Loop 324
106. Goat Lake 327

Chapter 7: A Detailed Guide to Outdoor Activities   . .330

Backcountry Huts 330
Backcountry Lodges 332
Backpacking in the
Canadian Rockies 334
Boating and Lake Canoeing .340
Camping 341
Canoeing the Easy Rivers   . .344

Cycling and Mountain Biking 348
Children's Programs 357
Fishing 358
Cross-Country Skiing 363
Downhill Skiing 370
Rafting 372
Scrambling 374

Chapter 8: Best of the Rockies 377

Best of the Walks 377
Best Spring and Fall Hikes . .379
Best Fall-Colour Hikes 379
Best Itineraries 379

Best of the Rockies on a
Splurge 384
Best of the Rockies on a
Budget 385

Sources 386
Bibliography 396
Index 397

Maps

1. Overview of Canadian Rockies 10
2. Overview of Banff National Park 22
3. Banff townsite 25
4. Lake Louise village 27
5. Cave & Basin Centennial Centre 61
6. Banff (Southwest) 67
7. Banff (Southeast) 74
8. Bankhead (Closeup) 87
9. Lake Minnewanka 89
10. Banff (North) 92
11. Rock Isle Lake 96
12. Bourgeau Lake 99
13. Johnston Canyon 100
14. Castle Mountain Area 104
15. Boom Mtn. & Storm Mtn. 107
16. Taylor Lake 109
17. Lake Louise (South) 111
18. Lake Louise (North) 121
19. Dolomite Pass & Bow Lake 135
20. Peyto Lake Viewpoint 139
21. Mistaya Canyon 141
22. Parker Ridge 144
23. Overview of Kootenay National Park 148
24. Fireweed Trail & Stanley Glacier 156
25. Marble Canyon 161
26. Overview of Yoho National Park 164
27. Takakkaw Falls 172
28. Yoho Valley 175
29. Emerald Lake 178
30. Lake O'Hara 181
31. Wapta Falls 186
32. Overview of Jasper National Park 188
33. Jasper townsite 191
34. Athabasca Glacier 209
35. Beauty Creek 214
36. Sunwapta Falls 216
37. Athabasca Falls 219
38. Jasper (Southeast) 221
39. Cavell area 226
40. Jasper (South) 230
41. Jasper (North) 240

42. Maligne Canyon 253
43. Medicine Lake 257
44. Maligne Lake (Closeup) 259
45. Maligne Lake 262
46. Miette Hot Springs 266
47. Overview of Kananaskis Country 270
48. Ptarmigan Cirque 282
49. Mt. Indefatigable 284
50. Black Prince Cirque 288
51. Many Springs 290
52. Grotto Canyon 292
53. Grassi Lakes 294
54. Burstall Lakes 298
55. Overview of Waterton Lakes National Park 300
56. Waterton townsite 303
57. Waterton (South) 315
58. Rowe Lakes 318
69. Crandell Lakes 321
60. Crypt Lake 323
61. Blakiston Creek 324
62. Goat Lake 327

LEGEND

mountain peak; ridgeline		picnic site; covered picnic site	
glacier		campground (tents)	
pond, lake		campground (trailers, RVs)	
creek, river; bridge; waterfall		campground (tents, trailers, RVs)	
1A 93A highway		hostel	
Trans-Canada Hwy. (Hwy. 1)		washroom; viewpoint	
Yellowhead Hwy. (Hwy. 16)		above 3500 m elevation	
road		3250–3500 m	
trailhead; number; turn-around		3000–3250 m	
24 trail shown on another map		2750–3000 m	
trail not described in this book		2500–2750 m	
railway		2250–2500 m	
railway (abandoned)		2000–2250 m	
provincial boundary		1750–2000 m	
international boundary		1500–1750 m	
park		1250–1500 m	
building		1000–1250 m	
P parking		below 1000 m	

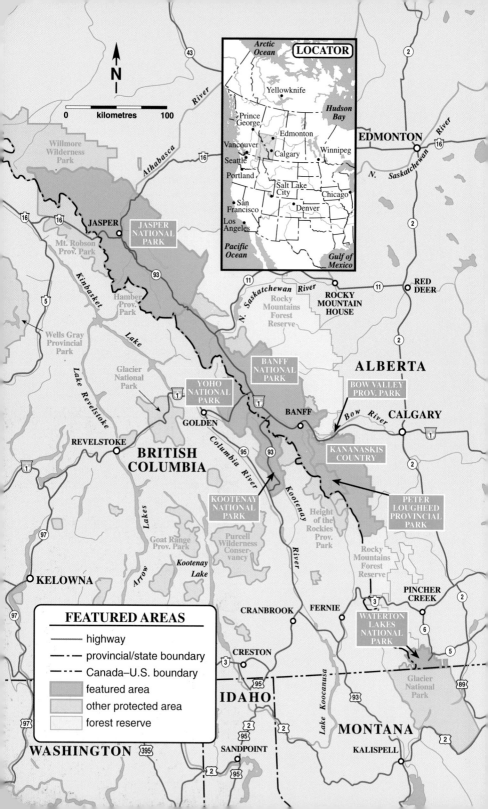

Introduction

'What's the best hike around here?'
'Where can I get away from the crowds?'
'Where's a good place to stay?'
'What can I do around here with my kids (or older parents)?'
'Where can I get a decent meal without paying a fortune?'
'How can I learn more about this area's history and wildlife?'

When we wrote the first edition of *The Canadian Rockies Access Guide* in 1987, the two most common questions visitors were asking of Parks Canada staff were 'Where are the washrooms?' and 'What's there to do here?'

Things have changed. Although the mountains haven't moved, the forces of increased tourism and commercialization in the Canadian Rockies have led to many more choices for today's visitor. The washroom question is as common as ever, but the question of 'What's there to do here?' has increasingly been supplanted by 'There's so much to do here! How can I decide on the best way to spend my time and my money?'

Our goal in revising this book is to answer that question for the approximately 10 million annual visitors to Canada's five stunning Rocky Mountain national parks and Alberta's equally stunning Kananaskis Country. It's an attempt to inform visitors of all ages and physical conditions of the many opportunities for actively enjoying the mountains. We invite you to participate in this landscape, not merely observe it from parking lots and tour buses.

There are many excellent new recreational and cultural opportunities for visitors to the Rocky Mountains. At the same time, increased commercialism and government cutbacks have led to the reduction of quality outdoor experiences in some areas. Planning is more important than ever to ensure a holiday tailored to your individual requirements for physical and spiritual renewal.

Moraine Lake and Valley of the Ten Peaks

visitor tips

Be a Responsible Visitor

The Canadian Parks Service needs help to protect the natural resources of these national parks. Please report any suspicious activities such as polluting, poaching, feeding or harassing wildlife, littering, removal of cultural artifacts or fishing violations by calling 1-888-927-3367.

Check That Area Code in 1999!

Effective January 25, 1999, the telephone area code of 403 for Alberta will no longer extend to all regions of the province. The area code 403 for the southern part of the province, including Banff, Calgary, Canmore, Lake Louise and Waterton Park, will not be changed.

Area codes for communities in the northern half of the province, including Edmonton, Hinton and Jasper, will be changed to 780. Callers will be able to use either the 403 or 780 area code between January 25, 1999 and July 12, 1999. Following that date, you must dial 780.

Canada's Rocky Mountains, especially the Banff townsite area, have become a wilderness with wine lists. We'll show you how to escape congestion and discover peace and solitude if that's what you're looking for. Plus, we have a few suggestions on where to get a good dinner to go with that wine after a great day in the mountains.

Walks and day hikes are the primary focus of this book. All of the trails described can be walked in a day, many of them in an hour or two. A few of the walks start from the vicinity of campgrounds, and are suitable for evening strolls. Some of our walk descriptions simply provide information about the flora, fauna and geology on short, graded strolls to popular viewpoints. Some guide the day hiker to areas seldom visited.

We also describe many other ways

to enjoy the mountains. You'll discover some of the best places to backpack, camp, cross-country ski, fish and enjoy other outdoor pursuits. This edition also contains new alpine hut and backcountry lodge sections and an expanded mountain bike section. Because more families with young children want to enjoy active holidays in the Rockies, we've included information on special children's programs, day camps and daycare. You'll also find a far more comprehensive section of ideas for rainy-day activities, as well as suggestions for where to eat and where to stay.

This edition also addresses the needs of the fastest growing segment of the travel sector, the 'cultural tourist.' Today's travellers not only want to enjoy active holidays in natural settings, they also seek an understanding of the history and culture of the area. They want to know about the best museums and historic sites. They want to learn about the art, literature and music of the area. See the 'Indoor and Rainy-Day Guide' sections of this book, plus overviews on subjects such as the art and paintings of the Rockies. We think visitors of all ages would enjoy the excellent Glacier Gallery at the Columbia Icefield, for example, as long as they time their visit right. You'll find out where to view Mt. Alberta's legendary ice axe in Jasper, where to peer into the replica workroom of one of Banff's most eccentric curators, and more. Please note that this book is not an attempt to include every activity available in the park.

Although the focus is on self-propelled travel and cultural/education programs, we do include some mechanized activities that have deep roots in the parks, such as the Columbia Icefield bus tours. We think it's important to recognize that not everyone can nor wants to climb a peak. If you're looking for information on where to ride your all-terrain vehicle, though, you won't find it here. We have tried to tailor our suggestions to those that are environmentally responsible in a fragile, pressured area. The impact of various human activities on different ecosystems in the parks is under an ongoing review and new recommendations might be forthcoming on responsible usage. Please see 'Sources' at the end of the book for ways to keep up-to-date on conservation issues.

How This Book Is Organized

For an overview of the best of what there is to do in the Rocky Mountain national parks (and Kananaskis Country), skim the sections at the beginning of each of the six chapters. You'll find everything from glacier walks to suggestions for historic cemetery rambles. Outdoor adventures are followed by indoor activities and a guide to what to do on a rainy day.

Some activities in the 'Outdoor Adventures' and 'Rainy-Day' guides, such as backpacking, bicycling, mountain biking and fishing, require more detailed information. Expanded descriptions of some of the major outdoor activities in the Rockies are found in chapter 7.

Medicine Lake and Colin Range

Lists of commercial outfitters providing guiding and other services are included; these are for readers' convenience and do not imply author endorsement.

Chapter 8 contains suggested itineraries. These itineraries include recommendations for the best longer walks and the best family walks. Also suggested is how to spend a day or two in Banff, Lake Louise, Yoho, Jasper and Kananaskis. Many of these itineraries are for people looking for rewarding but easy walks. You'll also find suggestions for how to have an economical trip—and how to splurge.

Chapters 1 to 6 contain our personal selections for the 106 best day hikes in the Canadian Rockies. We also tell you where to see wildlife in the vicinity, and often direct you to other nearby attrac-

Bow River, Banff National Park

tions. You'll also find information on avoiding bear conflicts, including new recommendations from Parks Canada experts regarding the use of pepper spray (see page 58).

This introduction has suggestions about footwear, what to bring, water, park regulations and the hiking season.

'Sources,' at the end of the book, lists helpful addresses for finding more information about the park. It includes Parks Canada addresses for each park, plus contacts for obtaining more information on accommodation and other commercial services. Web site addresses are included.

Getting the Most Out of This Book

If you have time before your trip, we suggest you browse through the book from beginning to end. You might find many surprising ways to enhance your holiday with such activities as attendance at the Canmore Folk Festival (held each August), an excursion to Alberta's new $14-million Western Heritage Centre in Cochrane, or even a quiet foray into the Lizzie Rummel Reading Room at the Lake Louise International Hostel.

Already arrived in the mountains? You'll find many suggestions for activities that require no advance booking. Also check at the nearest visitor information centre for updates on activities.

Travelling with children? You'll find listings for children's activities

Castle Mountain, Banff National Park

and programs under 'Children's Programs' in many of the individual park activity listings. Many park interpretive programs and guided activities are also designed for all ages. The itinerary section of this book, page 379, includes suggestions for outings well suited to families. Also see 'Children's Programs,' in chapter 7, for more information about children's day camps in the parks, etc.

Looking for additional help in pulling together your Rocky Mountain adventure? Since the last revision of this book, a new service sector area has developed in Banff: excursion planning for outdoor adventures such as rafting and hiking, as well as more traditional activities such as bus excursions. These companies will suggest activities, make reservations and assist with all other aspects of planning. See 'Activity Planners' in the 'Outdoor Adventures' sections for various parks. The *Where* publications are also helpful resources, and are widely distributed in the mountain parks.

What's the best way to spend your time here? This book has hundreds of answers.

Figuring Out Park Fees

Another change that has occurred since the last revision of *The Canadian Rockies Access Guide* involves national park entrance fees, which have risen substantially. You have a choice between purchasing a day pass or a Great Western Annual Pass.

A day pass is valid in all five national parks from date of issue until 4 p.m. the following day. The cost is $5 each for adults, $4 for seniors and $2.50 for children (except for Waterton, see below). Reduced rates are offered for groups of 2 to 10 persons: $10 for a group of adults and/or children; $8 for a group of seniors.

If you plan to travel to several national parks in western Canada, your best buy is a Great Western Annual Pass. It is valid for unlimited entry to all 11 national parks in western Canada, for one year from the month of purchase. The individual rate is $35 for adults, $27 for seniors and $18 for children. The group rate (2 to 10 persons) is $70 for adults and/or children and $53 for seniors.

Rates for Waterton Lakes National Park are slightly lower: day passes are $4 for adults, $3 for seniors and $2 for children; groups passes (2 to 10 persons) are $8 regularly and $6 for seniors. Annual group passes for Waterton: adults, $50 (includes adults and children); seniors, $38.

Passes are sold at park gates, visitor information centres, some campgrounds and hot springs. For extra convenience, you can order your passes ahead of time by phone (1-800-748-7275) or by e-mail: natlparks-ab@pch.gc.ca.

Emerald Lake and Michael Peak, Yoho National Park

Footwear

When we started hiking many years ago, we wore heavy, stiff leather boots designed more for general mountaineering or big-time backpacking than for hiking. They weighed several pounds each—and even after years of breaking in, produced blisters on long trails. Sometimes easy stretches of trail were agony, because it hurt to lift those leaden lumps at every step.

A few years later, we shifted to lighter, more flexible hiking boots. Walking felt easier, although an occasional blister still bubbled up. Then, for hiking many of the easy trails, we went even further and abandoned boots altogether. Running shoes weigh only a few ounces, are well-padded under the heel, and never seem to produce blisters.

However, running shoes do have a few problems: they tend to slide on wet rocks or muddy trails; they can't be waterproofed; and sometimes don't provide enough support on rough, rocky terrain.

Now we wear super-light hiking boots for most trails and sometimes even for backpacking—unless we're planning a lot of off-trail scrambling or climbing, or are heading out with really heavy loads. These light boots are made on a modified running shoe last, often by running shoe manufacturers. They are comfortable, sturdy and reasonably waterproof, with good traction.

However, running shoes remain a reliable option for most of the shorter trails in this book, especially in dry weather. Each walk contains a footwear recommendation.

What To Bring

For most of these short hikes, it doesn't matter much. Wear whatever you happen to have on. Don't let lack of special gear keep you from a rewarding experience. Many love to hike in shorts, even in fairly cool weather. Legs don't usually feel the cold like hands and feet do, and shorts provide freedom of movement. Jeans are adequate for a short stroll, although they tend to be tiring because the relatively stiff, tight material binds the legs in uphill walking. In cold weather, jeans give little protection and they feel especially unpleasant when wet. In cold, damp weather, synthetic fabrics or wool are highly superior.

For short hikes, it's still a good idea to bring a sweater and windproof/waterproof jacket, tied around the waist, if necessary. Mountain weather changes fast. You're likely to be warm while walking and cool off quickly when you stop.

Here's a suggested list for longer day hikes:

Day pack
Rain jacket (windproof)
Gloves
Compass
Guidebook
Map
Bear spray in holder
Camera

Sweater or pile jacket in stuff bag
Hat with brim
Wool toque
Lunch
High-energy snacks
Water bottle
Change of socks
Matches
Tissues
Insect repellent
Sunglasses
Sunscreen
First-aid kit
Pocket knife
Garbage bags

Water

Traditionally, hikers just drank from mountain streams when they felt thirsty. Nothing tasted better than the clear, icy water of a tumbling brook in the backcountry. These days, unfortunately, *Giardia lamblia* has reared its tiny, ugly head, and taken the romance right out of drinking.

Giardia is a parasite that contaminates water, causing stomach upsets and cramps in humans. It is widespread in western Canada and the U.S., and once contaminated the water supply for Banff townsite. The townsite problem has been alleviated by the construction of deep well pumps and a new 18-million-L (4-million-gal) reservoir with automatic controls and chlorination.

But Parks Canada says *giardiasis* continues to be a potential hazard in all the Rocky Mountain parks backcountry. They recommend that drinking water taken from rivers, lakes and streams be boiled for five minutes before use.

Day hikers aren't going to bring along a pot and stove for boiling. The alternative for walks longer than an hour or two is to bring water with you in canteens, supplemented possibly by containers of juice. Take a generous supply of liquid because dehydration is one of the fastest routes to fatigue. For long, hot hikes, we sometimes bring along iodine tablets to purify the creek water in our canteens. (We still drink the water in the high alpine regions where the danger of contamination is low.) Iodine doesn't taste good so we usually add some drink crystals to the canteen as well. For backpacking, you might add a filter to avoid a week of drinking only iodized water.

Garbage and Sanitation

Whatever you can pack in, you can also pack out. Take a garbage bag in your day pack for any leftovers, cans, bottles, foil or paper.

If there are no toilet facilities along the trails (and there usually aren't), defecation should be performed at least 100 m (328 ft) from water sources. Dig a small hole and cover it afterwards with soil.

Park Regulations

No permit is needed for day walks along the park trails, although a Wilderness Pass is required for overnight trips. See 'Backpacking in

Mule deer

Where to Find Wildlife

The easiest place to see animals in the mountain parks is along the highway. Drive out in the early morning or evening almost any place, except the Trans-Canada Highway, just before sunset, and you'll be rewarded. The Bow Valley Parkway (Hwy. 1A), the Banff-Windermere Highway (Hwy. 93), the Icefields Parkway (Hwy. 93) and Hwy. 16 in Jasper are likely to bring you close to elk, deer and bighorn sheep, maybe even a moose, coyote or bear—if you slow down and look. The best seasons are spring, fall and winter when much big game has moved from the subalpine forest into protected valleys.

A better place to see wildlife is in the backcountry—at least in the country away from the roads. You'll see different mammals and birds along many of the hikes in this book.

Although it might seem obvious, the best way to view wildlife is through binoculars or a telephoto lens. Don't get too close because close proximity is disturbing to wildlife. These animals are still wild and unpredictable. Any animal might bite if it feels threatened. Moose in rutting season (fall) might try to defend their territory. A moose cow can become aggressive if she feels her calf is threatened. Elk are common in the townsites and can be aggressive, especially if they think they are cornered.

Feeding of wildlife is illegal in national parks. Some animals have learned to panhandle for food. You do them no favour by feeding them. It disrupts their natural feeding patterns and makes them dependent on human handouts. It might even make them sick—or kill them—because they're getting the wrong kind of food.

wildlife

the Canadian Rockies,' page 334. Registration is also recommended (though not usually required) for 'risk activities' such as climbing, kayaking, skiing outside signed routes, or any travel on glaciers. By registering, wardens will know your itinerary, should you fail to return on time. Registration can be done at the visitor information centres in the national parks and at Warden Service offices. Your portion of the registration notice must be returned by the time and date recorded. After hours deposit boxes are located at the visitor information centres.

Fires aren't permitted, except in designated fireboxes and fireplaces. Dogs are supposed to be on a leash, and they aren't recommended anyway in the backcountry, because they can provoke bears and molest or annoy other animals. It's unlawful to feed wildlife, pick wildflowers or plants, or collect rocks or fossils.

Seasons

In winter, walks on paved roads are easily followed. Some of the other lower trails, especially within townsites, might have a beaten path and can be travelled without difficulty. Many of the others are best skied. See 'Cross-Country Skiing,' page 363.

Snow does linger in the mountains longer than on the prairies. By May, much of the snow has gone from the lower valley forest and some of the south-facing slopes. By June, trails begin to open below treeline, although they can still be extremely wet and muddy, especially at higher elevations and on north-facing slopes. It's a good idea to avoid the alpine or timberline zone until well into July. Even though the snow has melted along most of these high trails, the footing remains extremely wet, slippery and unpleasant. Walkers who use soft trails

When to Hike

Visitors to the mountain parks should be aware that the hiking season can end as early as the first week of September. One year, we woke up on Labour Day at Egypt Lake to find our tent almost collapsed under more than 25 cm (10 in) of snow. The hike out was a wet, dreary drudge—and that was the end of mountain adventures for the season.

Use the 'best season' recommendations that accompany each walk as guidelines only, based on averages for the terrain and elevation. The following terms are used in these recommendations:

'June *to* October' means June 1 to October 1.

'June *through* October' means June 1 to October 31.

Maligne Lake, Jasper National Park

under these conditions wear down the pathway until it becomes a ditch across the meadows. Then hikers begin to travel on the edge of the ditch and eventually create a second, parallel ditch and then maybe a third. The result is considerable destruction of the delicate environment.

Walking usually remains good through September, although an early snowfall can quickly blanket everything. Some years, the snow melts away. Some years, it doesn't. The hiking can remain fairly warm and dry well into October, but don't count on it.

In the mountains, all you can really count on is change. Weather conditions change, hour to hour, more rapidly than most other places. You can get rain, snow and sunshine on the same day. In the Rockies, warm, moist air from the Pacific often collides with cool, dry air from the plains. This collision can cause heavy rain or snow in many areas, depending on elevation and the locations of peaks and valleys. The mountains mix up the air flow.

The Columbia Icefield area gets an average of about 640 cm (250 in) of snow a year and 230 cm (90 in) of rain. Snow is recorded even in July and August. However, the Jasper Lake area, northeast of the townsite, has a semi-arid climate, including sand dunes, because it is located in a rain shadow. Rain tends to be pushed to either side of this small area or to fall before getting there.

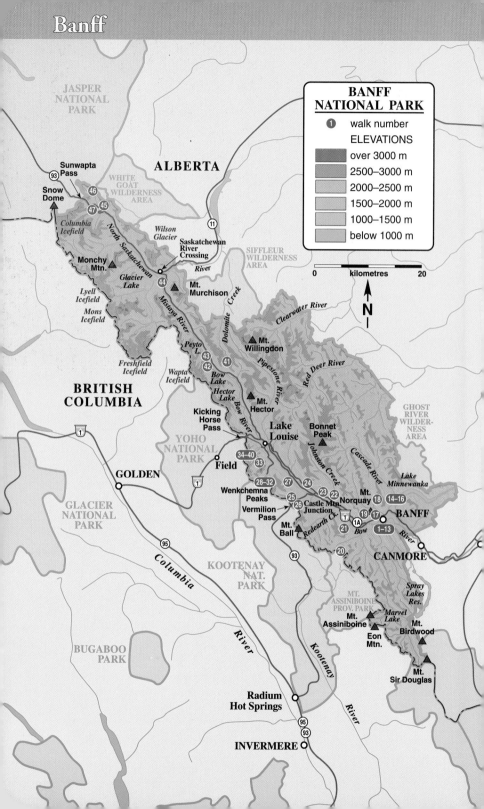

JASPER
NATIONAL
PARK

ALBERTA

**BANFF
NATIONAL PARK**

1 walk number
ELEVATIONS
over 3000 m
2500–3000 m
2000–2500 m
1500–2000 m
1000–1500 m
below 1000 m

Sunwapta
Pass
93
Snow
Dome
46
WHITE
GOAT
WILDERNESS
AREA
47 45

Columbia
Icefield

Wilson
Glacier

Saskatchewan
River
Crossing
11

SIFFLEUR
WILDERNESS
AREA

0   kilometres   20

N

Monchy
Mtn.

North Saskatchewan

Glacier
Lake

44 Mt.
Murchison

Dolomite Creek

Clearwater River

Lyell
Icefield

Mons
Icefield

Mistaya River

Mt.
Willingdon

Peyto
L.
43
42
41

Bow
Lake

Pipestone River

Red Deer River

GHOST
RIVER
WILDER-
NESS
AREA

Freshfield
Icefield

Wapta
Icefield

Hector
Lake

Mt.
Hector

Bow River

Lake
Louise

Bonnet
Peak

Cascade River

Lake
Minnewanka

**BRITISH
COLUMBIA**

Kicking
Horse
Pass

YOHO
NATIONAL
PARK

34–40
33

Johnston Creek

GOLDEN

1

Field

1

28–32 27 24

Wenkchemna
Peaks

23 Mt.
Norquay
18 14–16

GLACIER
NATIONAL
PARK

Vermilion
Pass

25
26 Castle Mtn
Junction

19 17

1A
BANFF

Mt.
Ball

Redearth Ck.

21 Bow

1–13

95

93

20

CANMORE

KOOTENAY
NAT.
PARK

Columbia

Spray
Lakes
Res.

BUGABOO
PARK

River

MT.
ASSINIBOINE
PROV. PARK

Mt.
Assiniboine

Marvel
Lake

Eon
Mtn.

Mt.
Birdwood

Kootenay

Mt.
Sir Douglas

Radium
Hot Springs

River

95
93

INVERMERE

Vermilion Lakes and Mt. Rundle

CHAPTER 1

BANFF NATIONAL PARK

Banff National Park, the most famous in Canada, offers everything for the sightseer, walker and outdoors person: glaciers, castellated peaks, deep forests, lakes, rivers, hot springs, wildlife and activities from waterfall ice climbing to downhill skiing, all accessed by 350 km (217 mi) of roads and 1300 km (806 mi) of hiking trails. If there is a price, it's that Banff is busier and more crowded than the four other Rocky Mountain parks: Kootenay, Yoho, Jasper and Waterton. About 4.7 million people visit Banff annually, compared with 2.2 million who visit Jasper, a larger park. Tourism in Banff has increased by 5.4 percent each year between 1950 and 1995. The Banff townsite, with a permanent population of about 8000 and a summer population of thousands more, has everything from art galleries to fudge shops on a teeming, throbbing main drag and rapidly expanding side drags.

The park, situated 114 km (71 mi) west of Calgary, encompasses 6641 sq. km (2656 sq. mi), and is cut by parts of two mountain ranges, the Front and Main ranges. Hikers ascending a peak could pass through three vegetation zones: montane, subalpine and alpine. Nearly 250 species of birds and 53 species of mammals exist in the park, including plenty of elk, moose, black bear, bighorn sheep and deer, plus 80 to 100 grizzly bears.

The oldest of Canada's national parks, Banff's origins go back to 1883 when railway workers discovered a hot sulphur spring near the south bank of the Bow River. A dispute soon arose over the ownership of the potentially profitable hot spring, and resulted in a takeover by the federal government and the creation of a reserve around the hot springs in 1885. The establishment of the reserve marked the beginning of Canada's national park system, which now comprises 39 national parks. The mountain parks are among the finest in the world.

In recent years, costs and commercial congestion within Banff townsite have risen substantially. You can still enjoy a peaceful, soul-restoring holiday in the park, but it could take some careful planning. If crowds bother you, avoid Banff townsite in peak summer months, if you can, and reserve accommodation well in advance. You might also want to consider basing your stay in quieter Lake Louise or in cabins along the Bow Valley Parkway (Hwy. 1A). The itinerary section of this book (page 379) contains many suggestions for beyond-the-beaten path destinations. Also see 'Sources' (page 386) for places to contact in advance for trip-planning information and handy web sites. Remember, though, that the cultural attractions of Banff townsite can compensate for the crowds. See the following listings on cultural and educational attractions for all ages. Children's programs are also available.

If you are flying to Alberta, note that there are direct or one-stop flights connecting Calgary with most major North American and European cities. A daily Airporter shuttle service runs between Calgary International and Banff. Bus service and car rentals are available in Calgary International Airport, Calgary and Banff. Brewster, Greyhound and Laidlaw bus lines provide regular coach service; taxi and limousine services are offered in Banff. For those romantics who like to travel by train, the Rocky Mountaineer, 1-800-665-7245, runs 41 different tours, including weekly service between Calgary and Vancouver in summer months.

Once you arrive in Banff National Park, begin your trip at the Banff Information Centre, 224 Banff Avenue, (403) 762-1550. This office is the place to go for most Parks Canada information, as well as information about accommodation and commercial activities. (The Banff/Lake Louise Tourism Bureau staffs a desk here. Ask for a copy of the *Official Visitor Guide*, published by the bureau for free.) Open 8 a.m. to 8 p.m. in summer; 8 a.m. to 6 p.m. in spring and fall; 9 a.m. to 5 p.m. in winter.

Can't find accommodation? The Banff/Lake Louise Tourism Bureau

BANFF TOWNSITE

H	Hospital	8	Banff Ave. Mall	20	Banff Park Museum
P	Parking	9	Sundance Mall	21	The Banff Centre
?	Information Centre	10	Park Avenue Mall	22	Cave & Basin
	Banff International Hostel	11	Town Centre Mall	23	Recreation Grounds
	Tunnel Mountain Campground	12	Caribou Corner Mall	24	Luxton Museum
1	Train Station	13	Whyte Museum	25	Cascade Gardens
2	Police Station (RCMP)	14	Kirby Lane Mall	26	Park Administration Building
3	Bus Depot	15	Clock Tower Village Mall	27	YWCA
4	Wolf & Bear Corner Mall	16	Public Library	28	Golf Course
5	Boating Facilities	17	Post Office	29	Upper Hot Springs
6	Cascade Plaza	18	Natural History Museum	30	Banff Springs Hotel
7	Bear St. Mall	19	Central Park		

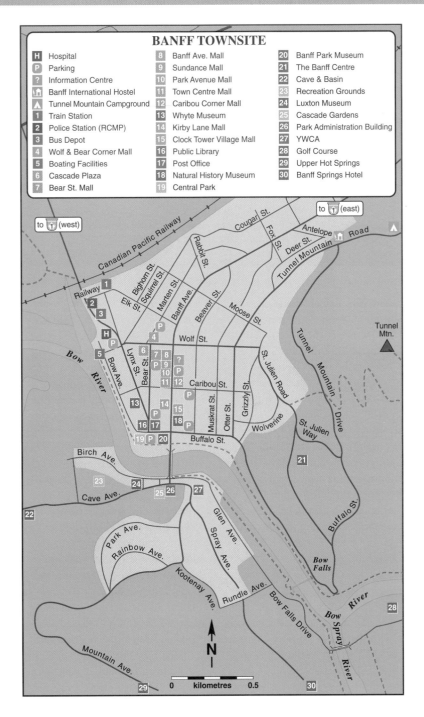

Moraine Lake Road

maintains a daily listing of available accommodation in the park in peak months. Ask at the Information Centre, (403) 762-0270.

No vehicle? Good news! It's becoming easier to be a pedestrian in Banff. In Banff townsite, Banff Transit Service offers frequent daily service ($1 for adults) in summer on two routes: the Banff Avenue–Banff Springs Hotel route and the Tunnel Mountain–downtown route. Check bus stops, the Information Centre and hotel desks for details. The availability of hiking shuttles is also increasing. See 'Guided Hikes' (page 33).

Lake Louise

Lake Louise Village has expanded in recent years into a busy commercial centre where you can buy souvenir T-shirts, wait in line for gas for 20 minutes, fight for a parking spot in Samson Mall as aggressively as you would in the big city, and be turned away from the campground, even though it's huge. A positive side exists as well. The Lake Louise International Hostel has been constructed, offering budget accommodation with deluxe trimmings— plentiful family rooms, wine with meals and spacious, tasteful surroundings—that are the envy of some larger commercial hotels. The Post Hotel has been renovated, enhancing its already well-deserved reputation as one of Canada's finest ski lodges. And there are many more things to do, both indoors and outdoors, including numerous guided walks that offer both outdoor adventure and education and special activities for kids.

For all of the activity, development at Lake Louise Village has, in our view, been fairly well contained. It's still a very small place, with a small-town feel, unlike neighbouring Banff townsite. If your schedule allows you to visit this area during off-peak weeks or hours, you'll find both peacefulness and unsurpassed mountain beauty. If you come seeking solitude during peak weeks, you can still be successful—but it will take more effort and planning.

The variety of outdoor activities in the Lake Louise area is truly outstanding, from gentle paddling on an alpine lake to world-class hiking and skiing (backcountry, cross-country and downhill). Those people who enjoy winter activities will usually find excellent snow conditions long into April. Lake Louise is also an excellent base for excursions up the Icefields Parkway (Hwy. 93) and into nearby Yoho and Kootenay national parks. An advantage to basing your stay here rather than in Banff townsite is that you'll have

less travelling to endure on the busy Trans-Canada from Banff to Lake Louise.

Start your visit by dropping into the Lake Louise Visitor Centre, (403) 522-3833, located just behind the Samson Mall in the Village of Lake Louise. The facility is the official centre for Parks Canada information on the area. Here, you can buy backcountry permits and get weather bulletins and bear warnings. In summer, the Banff/Lake Louise Tourism Bureau staffs a counter where you can obtain more information on commercial activities. The centre also has a theatre and interpretive displays. (See 'Indoor' section, page 51.) Open daily from 9 a.m. to 5 p.m. in winter and 8 a.m. to 8 p.m. in summer.

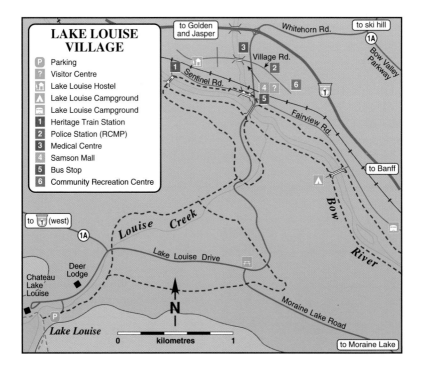

 This icon indicates activities that are in or around Lake Louise.

Outdoor Adventures

ACTIVITY PLANNERS: Don't have the time or inclination to plan your own outdoor adventure in the Rockies? Several companies will suggest activities, and make all the arrangements for you. Contact Summertime (and Wintertime) Activities & Excursions in Banff at (403) 762-0745 or 1-888-228-4889, Banff Adventures Unlimited at (403) 762-4554 or Good Earth Travel in Canmore at (403) 678-9358 or 1-888-979-9797. If you would like to plan your adventure travel activities and accommodation through the Internet, in North America and abroad, CAN*travel*, 'Western Canada's Travel Directory,' is a good source: www.cantravel.ab.ca. Also see 'Sources.'

ALPINE COURSES AND ROCK CLIMBING: Yamnuska Inc. Mountain School, (403) 678-4164, in Canmore offers a complete package of skiing, mountain leadership skills and survival courses, with accommodation, meals and technical

Canoeing on Vermilion Lakes

equipment provided. The school has a well-established reputation for safety and excellent instruction, often from climbers who have scaled the world's highest peaks. Mountain Magic Equipment, (403) 762-2591, in Banff is a good source of information on outdoor lessons and all-day climbs, and offers an indoor climbing wall. Check out the climbing wall at the Banff Community High School, 335 Beaver Street, (403) 762-1113. The school's wall is open to experienced climbers on an hourly basis. Major sporting goods stores in Banff rent climbing equipment. Also note that the Banff Springs Hotel, (403) 762-6895, has recently reintroduced professionally guided mountaineering trips for guests. (See 'Sources' for information on courses offered through the Alpine Club of Canada and Hostelling International.)

BACKPACKING: See chapter 7 (page 334) for recommendations on some of the best overnight trips in the backcountry.

BICYCLING: See chapter 7 (page 348) for bicycle rental locations and a guide to the best bicycle day trips and short trips around Banff National Park.

BOATING AND CANOEING: See chapter 7 (page 340 and 344) for boat and canoe rentals, rafting and a guide to the lakes and rivers around Banff townsite.

 Canoes or rowboats are available at the boathouse to the left

of Chateau Lake Louise, (403) 522-3511. Canoes and rowboats may also be rented at Moraine Lake in the neighbouring Valley of the Ten Peaks.

CARRIAGE RIDES: Tour Banff in a horse-drawn carriage. Banff Carriage Service has daily departures (weather permitting) from the Trail Rider Store, 132 Banff Avenue, (403) 762-4551.

CAVE AND BASIN: Don't miss experiencing where Banff began at the Cave and Basin, a national historic site, which also features several fine interpretive walks for all ages. A must for understanding the area's cultural history. (Guided tours daily in summer at 11 a.m. The pool is no longer open. See page 64.)

CEMETERY CREEPING: See 'Indoor and Rainy-Day Guide' (page 47).

CHILDREN'S PROGRAMS: Good news for parents. The Town of Banff sponsors a Summer Fun Program with eight weekly sessions from early July to late August. The program is open to school-age children and provides activities ranging from camping, hiking and canoeing to music and art, all under qualified supervision. You can enroll your kids for just one day, if that suits your schedule. (This camp is popular, so it's a good idea to reserve.) Daycare for children from 19 months to kindergarten is also available at the Banff Child Care

Centre, (403) 762-1229. Also see 'Evening Campground Programs' (page 32).

For programs in Lake Louise, inquire at the Lake Louise Visitor Centre. Also see 'Indoor and Rainy-Day Guide' (page 47).

COLUMBIA ICEFIELD EXCURSION: Here's a fine day trip from Banff—a must for many visitors. The Columbia Icefield, the largest ice cap south of the Arctic Circle, covers an area the size of Vancouver. You can see a small portion of it from the highway, or take a short walk along the lunar-like approach to the toe of the Athabasca Glacier, the most accessible glacier in North America (Walk 61). Brewster bus lines runs daily $9^{1}/_{2}$-hour round trips from Banff to the Icefield, early April to early November, $79 for adults and $39.50 for children (not including the 'snocoach'). A 'snocoach' tour, which takes you onto the glacier in a big-wheeled bus, is available from April 15 to mid-October weather permitting ($22.50 for adults and $5 for kids). The Icefield Centre, (403) 762-6767, which opened in May, 1996, contains the new Parks Canada Glacier Gallery, a 200-seat dining room and 32 hotel rooms. Also see page 195.

CRUISE DEVIL'S GAP: Daily cruises on Lake Minnewanka to Devil's Gap are perennially popular. Lake Minnewanka, 24 km (15 mi) long, is Banff's largest lake. Bear, deer and bighorn sheep may be seen along the shore. Tours in the glass-covered boats take about 1¹/₂ hours. They depart from the Minnewanka boat dock, which is 11 km (7 mi) north of the Banff townsite ($22 for adults, half-price for children). Dinner cruises are available by reservation, groups only. Drive the scenic Lake Minnewanka Road to the boat dock or take bus transportation to Minnewanka, which leaves from the downtown bus depot, Mount Royal Hotel and the Banff Springs Hotel. (There's a snack bar at the lake). Lake Minnewanka Boat Tours, (403) 762-3473.

DOGSLEDDING: In winter, you can get a taste of the Arctic by taking a dogsled tour. Enjoy the scenery as a 'musher' drives a team of seven to nine Alaskan Huskies, Siberians or Malamutes. Tours range from 30 minutes to five days. Mountain Mushers Dog Sled Company, (403) 762-3647.

DRIVES: Banff has 350 km (217 mi) of public roads. Most offer excellent views of the park's mountains, rivers and lakes. Near Banff townsite, we recommend the drives around the Banff Springs golf course, up to Mt. Norquay for a view of the town or along Vermilion Lakes Drive.

The most scenic route to Lake Louise is Hwy. 1A—the Bow Valley Parkway—with its interpretive stops and opportunities to see wildlife and to picnic along the way. At Lake Louise, be sure to take the side trip to Moraine Lake and the beautiful Valley of the Ten Peaks. The Icefields Parkway (Hwy. 93) from just north of Lake Louise to Jasper is one of the world's most scenic drives.

A favourite shorter trip is from Lake Louise to the Bow Summit. The Banff-Windermere Highway (Hwy. 93) through Kootenay National Park to Radium Hot Springs, B.C., provides an interesting longer excursion. Also, see the listing for the Great Divide Excursion (page 33).

Parks Canada publishes a brochure of suggested auto tours, available free from the Banff and Lake Louise information centres.

Mountain Mushers near Banff Springs Hotel

wildlife

What is a Wapiti?

The elk of the Canadian Rockies are called wapiti to avoid confusion with the European moose, which are also referred to as elk.

Larger than deer and smaller than moose, wapiti have a non-descript, knobby tail and a large, straw-coloured rump patch. They are the most common grazing animals in Banff and Jasper national parks. The wapiti once ranged across the United States. Eastern herds were killed off by hunters. Rocky Mountain wapiti came close to the same tragic end, and were almost extinct by the end of the 19th century. In 1917, 250 of the animals were imported from Yellowstone National Park for the restocking of the mountain parks. Most of the elk seen in these Canadian parks today are their descendants.

Wapiti are gregarious animals that congregate in herds of up to 80 in mating season, which starts in early September. The male works to attract females during this season by shaking its horns in the bushes, rolling in the mud, and bugling.

In recent years, encounters of the wapiti-human kind have become an increasingly serious problem in the Canadian mountain park communities, especially the Banff townsite.

To avoid an unfortunate elk encounter, follow these guidelines:

• Be especially alert during calving season from late May to late June, and when males are in rut (late August to mid-October).

• Be extremely cautious in wooded areas during calving season, especially in and around Banff townsite. A newborn calf may be hidden in the undergrowth.

• If you do encounter wapiti, maintain a healthy distance. The length of three buses is generally recommended.

• If you are charged, place something between you and the charging animal. A tree, automobile or post could provide the needed protection.

• If you are caught in the open with a wapiti charging, raise your arms above your head or hold up an object so that you appear taller than the animal. An umbrella, jacket or stick could be used. (Don't use this tactic in fall, because it might be seen as a challenge to a male in rut.)

Whatever you do, don't be like the tourist overheard in a cafeteria at the Banff Centre.

'I put my hand out to pat one of those stuffed elk,' she told her friends. 'It moved!'

EVENING CAMPGROUND PROGRAMS: You don't need to stay at Tunnel Mountain Campground to enjoy the special 'Family Night' programs presented each Wednesday evening in summer at the outdoor theatre in the Tunnel Mountain Tenting Campground. (The campground is a small city, so give yourself plenty of time to find the theatre.) Learn about Banff's bears, bugs and much more. Fun and free. Check at the Banff Information Centre, (403) 762-1550.

FISHING AND GUIDED FISHING: See chapter 7 (page 358) for where to fish, where to find fishing guides, and which lakes have which fish.

GOLFING: The Banff Springs golf course is often listed as one of the world's 10 most scenic. The beauty of the par-71, 27-hole velvet lawn under the cliffs of Mt. Rundle is enough to make even non-golfers consider taking up the sport. The late Stanley Thompson, one of the world's foremost golf architects, redesigned the original course in 1927. An adjoining nine holes and a new clubhouse opened in 1989. The clear air and the huge scale of the mountains often cause golfers to under-estimate the distance to the green. The ever-present elk lounging about the fairways don't contribute to low scores, but they're part of the attraction—and hazard—of this unique facility. For non-golfers, a scenic road winds around the course (beware of elk). The course is open daily 7 a.m. to 8 p.m. Tee-off reservations required. Lessons and golf equipment rentals are available at the pro shop, (403) 762-6801 for reservations. High season rates for 18 holes are $90, including the cart. Banff residents, however, gravitate to the 18-hole Canmore Golf Course, (403) 678-4784, which is scenic but less expensive. (More courses are scheduled to open soon in the Canmore area.) For golfers who don't mind an hour's drive, try the spectacular 36-hole Kananaskis Golf Course with its imported white sand and 18 water hazards. The course is 27 km (17 mi) south of the Trans-Canada on the Kananaskis Trail (Hwy. 40), 1-800-372-9201.

The 18-hole golf course, ranked among Canada's top 10, at Radium Hot Springs, is a 90-minute drive from Banff National Park and Lake Louise. Call 1-800-667-6444.

GONDOLA SIGHT-SEEING: The visitor who wants peak panorama without pain has a choice of two summer gondola lifts in Banff National Park, one at Sulphur Mountain and the other at Lake Louise, both with a teahouse at the top. (Wait for a good clear day, and don't expect solitude.) Short trails radiate from both of the lifts.

The gondola ride up Sulphur Mountain soars 2285 m (7495 ft) above the Banff townsite. At the top, you can stroll along the recently constructed Vista Trail (Walk 5) and visit an historic weather observatory.

There's also a trail up the mountain; those who walk up may ride down free. The ride takes only eight minutes. A modern teahouse with a licensed restaurant, coffee shop, gift shop and observation terraces is situated on top. The lift is 3.2 km (1.9 mi) from the townsite on Mountain Avenue, next to the Upper Hot Springs. Taxi service and Brewster bus service are available from the townsite. Open mid-May to early November, (403) 762-2523.

The Lake Louise Sightseeing Lift and Gondola will take you to 1075 m (3526 ft) on Mt. Whitehorn for views across the Bow Valley to Lake Louise and Valley of the Ten Peaks. Interpreters lead free nature hikes. You can work up an appetite before dining in the licensed Whitehorn Terrace Restaurant, (403) 522-3555. Daily hot buffets are offered in season for breakfast, lunch and dinner. Open June 1 to mid-September.

GREAT DIVIDE EXCURSION:

A great excursion from Lake Louise is to the Great Divide, the point where all waters flow either to the Atlantic or the Pacific. You can watch a stream here flow two ways: the east branch heads towards the Bow River, the South Saskatchewan River and Hudson Bay; the west branch towards the Columbia River and then into the Pacific Ocean. There are picnic tables right on the divide. Continue on Hwy. 1A past the Lake Louise road towards Kicking Horse Pass.

GUIDED HIKES: In the last few years, the number and variety of guided walks and hikes available has mushroomed. Most are both educational and fun. Even if you've walked Banff's trails many times, you'll learn something new—everything from the favourite hikes of famous painters to wolf mythology. The Friends of Banff National Park office in the Banff Information Centre is the first place to check for information. Daily guided hikes include the Vermilion Lakes stroll (Walk 5), the Cave and Basin Discovery Trail (Walk 2) and the (indoor) Banff Park Museum Wildlife Tour. These excellent tours are led by knowledgeable guides and are designed for all ages. A special 'Wonder Walk' is available for kids in summer; it begins at the

Banff Avenue and Cascade Mountain

front steps of the Cave and Basin. Pre-register at the Banff Information Centre.

Several evening research walks are presented in and around the townsite in summer and make an educational and fun outing for families. The Friends of Banff National Park offers these walks with White Mountain Adventures, a well-established tour company. Sample walks include 'Bears in Banff,' 'Elk, Moose and Other Hooved Animals' and 'Wolves—Myths and Realities,' where you walk in wolves' winter hunting grounds and learn about their intricate social structure. Check at the Banff Information Centre or call (403) 762-1550.

Here's a new offering that's great news for hikers: White Mountain Adventures also offers gentle half-day and day-long guided walks, as well as longer hikes. Walks are conducted daily from Banff with shuttles provided, (403) 678-4099.

White Mountain Adventures also provides shuttle service to Sunshine Meadows, an outstanding alpine area that could easily be the highlight of your trip. The Sunshine gondola no longer operates in summer, so the only access is by hiking or cycling a long, steep gravel road or taking a shuttle (see Walk 20). In winter, White Mountain conducts guided icewalks into Johnston Canyon, an exquisite world of frozen waterfalls (ice cleats included); field trips (either short snowshoe trips or walks) to discover the world of wolves in winter are also offered. Other companies offering guided interpretive hikes are Back of Beyond, (403) 678-6606, and Good Earth Travel Adventures, (403) 678-9358.

In the Lake Louise area, Parks Canada offers several excellent guided walks and tours. These tours include a leisurely two-hour stroll along Lake Louise, where you can learn about the natural and human history of the area, and a six-hour walking tour to the Plain of Six Glaciers (Walk 35). The tours are conducted several times a week for a reasonable fee. It's a good idea to register early. Check at the Visitor Centre, (403) 522-3833.

HISTORIC WALKING TOUR: Ask at the Information Centre for a free brochure entitled 'Banff's Historic Walking Tours.' The route takes you by many of the town's heritage buildings. The Whyte Museum of the Canadian Rockies, (403) 762-2291, also offers seasonal tours of historic areas.

HORSEBACK RIDING: If you've always wanted to ride a horse to breakfast, you have your chance in Banff. Holiday on Horseback offers one- to three-hour trail rides, breakfast rides, evening rides and covered wagon rides, as well as an

Trail riding near Canmore

imaginative selection of two- to six-day rides, including high-country fall colour excursions in September. The one- to three-hour rides start at the Banff Springs Hotel Corral, (403) 762-2848, and Martin Stables (Sundance Road), (403) 762-2832. Call for details on longer rides. If you enjoy home comforts with your horseback riding, consider a back-country ride and overnight stay at Sundance Lodge, a backcountry lodge. Illumination is by candlelight and propane lamp, water is heated by woodstove, but (joy of joys) hot showers are provided. The rides are hosted by Warner Guiding and Outfitting Ltd., in the business for 35 years. Call (403) 762-4551 or drop by the Trail Rider Store, 132 Banff Avenue.

In Lake Louise, Brewster–Lake Louise Stables offers a variety of horseback adventures, from hourly rides to all-day rides to Paradise Valley, Giant Steps, Lake Annette and Horseshoe Glacier. A special all-day high-line ride takes riders to both Lake Agnes and Plain of Six Glaciers teahouses, fine destinations indeed. Can't corral enough of the Old West? Inquire about the Brewster Cowboys' Barbecue and Dance Barn. Call (403) 522-3511 from Lake Louise or (403) 762-5454 in Banff for any of these Brewster-run activities. Lake Louise is also the starting point for 3- to 14-day trail rides from Timberline Tours, (403) 522-3743. Private trips of any length or group size may be arranged.

Banff a Family Business for the Brewsters

'Are you a real Brewster?'

That's a question the Brewsters of Banff get asked a lot. The legendary operators of Brewster Rocky Mountain Adventures can be found most days guiding pack trains, flipping steaks on barbecues or greeting cross-country skiers at a backcountry lodge.

The family business started in 1886 when John Brewster, an Irishman, arrived in Banff from Ontario. Deciding that the town would one day become a tourist mecca, he brought out his wife and family and began a dairy to supply the Banff Springs Hotel. His young sons Bill and Jim soon became expert mountain men, taking their first guests on a pack trip in 1892 at the tender ages of 12 and 10.

Before long, the Brewsters had established livery stables, a mercantile and grocery store, Banff's first opera house and Brewster Transport, which became one of the largest privately owned sightseeing companies in the world. Today, John Brewster's descendants operate Brewster Mountain Pack Trains, Brewster–Lake Louise Stables, the Kananaskis Guest Ranch, Shadow Lake Lodge and several other ventures.

history

HOT SPRINGS SOAKING: If you've never been to hot springs in the Canadian Rockies, prepare yourself for a treat. Banff's Upper Hot Springs, renovated in 1996, offers a great view of surrounding mountains from a poolside high above Banff townsite and an average water temperature of 38° C (100° F). Be warned that the springs are highly popular. During peak tourist season, you may want to go early in the day or later in the evening. The hot springs—3 km (1.9 mi) from the townsite on Mountain Avenue—are open year-round, 9 a.m. to 11 p.m. in summer and 10 a.m. to 10 p.m. in winter, except Saturday when they are open until 11 p.m. Call (403) 762-2056. Lockers are provided (a quarter is required) and towels and bathing suits can be rented. You can enjoy a cappuccino or snacks on the outside terrace or in the licensed restaurant. There's also a spa offering aromatherapy, body wraps, a steam room and massage. Call (403) 762-1515 for appointments. Brewster runs buses on the hour to the pool from the bus depot, Mount Royal Hotel and Banff Springs Hotel, from 9 a.m. to 6 p.m., May 1 until the end of October; $17 includes transport, pool admission and locker and suit rental. The springs are perhaps even more delicious in winter when mist rises from the warm water and ice forms on the railings. Perfect after a day's skiing.

If you enjoyed these hot springs, consider trying Radium Hot Springs in Kootenay National Park, page 153, and Miette Hot Springs in Jasper, page 199.

Radium Hot Springs, in particular, is a short drive from Lake Louise.

ICE CLIMBING: Ask at the Banff and Lake Louise information centres for information on guide services, conditions and routes. It's important to check on the condi-

Upper Hot Springs

tions of the routes since chinooks can seriously weaken waterfall ice in quick order.

ICE FISHING: See chapter 7 (page 358).

ICE SCULPTURE VIEWING:
Exquisite sculptures are crafted in winter months in front of the Chateau Lake Louise. They will have you hoping the weather stays cold.

ICEWALK: See 'Guided Hikes' (page 34) for information on the Johnston Canyon icewalk.

IN-LINE SKATING: You can rent in-line skates at Mountain Magic Equipment and the Ski Stop shop in the Banff Springs Hotel. The best local skating route is to Sundance Canyon (Walk 3).

KAYAKING: In Banff townsite, you can rent kayaks from Adrenalin Sports/Bactrax, (403) 762-8177.

LAKE O'HARA: At Lake Louise, you are very close to the renowned Lake O'Hara hiking area (Walk 56).

MOTORCOACH TOURING:
Brewster offers several bus excursions from Banff townsite:
• A three-hour round trip that stops at the hoodoos, Tunnel Mountain Drive and the Cave and Basin, where Banff's history began; $39 for adults, $19.50 for children.
• A four-hour round trip from Banff to Lake Louise, which goes by

Vermilion Lakes, Hole-in-the Wall and Johnston Canyon. At Lake Louise, time is allotted for walking on the trails or just enjoying the views; $44 for adults, $22 for children.
• The Columbia Icefield is an extremely popular one-day outing (see page 29 for listing).

Guided one-way and round trips are also offered on the scenic Icefields Parkway (Hwy. 93) to Jasper, one of the most beautiful highways in the world.

Visitors on their way to British Columbia may also choose Brewster's 'Cruisin' the Rockies Tour.' The three-day, two-night tour stops in Banff, Lake Louise and Roger's Pass, with nights in Calgary and Kamloops. Check with Brewster, (403) 762-6767 or 1-800-661-1152.

Brewster, (403) 762-6767, runs several bus excursions from Lake Louise:
• A 3½-hour trip goes across the Continental Divide into Yoho National Park to Takakkaw Falls, Emerald Lake, Kicking Horse Pass and the Natural Rock Bridge.
• A 7½-hour round trip goes to the Columbia Icefield, with time allowed for a 'Snocoach' ride on top of the Athabasca Glacier.
• An 8-hour, one-way trip goes to Jasper along the Icefields Parkway (Hwy. 93).

MOUNTAIN BIKING: See chapter 7 (page 351).

RAFTING: See chapter 7 (page 372).

RESEARCH ADVENTURES: One of the more illuminating ways to learn about the Rocky Mountains. You'll assist park wardens and researchers in programs from 7 to 14 days long. Assignments may involve helping a biologist track rare wolves, or learning how to monitor forest diversity. Call 1-888-979-9797.

SCRAMBLING: See chapter 7 (page 374).

SKATEBOARDING: Banff's new Skateboard Park, one of the largest in western Canada, opened in 1997 at the Banff Recreation Centre, Mt. Norquay Road, (403) 762-1235. The word is there's something for everyone and lots of potential for skin-splitting fun.

SKATING: Best bet is indoors at the Banff Recreation Centre on Norquay Road, where skate rentals are available, (403) 762-4454. In early winter, before the snow crusts on lake surfaces, you may be able to skate on Lake Minnewanka,

Vermilion Lakes or Lac des Arcs. Check at the Information Centre for ice conditions. There's also an outdoor rink at the Banff Springs Hotel, with a bonfire lit each evening.

 When the ice is cleared in front of Chateau Lake Louise, few places are as magical for skating. A bonfire is lit each evening and hot chocolate is provided. Roll on, winter!

SKIING (CROSS-COUNTRY): See chapter 7 (page 363), for the best trails for all levels, tips on what to take and warnings about avalanches.

SKIING (DOWNHILL): See chapter 7 (page 370).

SLEIGH RIDES: Holiday on Horseback, (403) 762-4551, offers daily sleigh rides in winter in the Banff townsite area.

In winter, sleigh rides to the end of Lake Louise are a popular activity for families—and lovers. Call (403) 522-3511 ext. 1210.

SNOWBOARDING: Local ski areas all have special snowboarding areas, with rentals and lessons. Parker Ridge has snow early in fall and late in spring.

Enthusiasts consider Lake Louise 'the biggest and best.'

SNOWSHOEING: A great way to observe the mysteries of how park animals hunt in winter. White Mountain Adventures offers guided half-day trips, snowshoes provided, (403) 678-4099.

Skiing, Lake Louise

Why Do We Feel So Good in the Mountains?

Is it the fresh air? The stupendous landscape that seems to shrink our individual cares? Or is it just that we're away from everyday concerns?

The reason why most of us feel a sense of well-being in the mountains probably has to do with those factors and many more. American science writer Winifred Gallagher explores this subject in her intriguing study, *The Power of Place*. She notes that it is 'just plain easier to breathe' in the mountains because there are fewer allergens and pollutants. Scientists who climb mountains also attribute well-being to the fact that there is less oxygen in the air at high altitudes, forcing deeper breathing, more oxygen to the brain and more efficient removal of carbon dioxide.

It's also thought that those who adjust well to altitudes over 2400 m (7872 ft) have a highly responsive gland in the neck's carotid artery that monitors oxygen in the blood and signals the brain to start hyperventilating if oxygen is scarce. Interestingly, the people who appear to respond poorly are endurance athletes, while 'sedentary slobs do fine.'

Of course, not everyone feels good out in the mountains and certainly not all the time. Through history, mountains have often been places more associated with lawlessness, monsters and evil spirits than with recreation and relaxation. (For a fascinating account of the influence of mountains, see Simon Schama's comprehensive survey, *Landscape and Memory*.)

Insomnia is a common problem, especially during a visitor's first 48 hours at higher elevation. So-called 'mountain sickness' is said to affect as many as 20 percent of visitors to the Colorado ski hills, for example, where altitude at base may be 2400 m (7872 ft) compared to 1500 m (4920 ft) in Banff and Jasper. Dryness is another irritant. (At the Banff Centre, there's a big demand for humidifiers from artists and musicians concerned about having their instruments, including their throats, dry out.)

Ah, and what about that common form of 'mountain madness,' the desire to quit that city job, buy mountain property based on a few happy days or weeks in these awe-inspiring surroundings, and start a new career baking chocolate chip cookies for tourists?

Lots of people have gone this route, and no doubt many are happy with their decisions. But stories of ill-considered property purchases and impulsive career changes are legion. Expensive housing, low pay and restricted career choices are just a few of the complaints. 'When I lived in Canmore, I never had any time to do the things I loved to do in the mountains,' one former mountain addict told us. After a year of trying to make a living there, he was happy to return to a well-paid city job. For a frank and sobering discussion of the dangers of resort town life, see Bob Sandford's informative insiders' guide, *The Book of Banff*.

The lesson? Enjoy your Rocky Mountain high, but don't let the lack of oxygen go to your brain.

Bicycling the Rockies

SWIMMING: Johnson and Herbert lakes in Banff are said to warm up enough for hardy swimmers, although to endure the cold, it probably helps to be under eight years old.

TENNIS: There are free tennis courts available to the public at the Banff Recreation Centre and the Banff Recreation Grounds, (403) 762-1113.

Indoor and Rainy-Day Guide

When clouds blanket Cascade Mountain and an all-day downpour sets in, resist the urge to move on immediately. Banff National Park is one of the few places in the Rockies where you can follow a day of mountain climbing with an evening at a live performance of the

Threepenny Opera or with a night out over Les Escargots à la bourguignonne. Rain can even be a blessing. It slows you down enough to discover what's happening right in the townsite.

A thick wallet is not essential to spending a rainy day in Banff townsite, although visitors who insist on sticking to Banff Avenue may be forgiven for thinking so. Banff townsite has the most spectacular hotel in western Canada—the Banff Springs, a best bet for lolling about on a rainy day—plus fabulous hot springs, several museums, fine alpine archives and a feast of festivals (a summer arts festival and television, mountain film and book festivals), all of which have larger centres turning shades of green. You could also make expeditions to nearby Canmore, an artists' mecca, to the new $14-million cowboy museum in Cochrane, to Radium Hot Springs or to Lake Louise.

Although Lake Louise Village is not nearly as lively as the Banff townsite, indoor and rainy-day activities can be found by the intrepid visitor. The Post Hotel or Chateau Lake Louise are two great places to start.

Before raindrops drive you back into your sleeping bag or RV, first give a thought to continuing with outdoor plans. The Banff and Lake Louise areas are among the best places in the Rockies for rainy-day walking. Numerous trails described in this book are fine for a wet day. See Rainy-Day Walks listed on page 54.

If rainy-day outdoor adventuring doesn't appeal to you, here's a menu of toasty-dry diversions.

ARCHIVES OF THE CANADIAN ROCKIES: Step back into the past in this comforting place, which seems far from the glitz of Banff Avenue. The public is welcome to browse through an extensive historic photograph collection, which includes scrapbooks of Hollywood's long-ago love affair with Banff, among other treasures. Nearby are many fascinating items, including books on mountain teahouses and local flora and fauna. A manuscript collection, oral history collection and research library on the Canadian Rockies are housed here. Part of the Whyte Museum, 111 Bear Street, Monday through Saturday, 1 p.m. to 5 p.m., except for Thursdays, 6 p.m. to 9 p.m. Closed Sundays. Call (403) 762-2291.

ART GALLERY AMBLES: The Whyte Museum of the Canadian Rockies displays paintings, drawings, sculptures—a wide range of art. Recent offerings include both international and local artists. The gallery, in the same building as the archives, is at 111 Bear Street. Hours are from 10 a.m. to 6 p.m. daily, mid-May to June 30; 10 a.m. to 9 p.m. daily, July and August; 10 a.m. to 6 p.m. daily, Labour Day to mid-October; winter hours, 1 p.m. to 5 p.m., Tuesday to Sunday; Thursday to 9 p.m. year-round. Call (403) 762-2291.

The Painter's Rockies

What do A. Y. Jackson, Lawren Harris, Arthur Lismer and J.E.H. MacDonald have in common?

Aside from being members of Canada's famous Group of Seven, they were also among the fine painters who have been enchanted by the landscape of the Canadian Rockies, and translated that enchantment into enduring works of art.

Glaciers, Rocky Mountains, by Lawren Harris, is one of the most stunning paintings of glaciers. Anyone who has been to Lake O'Hara will understand J.E.H. MacDonald's enthusiasm for the area, reflected in such lovely paintings as *Lake O'Hara, With Snow.*

The Canadian Pacific Railway, never a slouch at tooting its own horn, sponsored such painters as A.C. Leighton to stay at its hotels and paint the surrounding landscapes. Walter J. Phillips, Illingworth Kerr, Kathleen Daly and Frederick Henry Brigden are among others whose art was influenced by this profound landscape. Two early Banff artists of note were Catharine Robb Whyte and Peter Whyte, active outdoor persons who lived and painted in the area for decades. The former's *Mount Temple, Larches,* which captures one of the Rockies' most delicate and special sights, is a favourite of many.

Lisa Christensen's book, *A Hiker's Guide to Art of the Canadian Rockies,* is an excellent, award-winning companion guide to the paintings of this area. If you want to view fine Rocky Mountain art, visit the Whyte Museum of the Canadian Rockies in Banff.

Paintings, ceramics, weaving and slides are some of the visual art exhibits on display at the Walter J. Phillips Gallery, part of the Banff Centre. Includes works by Canadian and international artists, faculty members and students. Particularly known for photography and video. Combine a browse here with a stroll through some of the 27 acres encompassing the Banff Centre (Walk 7). The gallery is in the Jean and Peter Lougheed Building, Banff Centre. Open daily 12 p.m. to 5 p.m.; call for evening hours in summer. Closed Monday. (403) 762-6281.

BADMINTON: Try the gym at the Banff Community High School, (403) 762-1113; bring your own racquet. Or call the Sally Borden Building at the Banff Centre to book gym time. Racquet rentals available, (403) 762-6450.

BANFF CENTRE: One of the perks of a Rocky Mountain summer is the Banff Festival of the Arts, which includes music, theatre, dance, opera, film and visual arts. The centre, occupying 27 acres on Tunnel Mountain, is one of Canada's most prestigious post-graduate schools for professional artists. You can walk there from Banff

Avenue. Each summer from May to nearly the end of August, numerous performances are open to the public, including jazz, opera, chamber music, drama, movies and mime. Watch for special events. The Banff Festival of Mountain Films and the Mountain Book Festival are held each fall. The new Banff Centre for Mountain Culture presents an array of interesting events. (Everest mountaineer Jon Krakauer, author of *Into Thin Air*, gave a slide show and reading there recently.) These and other activities too numerous to list are open to the public year-round. For events information, check the local papers or call the box office, (403) 762-6300 or 1-800-413-8368.

BANFF HERITAGE HOMES TOURS: Glimpse what life was like in Banff in the first part of the 20ᵗʰ century. Daily guided tours are given in summer (except Tuesdays) through two log homes, one belonging to Col. A. and Pearl Brewster Moore, built in 1907, the other the home of Catharine and Peter Whyte, built in 1930–31. The Moore house displays native art, eastern American antiques and equine gadgets. The Whyte home reflects the family's lives as artists, skiers, travellers and collectors. Check times and register in advance at the Whyte Museum, 111 Bear Street, (403) 762-2291.

BANFF SPRINGS HOTEL: Never mind if it's pouring rain. While the Scottish baronial exterior of the Banff Springs Hotel impresses, its interior warms. This hotel is perhaps the most magnificent hotel in western Canada and deserves a peek inside, rain or shine. The styles are so diverse that 30-minute guided tours of the hotel—the largest in the world when it was built in 1888—are conducted daily year-round. Meet at the concierge's desk at 5 p.m.—call (403) 762-2211.

The hotel, nestled between Rundle and Sulphur mountains and the confluence of the Bow and Spray rivers, looks out on one of the most beautiful scenes in the Rockies. Find a writing desk looking out on all of this beauty and compose a long letter (or e-mail) home, or read a romantic novel. The setting's perfect. If you're in the mood for pampering, treat yourself to a visit to Solace—the spa. (See 'Spas' listing for details.)

Cave and Basin observation deck

Banff Springs Hotel

'If we can't export the scenery, we'll import the tourists.'

Those famous words, spoken by William Van Horne, general superintendent of the Canadian Pacific Railway (CPR), heralded the beginnings of the hotel.

After the discovery of the hot springs below Sulphur Mountain in 1883, the government declared a 26-sq.-km (10-sq.-mi) block around the hot springs a national reserve and proposals were made to expand the park.

Van Horne foresaw the fabulous tourism potential of the park and predicted that wealthy people travelling by rail would enjoy the mountain playground. In 1887, he made plans for a hotel at the confluence of the Bow and Spray rivers.

The 250-room hotel was the largest in the world when it was finished in 1888, but by 1910 the CPR decided to build anew. Designed in the Scottish baronial tradition, a new central stone section was completed in 1913. The original north wing burned down in 1926, and the original south wing was demolished and rebuilt in 1928.

Inside, decor ranges from Spanish in the Alhambra Dining Room to 15th-century gothic in Mount Stephen Hall. The designers tried to imitate the furniture found in European castles of the time. The oak panelling is from Michigan, the glass in the Riverview Lounge is from the former Czechoslovakia and the Stephen Hall flagstone is from Indiana.

A Royal Guest List

What do you think of this aristocratic guest list? Guests who have stayed at the Banff Springs Hotel over the years include Lord Stanley, a former Governor General of Canada, and Lady Stanley in 1889, the Duke and Duchess of Connaught (who were canoeing on the Bow River when they learned the First World War had broken out), the King and Queen of Siam in 1930, King George VI and Queen Elizabeth (the Queen Mother) in 1939 and their daughter, Queen Elizabeth II in 1959.

Makes you glad they keep the silver polished up there.

BOOK IT: Outdoorsy types will find the Banff Book and Art Den, 110 Banff Avenue, well-stocked with maps and books on outdoor adventure and mountain lore—everything from bears to Bonington. Same-day copies of the Sunday *Los Angeles Times* and *New York Times* are also available, but dash down early. The Whyte Museum of the Canadian Rockies has a fine selection of books about the area. The Banff Public Library, 101 Bear Street, is also a good place to browse in the books and magazines on a rainy day. The reading room in the Banff Park Museum, at the north side of the Banff Avenue Bridge, is a wonder and open to the public.

facing page: Banff Springs Hotel

arts

The Literary Rockies

For generations, the landscape of the Canadian Rockies has inspired writers to scale literary heights.

The famed American poet William Stafford was inspired by his travels here to pen 'The Woman at Banff.' The poem contains two elements foreign writers love: bears and moose.

Ralph Connor, judged by some as Canada's most successful novelist of the early 20th century, was inspired by his missionary work in Canmore and Banff to pen numerous best-sellers. The Lethbridge-born writer Howard O'Hagan is acknowledged by many as Canada's premiere literary 'mountain man.' His 1939 novel, *Tay John*, celebrates the blonde giant, 'Tete Jaune,' for whom Yellowhead Pass is named. O'Hagan's short stories are also acclaimed and stand the test of time better than many. See *The Woman Who Got On At Jasper Station and Other Stories*. Another mountain man of literature is conservationist Andy Russell, whose acclaimed non-fiction books include *Adventures with Wild Animals*, *Grizzly Country* and *Horns in the High Country*. Former Parks Canada employee, Sid Marty, gained international acclaim for *Men for the Mountains*, an immensely readable account of his often-harrowing days as a warden.

A reading of *Icefields*, Thomas Wharton's award-winning, evocative novel of early days of exploration at the Columbia Icefield, will enrich the experience of visiting this area. Two other fine novels set in the Crowsnest Pass area of the Rockies are Peter Oliva's *Drowning in Darkness* and Roberta Rees' *Beneath the Faceless Mountain*.

If you're itching to rub shoulders with literary luminaries, plan to attend the annual PanCanadian WordFest Banff-Calgary International Writers' Festival usually held in mid-October. The event features readings in both Calgary and Banff, and attracts such internationally known writers as Margaret Atwood. Hard on its heels is the Banff Festival of Mountain Books, usually held in early November in conjunction with the Banff Festival of Mountain Films.

If you are a serious writer interested in honing your skill in these inspiring surroundings, investigate programs offered in Banff by the Banff Centre and in Jasper at the Jasper Palisades and the nearby Black Cat Guest Ranch. Call the Writers' Guild of Alberta, (403) 422-8174.

BOWLING: There's a four-lane, five-pin bowling centre, open to the public, at the Banff Springs Hotel Bowling Centre, 405 Spray Avenue, (403) 762-6892.

CANMORE EXCURSION: For a change of scene, head for Canmore, an old coal-mining town established in 1883. It's situated beneath the famous Three Sisters mountains in the Bow Valley, 25 km (15.5 mi) east of Banff townsite on the Trans-Canada. Canmore isn't as flashy, expensive or crowded as Banff. It's more low-key, although it's filled with artists, film-makers and outdoor lovers who enjoy the mountains. And the town is the gateway to some gorgeous hiking areas. (See Kananaskis Country, chapter 5, page 271.) The Canmore Nordic Centre, host of the nordic skiing events for the 1988 Winter Olympics, is an attraction. Some old buildings from the coal-mining days still stand. The town stages the superb, family-oriented Heritage Days Folk Festival the first weekend in August, with ethnic food and crafts as well. The event draws people from as far away as Europe.

CAVE AND BASIN: This national historic site is where Banff National Park began. The centre features a walk into the reconstructed cave where the springs were first found (kids will especially love this), as well as a cafeteria, historical exhibits, excellent videos about the park, computer games about the past and cozy nooks for curling up with a book. See Walks 1 and 2 and sidebar, page 64.

CEMETERY CREEPING:
Although not to everyone's taste, tombstone aficionados will be tickled to find the graves of persons famous in local history: Brewster, Whyte and early Banff guides for starters. Check at the Whyte Museum for guided tours, reputed to be excellent, or go on your own.

(A guidebook, *Rest in the Peaks*, by E.J. Hart and Hélène Deziel-Letnick, is available at the Whyte Museum gift shop.) From Banff Avenue, turn left before the Banff Avenue Bridge and go up three blocks to the corner of Otter and Buffalo.

CHATEAU LAKE LOUISE: Rain or shine, the most genteel way to cap a fine afternoon might be with afternoon tea in the lobby of the Chateau Lake Louise. Served from 1 p.m. to 3 p.m. in summer.

The restaurants of the Chateau are legion, and the view from most of them can make it hard to focus on the food. The most formal is the Edelweiss Dining Room (jacket required) with pan-fried trout or seared venison medallions. The large Victoria Dining Room upstairs offers a buffet and a large dinner menu. The Tom Wilson Room on the seventh floor features Italian fare, and the Poppy Room downstairs is casual and relatively inexpensive. The Walliser Stube is a Swiss wine bar with raclette, fondues and simple fare such as hearty barley soup.

CHILDREN'S PROGRAMS:
There are a variety of children's programs in the Banff townsite (see 'Outdoor Adventures' section, page 29).

During winter, some Lake Louise hotels offer kids' nights, with special programs and qualified care.

CLIMB A WALL: The climbing wall at the Banff Community High School is open to experienced climbers on an hourly basis; 335 Beaver Street, (403) 762-1113.

COCHRANE COWBOY CAPER: Absolutely pouring? Be an urban cowboy. Head east to the town of Cochrane, a scenic one-hour drive east of Banff townsite, where the $14-million Western Heritage Centre rounds up and entertains visitors everyday. (Take Hwy. 1A from Canmore for the best scenery.) The centre, the only one of its kind in Canada, was a decade in planning, and is the first major Canadian attraction dedicated to the history of western life. Exhibits showcase the old, new and future West, blending computer technology with cowboy romance. You can try your hand at milking a fibreglass cow, use computer technology to wield an electronic scalpel and 'save' a calf's life, watch a retired rancher demonstrate leather tooling, and even see yourself as a 'virtual cowboy' through the use of blue-screen technology. Not your usual cowpoke collection of artifacts. Special seasonal events, such as a 'Cowboy Christmas,' are also offered. Call (403) 932-3514 for times.

CRUISE DEVIL'S GAP: Depending on how low the cloud cover is, a cruise on Lake Minnewanka, just outside of Banff townsite, is a possibility even in the rain. The boats are covered. See 'Outdoor Adventures' (page 29).

DINING IN BANFF: Drowning rainy-day blahs in a flat-out feast in Banff townsite isn't such a bad idea, if you can afford it. After all, you can always burn away the calories by striking up Sentinel Pass tomorrow. The Chamber of Commerce on Banff Avenue distributes a booklet called *Dining in Banff*, with menus from local restaurants, but alas, few prices. Be forewarned: Eating in Banff is not cheap.

Casual: For a relaxed, affordable meal, we like Giorgio's Trattoria, at 219 Banff Avenue. Italian specialties, such as pizza cooked in a wood-burning pizza oven and pasta, are featured, (403) 762-5114. (Reservations for eight or more only; you may have to line up, but the line usually moves fast.) Coyotes Deli & Grill, featuring southwestern fare, is a favourite with locals; 206 Caribou Street, (403) 762-3963. For a great sandwich or a casual meal (shepherd's pie comes to mind), Evelyn's Coffee Bar, 201 Banff Avenue, is satisfying, if often crowded. And when the crowds on Banff Avenue tire you out, you can often squeeze into an enjoyable nook at the Fine Grind, 137 Banff Avenue, for coffee, spanokopita, salads, chili and other light fare. Or take a hike up to the Banff Centre and have a sandwich, homemade soup, specialty coffee or baked goods at La Palette, Donald Cameron Hall. It's tiny, easy on the budget, full of art supplies, and the eavesdropping is great; the person next to you may have been studying at the Juilliard last week.

The cafeteria in the Mineral Springs Hospital is open to the public for lunch only, and is said to have the best hospital food in Canada (perhaps because of an insistence on fresh ingredients and the abundance of great chefs who gravitate to town). Local professionals know what's good and often congregate here.

Splurge: If you're pursuing a peak dining experience, Buffalo Mountain Lodge has a reputation for dishing out some of the finest cuisine in the Rockies. It specializes in regional cuisine such as northern caribou with apple fig chutney and mushroom crusted beef tenderloin. Tunnel Mountain Road, (403) 762-2400. Le Beaujolais also achieves gastronomic heights. Try home-smoked B.C. salmon with creme fraiche or Chateaubriand of Alberta beef. At the corner of Banff Avenue and Buffalo Street, (403) 762-2712. Try the new Ticino's for Swiss-Italian food, at the High Country Inn, 415 Banff Avenue, (403) 762-3848. The Grizzly House, 207 Banff Avenue, (403) 762-4055, still serves the original fondue dinner but has added some unusual variations: shark, alligator and rattlesnake, to name a few. Or head to the Banff Springs Hotel. Diners are often surprised at what good value can be found at the hotel's various eateries, especially the smaller ones: the renowned Samurai (Japanese food), Grapes Wine Bar (wine, salad and cheese) and Waldhaus (fondues).

Breakfast: If you have plain but hearty breakfast fare in mind (we usually do), the Rundle Restaurant at 319 Banff Avenue, across the street from the Banff Information Centre, delivers what it promises: good service and good, plain food any time of day. The Clubhouse Restaurant, overlooking the Banff Springs golf course, offers one of

The Town Centre building, Banff townsite

the most affordable breakfasts in town and a deluxe view for all diners. Reservations recommended for lunch and dinner. A shuttle is available every half hour from the Banff Springs Hotel lobby, (403) 762-6868.

DINING IN LAKE LOUISE:

According to the locals, it's a crime to pass through Lake Louise Village without stopping at Laggan's, a popular bakery/deli. Grab a table (you may rub shoulders with someone just down from climbing Temple) and enjoy the frenetic but friendly scene. You can get a sandwich on whole-wheat for $3.75. (Laggan's doesn't add eggs, artificial colourings, flavours or preservatives to their bread.) Laggan's is also a great place to hit before going on a picnic. Stock up on baked goods ranging from lemon poppyseed bread to apple strudel and sourdough bread. (Psst! Don't wait in line as you go in the front door. There's often a second, faster line at a second cashier at the far end around the corner.)

Bill Peyto's Cafe in the new and gorgeous Lake Louise International Hostel is also popular with travellers. (Open to the public.) You can get French toast with maple syrup and fruit for $5.95, soup of the day with whole-wheat bread for $4.15 and spaghetti Bolognese (with meat) for $7.95. And yes, there is a liquor licence.

Looking for something more upscale? The Lake Louise Station Restaurant is (surprise) in a restored log station built in 1910 and in two Canadian Pacific Railway (CPR) dining cars from a later era. You can get beef stew or Station Kabobs for lunch. Dinner fare includes venison or oven-roasted halibut. The Baker Creek Bistro on the Bow Valley Parkway (Hwy. 1A), 15 km (9.3 mi) east of Lake Louise, serves up gourmet food such as grilled muscovy duck breast. Quaint surroundings. Reservations recommended, (403) 522-2182. For one of the finest dining experiences in the Rockies, head for the renowned Post Hostel, (403) 522-3989. In *Gourmet's* words, 'the standards of excellence of Swiss brothers George and Andre Schwarz are a benchmark for the area.' For a casual drink, the Outpost Pub is warm and distinctive. For a real treat, have breakfast at the Post. The orange juice will be freshly squeezed, you'll feel like royalty, and while it may dent your budget, it won't break it. Also see 'Chateau Lake Louise' listing for more dining possibilities.

FITNESS CENTRES: If you're not getting in enough hiking or other strenuous activities, there's no need to disrupt your normal fitness routine while in the Rockies. The well-equipped Banff Community Fitness Centre at the town high school is open to the public. The gym is also available for most sports from September through June on evenings and weekends and also during the day in July and August, (403) 762-1113. The Sally Borden Centre at the Banff Centre has a weight room, bicycles, step machines, a gym, drop-in classes, equipment rental, sauna, jacuzzi, a gorgeous glass-enclosed swimming pool and much more. Open to the public, (403) 762-6450.

GUIDED AUTO TOURS: The scenery won't be as great on a rainy day but at least you'll be dry. Parks Canada publishes a brochure on suggested drives in the park. Also see 'Outdoor Adventures' (page 30) for recommendations. The number of commercial operators offering guided tours in the park has sky-rocketed in recent years. For the most up-to-date listing, check the *Official Visitor Guide* published by the Banff/Lake Louise Tourism Bureau. Free at the information/ visitor centres.

HOSTEL TOUR: Even if hostels aren't your thing, it's worth taking a look at the Lake Louise International Hostel to see just how good hostelling can get. The hostel, built in partnership with the Canadian Club of Canada, has 150 beds (including family rooms), a licensed cafe and a spacious upper lounge. In the Lizzie Rummel Reading Room, you can hunker down with old issues of the *Canadian Alpine Journal* and many other fascinating mountain-related journals and books. Located on Village Road, (403) 522-2200.

HOT SPRINGS (BANFF): Not to be missed, and you can enjoy them in any weather. See Hot Springs listing (page 36).

INTERPRETIVE EXHIBITS AND VIDEOS: The Lake Louise Visitor Centre is also an interpretive centre, with a theatre showing videos about the area's natural and cultural history, plus displays of the geology of the area.

Mountain Geology: How Cirques Are Formed

In the interpretive centre at Lake Louise, visitors can learn about geological features such as cirques. These natural depressions in the sides of mountains tend to be widened and deepened by the freezing and thawing of water. These depressions become natural channels for glaciers, which pick up boulders as they travel down the mountain-side and scratch and gouge away the rock at their base. Because the erosion is greatest in the centre of the glacier, a bowl-shaped depression tends to be created under all that ice and snow. The most striking peaks in the Rockies got their pyramid-like shape largely because of cirque glaciers that cut away the mountain from several angles.

Glaciers in the Canadian Rockies are generally retreating and the ones that created the cirques on the sides of many mountains have long since vanished. In the front ranges, for example, few of the peaks bear glaciers—the winter chinook winds prevent the snowfall accumulation from becoming deep enough to form long-lasting ice.

geology

LAUNDRY: Unromantic but practical. The Cascade Plaza Laundromat in the Cascade Plaza on Banff Avenue provides a drop-off and dry-cleaning service. Parking may be less of a hassle, however, at the Chalet Coin Laundry on Tunnel Mountain, where you can swim and frolic on the waterslide while your clothes are rinsing.

MOUNTAIN LECTURES, LORE, READINGS: The Whyte Museum of the Canadian Rockies holds intriguing programs every Thursday night at 7:30 p.m., from October to March and July to August, (403) 762-2291. Also contact the Banff Centre and the Banff Information Centre and/or check local publications.

MOVIES: The Lux Theatre screens first-run movies and also less commercial fare. Wolf and Bear streets, (403) 762-8595. Film buffs should also check public screenings at the Banff International Television Festival, usually held in June, (403) 678-9260, and the Banff Festival of Mountain Films in early November, (403) 762-6125.

MUSEUMS:

Banff Park Museum: Don't miss western Canada's oldest and best preserved early museum located in the Banff townsite. The structure itself has been described as 'the most handsome of western public buildings.' Built in 1903 by the Canadian Pacific Railway (CPR) as a research facility and tourist attraction, the museum is constructed in the architectural style called 'railroad pagoda.' Recently restored, it features trestle-like internal supports, a lantern skylight and an exquisite reading room open to the public.

The museum conducts excellent daily tours that the whole family will enjoy. Natural history treasures include a (stuffed) grizzly bear, mountain sheep and wolves. You can also peek into the office of the eccentric first curator, Norman Sanson. The museum is interesting not only as an architectural and natural history showpiece, but as an insight into how wildlife management has changed in the parks. Learn about the days when the museum kept a zoo in Central Park, complete with coyotes, foxes and elk! Situated just off Banff Avenue beside the Banff Avenue Bridge. Open 10 a.m. to 6 p.m. daily in summer; daily tours at 11 a.m. and 3 p.m. Open 10 a.m. to 5 p.m. daily, September to May; daily tour at 3 p.m. Admission fee, (403) 762-1558.

Luxton Museum of the Plains Indians: The Luxton Museum in Banff townsite is operated by the Buffalo Nations Cultural Society, and explores the heritage of the native peoples of the Northern Plains and the Canadian Rockies. The museum, at 1 Birch Avenue, is situated in a log building across Banff Avenue Bridge (turn right).

arts

The Rockies See Stars

Besides Hollywood, what do Marilyn Monroe, Bing Crosby, James Stewart and Betty Grable have in common with Margot Kidder, Arnold Schwarzenegger and Sir Anthony Hopkins?

They've all appeared in films shot in and around the Canadian Rockies, a drawing card for Hollywood since the 1920s. Walter Brennan was one of the first big stars, appearing in *The Alaskan* with Anna May Wong. Betty Grable filmed *Springtime in the Rockies* in Banff National Park in 1942. In 1946, Billy Wilder directed *The Emperor Waltz* in Jasper, starring Bing Crosby. The film was shot at Mt. Edith Cavell; some of the trees were brought in from Hollywood! James Stewart visited the Rockies in 1953 for *The Far Country*, which was shot at the Columbia Icefield, Mt. Edith Cavell and Moberly Flats in Jasper.

In the same year, Otto Preminger filmed *River of No Return*, starring Marilyn Monroe, Robert Mitchum and Rory Calhoun. Even Joe Dimaggio is reported to have appeared in Banff that star-struck summer, calling on Monroe at the Banff Springs.

In more recent years, the Rockies have been the setting for parts of *Dr. Zhivago*, the Superman films (in nearby Kananaskis Country), Robert Altman's *Buffalo Bill and the Indians*, starring Paul Newman, the Oscar-winning *Unforgiven*, with Clint Eastwood, and *Last of the Dog Men*, with Tom Berenger and Barbara Hershey.

The Canadian-made television series, *Destiny Ridge*, began shooting in Jasper in 1993. Alex Baldwin and Sir Anthony Hopkins filmed *The Edge* in 1996, staying in Canmore. The Canadian Rockies celebrates its star-struck appeal each June at the annual Banff International Television Festival and the Banff Festival of Mountain Films in late fall.

Life-size displays show how native peoples made pemmican, performed the Sundance and experienced vision quests. Other exhibits explore such subjects as the importance of eagles to North American native cultures. Look for hand-crafted beadwork in the gift shop. Open 9 a.m. to 7 p.m. Admission fee; (403) 762-2388.

Natural History Museum: This museum contains displays, audio-visuals and models to give glimpses into the geological and natural history of the area. There's an exhibit on the Castleguard Cave, one of the largest caves in North America. One display depicts hoodoo formation; another small exhibit focuses on mountain forests. Clock Tower Village, 2nd floor, 112 Banff Avenue; open 11 a.m. to 7 p.m. daily, (403) 762-4747. Free.

The Whyte Museum of the Canadian Rockies: While in Banff townsite, head here for an introduction to the human history and culture of Banff National Park. Heritage exhibits take you back to early settlement days; art exhibits change frequently. There are also Thursday night lectures (see Mountain Lectures, page 52). The museum has an excellent gift shop, with many books about the cultural and natural history of the area, as well as local art and quality jewellery. A great place to stock up on Christmas stocking stuffers. The Lizzie Rummel Tea Shoppe is open in summer; 111 Bear Street, (403) 762-2291.

NIGHT LIFE: Kick up your heels to DJ music at Silver City, 110 Banff Avenue. Locals often congregate in the upstairs pub at Melissa's, 218 Lynx Street. If western music is your thing, Wild Bill's Legendary Saloon, 201 Banff Avenue, is the place to see some top talent. For truly dignified watering holes, the Rundle Lounge, a piano lounge, or the Grapes wine bar, both on the mezzanine level at the Banff Springs Hotel, rate high. Visitors also rave about the Larkspur Lounge in the Rimrock Resort Hotel.

POST IT: *Esquire Magazine* called Lake Louise's Post Hotel 'the world's most perfect ski lodge,' and it's easy to see why. Relax for a while in the lovely lounge area. Connive to linger by staying for afternoon tea or retiring to the Outpost Pub.

RAINY-DAY CYCLING: Although people who haven't tried it might cringe at the suggestion, bicycling in the rain can be enjoyable, as long as you have a waterproof poncho or jacket and a warm, dry place at the end. The action of cycling usually keeps the body warm, at least in summer. A fine and mostly flat cycle from Banff townsite follows the Bow Valley Parkway (Hwy. 1A). See chapter 7 (page 348). The Canmore Nordic Centre has challenging mountain bike trails and a warm, dry area to gulp down a hot drink and watch the showers come down.

RAINY-DAY WALKS: In Banff townsite, the short, interpretive Fenland Trail (Walk 4) is a fine choice for a rainy day. So are the Cave and Basin Marsh Trail (Walk 1) and Discovery Trail (Walk 2) by the Cave and Basin Hot Springs. Amble through the Centennial Centre with its exhibits and films, then drive to the Upper Hot Springs to chase the chills away with a blissful soak in the naturally heated pool. Or stroll through the remains of Bankhead, a coal-mining ghost town near Banff (Walk 14). Further afield, prowl Johnston Canyon (Walk 22), Marble Canyon (Walk 50) or the Paint Pots (Walk 51), where you see much the same thing in sun or showers.

In Lake Louise, the Lakeshore Trail (Walk 34) and Consolation Lakes (Walk 30) are fairly short and inspiring. If you are more energetic, take a jaunt to a teahouse: Lake Agnes (Walk 38) or

Plain of Six Glaciers (Walk 35). The hot soup will taste all the better for the rain!

RACQUET SPORTS: A number of lodges and inns have racquetball and squash facilities and make them available to non-guests. Inquire at the Banff Information Centre.

SHOPPING: In Banff, the Whyte Museum of the Canadian Rockies operates a gift store with tasteful and reasonable souvenirs, 111 Bear Street. If you want to see how millionaires shop, visit the boutiques in the Banff Springs Hotel.

In summer, the Friends of Banff Park operates a gift shop in Lake Louise's Visitor Centre, a good place to get a head-start on Christmas shopping. (All profits go towards preservation of the park.) Other shopping is concentrated in the Samson Mall, a better-than-average development of fieldstone and wood. Spend some time browsing in the splendid Woodruff & Blum bookstore, which has an extensive selection of outdoor and nature guides to the area, as well as everything from literary fiction to kids' books. You can also pick up topographical maps, newspapers,

Banff Avenue

magazines, posters and cards. The mall also has a sportswear store, a photography store, takeout chicken and pizza places, homemade ice cream and candy stores, a post office, public showers, a liquor store and an Alberta treasury branch, among others. Check the Chateau for upscale shopping.

SHOWERS: A great indoor activity. If you don't have access to a shower or are staying at a campground without showers, your group can arrange for them at a campground with these facilities. The group fee is $5. Ask the campground attendant. In Lake Louise, showers are also available in Samson Mall.

SKATING: The Banff Recreation Centre offers indoor public skating from the end of April to August. Skate rentals available, (403) 762-1238 for times.

SPAS: If you haven't been to Banff townsite for a while, the big news here is 'Solace,' the $12-million spa facility opened at the Banff Springs Hotel in 1995. This 3150-sq.-m (35,000-sq.-ft), 16-room, European-style spa is steeped in luxury, from mineral whirlpools and indoor/outdoor saltwater pools to cascading waterfalls. For many visitors to Banff, the ultimate pampering experience is a visit here. Most spa amenities, including use of the mineralized pool and the aquatic, cardio and aerobic centres, are open to non-guests for $30 daily. Take your pick of pleasures as diverse as an all-natural Italian Fango Mud facial ($75) to a Moor Mud Wrap ($100) or a Thalassobath ($50), which uses 'the healing properties of the sea' to relax and detoxify the body. (And if you're out of ideas for that birthday or anniversary gift, here's one.) Call (403) 762-1772.

SPORTS INJURY THERAPY: The Banff & Canmore Sports Injury Clinics assist with short-term and long-term help, (403) 762-3734 in Banff, (403) 678-6205 in Canmore.

SWIMMING: Try the glass-topped pool at the Sally Borden Building, Banff Centre. Call for public hours, (403) 762-6450. See 'Banff Springs Hotel' listing (page 43) for a phone number to call about the hotel's pool.

TEA TIME: Enjoying high tea seems the most civilized way to watch the rain (or even the sun) beat down. Sip away at the Banff Springs Hotel, perhaps combining tea with a hotel tour. Tea served from 2:30 p.m. to 4:30 p.m. daily, from July to September, in the Van Horne Room on the mezzanine level.

Or drive to the Post Hotel in Lake Louise for its afternoon tea, home-made custard pie, with fresh fruit, and cake of the day. Daily from 2:30 p.m. to 5 p.m. The Chateau Lake Louise also serves afternoon tea in the lobby, with beautiful views over the lake and Victoria Glacier, from 1 p.m. to 3 p.m. in summer.

Upper Hot Springs

WATERSLIDES: Two indoor waterslides (in Banff townsite) at Douglas Fir Resort on Tunnel Mountain are open to the public. There's also a jacuzzi, steam room and fitness room. Call (403) 762-5591 for times.

wildlife

Be Sensible about Bears

There's something bigger and stronger and faster than you out there. Thousands, maybe millions, of visitors to the mountain parks never venture out of the parking lot because of their fear of bears. But for all of those horror stories of grizzly attacks, studies show that you're far safer on mountain trails than driving on the highway. Most experienced hikers feel more secure alone on any trail in

black bear

the national parks than on city streets. It's estimated that there is only one bear injury for every two million park visitors. So if you allow yourself to be frightened away from exploring, you're missing so much—for so little reason.

But it is true that bears, especially when startled or made to feel threatened, can be fearsome, even life-threatening.

The black bear is a more common sighting in the Rockies than the grizzly, which can be distinguished by the hump on its back and its dished-in face. Highway bear encounters—a common cause of traffic jams—can bring out the worst in visitors, who are tempted to get out of their cars and approach the bears or, worse yet, offer them food. If a bear approaches while you are in a vehicle, stay in your car and roll the windows all the way up. These bears have learned to tolerate traffic and humans because they associate people with food. They are problem bears, caused by problem people. Such bears are more dangerous and unpredictable than wild ones.

In recent years, the use of bear repellents has become popular. A study by bear experts Stephen Herrero and Andrew Higgins of the University of Calgary examined the use of bear sprays in 66 incidents between 1988–94. In 94 percent of cases involving aggressive bears, the spray stopped the aggressive behaviour that was displayed immediately before the spray was released.

While it's wise to carry bear spray, it's equally wise to regard it as a last resort. Be sure it is accessible, check the expiry date, don't let it freeze or carry it with the safety clip off, and don't carry it in the cabin of an aircraft. Bear spray is available on a rental basis; ask your lodge operator.

If camping, don't cook in or around the tent, keep a clean camp and store food in your vehicle or high in a tree well away from camp. When hiking, make enough noise that any bear in the area will know you are coming. Some

grizzly bear

people wear bells; some just talk a lot. If you are travelling into the wind, the bear might not get your scent until you are close.

facing page: Lower Waterfowl Lake

1. Cave and Basin Marsh Trail

Minnows and mallards

Watercress growing outdoors in January? Six species of wild orchids? Robins in winter? This lavishly interpreted trail is a microcosm of rich marshland warmed by thermal springs from Sulphur Mountain.

access

In Banff townsite. Trailhead sign is north of the Cave and Basin buildings at the end of Cave Avenue, 1.6 km (1 mi) west of the Banff Avenue Bridge.

Map: page 61
Distance: 1-km (0.6-mi) loop
Time: 20–25 minutes
Rating: Easy
Max. elevation: 1383 m (4536 ft)
Elevation loss: Negligible
Footwear: Anything
Best season: Year-round

Keep right on the boardwalk, which soon crosses a tiny, steamy stream. This warm run-off from Sulphur Mountain's hot springs keeps moss and watercress growing year-round. Six species of orchids flourish here in spring.

Just below the stream, free telescopes are provided to help you search for animals and birds in the marsh and view the surrounding peaks across the Bow River flats.

Birdwatching blind

Directly ahead is Mt. Norquay—the distinctive, needle-like pinnacle of Mt. Edith rises to its left, and the slate grey Cascade Mountain glistens to its right. The spiky Sawback Range thrusts upwards to the northwest.

At the bird viewpoint, summer visitors might spy yellowthroats, ruby-crowned kinglets, red-winged blackbirds, teals, snipes or mallards. The ice-free marsh also attracts birds, such as the killdeer, that would otherwise fly south for winter.

The boardwalk leads down to a platform on the edge of the marsh—a tangle of willows, sedges, water lilies, duckweeds, cattails and rushes in a lush environment warmed by the water from the hot spring. A birdwatching blind occupies the end of the boardwalk, allowing visitors to scan for ducks, warblers, juncos and many other birds. In fact, 80 percent of Banff's bird species can be found here in the course of a year.

Follow the boardwalk and trail back to the Cave and Basin buildings.

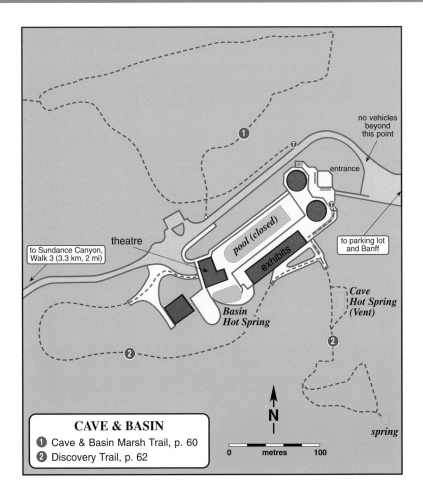

to Sundance Canyon,
Walk 3 (3.3 km, 2 mi)

theatre

no vehicles
beyond
this point

entrance

pool (closed)

exhibits

to parking lot
and Banff

*Basin
Hot Spring*

*Cave
Hot Spring
(Vent)*

N

spring

CAVE & BASIN

❶ Cave & Basin Marsh Trail, p. 60
❷ Discovery Trail, p. 62

0   metres   100

Banff's Unique Ex-minnow

Many years ago, some aquarium enthusiasts in Banff wanted to see what would happen if tropical fish, such as the sailfin molly, were released into warm waters near the outlet of Banff's famed hot springs. Unfortunately, the tropical fish flourished at the expense of some native species. The experiment spelled disaster for the Banff longnose dace, a native minnow adapted to warm water. Because of the introduction of the aquarium fish, the Banff longnose dace, which was found nowhere else on Earth, is now believed to be extinct—a stark reminder of the dangers of tampering with nature's delicate balance.

wildlife

2. Discovery Trail—*Hike to a hole*

A very short route to a very important site: the mysterious hole in the ground that the McCardell brothers and their partner, Frank McCabe, stumbled across in 1883. Their discovery led indirectly to the formation of Canada's national park system.

access

The route begins at the stairs to the left of the main entrance to the Cave and Basin buildings, which are in Banff townsite at the end of Cave Avenue, 1.6 km (1 mi) west of the Banff Avenue Bridge.

Map: page 61
Distance: 1 km (0.6 mi)
Time: 15 minutes
Rating: Easy (some stairs, wheelchair access is from the rear of Cave and Basin buildings)
Max. elevation: 1395 m (4576 ft)
Elevation gain: Negligible
Footwear: Anything
Best season: Anytime (stairs and boardwalk not maintained in winter)

Take the wide stairs behind the elegant Cave and Basin buildings, and keep left to reach a very important hole in the ground. You can peer down into the cave just as the three young Canadian Pacific Railway (CPR) workers did in 1883. (Well, maybe not exactly as they did—there's now a grate over the hole, a fence around it, a paved trail and the sound of visitors below.)

These three workers had been prospecting in the valley when they stumbled on the warm stream that can be seen on Walk 1. Following the stream, they came across the basin pool and then found a mysterious hole in the ground, which had sulphurous vapour arising from the depths. On the next visit, one of the men—William McCardell—climbed into the hole on a tree trunk and found a cave of hanging stalactites and a clear hot spring bubbling up from below. He stripped and became one of the first of many bathers. It might have been his first bath in some time. In a frontier where plumbing

Cave and Basin

The Basin

was unknown, hot water could be liquid gold.

Although McCardell, his brother Tom and partner Frank McCabe did not grow rich, their discovery led indirectly to the formation of Canada's national parks system (see sidebar, page 64).

Past the hole in the ground, the trail leads to a spring where hot water bubbles from the rock. The route terminates at an odiferous hot pool surrounded by deposits of tufa, a rock that looks like a dark sponge. Tufa consists primarily of calcium and magnesium compounds that crystallize when the warm, mineral-filled waters reach the surface of the ground.

Return past the hole in the ground, and turn left to circle above the original basin that served as a warm swimming and soaking hole before the rectangular pool was built. Stairs lead back to the main Cave and Basin buildings.

history

Hot Water Was Gold

'The beautiful glistening stalactites that decorated this silent cave were like some fantastic tale of the Arabian Nights .... They had attained such perfection, that it must have required myriads of years to shape them to the size they had developed into.'

That's how William McCardell described the experience of discovering sulphur hot springs within a misty cave. The year was 1883. He'd stumbled across the Cave and Basin while prospecting for minerals on the slopes of Sulphur Mountain.

The three railway workers were not the first to see these springs, but they were the first to try to profit from them. The Stoney knew of the two mineral hot springs, and legend says that arthritic grizzly bears used to soak their aching bones there.

Soon after the discovery of the springs, ownership of this land caused a dispute, which caught the federal government's attention. The government stepped in, and in 1885, 26 sq. km (10 sq. mi) around the springs were formally set aside as a reserve (the Banff Hot Springs Reserve). This land was the beginning of Canada's superb national park system. In 1887, the area became the Rocky Mountains Parks Reserve.

That same year, bathhouses were erected beside the Basin and at the entrance to the Cave. In 1914, a large stone building was added. The springs were hailed as a cure for everything from syphilis to mercury poisoning. At one time, crutches and canes were nailed to nearby trees by those who attributed cures to the sulphur-laden water.

The Cave and Basin was extensively renovated and the pool was refurbished for the 100th birthday of Canada's national park system in 1985. Bathers could cavort in turn-of-the-century bathing costumes. Yet the rebirth of this golden area lasted only half a decade. In 1990, Parks Canada 'permanently' closed the pool because of cracked and loose tiles and crumbling cement. Parks said that it could no longer afford to operate the pool—costs were increasing and the number of bathers were dropping, partly because the pool was smaller and the water cooler than the newer, more successful Upper Hot Springs.

Nonetheless, the Cave and Basin buildings remain in their 19th-century glory (admission fee applies), although filled with a mixture of the old and the new. Here, fascinating photo galleries and Edwardian-era exhibits combine with computer games about the park and its history. The old bathhouse contains a small theatre with a continuous film presentation.

And if the McCardell brothers could get a look at the expensive stores on Banff Avenue today, they'd understand where the real gold is found.

3. Sundance Canyon—*A wild, romantic canyon*

An impressive overhanging canyon, waterfalls, cascades, huge boulders, a viewpoint overlooking the Bow Valley and the rugged Sawback Range behind make this walk rewarding. The 3.2-km (2-mi) approach, however, is on a paved road, now closed to non-authorized motor vehicles. This portion is probably best travelled by bicycle or even roller blades or skateboard—anything to prevent sore feet from the hard, constant surface. The approach is wheelchair accessible.

Map: page 67
Distance: 9.5 km (5.9 mi) return
Time: 3 hours
Rating: Moderate
Max. elevation: 1463 m (4799 ft)
Elevation gain: 60 m (197 ft)
Footwear: Walking/running shoes
Best season: April to October

access

In Banff townsite, cross the Bow River on the Banff Avenue Bridge, then turn right and follow Cave Avenue 1.6 km (1 mi) to the large parking lot at the end.

Walk past the Cave and Basin buildings onto the old paved road. The road parallels the Bow River closely and provides excellent views across to the sharp-toothed Sawback Range. Most prominent in the range is the pinnacle of Mt. Edith directly opposite you. Coyote, moose and elk can sometimes be seen along the route.

The road curves left away from the river and into the forest, gradually ascending Sundance Creek to a picnic area, where the road ends.

Here, Sundance Creek has eroded a soft layer of rock and dips sharply to the west. Large boulders have fallen into the stream where it undercut the rock. The loop trail crosses the creek on a footbridge, and then climbs past an overhanging cliff, ascending along the creek's cascades. This canyon was part of the setting for a novel by Ralph Connor who depicted it as the site of a Sundance ceremony by native peoples.

The trail ascends steeply on short flights of stairs and crosses the stream again at a fascinating viewpoint—water cascades everywhere in the boulder-strewn stream-bed.

Cross the creek and climb gradually above the canyon to reach a viewpoint over the Bow Valley, with the rugged, steeply tilted Sawback Range behind the valley. Beyond the viewpoint, the trail switchbacks steeply down to the road, looping back to where you started.

Coyote

4. Fenland Nature Trail—*Marshland habitat*

This self-guiding nature trail, which loops around a lazy bend in Forty Mile Creek on the Bow River flats, is a surprise. Although it simply traverses unspectacular woodland and marsh on the edge of Banff townsite, the trail is consistently interesting. Deer, beavers, red-winged blackbirds and a variety of waterfowl are seen along these pleasant paths. Stay away in prime mosquito season. The trail is usually closed from mid-May to late June to protect this sensitive elk-calving habitat.

Map: page 67
Distance: 2.2-km (1.4-mi) loop
Time: 30 minutes
Rating: Easy
Max. elevation: 1382 m (4533 ft)
Elevation gain: None
Footwear: Anything
Best season: May through October (trail closed in mid-May to late June)

access

In Banff townsite, take Lynx Street north towards the Trans-Canada Highway, following the signs. Cross the railway tracks and the bridge over Forty Mile Creek. The parking and picnic area is on the west side right after the bridge.

The trail crosses Forty Mile Creek and leads into a thick forest of white spruce, an area of rich, river-bottom soil. Turn left. This fen environment consists of damp soil, grasses and sedges. An abandoned river channel—now fragmented into ponds—runs through the middle. It is prime habitat for beavers, which eat the young growth of aspen trees. Deer and elk keep the shrubs trimmed.

Forty Mile Creek

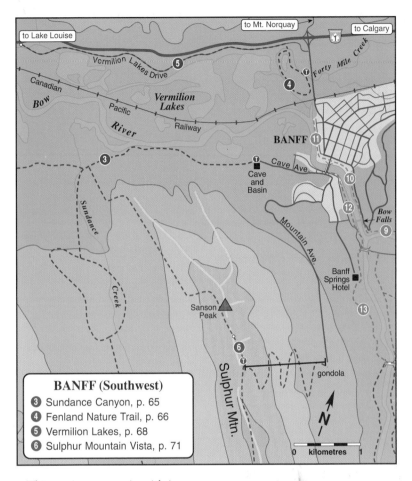

to Mt. Norquay
to Lake Louise
to Calgary
Vermilion Lakes Drive ⑤
Forty Mile Creek
④
Canadian
Bow
Pacific
Vermilion Lakes
River
Railway
BANFF ⑪
③
Cave Ave.
Cave and Basin
⑩
⑫
Bow Falls
⑨
Sundance
Mountain Ave.
Banff Springs Hotel
Creek
Sanson Peak
⑬
⑥
Sulphur Mtn.
gondola

BANFF (Southwest)
③ Sundance Canyon, p. 65
④ Fenland Nature Trail, p. 66
⑤ Vermilion Lakes, p. 68
⑥ Sulphur Mountain Vista, p. 71

N

0   kilometres   1

This semi-open terrain with its aquatic plants and willows used to be a favoured place for moose but few of them are seen here anymore, possibly because of the rapidly increasing congestion and development around the townsite. However, elk are far less reclusive than moose and remain common.

The trail follows the creek and you can look across it to the vast marshy area that culminates in the Vermilion Lakes. You pass a bridge leading to Vermilion Lakes Drive (Walk 5) and loop back to the start.

red-winged blackbirds

♂

♀

67

5. Vermilion Lakes—*Muskrats and mergansers*

Although the somewhat busy road edging Vermilion Lakes is well known as one of the finest short drives in the Banff area, it also makes an unforgettable wetlands walk, which is accessible right from Banff townsite. You can't feel or really see this interesting terrain from a car; a bicycle is excellent here. There's no foot-trail and walkers are forced to use the road, but traffic is slow moving. Parks Canada plans to close the road at First Vermilion Lake in 1999 and turn the remainder of the route into a footpath.

Map: page 67
Distance: 9.2 km (5.7 mi) or less return
Time: 2¹/₂–3 hours
Rating: Moderate
Max. elevation: 1386 m (4546 ft)
Elevation gain: None
Footwear: Walking/running shoes
Best season: April through October

access

In Banff townsite, take Lynx Avenue north towards the Trans-Canada Highway, following the signs. Cross the railway tracks and the bridge over Forty Mile Creek. The parking and picnic area are on the west side right after the bridge.

Cross Forty Mile Creek on a footbridge and enter a thick forest of white spruce in an area of rich river-bottom soil. Turn right and follow the creek to a second bridge that leads to paved Vermilion Lakes Drive. This first portion of the trail is also part of the Fenland Nature Trail (Walk 4).

The road follows the shorelines of the three lakes, which are connected by ponds and marshland. The lakes were formed by water from the Bow River backing up onto the valley flats. From one of its most dramatic angles, knife-edged Mt. Rundle rises behind the townsite. On its right is Sulphur Mountain, believed to be the source of the warm springs that surface on the other side of Vermilion Lakes.

The wetlands around the three lakes are a habitat for beavers, muskrats and many of the park's 238 bird species.

A Bird-Finding Guide to Canada notes that the Vermilion Lakes are probably 'the most important area in the park for migrating waterfowl.' Between April and late May, feathered visitors include tundra swans, common and hooded mergansers and red-necked grebes. The bald eagle nests nearby. Some ducks stay all winter on the warm spring water.

Lowbush cranberry, red osier dogwood, duckweeds, common cattail, rushes, sedges and even orchids can be found in this rich habitat.

In winter, watch for wolf tracks. Coyotes prowl the frozen shoreline, and you might see sheep grazing on Mt. Norquay. Nearby should be chickadees, woodpeckers and waxwings plucking berries from scattered juniper bushes.

The road continues to a dead-end below the highway.

facing page: First Vermilion Lake and Mt. Rundle

history

The First People in the Rockies:

The first people to visit the Rockies camped and hunted in the mountains during summer months, and made camp at such places as the warm south side of the Vermilion Lakes, returning to the same sheltered locations century after century.

Evidence indicates that people visited the area as long ago as 12,000 BC. The Clovis Point, or arrowhead, dating from 12,000 to 11,000 BC, has been found along the upper drainages of the North Saskatchewan River. It's known that a band of hunters camped on the slopes of Mt. Edith by the Vermilion Lakes about 10,500 years ago.

They lived there at the end of the last Ice Age, known as the Pleistocene Epoch. The last ice sheets were rapidly receding from all of Alberta, exposing terrain that had been covered for hundreds of centuries. Mammoths, lion-like cats, camels and giant bison now began to vanish. The first people to the Vermilion Lakes area were likely mammoth hunters and nomadic hunter-gatherers who ventured into the mountains during the warm months and retreated to the plains during winter.

As the ice retreated, foraging for food in the mountains increased. By the late 18th century, many tribes were present in the Rockies, partly pushed from the plains by the advent of the fur trade: Sarcee, Beaver, Blood, Blackfoot, Kootenai and Salish, among others.

As the fur trade declined, interest in the Rockies as a tourism area increased, spurred by the completion of the Canadian Pacific Railway (CPR) in 1885. In 1887, Banff was officially designated as the Rocky Mountains Parks Reserve.

common muskrat

6. Sulphur Mountain Vista Trail

A most accessible ridge

Anyone can do a rewarding ridge walk—with a little cash. It begins after an eight-minute gondola ride whisks the visitor to a futuristic-looking teahouse on top of Sulphur Mountain (above Banff townsite). An easy boardwalk trail leads to Sanson Peak along the ridge of Sulphur Mountain. The trail offers good views, excellent interpretive panels explaining the natural features of the area and a look at an historic weather observatory. The toughest part is waiting in line for the gondola during busy summer months.

Map: page 67
Distance: 2 km (1.2 mi) return
Time: 30 minutes (after gondola ride)
Rating: Easy
Max. elevation: 2295 m (7527 ft)
Elevation gain: 30 m (98 ft)
Footwear: Walking/running shoes
Best season: May to October

access

From the Information Centre in Banff townsite, drive south on Banff Avenue across the bridge. Turn left on Spray Avenue and then take the first right onto Mountain Avenue. Follow the signs 3.2 km (2 mi) to the Sulphur Mountain Gondola Lift. The gondola is open year-round. The very fit could hike up a steep, 5-km (3.1-mi), wooded trail on the east side of Sulphur Mountain—an elevation gain of 650 m (2132 ft). This trail starts from the Upper Hot Springs parking area and takes about two hours one-way. The ride down on the gondola is free.

From the top of the gondola lift, start at the boardwalk at the north side of the tea-house. Panoramic views of the Bow Valley can extend 145 km (90 mi) on a clear day. Use a polarizing lens for photos that otherwise tend to turn out hazy.

A major rehabilitation program began here in 1994 to rejuvenate native plants and wildflowers. Wild strawberry, columbine, moss campion and scorpion weed survive at this altitude, clinging close to the ground in broad, protective mats.

The boardwalk winds past stunted fir and spruce, and then heads up a wide, rocky section often exposed to the wind. A small observation deck identifies 17 peaks of the Bow Valley. Several picnic tables are spread along the trail. Be warned that chipmunks, golden-mantled squirrels and bighorn sheep vie for the visitor's attention, sometimes for his lunch. Be hard-hearted. Feeding animals in the park is not only illegal, it destroys their natural feeding patterns and makes them sick and dependent on hand-outs.

71

Sulphur Mountain and teahouse

north and Norquay to its left. Tiny Tunnel Mountain is east; deep blue Lake Minnewanka shimmers far beyond. The high mountain north of the lake is Mt. Aylmer.

The station was established to study wind and other high-altitude weather conditions. It is named after Norman Sanson, curator of the Banff Park Museum, who opened the observatory in 1903. The interior of the station has been refurbished to resemble the way it looked during Sanson's life. You can't go inside, but you can peer through a large glass window to view his bunk bed, desk, phone, bottle of beer, coalbuckets and other relics.

The walk culminates at the site of an abandoned government meteorological station where Sulphur Mountain offers its most dramatic views: the wide Bow Valley (the Bow River a slim thread slicing through it), the sharp-toothed Sawback Range across the river, slate grey Cascade rising to the

On your return, you could explore the South Ridge Trail, which starts on the south side of the teahouse. You could also get a snack or a casual meal in the self-serve Summit Restaurant. A breakfast buffet ($7.95) is served from 8:30 a.m. to 10 a.m. until mid-September.

history

Sanson, the Weather Man 'Gone up Sulphur!'

Employees at the Banff Park Museum in the early part of the 1900s became accustomed to seeing that note posted on curator Norman Sanson's door. Starting in 1903, the meticulous, self-educated meteorologist (1862–1949) climbed up to the Sulphur Mountain Weather Observatory to take more than 1000 readings over 36 years. After the 1000th trip, friends got together to prepare him a well-deserved breakfast at the top!

Shy and a little taciturn, Sanson's passionate curiosity led him to many discoveries, including a new order of ice bug, *Grylloblatta,* found in late spring snow on Sulphur Mountain in 1914. Fascinating samples from Sanson's journals can be read at Sanson Peak. You can also peer into his workroom at the observatory, built in 1903 and recently refurbished.

7. Tunnel Mountain—*The tiny mountain*

One of the few mountain summits in the Canadian Rockies that can be readily ascended by the casual walker, Tunnel Mountain is accessible right from Banff Avenue. You can fortify yourself for the outing with a latté. The views over Banff townsite, the golf course and Bow Valley are outstanding considering the relatively easy ascent.

Map: page 74
Distance: 4.6 km (2.9 mi) return
Time: 2–3 hours
Rating: Moderate
Max. elevation: 1691 m (5546 ft)
Elevation gain: 275 m (902 ft)
Footwear: Walking/running shoes/light hiking boots
Best season: May to October

access

Strollers approaching on foot from the townsite can reach the trail most easily by walking up Wolf Street, which leads off Banff Avenue just before the Information Centre. After four blocks, turn right at the end of the street and take the upper fork (St. Julien) towards the Banff Centre. The trail begins from a parking lot just below the centre and climbs steadily through open forest to Tunnel Mountain Drive. The route is dry; take water.

Hikers with cars can save some steep climbing by taking Tunnel Mountain Road (see Walk 8) up from the townsite. Park at the first viewpoint on the left side above the Banff Centre (limited parking). The trail begins a few metres further up the road on the right.

The wide, well-maintained trail climbs steadily from the viewpoint through a dry forest. Views of the townsite below, the Vermilion Lakes and the relatively level Bow Valley gradually open up. You begin to catch glimpses of the Scottish baronial splendour of the Banff Springs Hotel, which is set between the distinctive 'writing-desk' slope of Mt. Rundle and the long, wooded ridge of Sulphur Mountain opposite.

A little further up, you can see south to where the Spray River enters the Bow River just below the falls. The trail soon reaches the top of the ridge, now rocky and mostly open. It turns abruptly and swings around to the Rundle side. Many of the trees up here are stately, old Douglas-fir,

red-breasted nuthatch

73

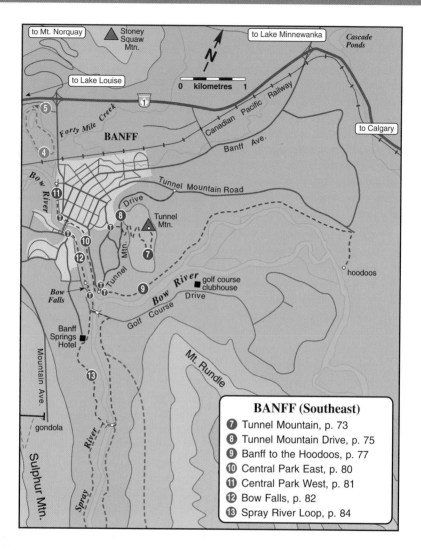

to Mt. Norquay
Stoney Squaw Mtn.
to Lake Minnewanka
Cascade Ponds
to Lake Louise
0 kilometres 1
Canadian Pacific Railway
to Calgary
Forty Mile Creek
BANFF
Banff Ave.
Bow River
Tunnel Mountain Road
Drive
Tunnel Mtn.
Bow River golf course
clubhouse
hoodoos
Golf Course Drive
Bow Falls
Banff Springs Hotel
Mt. Rundle
Mountain Ave.
gondola
Sulphur Mtn.
Spray River

BANFF (Southeast)
7 Tunnel Mountain, p. 73
8 Tunnel Mountain Drive, p. 75
9 Banff to the Hoodoos, p. 77
10 Central Park East, p. 80
11 Central Park West, p. 81
12 Bow Falls, p. 82
13 Spray River Loop, p. 84

survivors of fires that downed lesser trees. This tree of the montane zone has thick, fire-resistant bark.

The trail soon reaches the top of the rocky ridge, providing views on both sides. Although the high point is partially treed and contains only the footings for a former lookout tower, you can walk a few metres on either side to gain better views. On the west, the whole of the town is at your feet. On the east, Rundle rises massively above the elk-dotted green of the golf course.

8. Tunnel Mountain Drive—*All-season route*

Here's a rarity: a route that's fine in any weather—it's a paved road, not a trail. You could simply drive or bicycle the distance and park at the viewpoints. Yet Tunnel Mountain Drive is popular with strollers. The viewpoints over the Banff townsite and across to the Banff Springs Hotel are excellent. Traffic is usually moderate. In winter the road is closed to vehicles past the Banff Centre.

Map: page 74
Distance: 4.7 km (2.9 mi) one-way
Time: 1¹/₂–2 hours
Max. elevation: 1493 m (4897 ft)
Elevation gain: 90 m (295 ft)
Rating: Moderate
Footwear: Light walking shoes/ running shoes
Best season: Year-round

access

In Banff townsite, walk down Banff Avenue and turn left on Buffalo, the last street before the bridge over the Bow River. You could also drive to the small parking lot, 2 km (1.2 mi) up the road where Walk 9 (Banff to the Hoodoos) starts. Or do the route in reverse, starting from the motel village on Tunnel Mountain Drive. Another alternative is to start at the Banff Avenue Bridge and follow Walk 10 (Central Park East trail).

Buffalo Street leads past some fine old homes overlooking the river. You begin to climb, with views opening up to Sulphur Mountain opposite and the long Spray Valley. You soon come upon one of the most impressive views anywhere of the Banff Springs Hotel. Beyond the viewpoint is the start of the trail along Bow River to the Hoodoos (see Walk 9). Take this trail on the return for a more varied loop.

The climbing gets steeper as you pass the Banff Centre. Visitors might enjoy stopping at the Walter

Banff Springs Hotel

red squirrel

good viewpoint as well as the trail to the summit of Tunnel Mountain from the townsite (see Walk 7). Below are the Banff townsite, the flat Bow Valley and the Vermilion Lakes, all of which reveal the incredible natural and man-made diversity of the area. Stairs and a switchbacking trail lead back to town. The drive twists around the cliffs of Tunnel Mountain, descends slightly and reaches a T-junction and store. Left is a direct route back to Banff townsite. Right are the campgrounds, hoodoos and access to Walk 9.

J. Phillips Gallery in the Jeanne and Peter Lougheed Building, where Canadian and international artists exhibit paintings, ceramics, weaving and photography (closed Mondays). Near the top of the slope is a

The Tunnel That Never Was

There's no tunnel in Tunnel Mountain; never has been. When surveyors for the Canadian Pacific Railway (CPR) first examined the route up the Bow Valley in 1882, they planned to dig a 270-m (900-ft) tunnel under the mountain. But surveyor C.A.E. Shaw was later commissioned to re-examine the proposed route and see if he could save the company money. He rerouted the line along the Cascade trench, where the Trans-Canada Highway now goes. And so the CPR situated 'Siding 29'—the beginnings of Banff—at the foot of Cascade Mountain. However, the community of Banff grew up close to the Bow River where the Cave and Basin hot pool was the major attraction. The CPR later relocated its station.

history

9. Banff to the Hoodoos—*Walking among giants*

This scenic, easy trail right from Banff townsite has an intriguing destination. The walk has constantly changing vistas of mighty Mt. Rundle, the Tunnel Mountain cliffs and the picturesque Bow River Valley, and ends at the earthen hoodoos on Tunnel Mountain Road.

Map: page 74
Distance: 4.8 km (3 mi) one-way
Time: 1–2 hours
Rating: Moderate
Max. elevation: 1417 m (4648 ft)
Elevation gain: 45 m (148 ft)
Footwear: Walking/running shoes
Best season: June through October

access

In Banff townsite, drive or walk south on Banff Avenue and turn left on Buffalo, the last street before the Banff Avenue Bridge. Continue up Buffalo for 1.7 km (1.1 mi) to the small parking lot at a sharp bend in the road. The trail descends on steps from the parking lot.

The pine-needled trail descends gently to the Bow River with Mt. Rundle dominating to the right at 2864 m (9394 ft). The mountain is named for Rev. Robert Rundle, a Wesleyan missionary to the native peoples of the Northwest from 1840–48. Sandy beaches along the bank make good picnic spots.

Hoodoos and Bow River

The route soon leads under the rubble-strewn cliffs of limestone Tunnel Mountain, which geologists believe was once part of Rundle.

The trail follows a river side-channel for a while, then climbs a low bluff overlooking the Bow Valley, Mt. Rundle and the Spray Valley to the right. Descending the bluff, leave the cliffs behind and walk through flat Tunnel Mountain Meadows. The meadows are a good place to spot deer, elk and coyote and get an unusual perspective on Mt. Rundle, which appears as a big, grey wall. Rundle's long ridge has seven distinct high points. Only in the last 35 years have all of them been conquered from the challenging east side.

The path climbs to Tunnel Mountain Road and continues on its right edge to a lookout, then slips into the woods again. You'll soon enjoy the first views of the hoodoos on the south bank. An asphalt trail goes to a second and better viewpoint, with a panorama of the Bow and Spray valleys.

An alternate route back to the start is on or alongside the road itself. A trail follows the road back to Tunnel Mountain Motel Village. Turn left on the scenic Tunnel Mountain Drive (Walk 8), and follow this quieter road back to the parking lot.

geology

Hoodoo Viewpoint

The 0.6-km (0.4-mi) stroll from Tunnel Mountain Road opposite the vast campgrounds is a must for first-time visitors. The viewpoint offers a close-up look at the hoodoos as well as good views across to the Bow and Spray valleys and Mt. Rundle.

Native peoples thought the hoodoos were giants who slept by day and awoke at night to throw rocks down on unsuspecting travellers. Geologists say the hoodoos are actually columns of silt, gravel and rocks cemented together by dissolved limestone. The uncemented material slowly washed away, leaving the hoodoos.

The Bow River is a silvery, winding ribbon beneath the viewpoint. Follow the asphalt path to a second viewpoint, with its better views of the hoodoos and the Banff Springs Hotel. From this perspective, the hotel seems to be nestled in the notch between Mt. Rundle and Tunnel Mountain. The path loops around a third viewpoint—worthwhile for views back on Cascade and another perspective on the hoodoos.

Limber Pine

Limber pine, not common in the Canadian Rockies, can be found on rocky outcroppings in the montane zone. Look for these trees at the Hoodoos viewpoint in Banff or above Waterton Lake on the Lower Bertha Falls trail (Walk 99). This tree often has crooked trunks and large, uneven crowns. The needles are 3–8.8 cm (1¹/₂–3¹/₂ in) long, in bundles of five. Cones are up to 20 cm (8 in) long. Under park regulations, only squirrels are allowed to gather them.

biology

Viewpoint offers close-up view of hoodoos

10. Central Park East
Escape from Banff Avenue

Escape frenetic Banff Avenue and stroll along the fast-moving Bow River on this little outing, suitable for almost everyone. A good remedy for souls tattered by tourism's more commercial face.

access

In Banff townsite, start at Central Park on the north side of the Banff Avenue Bridge. Park behind the Banff Park Museum on Buffalo Street, just off Banff Avenue.

Map: page 74
Distance: 2 km (1.2 mi) return
Time: 30 minutes
Rating: Easy
Max. elevation: 1383 m (4536 ft)
Elevation gain: Negligible
Footwear: Anything
Best season: April to October

Turn left onto the asphalt path behind the Banff Park Museum next to the river, and walk under the bridge, where cliff swallows nest. Note the faces carved into the side of the bridge. Benches and picnic tables are situated beside the Bow River.

At this point, the Bow River goes from tranquil meandering to an aggressive rush for the plunge over Bow Falls. The water is usually silty in early summer and turns a darker green later in the season as silt particles settle. The path leads through trees, past some lovely old houses, then narrows, turns to dirt and curves along the river.

You can hear the rumbling falls ahead as the trail climbs a steep bank and comes out along Buffalo Street. The walker is rewarded with excellent views of the venerable Banff Springs Hotel, rising like a castle across the Bow River.

Walkers now have several choices: return the same way; return on the road that goes past the interesting Banff cemetery; or continue up Buffalo Street and Tunnel Mountain Drive for a view of Bow Falls and perhaps the highly recommended walk up to the Hoodoos (Walk 9) for a longer outing.

wildlife

Cliff Swallows

Think of cliff swallows as bridge groupies. They congregate, sometimes by the thousands, on the underside of bridges where they carefully build mud nests. They transport their building material beakful by beakful.

11. Central Park West—*The easiest stroll*

Instead of the skyscrapers of Manhattan's Central Park, you get high peaks and a placid river. The stroll is short, level and peaceful—for downtown Banff.

access

In Banff townsite, head down Banff Avenue and turn right on Buffalo Street, just before the bridge. A parking lot is to the right of the Banff Park Museum.

Map: page 74
Distance: 1 km (0.6 mi) return
Time: 20 minutes
Rating: Easy (wheelchair accessible)
Max. elevation: 1383 m (4536 ft)
Elevation gain: None
Footwear: Anything
Best season: Anytime

Behind the Banff Park Museum, follow the riverside path to the right along the Bow River, past benches and overhanging trees that tempt you to stop and contemplate this peaceful setting.

The Bow, fed by the glaciers above Bow Lake and Lake Louise and by hundreds of mountain brooks, rises in turbulence, and then slows in the relatively level Bow Valley en route to far-off Hudson Bay. In spring, the river looks thick and brown with mud and glacial silt. Later in summer, it turns a green-blue.

Across the water rises the wooded ridge of Sulphur Mountain. Its subterranean depths are believed to be the source of the hot springs (see Walk 1). Note the warning signs across the river telling boaters to go no further. The river current soon picks up beyond the bridge, and a canoe can be swept over Bow Falls. A few people have survived the plunge; others have not.

The Whyte Museum of the Canadian Rockies is on the right as you continue. You also go by some of Banff's most gracious homes along riverside Bow Avenue. The trail soon ends at a boathouse, where you can rent a canoe or rowboat and experience the area in another equally rewarding way. Some walkers continue by road to the Fenland (Walk 4) and Vermilion Lakes (Walk 5) trails.

Banff townsite

12. Bow Falls Trail—*Best way to the falls*

The trail is a short, easy walk to the thundering falls and the famous Banff Springs Hotel. Both are best approached gradually and savoured.

access

In Banff townsite, park at Central Park, on the north end of the Banff Avenue Bridge. This walk starts by the Banff Park Museum, the building that looks like a train station in search of a train.

Map: page 74
Distance: 2.4 km (1.5 mi) return
Time: 25 minutes
Rating: Easy
Max. elevation: 1384 m (4540 ft)
Elevation gain: Negligible
Footwear: Walking/running shoes
Best season: May to October

W alk south across the bridge. The graceful structure at the end is the Park Administration Building with the beautiful Cascade Gardens behind it. Turn left along the river, heading through groves of fir and patches of bunchberry and wildflowers, including yellow cinquefoil.

Ahead you can see the rooftops of the Banff Centre on Tunnel Mountain. Mt. Rundle looms to its right. (In June, 1841, Rev. Robert Rundle ascended the Bow Valley, camped near the foot of Cascade Mountain, and visited the Bow Falls.)

You view the falls tumbling below, perhaps a more dramatic vantage than from the official viewpoint downstream. The water roars over rock steps in the river, although the high water levels of spring make it look like a continuous plunge. Once the falls were much higher than today. Over thousands of years, they have worn down the rock barrier from the height of the left bank.

Steller's jay

Descend to the busy parking lot where there's a promenade and benches. Walkers continuing on to the Banff Springs Hotel can go through the parking lot and follow signs up the stairs to the hotel. (The stairs are closed in winter.) Half-hour guided tours of the hotel are held daily, year-round. Meet at the concierge's desk at 5 p.m.

Brett of Banff

The striking Park Administration Building at the head of Banff Avenue was not the first to occupy the site. Dr. Robert Brett operated the Brett Sanitorium Hotel and Hospital here until the early 1900s. Wealthy guests soaked in the hot sulphur water, piped in from the springs above, and attributed curative powers to these mineral baths.

Cascade Gardens, located behind the building, offers a tranquil sanctuary in summer for fatigued visitors. Built in 1934 as a Depression-era project, it was originally intended by Toronto architect Howard Beckett to illustrate the successive eras of geological time. (Later research indicates that, geologically speaking, the representation is not accurate.) Nevertheless, the gardens are certainly scenic with their decorative pools and streams and thousands of poppies, golden columbines and delphiniums.

history

Bow Falls

13. Spray River Loop—*Mellow woodland stroll*

The Spray River Valley, upstream from the Banff Springs Hotel, isn't spectacular. The trail along the river simply provides gentle woodland walking that is easily accessible from Banff townsite. It also makes a good family bike route in dry weather. Horses can churn up the trail in wet weather.

Map: page 74
Distance: 3.2 km (2 mi) return
Time: 1½ hours
Rating: Moderate
Max. elevation: 1371 m (4496 ft)
Elevation gain: Negligible
Footwear: Walking/running shoes (light hiking boots in wet conditions)
Best season: May through October

access

Cross the Banff Avenue Bridge, turn left onto Spray Avenue, and turn left again at the sign for the golf course. Park at Bow Falls.

Cross the Spray River below the Banff Springs Hotel and watch for signs for the Spray River trail on the right just past the first fairway. The path leads into the woods and alongside the Spray River. Profusions of harebells, purple asters and arnicas brighten the bank—compensation for the damage that horses do to the trail. There are pleasant picnic places along the river.

At the 1.5-km (0.9-mi) mark, turn right and cross a wooden bridge by an abandoned quarry. Here, rocks were cut for the building of the Banff Springs Hotel, the Banff Post Office and the Park Administration Building. (A longer loop trail continues for a further 4.4 km [2.7 mi] up the river to a second bridge and returns on the other side. The total distance of this longer route is 13.5 km [8.4 mi].)

Across the bridge, turn right and loop north back to the Banff Springs Hotel on a less-interesting fireroad out of sight of the river. The road ends at a locked gate just before the Banff Springs Hotel at the end of Spray Avenue. To return to the Bow Falls parking lot, you could enter the hotel, descend to the arcade level, exit above the pool, and follow the walkway to stairs leading down to the Bow Falls and Spray River Bridge.

black bear

Spray River and Banff Springs Hotel

Sporting Illusions

At the Banff Springs Hotel, golfers can blame nature for a bad day. Optical foreshortening, caused by the clear air and the huge mountains towering over the course, often causes golfers to under-estimate the distance to the green, just as hikers misjudge the distance to their destination. Or golfers could simply blame the ubiquitous elk.

The golf course was started in 1911 by the Canadian Pacific Railway (CPR). German prisoners-of-war extended the course to 18 holes during the First World War. But in 1927, the course was redesigned by Stanley Thompson, one of the world's foremost golf architects. In 1989, an additional nine holes (the Tunnel 9) and a new clubhouse and restaurant were added.

history

14. Bankhead Historical Loop

Life in the pits

An excellent interpretive trail evoking the life of Bankhead, a once-thriving coal-mining town abandoned in 1922. The entrance looks unassuming— but persevere. Amidst these old buildings, rusting machinery, rubble and grass-covered foundations, the imagination takes flight. Indeed, walking here at dusk can be likened to exploring the remains of a 20ᵗʰ-century cliff community.

Map: page 87
Distance: 1.1-km (0.7-mi) loop
Time: 25–30 minutes
Rating: Easy
Max. elevation: 1417 m (4648 ft)
Elevation gain: Negligible
Footwear: Anything
Best season: May to October

access

Bankhead is on Lake Minnewanka Road, 3 km (1.9 mi) north of the Trans-Canada Highway, opposite Banff townsite. There's a sign for the Bankhead parking lot. The trail starts to the right of a viewpoint.

The trail descends steps to the main tunnel entrance to the mine, where the coal was extracted on A-Level, B-Level and C-Level, each a tunnel following the coal seams deep under Cascade Mountain. Miners were each assigned a numbered mining lamp at the lamphouse at the beginning of each shift. If a miner's lamp was missing at the end of the day, a search would be started.

Keep right over a tiny wooden bridge on an easy cinder trail to reach the transformer building. Peer inside for a depiction of life and times in an old mining town. The miners were mostly immigrants from Poland, Italy, Russia, Germany, Ireland and China. At Bankhead's peak, 275 men worked below ground and 195 above,

Narrow-gauge coal train

producing 400 carloads of coal a day.

The trail winds through bare foundations, by the remains of the power house that supplied the electricity for Banff townsite and the briquetting plant. The plant converted easily broken Cascade coal into a form more easily used for heating.

The trail loops back past slag heaps and the shantytown behind the heaps, where the Chinese lived. Wild rhubarb, spread from the abandoned gardens of Chinese workers, grows on these slag heaps.

It's said that when the town opened a cemetery, no one wanted to be the first to be buried in it. A friendless Chinese labourer, the town's only murder victim, became its only occupant. His remains were later shipped back to China.

Near the conclusion of the walk is a narrow-gauge coal train.

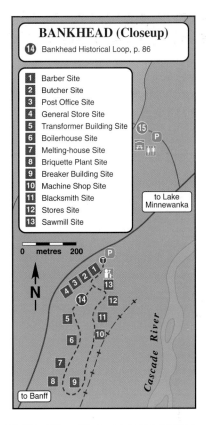

BANKHEAD (Closeup)

14 Bankhead Historical Loop, p. 86

1 Barber Site
2 Butcher Site
3 Post Office Site
4 General Store Site
5 Transformer Building Site
6 Boilerhouse Site
7 Melting-house Site
8 Briquette Plant Site
9 Breaker Building Site
10 Machine Shop Site
11 Blacksmith Site
12 Stores Site
13 Sawmill Site

0 metres 200

N

to Lake Minnewanka

Cascade River

to Banff

Ghosts of Bankhead

Early in the 20th century, a coal-mining town called Bankhead flourished under Cascade Mountain near Banff townsite.

Between 1904 and 1922, Bankhead was not only bigger than Banff, it was also Alberta's most modern town. More than 1200 people lived in 90 homes. There were tennis courts, a skating rink and a library. Coal production hit 200,000 tons a year.

The boom withered in the 1920s, partly because of the expense of processing the brittle coal, which had to be compressed into 'briquettes' to be usable. To these difficulties were added labour problems and poor markets.

By 1922, Bankhead had become a ghost town. The last resident of Bankhead was a Danish caretaker in charge of safeguarding the remaining houses. It was said that he also scared away 100 ghosts.

history

15. Upper Bankhead—*Mines and glaciers*

This trail has everything, except ease. You start at historic Bankhead, pass an abandoned coal mine and an overlook to Lake Minnewanka, and reach a cirque deeply cut into the cliffs of mighty Cascade Mountain. The route is moderately steep throughout. Bring a canteen.

Map: page 89
Distance: 8 km (5 mi) return
Time: 4 hours
Rating: Strenuous
Max. elevation: 1935 m (6347 ft)
Elevation gain: 472 m (1548 ft)
Footwear: Light hiking boots
Best season: Mid-June to October

access

From Banff townsite, drive back to the Trans-Canada Highway, then north up the road to Lake Minnewanka. At 3.5 km (2.2 mi) from the junction just past the turnoff for the Bankhead exhibit, take the left entrance to the Upper Bankhead parking lot, which is beside a pleasant picnic area.

The trail climbs moderately steeply to the upper remains of the once-thriving coal-mining operation of Bankhead and past the concrete shell of an old mine building. Behind are several fenced-off mine shaft holes. To the right, on another mini-ridge of coal tailings, is a good overlook towards Lake Minnewanka and down the Bow Valley towards Canmore.

The route leads through deeper forest and over a wooded ridge, then levels off as views open up over the valley. Suddenly, you round a corner and the cirque looms up before you—grey, gloomy and imposing, its massive walls rising above talus slopes. It's called C-Level Cirque because the mine shafts following the coal seams under Cascade Mountain were simply called A-Level shaft, B-Level and C-Level.

The main trail ends above a small pond overlooking the boulder-strewn bowl in the rocks, one of several cirques cut into the sides of Cascade by ancient glaciers. A rougher trail continues up on the right side of the cirque to provide even better views of this natural amphitheatre.

Fall at Bankhead

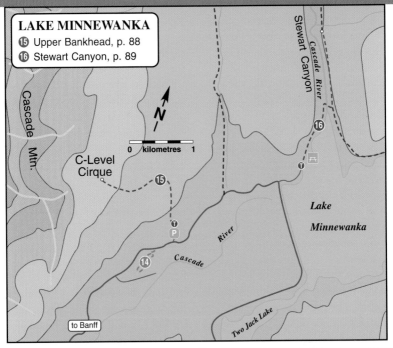

LAKE MINNEWANKA
- ⑮ Upper Bankhead, p. 88
- ⑯ Stewart Canyon, p. 89

16. Stewart Canyon——*A little fjord*

A beautiful inlet that resembles a miniature fjord. A shady path along the lakeshore, the shimmering blue of Lake Minnewanka and the grey and white of the mountains visible through the forest. These scenes are not spectacular or awe-inspiring as the Rockies go, yet they constitute a fine family stroll.

Map: above
Distance: 2–4 km (1.2–2.5 mi) return
Time: 45 minutes to 1½ hours
Rating: Easy
Max. elevation: 1493 m (4897 ft)
Elevation gain: Negligible
Footwear: Almost anything
Best season: May to October

access

The interchange for Lake Minnewanka Road is 3.2 km (2 mi) north of Banff townsite. Drive 7 km (4.3 mi) up to the lake and park at the Minnewanka day use area. Walk down the road above the boat ramp and picnic area to begin at the trailhead information kiosk.

Follow the asphalt path through a grassy picnic area near the lake, a pleasant spot with scenic coves to explore and boulders for children to climb. Some of these limestone rocks contain fossil imprints. The lake is the largest in Banff (24 km [15 mi] long and 1.5–3 km [0.9–1.9 mi] wide); the grey cliffs of Mt.

Inglismaldie (on the right) and Mt. Girouard dominate the far side of the lake. The first mountain is named for a Scottish castle; the second for Col. Sir Edward P. Girouard, a prominent officer during the Boer War (1899–1901).

At the far end of the picnic area, a wide path leads through lodgepole pines and past a gravel beach covered with driftwood. The whole scene—the robin's egg–blue water seen through the pines—appears more Mediterranean than western Canadian.

Minnewanka is a native peoples' name meaning 'Lake of the Water Spirit.' The route along the north shore was once used by native peoples travelling into the mountains from the plains through the gap at the far end of the lake.

The cold lake usually supports a sizable population of loons and other waterfowl in spring and fall. Watch for mountain bluebirds along the trail.

The trail reaches Stewart Canyon in less than 1 km (0.6 mi) and crosses it on a scenic bridge. Here are the best views of this interesting inlet, with its sheer grey walls of limestone carved by the Cascade River. This river does not naturally flow into Lake Minnewanka. In earlier days, the lake did not extend this far down the valley. When the level of Minnewanka was raised in 1941 to provide hydro-electric power, the head of the lake was pushed south and the river canyon became a steep-walled inlet.

Though many will go no further than the bridge, good views of the canyon can be obtained by following a path to the left. The main path straight ahead leads down the lake and to lofty Aylmer Pass above it.

OPTION: Notice how the somewhat murky lake water suddenly turns clear where it meets the flow from the Cascade River. The further you go up the canyon, the faster-moving the water is. The canyon is a good place to spot bighorn sheep. In about 1 km (0.6 mi), the trail finally descends to the river at the end of the canyon, a favourite place for trout fishermen. A rocky clearing beside the river provides a natural area for a backcountry picnic.

Stewart Canyon

17. Stoney Squaw Lookout—*Bow Valley views*

Stoney Squaw is only a pimple of a mountain between Mt. Norquay on the left and Cascade on the right. But its lookout, reached on a relatively short and easy trail, offers a superb panorama of the Banff area.

access

The trailhead is at the entrance to the main parking lot at the Banff/Mt. Norquay ski area, 5 km (3.1 mi) north from Banff townsite on Mt. Norquay Road. Mule deer and bighorn sheep are commonly seen along this drive.

Map: page 92
Distance: 4.6 km (2.8 mi) return
Time: 1½ hours
Rating: Moderate
Footwear: Walking/running shoes/light hiking boots
Max. elevation: 1883 m (6176 ft)
Elevation gain: 176 m (577 ft)
Best season: June to October

The pine-needled path starts through mixed forest, moving up the west side of Stoney Squaw on a moderate grade. The name refers to a Stoney woman standing beside her Stoney Chief, the former name for Cascade Mountain.

Continue through stands of Douglas-fir and white spruce until the trees thin out and views begin to appear down to the Banff townsite and the Spray Valley to the south. The path proceeds on to the lookout, where the forest opens to an excellent view of 2998-m (9833-ft) Cascade Mountain. To its south and west, the striking outlook encompasses the Bow Valley, tiny Tunnel Mountain, Mt. Rundle, Spray Valley, Sulphur Mountain and the Trans-Canada Highway.

Vermilion Lakes from Stoney Squaw Lookout

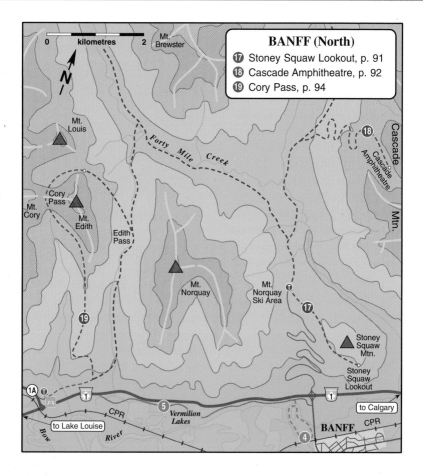

BANFF (North)
⑰ Stoney Squaw Lookout, p. 91
⑱ Cascade Amphitheatre, p. 92
⑲ Cory Pass, p. 94

18. Cascade Amphitheatre

Playground of the gods

Although the Cascade Amphitheatre route is long and fairly tough, it leads to an extraordinary bowl cut deep into the limestone cliffs of Cascade Mountain. Here's a location that invites the more experienced hiker to wander the edges of the mountain's steep talus slopes and boulder fields or seek the high ridge above.

Map: above
Distance: 12.8 km (7.9 mi) return
Time: 6 hours
Rating: Strenuous
Max. elevation: 2194 m (7196 ft)
Elevation gain: 610 m (2000 ft)
Footwear: Light hiking boots
Best season: July to September

access

From Banff townsite or the Trans-Canada Highway, take the Mt. Norquay turnoff north and drive up the steep, switchbacked road to the main parking lot at the Banff/Mt. Norquay ski area. The trail begins at the far end of this vast lot.

Walk down the narrow road from the parking lot and keep straight past the Mystic chairlift; then follow the trail sign to the right. The road leads into the trees again beyond the ski area, and descends gradually through a pleasant forest to cross vigorous Forty Mile Creek.

The road becomes more of a trail and begins to climb in earnest, switchbacking up the western flank of Cascade Mountain with occasional views across the valley to Mt. Norquay and a glimpse up Forty Mile Creek to the striking tower of Mt. Louis. At 4 km (2.5 mi), the trail to Elk Lake continues straight ahead. The Amphitheatre route goes right, climbing more steeply now and switchbacking steadily through a lodgepole pine forest before levelling off at the beginning of the cirque.

A rough trail leads right to the crest of the Cascade Ridge; it is a late-summer scramble route to the top with one tricky part at the false summit. *Not* for the casual hiker. Most hikers will be content with the barren splendours of the meadows and amphitheatre ahead.

The terrain grows more desolate as you enter the amphitheatre, a cirque hollowed out by glaciers that have long since retreated. To the west, views open up to Mt. Brewster. The trail wanders on for a while, gradually becoming indistinct among the large boulders.

Cascade Amphitheatre

19. Cory Pass—*Glimpse of the gargoyles*

This wild, desolate pass overlooks jagged rock formations that sometimes resemble gargoyles. It offers wide views over the Bow Valley and most especially behind the pass to the magnificent spike of Mt. Louis, one of the most striking mountains in Banff. This trail has everything, except ease. The ascent is long and steep, the trail rough in places, often with snow lying over the path on the final section even in mid-summer. The hike is often done on a loop with the return on the Edith Pass trail.

Map: page 92
Distance: 13.5 km (8.4 mi) return
Time: 6 hours
Rating: Strenuous
Max. elevation: 2371 m (7777 ft)
Elevation gain: 981 m (3218 ft)
Footwear: Light hiking boots
Best season: Mid-July to late September

access

From Banff townsite, drive west on the Trans-Canada Highway for 6 km (3.7 mi) to the Bow Valley Parkway (Hwy. 1A). Turn onto the parkway and take the first road right up a hill to the Fireside picnic area. The trail begins at a bridge over the creek.

The route parallels the Trans-Canada, climbing slightly. In about 1 km (0.6 mi), you reach a patch of Douglas-fir, where the Cory Pass trail branches left while the trail to Edith Lake continues straight. The route to Cory Pass begins to climb steeply and relentlessly, soon gaining the crest of a semi-open, grassy ridge of Mt. Edith (2554 m, 8377 ft). The mountain is named after Edith Orde, who visited Banff in 1886 with Lady Macdonald, wife of Canada's first prime minister. Mt. Cory (2790 m, 9151 ft) is named for William Cory, deputy minister

of the Department of the Interior, from 1905–30.

The lung-pounding ascent is partly compensated for by the expanding views, with the Vermilion Lakes and much of Bow Valley visible below. The route levels off slightly at the top of the ridge, but climbs again as it traverses Mt. Edith, where views open up into the valley.

The trail goes over several rocky knobs, descends steeply for a few metres through a crack in the rock (the route can be obscure) and climbs again. The terrain gradually opens up as you begin the long ascent above Cory Valley, the pass ahead looking inhospitable even on a sunny day. There are few switchbacks as the trail ascends the pass under the crumbling cliffs of Mt. Edith, where snow patches may lie across the trail well into July.

The top, which is well above timberline, is a spectacular, rugged and usually cool place that funnels the winds between Mt. Cory on the west side and Mt. Edith on the east. You can climb a little higher on the ridge to the right for better views of

Valley of the Gargoyles

the rock needles over the other side that might be compared to gothic-carved gargoyles.

These mountains are part of the aptly named Sawback Range whose rocks stick up almost vertically. Most dramatic of these spires is Mt. Louis, visible on the other side of the Gargoyle Valley, which is a chal-lenging ascent for rock climbers. The mountain is named after Louis Stewart, a professor at the University of Toronto who explored the Rockies with A.P. Coleman in the late 19th and early 20th centuries. Far beyond Banff, you can see the lofty pyramid of Mt. Assiniboine.

20. Rock Isle Lake—*Alpine splendour*

The Sunshine Meadows are one of the most glorious and accessible alpine areas in the Canadian Rockies. More than 400 species of alpine flowers bloom at Sunshine amidst staggering views. This trail is one of the area's easiest and most popular walks. Strong hikers have the option of continuing close to the crest of the Continental Divide as far as Citadel Pass. Note that the gondola lift does not operate in summer. Access to Sunshine is by shuttle bus from either the Banff townsite or the parking area at the foot of the gondola lift.

Map: below
Distance: 3.2 km (2 mi) return
Time: 1¹/₂ hours
Rating: Moderate
Max. elevation: 2280 m (7478 ft)
Elevation gain: 100 m (328 ft)
Footwear: Running/walking shoes/light hiking boots
Best season: July to mid-September

access

White Mountain Adventures runs a shuttle bus service up the steep road (closed to private vehicles) to Sunshine Village from June to September 30; $17 for adults, $8 for children. Call (403) 678-4099 for times. Although you can take the bus from Banff for $35, visitors with their own vehicles usually meet the bus at the gondola parking lot. Turn off the Trans-Canada Highway at the Sunshine interchange, 9 km (5.6 mi) west of Banff, and drive 9 km (5.6 mi) to the parking area at the end of the road. (You could hike 6 km [3.7 mi] up the steep road to Sunshine Village from the parking area. Personally, we think life's too short for such a long and monotonous grind.)

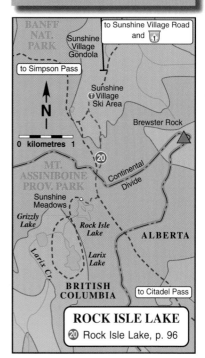

ROCK ISLE LAKE
20 Rock Isle Lake, p. 96

Start at the Sunshine Village interpretive centre and follow the path past the Strawberry Chairlift (not operating in summer). You begin a moderately steep ascent out of this timberline valley, making a quick transition from a subalpine forest of larch, fir and spruce to the bare meadows of the alpine region.

The trail takes you past wet hollows containing moisture-tolerant plants. Some of the hollows might be covered with snowdrifts even in mid-summer. A yearly snowfall of 6.5 m (21 ft) is not uncommon. The small plants survive in thin, dry and dusty soil, buffeted by strong winds for much of the short summer.

Hikers start to see views of the imposing pyramid of Mt. Assiniboine to the southeast. The trail climbs over a small rise marking the Continental Divide and the boundary between Alberta and British Columbia. Beyond the divide, the tiny alpine streams all flow towards the Pacific.

A trail leads off left into Mt. Assiniboine Provincial Park, and the Rock Isle Lake Trail descends past the burrows of hundreds of aggres-sive ground squirrels to a small lake, a gorgeous spot on a sunny day. Benches and an observation deck have been built above the lake.

OPTIONS: Hikers with the time and energy could explore the stunning plateau further by continuing on the loop trail to Grizzly Lake or Larix Lake, although this choice involves a descent (and an ascent on the return) back into the subalpine forest.

The most scenic option is to continue above Rock Isle Lake on the high route to Citadel Pass, a total distance of 18 km (11 mi) from Sunshine Village. This popular route stays mostly above treeline, providing outstanding views and wildflower displays. Just leave enough time to return and catch your bus back down.

Rock Isle Lake

Early fall snow covers Bourgeau Lake approach

21. Bourgeau Lake—*Land of the rock rabbit*

Although the climb to Bourgeau Lake is long and steep, the day walker passes waterfalls and cascades, and finally attains a gorgeous timberline meadow and a small lake set amid rugged rock walls and scree slopes. The trailhead is close to Banff townsite, and there are good views for much of the ascent. For strong hikers only.

access

From Banff townsite, drive 11.4 km (7 mi) north on the Trans-Canada Highway to the Bourgeau Lake parking lot.

Map: page 99
Distance: 15.2 km (9.4 mi) return
Time: 6 hours
Rating: Strenuous
Max. elevation: 2148 m (7045 ft)
Elevation gain: 747 m (2450 ft)
Footwear: Light hiking boots
Best season: July to mid-September

The trail climbs easily at first above Wolverine Creek through a lodgepole pine forest, gradually entering the steep valley. Views open up as the trail crosses old slide areas. You can also see back across the Bow Valley to the sharp-toothed Sawback Range whose rocks are laid nearly vertically.

The lodgepole forest gradually turns to spruce as elevation increases. This transition is about half-way in terms of distance, although the hardest climbing is yet to come. The trail works its way up well above the stream, passing under the broken, brown cliffs of Mt. Bourgeau. A series of spectacular cascades looms ahead. The climbing gets steeper as the trail switchbacks through a series of rock bands to get above the cascades.

As you gain the upper floor of the valley, you cross a grassy meadow, which is under impressive, rugged slopes set between a continuation of Mt. Brett to the right and Mt. Bourgeau to the left (2918 m, 9571 ft). The first mountain is named for Dr. R.G. Brett, the energetic Canadian Pacific Railway doctor and Banff pioneer who became lieutenant governor of Alberta. The latter is named for Eugene Bourgeau, botanist with the famous Palliser Expedition (1857–60).

This valley is a typical glacial cirque, carved out by the ice. The glacier has long since retreated, leaving a lake where it created a depression in the rock.

The trail continues over meadows spangled with wildflowers to reach icy, boulder-strewn Bourgeau Lake, set under forbidding limestone rock walls and steep scree slopes. The rocks shelter colonies of pikas, also known as rock rabbits.

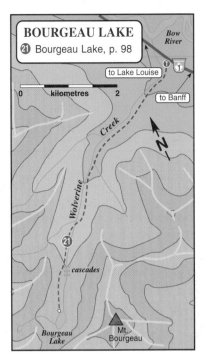

BOURGEAU LAKE
㉑ Bourgeau Lake, p. 98

Bow River

to Lake Louise

to Banff

0   kilometres   2

N

Wolverine Creek

㉑

cascades

Bourgeau Lake

Mt. Bourgeau

Pika

22. Johnston Canyon—*Most-visited canyon*

This narrow, dark gap cut by rushing, crystal waters is probably the most visited canyon in the Canadian Rockies. Yet relatively few venture beyond the first cascade—and that's a pity. The path features seven waterfalls, an optional walk through a wet tunnel and a close-up look at the Upper Falls, twice the size of the Lower Falls. For those with extra energy, the hike to the jade-green Inkpots is a pleasant half-day option.

access

Johnston Canyon is 25 km (16 mi) north of Banff townsite on the Bow Valley Parkway (Hwy. 1A). The trail starts from the large parking area on the east side of Johnston Creek.

Map: below
Distance: 2.2 km (1.4 mi) return to Lower Falls; 5.4 km (3.3 mi) return to Upper Falls; 11 km (7 mi) return to Inkpots
Time: 40 minutes (Lower Falls); 1¹/₂ hours (Upper Falls); 4¹/₂ hours (Inkpots)
Rating: Easy to Lower Falls (wheelchair-accessible paved trail); moderate to Upper Falls and Inkpots
Max. elevation: 1647 m (5402 ft) at Inkpots
Elevation gain: 243 m (797 ft) to Inkpots
Footwear: Anything to Lower and Upper Falls; light hiking boots to Inkpots
Best season: Mid-May to October

The wide asphalt trail starts up gently through a lush, mossy forest beside vigorous Johnston Creek and enters the canyon. In this narrow canyon cut into 350-million-year-old limestone, the world seems to consist only of rock and the sound of swirling water. In some places, the canyon walls are more than 30 m (98 ft) high and less than 6 m (20 ft) across. Each year, rushing water wears away 2 mm (0.1 in) of limestone, scouring the canyon's face into myriad shapes.

The elaborate trail in this section consists of a suspended walkway bolted onto the side of the cliff, partway up the canyon wall. Black swifts, found only in a few places in Alberta, nest in the canyon walls. Look for them in early morning or

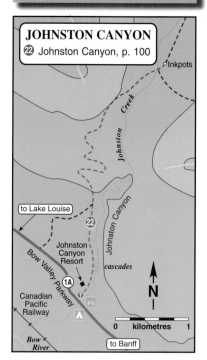

JOHNSTON CANYON
㉒ Johnston Canyon, p. 100

Inkpots

Johnston Creek

to Lake Louise

㉒

Johnston Canyon Resort

Johnston Canyon

cascades

Bow Valley Parkway

1A

Canadian Pacific Railway

N

0   kilometres   1

Bow River

to Banff

at dusk, especially by the lower falls. Watch also for American dippers, or water ouzels, flying just above the water to feed or bobbing up and down at the side of the stream.

Pass under an overhanging cliff of solid limestone to the Lower Falls, which swirl into a green pool against copper-coloured cliffs. Cross the small bridge to the other side of the canyon, and go through a tiny, dark rock passage where the creek once flowed for a misty, close-up of the falls.

The trail continues past pretty Twin Falls, keeping to the right for a close-up view of the impressive Upper Falls.

In winter, the canyon becomes a world of frozen waterfalls and pillars of blue ice. Guided interpretive walks, partly along the canyon bottom to the Upper Falls, are offered daily by White Mountain Adventures. Call (403) 678-4099.

OPTION: For the Inkpots alternative, continue up the wide pathway away from the falls until you reach a fireroad. Turn right onto the fireroad, which cuts uphill through thick forest. Calypso orchids (or Venus'-slippers) bloom here in June, their purplish-pink flowers delicately shaped like tiny slippers. Asters, arnicas, Indian paintbrushes and other wildflowers adorn the trail and meadows ahead. A clearing offers views of the Bow Valley.

The path opens into a beautiful, wide valley. The Inkpots, only a few steps further, are small natural springs, usually bright blue or jade

Johnston Canyon icewalk

in colour, that are maintained at a constant temperature of 1° C (34° F).

The glaciers have since retreated and disappeared hereabouts, but glacial till is everywhere. Water that flows into the Inkpots probably travels through this till, picking up the 'rock flour' ground by ancient glaciers. This flour is suspended in the water and catches the light, changing the colour of the water on the surface to stunning shades of blue or jade.

23. Silverton Falls—*The unknown falls*

Silverton Falls is higher and more spectacular than any single waterfall in tourist-crowded Johnston Canyon nearby. Yet it isn't often visited by the thousands who travel the Bow Valley Parkway (Hwy. 1A). The route to the falls is an easy trail that loses its snow faster than many others in spring. The ideal time for a visit is in late spring or early summer when the creek's water volume is highest.

access

Follow the Trans-Canada Highway to Castle Mountain Junction, 28 km (17 mi) northwest of Banff townsite, at the intersection with Hwy. 93. Turn east towards the Bow Valley Parkway (Hwy. 1A), and then turn right at the store and cabins. Just south of this junction, turn left beside a warden station into the parking lot for the Rockbound Lake Trail.

Map: page 104
Distance: 2.5 km (1.6 mi) return
Time: 45 minutes
Rating: Easy
Max. elevation: 1524 m (4999 ft)
Elevation gain: 76 m (249 ft)
Footwear: Walking/running shoes/light hiking boots
Best season: May to October

Continue up the wide trail to Rockbound Lake for about 195 m (640 ft). Watch for a smaller trail leading right. The trail heads through a thick growth of lodgepole pine to Silverton Creek and a T-intersection. The right branch follows the creek to the base of the lower falls. The left branch immediately switchbacks up to a fine viewpoint half-way up the falls and separated from the wild rush of water by only a few metres.

Above, water is forced through a narrow gap in the rock and down five waterfalls in the cliff, although the last plunge is out of sight. This creek, named for the silver mining boom that hit this area in 1883, drains Rockbound Lake behind Castle Mountain.

history

Boom Times at Silver City

The boom started in 1882 after a Stoney man showed prospector J.J. Healy a chunk of ore high in silver and copper. Healy staked a claim and word got around, as word always does. By 1883, there were 175 wooden buildings, including five stores, three hotels, two saloons and three butcher shops, plus numerous tents in what was called Silver City. But no silver. By 1885, Silver City was a ghost town.

meadow vole

facing page: Silverton Creek

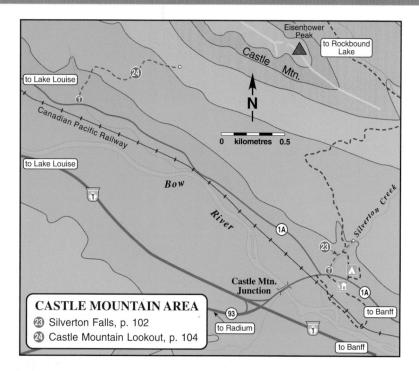

CASTLE MOUNTAIN AREA
- **23** Silverton Falls, p. 102
- **24** Castle Mountain Lookout, p. 104

24. Castle Mountain Lookout

To the castle walls

Castle Mountain is among the most magnificent peaks in Banff with its towers, terraces and sheer walls. The lookout trail climbs to the base of the great walls and provides outstanding views over the wide Bow Valley.

access

From the Trans-Canada Highway, turn east at Castle Mountain Junction, 28 km (17 mi) northwest of Banff townsite, then left on Hwy. 1A, the Bow Valley Parkway. At about the 5-km (3.1-mi) mark from the junction, turn right onto a paved road leading to a parking area.

Map: above
Distance: 7.2 km (4.5 mi) return
Time: 3½ hours
Rating: Moderate
Max. elevation: 1900 m (6232 ft)
Elevation gain: 436 m (1430 ft)
Footwear: Walking/running shoes/light hiking boots
Best season: May to October

The hiking on a fireroad is moderate at first. It becomes steeper and passes the remains of an old cabin as the trees begin to open to reveal the valley below. The road reverts to a narrow trail and begins to switchback up rocky, mostly open slopes and flower-filled meadows below the cliffs.

At about 3.6 km (2.2 mi), the trail finally pushes through a band of rock, levels off atop a rock pitch and reaches what used to be a fire lookout. Lookouts have been replaced with aerial patrols, and the old place burned down anyway. It is a great spot to contemplate the glacier-gouged Bow Valley and the impressive peaks across it, such as rugged Storm Mountain—which often seems to create its own bad weather.

How a Castle Became a General

The prominent peak on the north side of the Bow Valley half-way between Banff and Lake Louise had long been called Castle Mountain for its impressive ramparts and towers. But following the Second World War, it was re-named Mt. Eisenhower after the American general who later became the U.S. president. When told of the honour, he is said to have replied that there already was a mountain named after him: 'Old Baldy.' Only recently has the name reverted back to Castle Mountain, although the first and most prominent rocky spire on the south end of the ridge is still called Eisenhower Peak.

Castle Mountain is a perfect example of a 'layer' or 'castellated' mountain composed mostly of horizontally laid sedimentary rock. Erosion creates the great towers and pinnacles. The softer rock gradually drops away, leaving an upstanding core of more resilient rock.

Rocky facts

Castle Mountain

25. Boom Lake Trail—*Boom of beauty*

Clear Boom Lake is dramatically set below Chimney Peak, Boom Mountain and Mt. Quadra, framed by dark timber and a white glacier. The outing is reasonably short without major climbing and could be suitable for families. Although the approach to the lake is easy, views along the way are non-existent.

Map: page 107
Distance: 10.2 km (6.3 mi) return
Time: 3–3¹/₂ hours
Rating: Moderate
Max. elevation: 1892 m (6206 ft)
Elevation gain: 185 m (607 ft)
Footwear: Light hiking boots
Best season: June to October

access | **From Banff townsite, drive 28 km (17 mi) northwest on the Trans-Canada Highway to Castle Mountain Junction. Turn left on Hwy. 93 and travel 6.2 km (4 mi) up Vermilion Pass. Boom Lake parking lot is on the right at a picnic area. Start at the north end, crossing over a wooden bridge.**

The walk begins on a wide road, veering left for a short steep section onto a trail embowered by lodgepole pine, white spruce and fir. South are tantalizing views of Storm Mountain, named by G.M. Dawson in 1884 after the storm clouds so often seen on the summit.

The trail then soon levels off. The air seems especially fragrant, a tumbling stream echoes below, and an 'away from it all' feeling prevails at last. The lodgepole pines give way to the denser, damper subalpine forest.

Shortly before the lake, the walker has a choice of going right through a small rock slide area, or continuing left on the wide trail. They both go the same way, although the left-hand route is easier.

Boom Lake is long, narrow and aqua-green, forested at its edges and strewn with rubble on the north side. Small cutthroat and rainbow trout can be caught. Early in the season, avalanches drop from Boom Mountain on the south side. Mt. Quadra dominates the panorama to the northwest, and to the right are the forested lower slopes of Bident Mountain.

Boom Lake

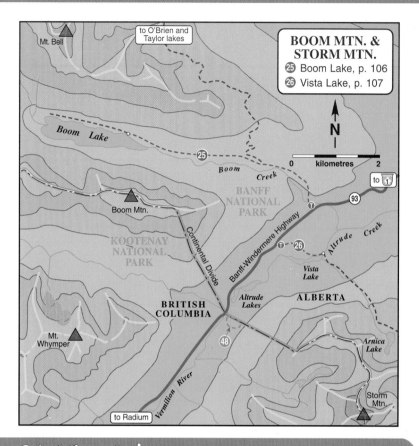

**BOOM MTN. &
STORM MTN.**
㉕ Boom Lake, p. 106
㉖ Vista Lake, p. 107

N

0   kilometres   2

to ①

Mt. Bell

to O'Brien and
Taylor lakes

Boom Lake

㉕

Boom Creek

BANFF
NATIONAL
PARK

Boom Mtn.

93

KOOTENAY
NATIONAL
PARK

Continental Divide

Banff-Windermere Highway

㉖

Altrude Creek

Vista
Lake

BRITISH
COLUMBIA

Altrude
Lakes

ALBERTA

Mt.
Whymper

48

Arnica
Lake

Vermilion River

to Radium

Storm
Mtn

26. Vista Lake—*Fire and rebirth*

Descend through the fascinating renewal of a forest, following the devastation of a 1968 forest fire, to reach a vivid green lake under the imposing heights of Storm Mountain. The trail is short and open to grand views all the way.

access

From the Trans-Canada Highway at Castle Mountain Junction, 28 km (17 mi) northwest of Banff townsite, take Hwy. 93 for 4 km (2.5 mi) up Vermilion Pass. Near the top of the hill is a scenic turnoff on the left, with Vista Lake visible below.

Map: above
Distance: 2.8 km (1.7 mi) return
Time: 1½ hours
Rating: Moderate
Max. elevation: 1700 m (5576 ft)
Elevation loss: 130 m (426 ft)
Footwear: Walking/running shoes
Best season: June to October

The trail edges down the side of the steep hill through the burn. Ahead looms the imposing bulk of Storm Mountain, its reddish-brown quartz sandstone deeply cut by great cirques. This

107

Heart-leaved arnica

Luxuriant new growth now dominates, although some grey, dead trees and fireweed remain in the aftermath of a devastating forest fire.

The route passes a small hoodoo composed of conglomerate material —clay and stone—that has remained cemented together while the soil around it has eroded.

The trail soon reaches the lake where cutthroat trout might be caught. The trail follows the shore to the stream outlet that is crossed on a bridge.

OPTION: The trail from Vista Lake continues for another 3.6 km (2.2 mi) to Arnica Lake, a strenuous option for strong hikers, with an elevation gain of 550 m (1804 ft). The route climbs a bare ridge with gorgeous views, and passes under the gloomy cliffs of Storm Mountain to reach the small, sub-alpine lake surrounded by larches.

The name 'arnica' refers to a common wildflower of this subalpine, spruce-fir forest. The heart-leaved arnica, the most widely distributed, is a member of the daisy family and bears yellow, daisy-like flowers from long stems.

Views open up on the ridge beyond the lake and the trail descends in 1.4 km (0.9 mi) to Upper Twin Lake and a camp-ground and the more scenic Lower Twin—a rocky tarn whose meadows contrast vividly with the grey cliffs of Storm Mountain.

mountain does seem to gather the storms; it's often enclosed in dark clouds when other peaks around are clear.

On July 9, 1968, lightning struck this area and the resulting fire burned 2464 ha (6160 acres). Now, animals and a new succession of plants and trees have invaded the burn and the forest is slowly renewed.

27. Taylor Lake Trail—*Dramatic cirque*

The hike is a steady uphill trudge through thick subalpine forest. But the reward is Taylor Lake's dramatic setting under the backdrop of Mt. Bell and an optional side trip to a splendid meadow of alpine flowers.

access

From Banff townsite, drive 36 km (22 mi) west on the Trans-Canada Highway or 8 km (5 mi) west of Castle Mountain Junction. Start at the Taylor Creek picnic area and parking lot. Cross a wooden bridge; the trailhead is to the right.

> **Map:** below
> **Distance:** 12.6 km (7.8 mi) return
> **Time:** 4 hours
> **Rating:** Moderate
> **Max. elevation:** 2057 m (6747 ft)
> **Elevation gain:** 579 m (1899 ft)
> **Footwear:** Light hiking boots
> **Best season:** July to mid-September

The trail heads up gradually on an abandoned fireroad along rushing Taylor Creek. It begins in the lower subalpine, which gradually gives way to stunted fir and Engelmann spruce.

After considerable forest trudging, the walker will be relieved when dramatic views open to Mt. Bell on the left and Panorama Ridge on the right, the latter separating Bow Valley from the rugged Consolation Valley to the west. Cross a poten-

tially mushy meadow before coming to a camping area in the trees and then to Taylor Lake in a small, gem-like, forest-fringed cirque. The lake, bounded by meadows and subalpine forest, is set under the steep cliffs of Mt. Bell.

OPTION: While a route also leads 2 km (1.2 mi) south to O'Brien Lake, the way can be difficult. Easier and more rewarding is the short hike to the north from the campground on the Panorama Ridge Trail. In just a few minutes, the trail leads to an extensive wildflower meadow under Panorama Ridge.

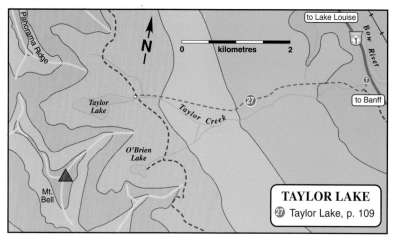

TAYLOR LAKE
27 Taylor Lake, p. 109

28. Moraine Lake Viewpoint—*Priceless view*

The walk up to Moraine Lake Viewpoint is one of the shortest in this book; the panorama it offers is not to be missed. The path ascends a huge rockpile under the imposing Tower of Babel to a magnificent vantage point on the turquoise-green lake framed by jagged peaks. This view was once depicted on the back of Canada's $20 bill. Here, it's free.

Map: page 111
Distance: 0.7 km (0.4 mi) return
Time: 15–20 minutes
Rating: Easy
Max. elevation: 1950 m (6396 ft)
Elevation gain: Negligible
Footwear: Walking/running shoes
Best season: June to October

access

From the Trans-Canada Highway at the Lake Louise intersection in Banff National Park, turn west on Hwy. 1A and drive 1.1 km (0.7 mi) up the hill towards Lake Louise. Turn left (south) on the Moraine Lake Road, which ends in 12.4 km (7.7 mi) at a large parking lot. The trail begins on the south end of the parking lot at the sign for Consolation Lakes.

dark-eyed junco

The walk starts in a dramatic setting, under the reddish, aptly named Tower of Babel. Geologists now believe that the rock debris that dams this end of the lake fell from this mountain. However, Walter Wilcox, who named the lake in 1893, believed the debris to be a moraine, a deposit of debris carried by a glacier or pushed ahead by it—hence, Moraine Lake. It is a good name, even if it is scientifically wrong.

The path soon opens out onto a panorama of Moraine Lake. The 10 peaks, east to west, are Fay, Little, Bowlen, Tonsa, Perren, Allen, Tuzo, Deltaform, the tallest, Neptuak and Wenkchemna.

You can climb down to the water's edge, if you want. On a sunny day, it's a great place to sketch, read, or just soak in the splendour, though not the solitude.

Moraine Lake

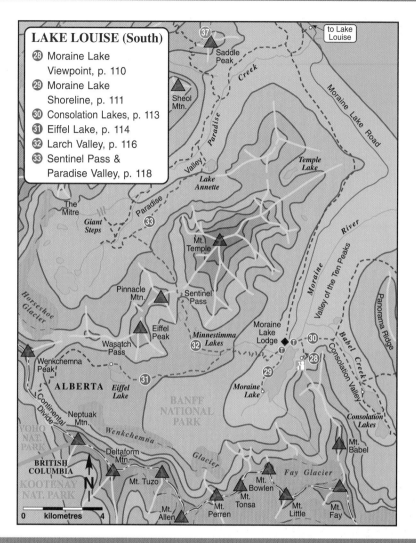

LAKE LOUISE (South)

28 Moraine Lake
Viewpoint, p. 110
29 Moraine Lake
Shoreline, p. 111
30 Consolation Lakes, p. 113
31 Eiffel Lake, p. 114
32 Larch Valley, p. 116
33 Sentinel Pass &
Paradise Valley, p. 118

to Lake
Louise

Saddle
Peak

Creek

Sheol
Mtn.

Moraine Lake Road

Paradise

Valley

Lake
Annette

Temple
Lake

The
Mitre

Giant
Steps

Paradise

33

River

Mt.
Temple

Horseshoe
Glacier

Pinnacle
Mtn.

Sentinel
Pass

Moraine

Valley of the Ten Peaks

Panorama Ridge

Eiffel
Peak

Wasatch
Pass

Minnestimma
Lakes

32

Moraine
Lake
Lodge

30

Babel Creek

Consolation Valley

Wenkchemna
Peak

28

29

ALBERTA Eiffel
Lake

31

Moraine
Lake

Continental Divide

Neptuak
Mtn.

Wenkchemna

BANFF
NATIONAL
PARK

Consolation
Lakes

YOHO
NAT.
PARK

Deltaform
Mtn.

Glacier

Mt.
Babel

**BRITISH
COLUMBIA**

KOOTENAY
NAT. PARK

N

Mt. Tuzo

Fay Glacier

Mt.
Bowlen

0   kilometres   4

Mt.
Allen

Mt.
Perren

Mt.
Tonsa

Mt.
Little

Mt.
Fay

29. Moraine Lake Shoreline—*Lakeshore stroll*

Turquoise Moraine Lake, set in the commanding Valley of the Ten Peaks, is regarded by many as more dramatic and striking than its more famous sister, Lake Louise. A pretty lakeshore stroll, suitable for all ages, meanders along its wooded west shore. The path is just long enough to stretch your legs or work off dinner.

Views are fewer than one might expect, however. If panoramas are a priority, take the short stroll to Moraine Lake Viewpoint (Walk 28) or the longer Larch Valley trail (Walk 32). Canoes can be rented and fishing is permitted in season with a Parks permit.

Banff: Lake Louise

access

From the Trans-Canada Highway at the Lake Louise intersection in Banff National Park, turn west on Hwy. 1A and drive 1.1 km (0.7 mi) up the hill towards Lake Louise. Turn left (south) on the Moraine Lake Road, which ends in 12.4 km (7.7 mi) at a large parking lot. The walk starts on the asphalt path at the south end of parking lot.

Map: page 111
Distance: 3.2 km (2 mi)
Time: 30–40 minutes
Rating: Easy
Max. elevation: 1900 m (6232 ft)
Elevation gain: Negligible
Footwear: Walking/running shoes
Best season: Mid-June to October

On this walk, the most fabulous views are at the beginning, even before you reach Moraine Lake Lodge. The spectacle of the green lake set against the magnificent backdrop of the Valley of the Ten Peaks is exquisite indeed.

On the other side of the boat launch, take the lower trail left at the junction with the trailhead sign for Larch Valley. Mt. Fay, the first of the 10 numbered peaks, is to the left. To its right are Little, Bowlen, Tonsa, Perren, Allen, Tuzo, Deltaform (the highest of the 10), Neptuak and Wenkchemna. The pink rock pile visible on the east shore is composed of shale and quartz sandstone.

The pleasant path is strewn with wildflowers in summer, and winds through an open forest with lake views. As one walks, Moraine's colour, the result of suspended rock particles, seems to change from teal-blue to turquoise and green.

Dippers and harlequin ducks can sometimes be seen on the lake. The forest becomes mossy and marshy, and better views of hanging Fay Glacier appear ahead. Near the end of the walk, you might hear the rumble of a glacial stream. The trail heads into cool, dense forest before ending at the stream, which drains Wenkchemna Glacier.

Moraine Lake and Valley of the Ten Peaks

30. Consolation Lakes—*Rock hopper's delight*

Most of the spectacular subalpine lakes in the Banff backcountry can only be reached after hours of hard uphill slogging. The lower of the Consolation lakes, as scenic as any lake in the Rockies, is easily attained on a wide, gentle trail from popular Moraine Lake. It's a good way to escape the crowds that drift through the Lake Louise-Moraine Lake area in summer, and you don't have to strain yourself to do it.

Map: page 111
Distance: 6.4 km (4 mi) return
Time: 2¹/₂ hours
Rating: Moderate
Max. elevation: 1950 m (6396 ft)
Elevation gain: 94 m (308 ft)
Footwear: Walking/running shoes
Best season: Mid-June to October

access

From the Trans-Canada Highway at the Lake Louise intersection in Banff National Park, turn west on Hwy. 1A and drive 1.1 km (0.7 mi) up the hill towards Lake Louise. Turn left (south) on the Moraine Lake Road, which ends in 12.4 km (7.7 mi) at a large parking lot. The trail to the lower of the two Consolation lakes begins from the lower parking lot.

Babel Creek in Consolation Valley

The trail climbs briefly over part of the huge rock pile that blocks the end of the lake. The Consolation Lakes trail soon branches left, away from the rocks, while the route straight ahead continues to a viewpoint overlooking the gorgeous lake (see Walk 28).

The trail traverses a boulder field under the imposing and crumbling heights of Mt. Babel. Behind you, to the northwest, is the sprawling mass of Mt. Temple (3547 m, 11,634 ft), a most imposing pyramid. The trail gradually ascends beside vigorous Babel Creek, enters a forest of spruce and subalpine fir

and terminates in a vast area of boulders at the end of the lake. It's fun to hop from rock to rock and get close to the water. On the right, long scree slopes descend to the lake, while glacier-hung Mt. Bident and Mt. Quadra tower behind it.

This lake is the lower of the two. Determined hikers could reach the second one by walking far enough back down the creek to gain the other side, and then following a rough trail along the left shore and over the moraine that divides the two small lakes. Most hikers, however, should console themselves with lower Consolation Lake.

113

31. Eiffel Lake—'Peer of any lakes'

'The peer of any lakes in the Rocky Mountains.' The first European exploration party into this upper valley in 1899 thus described the barren Eiffel Lake. The lake lies among the last stands of larches and the desolation of rubble under the wall of the Wenkchemna Peaks, otherwise known as the Valley of the Ten Peaks.

Map: page 111
Distance: 11.2 km (6.9 mi) return
Time: Day trip
Rating: Strenuous
Max. elevation: 2270 m (7446 ft)
Elevation gain: 384 m (1260 ft)
Footwear: Light hiking boots
Best season: Mid-July to mid-September

access

From the Trans-Canada Highway at the Lake Louise intersection in Banff National Park, turn west on Hwy. 1A and drive 1.1 km (0.7 mi) up the hill towards Lake Louise. Turn left (south) on the Moraine Lake Road, which ends in 12.4 km (7.7 mi) at a large parking lot. The trail to Eiffel Lake begins near the lakeside just beyond the lodge. Take the right fork up the hill.

The initial trail is wide and well-graded as it switchbacks up the steep slopes. The trail offers occasional views down to the stunning emerald-green of Moraine Lake and across the lake to Wenkchemna Glacier, its ice protected from the sun under rock fall and dirt accumulated over the years. This covering keeps the ice from melting at the same rate as most other glaciers.

At 3.2 km (2 mi), the Sentinel Pass trail leads off to the right. Keep straight for Eiffel Lake, the trail neatly following the contour of the hillside under crumbling Eiffel Peak. Among the usual alpine fir and Engelmann spruce are larches, which turn a most spectacular yellow in fall before losing their needles, the only coniferous trees to do so.

There are wonderful views back to Moraine Lake as the forest gradually opens up, revealing the glacial rubble and rock fall below. The hillside becomes more rocky and rugged as you go along, now passing under the broken cliffs that lead up to the trail-less Wasatch Pass (an easy scramble) and Paradise Valley beyond. The trail climbs slightly above the lake, crossing a rock slide and leading to a natural rock bench with a back-rest right on the trail; it is a perfect spot to contemplate this stunning alpine area.

Eiffel Lake is set among enormous boulders that tumbled down from Neptuak Mountain. This view is the one, more or less, that explorer Walter Wilcox saw when he first encountered this area in 1893 and named it 'Desolation Valley.' Had he seen Moraine Lake first, his designation might have been different.

Eiffel Lake environs

OPTION: Strong hikers can continue beyond the lake, climbing only slightly as the trail follows the right edge of the valley. It works its way along an old lateral moraine, and keeps well away from the avalanche-prone slopes on the side.

The ultimate destination is visible 4 km (2.5 mi) above Eiffel Lake: Wenkchemna Pass at the top of broad, rocky meadows. To the right are crumbling tower-like crags with little waterfalls coming off them. Across the valley rises Deltaform and Neptuak. The trail curves left towards the middle of the valley floor, passing near more rock-bound ponds and beginning its ascent of the pass. These rocky meadows might be snow-covered until mid-summer, and the snowcover often returns early in fall.

In good weather, the route, which zig-zags steeply up to the low point in the barren, windswept pass, is unmistakable. Views are grand back down the whole valley and west into Yoho National Park, to the barren Eagle Eyrie and the icefield leading to Opabin Pass and Lake O'Hara.

115

32. Larch Valley—*The golden meadows*

This highly popular trail rises rapidly above Moraine Lake to delightful subalpine meadows that are set against the jagged backdrop of the Valley of the Ten Peaks. Families will find it an ideal way to enjoy sublime mountain views. In September, when the larches have turned gold and the sun is shining, Larch Valley is one of the most exquisite spots in the Rockies—and one of the busiest trails.

Map: page 111
Distance: 8 km (5 mi) return
Time: 3–3½ hours
Rating: Moderate
Max. elevation: 2275 m (7462 ft)
Elevation gain: 375 m (1230 ft)
Footwear: Light hiking boots
Best season: Mid-July to late September

access

From the Trans-Canada Highway at the Lake Louise intersection in Banff National Park, turn west on Hwy. 1A and drive 1.1 km (0.7 mi) up the hill towards Lake Louise. Turn left (south) on the Moraine Lake Road, which ends in 12.4 km (7.7 mi) at a large parking lot. From here, take the asphalt path past Moraine Lodge. Follow the sign to Larch Valley and turn right at the second sign to Wenkchemna Pass, Larch Valley and Sentinel Pass.

The first part of the trail bolts up steeply, with tantalizing glimpses through the trees of Moraine Lake below. In 1893 explorer Walter Wilcox climbed a ridge and recorded his impressions of 'one of the most beautiful lakes I have ever seen. … No scene has ever given me an equal impression of inspiring solitude and rugged grandeur.'

The lake was Moraine, and its colours of mingled robin's egg–blue and green make it equally beautiful today. At the 3.2-km (2-mi) mark, the trail reaches the junction with the Eiffel Lake trail. Keep right and enter a subalpine environment of alpine larches, feather mosses, arnicas, bunchberries and heathers. Views soon open onto the lower Larch Meadows. Mt. Fay, with its hanging glacier, dominates the skyline.

Cross a small stream and continue to the upper Larch Valley, gradually leaving the trees behind to emerge into an area of meadows, delicate pools and, for a short time in summer, tiny alpine flowers. See Walk 33 for the route over Sentinel Pass to Paradise Valley.

short-tailed weasel

Larch Valley

The Allure of Larches

Many Albertans consider fall the most beautiful time to be in the Canadian Rockies, partly because in that season larches turn to gold. The larch is Canada's only deciduous conifer, shedding its soft needles in fall. These needles come in bunches of 30 to 40 on dwarfed, knob-like branches. The alpine larch, one of 10 species of larch, grows in Alberta and southern British Columbia at higher elevations. In Banff National Park, larches are found only in a restricted range at timberline.

The sight of a mountain slope blazing with bright golden larches set against dark green evergreens is truly wondrous. The Banff artist Catharine Robb Whyte captures this beauty in her painting, *Mount Temple, Larches*, 1940. (The painting is at the Whyte Museum of the Canadian Rockies in Banff; also see *A Hiker's Guide to Art of the Canadian Rockies*, by Lisa Christensen.)

biology

117

33. Sentinel Pass and Paradise Valley

Path to Paradise

Peak-rimmed alpine meadows, a pinnacled mountain pass, delicate lakes and pools—these are the rewards of the popular Sentinel Pass trail. The demanding all-day hike over the pass is one of tremendous beauty, plus considerable toil. Snow can last well into summer and cover the other side of the pass by early September.

access

From the Trans-Canada Highway at the Lake Louise intersection in Banff National Park, turn west on Hwy. 1A and drive 1.1 km (0.7 mi) up the hill towards Lake Louise. Turn left (south) on the Moraine Lake Road, which ends in 12.4 km (7.7 mi) at a large parking lot. From the parking lot, follow the asphalt path past Moraine Lodge. Turn right in about 50 m (164 ft) onto the trail to Larch Valley.

Map: page 111
Distance: 20.1-km (12.5-mi) loop to Moraine Lake Road via Paradise Valley; 11.6 km (7.2 mi) return to Sentinel Pass
Time: Long day trip
Rating: Strenuous
Max. elevation: 2600 m (8528 ft)
Elevation gain: 700 m (2296 ft)
Footwear: Light hiking boots
Best season: Late July through September

For details of the approach to Larch Valley, see the preceding route (Walk 32, page 116). In Larch Valley, the trail leads quickly into the magical subalpine meadows that are rimmed with the tops of the Ten Peaks. It continues past tiny ponds towards the upper meadows. Pinnacle Mountain dominates views on the left, while Mt. Temple looms on the right, the highest—3647 m (11,962 ft)—in the Lake Louise area and 10th highest in the Canadian Rockies. Named for Sir Richard Temple, a visitor to the Rockies in 1884, it was first climbed in 1894 by members of the Yale Lake Louise Club, a

Upper Larch Valley

merry band of alpinists who explored extensively in the area. The forbidding north face was not conquered until 1966 when a party led by Brian Greenwood, of Calgary, forced a route.

The trail begins to attack the slope on the right side of the valley, heading for a huge zig-zag on the bare slope under the pass far ahead. Snow often lies across the trail into summer, although there's usually a well-stamped trail across steep patches. Walkers will have to judge the safety of a crossing for themselves.

The top of the pass offers a tremendous view ahead to Paradise Valley and back over the Valley of the Ten Peaks.

The walk over the pass down to Paradise Valley can be treacherous. Snow usually remains on the initial steep and rugged descent until early July, and it returns as early as Labour Day.

Pick your way carefully down the steep slope past gothic sentinels, strange needle-like formations of Pinnacle Mountain.

The trail stops its relentless descent above the valley floor (an alternate route continues down towards Giant Steps). Keep right and cross a large avalanche area, the last major panorama on this walk.

The trail then descends through open forest to Lake Annette. This small lake is situated under the gloomy, awesome cliffs of Mt. Temple. Huge avalanches break the silence of sunny summer afternoons.

The route descends quickly to the valley floor and follows tumbling Paradise Creek under Sheol Mountain and Saddle Mountain. Pay close attention to the signage at the junctions just above the Moraine Lake Road.

The parking lot on the Moraine Lake Road is 2.4 km (1.5 mi) south of the junction with the Lake Louise access road. It's 10 km (6.2 mi) from the parking lot back to Moraine Lake. Don't plan on walking 10 km on a paved road after that long trail. Your feet will die a thousand deaths.

How to Arrange a Sentinel Pass– Paradise Valley Loop

One difficulty with this marvellous walk is the need to arrange transportation back to Moraine Lake from the Paradise Creek parking area. While we don't recommend hitchhiking, necessity has sometimes dictated it here. A safer, surer alternative is to arrange for a taxi shuttle (403-522-2020 at Lake Louise) to take you to the start of your hike after you leave your car at the Paradise Creek parking area.

An enjoyable alternative is to hide bicycles in the woods (locked to a sizable tree near the Paradise Valley parking lot). Leave your car at Moraine Lake at the start of the route. At the end, cycle back to the lake.

Visitor tips

34. Lakeshore Trail—'The most beautiful lake'

'As a gem of composition and colouring it is perhaps unrivalled anywhere,' Sir James Outram wrote of Lake Louise in the early 1900s. His assessment endures. A Florida newspaper recently called Lake Louise 'the most beautiful lake in the western hemisphere.' The shimmering peacock-blue lake, with the sun catching Victoria Glacier at one end and stately Chateau Lake Louise at the other, simply is the Canadian Rockies to many.

Yet you can't really appreciate the lake and its surrounding peaks and glaciers amidst the milling crowds in front of the Chateau. A much better way is to arrive in early morning (when picture-taking is best anyway) and stroll along the lake's right shore. This walk is for anyone. Parents have pushed prams through the rougher section at the end.

Map: page 121
Distance: 3.8 km (2.4 mi) return
Time: 40–60 minutes
Rating: Easy
Max. elevation: 1732 m (5681 ft)
Elevation gain: Negligible
Footwear: Walking/running shoes
Best season: July to October

access

From the Trans-Canada Highway at the Lake Louise Village intersection, drive 8 km (5 mi) up the steep road to Lake Louise. From the big parking lots, walk down to the lake and turn right on the asphalt path in front of the hotel. (Canoes are available for rent at the boathouse to the left of the Chateau, and there is a dock at the southwest end of the lake. You can also rent horses.)

Walk past the Chateau gardens, which in summer are spangled with the reds, oranges and yellows of Icelandic and Shirley poppies, as well as lilies, purple delphiniums, violets and many others. Across the lake, Mt. Victoria and the gleaming Victoria Glacier overwhelm the landscape. On the immediate left is Fairview Mountain and to the right, the Beehives.

Keep on the lower lakeside trail, where the formal gardens give way to a path fringed by daisies, asters and other wildflowers.

The lake's colour seems to change constantly, the result of suspended rock flour particles from Victoria Glacier catching the sun's rays like a spectrum. Early summer sees the lake a clear blue; it turns progressively greener through the season as more silt accumulates in the lake.

This lake, along with many others scooped out by glaciers in the Rockies, is finger-shaped. It's less than 0.5 km (0.3 mi) wide and 2.5 km (1.6 mi) long and up to 75 m (246 ft) deep. The water never warms up in summer.

Views back to the Chateau emerge; the old grey lady of the Rockies is perched on an old moraine like a duchess on a beach chair. The Canadian Pacific Railway (CPR) first built a one-storey log

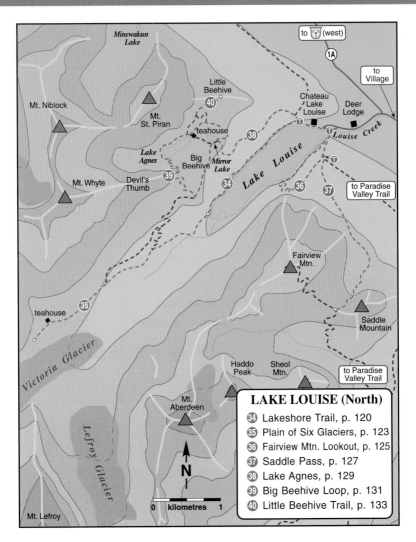

LAKE LOUISE (North)
- ③④ Lakeshore Trail, p. 120
- ③⑤ Plain of Six Glaciers, p. 123
- ③⑥ Fairview Mtn. Lookout, p. 125
- ③⑦ Saddle Pass, p. 127
- ③⑧ Lake Agnes, p. 129
- ③⑨ Big Beehive Loop, p. 131
- ④⓪ Little Beehive Trail, p. 133

building here in 1890, and quickly followed it with a full-scale Tudor wooden chateau. All except one section, the concrete Paynter Wing, burned down in 1924 and was replaced by the current brick addition. The hotel is open year-round.

A semi-circle of mountains surrounds the lake including, from left to right, Fairview, Aberdeen, Lefroy, Victoria, Whyte, Niblock and St. Piran. From the walker's perspective, Fairview looms closest across the lake on the left. The lookout above the lake under Fairview makes a wonderful destination from which to view everything (see Walk 36).

The path becomes a bit rougher, following a wall of pink-stained quartzrose sandstone, where climbers can often be seen on routes such as Wicked Gravity and

121

Lake Louise

Exquisite Corpse. At the end of the lake, a profusion of braided streams pour in amidst a mass of glacial rubble. Note the colour contrast as the clear meltwater enters the opaque lake.

Wilson's Wonder

In 1882, Tom Wilson, a CPR worker, was camping at Laggan, as the former Lake Louise station was called, when he heard the sound of distant thunder. The thunder, the Stoney told him, came from an immense white mountain nearby, above 'The Lake of Little Fishes.' Intrigued, Wilson decided to investigate. The next morning, he became the first non-native to see Lake Louise. Wilson, it was said, recalled the wonder of this moment for the rest of his life.

'For some time we sat and smoked and gazed at the gem of beauty beneath the glacier,' he wrote. Although Wilson renamed it 'Emerald Lake,' the name was later changed to Louise in 1884 after Princess Caroline Alberta Louise, daughter of Queen Victoria and wife of the governor general of Canada.

Today, the lake is surely as beautiful as the day Wilson first gazed on it. But don't expect solitude. It has been visited by more than 100 million people, and the number keeps climbing at a rate of 1.6 million a year.

history

35. Plain of Six Glaciers—*Glaciers and biscuits*

Six glaciers, the starkness of glacial rubble, panoramas of turquoise Lake Louise, the startling thrust of great peaks and deep rumbling avalanches are the rewards awaiting the walker on this classic trail. The appetite-rousing walk leads up to a rustic tea-house near the top, which serves teas, homemade soups and hot baking powder biscuits. If you only have time for one walk in the Rockies, and don't mind sharing it with horses and many other hikers, this would be an excellent choice.

access

From the Trans-Canada Highway at the Lake Louise intersection, drive 8 km (5 mi) up the steep road to Lake Louise. From the large parking lots, walk down to the lake and head right along the shore past the flower gardens and snack bar concession. The trail starts at a sign just right of the Chateau.

Map: page 121
Distance: 11 km (7 mi) return
Time: 5 hours
Rating: Moderate
Max. elevation: 2263 m (7423 ft)
Elevation gain: 471 m (1545 ft)
Footwear: Light hiking boots
Best season: July to October

The first section is described in Walk 34 (page 120). From the end of Lake Louise, enter an area of fir, spruce and wild strawberries, followed by an overgrown avalanche area. Some tiny paths lead to clearings by the glacial stream. Continue past shrubbery laced in summer with yellow cinquefoil, harebells, Indian paintbrush, western anemone and purple saxifrage.

The next portion ascends gradually through trees, and the walker starts to reap the rewards of toil. The trail enters a vast, open plain of deadfall and lateral moraines, which were deposited by the Victoria Glacier as it receded during the 19th century.

The next portion is rough, like a trip through a gravel pit. The trail then switchbacks briefly through the trees before arriving at the teahouse.

Here is one of the two surviving teahouses in Banff National Park that were built at the turn of the 20th century by the Canadian Pacific Railway (CPR). This teahouse is open from late June to early September.

Although weary walkers might be tempted to turn back at the teahouse, they should probably persist for another 30 minutes to the end of the trail.

The trail stops on a barren south-facing slope at the end of the moraine. You might hear the crashing of avalanches from the Upper Lefroy and Upper Victoria glaciers on warm summer afternoons.

Vistas are stupendous. Looming ahead, from left to right, are the black Mitre, shaped like a bishop's hat, lofty Lefroy at 3420 m

Lake Louise from Plain of Six Glaciers

(11,218 ft) and snow-benched Mt. Victoria at 3464 m (11,362 ft). The six glaciers visible are, from left to right, Aberdeen Glacier, Upper Lefroy Glacier, Lower Lefroy Glacier, Upper Victoria Glacier, Lower Victoria Glacier and Pope's Glacier.

Abbot Hut

At the end of the Plain of Six Glaciers trail, the sharp-eyed will spot Abbot Hut between Mt. Victoria and Mt. Lefroy. The hut was the highest building in Canada when constructed in 1922 for $30,000. It was named after Phillip Abbot, an attorney for the Wisconsin Central Railway who plunged to his death in this pass on August 3, 1896, becoming the first-recorded climber to die in the Rockies. The glacier going up to the hut—a refuge for serious climbers—has the reassuring name of 'Death Trap.' In 1992, the shelter was designated a National Historic Site.

history

36. Fairview Mountain Lookout

Early morning splendour

The splendour of Lake Louise is best seen at sunrise before the hordes of tourists begin to stir. Mist still curls over the water and the early light etches Victoria Glacier and mountains beyond in startling clarity. Although the Beehives and other high vantage points are probably too difficult to reach before breakfast, the Fairview lookout can be attained in about 30 minutes, even in dim light. The trail's just long enough to make you hungry for breakfast, and is a splendid spot to observe the colours of Lake Louise and the wide expanse of the Bow Valley beyond—before breakfast, lunch or dinner.

Map: page 121
Distance: 3.5 km (2.2 mi)
Time: 1–2 hours
Rating: Moderate
Max. elevation: 1825 m (5986 ft)
Elevation gain: 93 m (305 ft)
Footwear: Walking/running shoes/light hiking boots
Best season: Mid-June to October

access

From the Trans-Canada Highway at the Lake Louise intersection in Banff National Park, drive 8 km (5 mi) up the steep road to Lake Louise. From the vast parking lots, walk down to the shore of the lake and turn left along the shore towards the boathouse. Before you reach the boathouse, take the wide trail that enters the trees and begins climbing.

The trail begins as the main route to Saddle Pass, and climbs gradually through a thick, mossy forest. At 0.4 km (0.2 mi), take the right fork and ascend, sometimes steeply, through the forest under the cliffs of Fairview Mountain.

The trees open up at a good viewpoint with an observation platform high above the lake. The views are inspiring, to say the least.

Lake Louise is in a hanging valley above the wide, U-shaped Bow Valley trench. The lake, hollowed out by glaciers, is more than 80 m (262 ft) deep in places, and the water temperature doesn't rise much above freezing. Its dazzling colour is

Chateau Lake Louise

dependent on the lake's depths and the 'rock flour' suspended in the water. The glaciers high on the slopes of Lefroy and Victoria grind up rock as they move gradually down the slopes. When the ice melts at the bottom, the streams carry this rock flour into the lake, changing Louise's colour, as a tablespoon of milk changes the colour of a glass of water.

In summer, when the ice finally goes out, the lake is a robin's egg–blue. Later, it seems to turn greener or aquamarine, delectable shades that are best appreciated from such vantage points as these.

The easiest and shortest way back is the route you arrived on. For more variety, a true loop can be made by descending steeply from the lookout down to the Lake Louise shoreline. Turn right at the bottom and follow the trail—much quieter than the tourist-clogged route on the far side—back to the boathouse and the Chateau.

Lake Louise: One of the most visited sites in the Rockies

37. Saddle Pass—*More than a fair view*

The pass between Saddle Mountain and Fairview Mountain, although not the most popular choice for day walks in the Lake Louise area, does provide extraordinary views across to the awesome north face of Mt. Temple and the black cliffs of Sheol Mountain. The pass is a grassy meadow, lush with wildflowers. The trail to it is fairly steep.

Map: page 121
Distance: 7.2 km (4.5 mi) return
Time: 4 hours
Rating: Strenuous
Max. elevation: 2300 m (7544 ft)
Elevation gain: 570 m (1870 ft)
Footwear: Light hiking boots
Best season: July to October

access

From the Trans-Canada Highway at the Lake Louise intersection, drive 8 km (5 mi) up the steep road to Lake Louise. From the vast parking lots, walk down to the lake and turn left along the shore towards the boathouse. Before you reach the boathouse, take the wide trail that enters the trees and begins climbing.

The trail climbs gradually through a thick, mossy forest. The side trail to Fairview lookout heads right at 0.4 km (0.2 mi). Continue straight. The trail begins to switchback more steeply before levelling off somewhat as it crosses open avalanche paths, which provide views of the Bow Valley.

The route zig-zags around the lower slopes of Fairview, and then turns straight for little Saddle Mountain.

The terrain opens up in rocky meadows below Saddle, home of numerous ground squirrels, pikas and marmots. The route rises gradually almost to timberline through this beautiful meadow, reaching the top of the pass at 3.6 km (2.2 mi). The black mass of Temple, with its snow field near the summit, looms before you.

While it first appears that Temple rises up from the top of the pass, you soon discover that the base of it lies some distance away, separated from Saddle Pass by the wide Paradise Valley (see Walk 33). Closer at hand are the imposing black cliffs of Sheol Mountain.

Although a trail continues down the other side of Saddle Pass into Sheol and Paradise valleys, most walkers will probably be content with these glorious heights and inviting meadows.

Strong hikers could turn either left from Saddle Pass to ascend low-angled Saddle Mountain, which provides good views in all directions, except up the valley beyond Lake Louise.

Fairview Mountain at 2774 m (9099 ft) is a stiffer ascent on loose scree slopes above Saddle Pass, and the views from the barren top are simply magnificent. For strong, experienced hikers only.

Columbian ground squirrel

38. Lake Agnes—*The most popular hike*

The hike to Lake Agnes is reputed to be the most popular in the Canadian Rockies, and it's easy to see why. It departs from what may be Canada's second most visited tourist attraction (after Niagara Falls): the famous Lake Louise. It ascends for 4 km (2.5 mi) on a wide trail to a fascinating, scenic subalpine lake, where there's a rustic teahouse offering homebaking and tea, like the many chalets high in the Swiss alps. There are stunning views, plus a waterfall-cascade below the teahouse. Once you've had a snack at the teahouse, you should have the energy to explore the lake and nearby Beehives (see Walks 39 and 40). The disadvantage is little solitude.

Map: page 121
Distance: 7.2 km (4.5 mi) return
Time: 4 hours
Rating: Moderate
Max. elevation: 2125 m (6970 ft)
Elevation gain: 400 m (1312 ft)
Footwear: Light hiking boots
Best season: July to October

access

From the Trans-Canada Highway at the Lake Louise intersection in Banff park, drive 8 km (5 mi) up the steep road to Lake Louise. From the vast parking lots, walk down to the lake, and then along the shore past the hotel grounds. The Lake Agnes trail leaves the paved Lakeshore Trail, just past the hotel.

The trail is wide and well-graded through thick sub-alpine forest with occasional glimpses of Lake Louise. At the 3-km (1.9-mi) mark, you reach Mirror Lake, a tiny tarn set below the cliffs of the Big Beehive. From here, the left-hand trail takes a high-level route along to the Plain of Six Glaciers (Walk 35). Take the right-hand route that switchbacks up into more open country, views improving every minute. Behind you is the wall of Fairview Mountain towering over Lake Louise, its ridge rising into the glaciated and sharper peaks of Mt. Aberdeen and Mt. Haddo. You can also see up Louise Creek to the glacier-capped heights of Mt. Victoria and the great thrust of Mt. Lefroy.

Ahead, a waterfall tumbles down from Lake Agnes—your destination—under the Big Beehive. At the first junction above Mirror Lake, keep straight and traverse along under cliffs towards Bridal Veil Falls; then take the stairs that ascend the cliff.

The teahouse at the top of the stairs, whose menus once described it as the 'highest tea room in Canada,' usually offers homemade soup and an assortment of teas. You can get sandwiches on home-made bread, cookies and cake. (Pioneer explorer and map-maker Walter Wilcox called Lake Agnes 'a wild tarn imprisoned by cheerless cliffs.' He didn't have the advantage of sitting on a teahouse balcony eating cake.)

129

Lake Agnes Teahouse

The lake was named for Lady Agnes Macdonald, wife of Canada's first prime minister. To the left as you look down the cirque lake, once carved out by a small glacier, rises the distinctive, conical Big Beehive, a huge, grey, horizontally layered rock wall. For the trail to the Big Beehive, see Walk 39. Behind the teahouse, on top of the falls, is a stunning view down to Lake Louise. The stroll down Lake Agnes from the teahouse, with its changing perspectives on the Beehives, is highly recommended.

common raven

39. Big Beehive Loop—*View from a beehive*

'I have never seen this glorious ensemble of forests, lakes and snowfields surpassed in an experience on the summits of more than 40 peaks and the middle slopes of as many more in the Canadian Rockies.' Walter Wilcox, an early explorer of these regions, was describing his first view from the Beehive area. To experience what Wilcox felt, you must journey beyond the cozy, gorgeous confines of Lake Agnes and toil up at least one of the unusual 'beehives.' The trail past the largest and best Beehive can be combined with a loop back to Lake Louise on the lower stretch of Plain of Six Glaciers trail (Walk 35), and then along the shore of Lake Louise, a route consistently varied and interesting. There are so many options in this fascinating area, you can tailor your route to how you feel.

access

From the Trans-Canada Highway at the Lake Louise intersection in Banff park, drive 8 km (5 mi) up the steep road to Lake Louise. From the vast parking lots, walk down to the lake, and then along the shore past the hotel grounds. The Lake Agnes trail leaves the paved Lakeshore Trail, just past the hotel.

Map: page 121
Distance: 11.5-km (7-mi) loop (variations possible)
Time: 6 hours
Rating: Strenuous
Max. elevation: 2235 m (7331 ft)
Elevation gain: 504 m (1653 ft)
Footwear: Light hiking boots
Best season: Mid-July to October

Follow the route described for the Lake Agnes trail (Walk 38) as far as the teahouse. To the left of the cirque lake, which was carved out by a small glacier, rises the distinctive, conical Big Beehive, a huge, grey, horizontally layered rock wall. That is your destination on this loop, 2.1 km (1.3 mi) ahead. From the teahouse, follow the trail around the right side of Lake Agnes, gaining impressive views of Mt. Whyte and Mt. Niblock, which soar steeply above the dark green waters. The trail switchbacks steeply up the side of Big Beehive, passing between the

deer mouse

131

Beehive and a promontory known as the Devil's Thumb. The exertion is rewarded with grand views back over the lake and Mt. St. Piran, one of the most easily climbed peaks around.

From the flat, larch-covered top of the semi-wooded Beehive ridge, a side trail wanders left to the Big Beehive Viewpoint. Don't omit it. The trail is somewhat indefinite, but it doesn't matter. Keep generally to the right and pick your own route to the edge of the Beehive, 150 m (492 ft) above Lake Agnes, as the rock drops.

Near the edge of the cliff is an open-sided, red-roofed log shelter providing views from safety and comfort. Lake Louise is a marvel from here—maybe the best spot of all to contemplate this milky masterpiece, sometimes called one of the top 7 or 10 natural landscapes in the world. Across the lake rise

the cliffs of Fairview Mountain and behind them, the north wall of Mt. Temple. Directly below is tiny Mirror Lake. To the right, the great glaciated walls of Mt. Lefroy and Mt. Aberdeen form the backdrop to Lake Louise.

From the junction with the main trail (6.7 km, 4.2 mi), you could turn back to the teahouse the way you came, but we recommend an alternate loop back to Lake Louise, unless you urgently require more tea. Turn left and descend the other side of the Big Beehive, dropping steeply through the subalpine forest to the Highline Trail, 3.1 km (1.9 mi) from Lake Agnes. The left fork will take you back to Mirror Lake and the descent to Lake Louise again. It saves a couple of kilometres of walking.

OPTION: For a slightly longer loop with more variety, go right, heading gradually downhill. You'll reach a trail junction in 0.7 km (0.4 mi). Although the route straight ahead goes on to the Plain of Six Glaciers Viewpoint, that would make for a total loop of almost 20 km (12.4 mi), an extremely long day. Most walkers who have already come over Big Beehive prefer to take the left branch, and descend steeply on switchbacks for almost 1 km (0.6 mi) down to Louise Creek and the Plain of Six Glaciers trail. (See Walk 35 for the continuation of the trail up the Plain of Six Glaciers.) Go left at the bottom back towards Lake Louise, and follow the heavily travelled route to return to the hotel.

Mirror Lake and the Big Beehive

40. Little Beehive—*Ultimate Bow Valley views*

For the day walker who has already reached scenic Lake Agnes and the cozy teahouse above Lake Louise, the side trail to Little Beehive involves less than I km (0.6 mi) each way; it provides perhaps the best view anywhere of the wide, U-shaped Bow Valley and hundreds of peaks north to the Columbia Icefield and south towards Banff townsite. It also offers views down to the astonishing turquoise of Lake Louise, one of the finest sights in the Canadian Rockies.

Map: page 121
Distance: 1.8 km (1.1 mi) return from Lake Agnes
Time: 1 hour
Rating: Moderate
Max. elevation: 2246 m (7367 ft)
Elevation gain: 121 m (397 ft) from Lake Agnes
Footwear: Light hiking boots
Best season: Mid-July to October

access

From the Trans-Canada Highway at the Lake Louise intersection in Banff park, drive 8 km (5 mi) up the steep road to Lake Louise. From the vast parking lots, walk down to the lake, and then along the shore past the hotel grounds. The Lake Agnes trail leaves the paved Lakeshore Trail, just past the hotel.

Follow the Lake Agnes trail (Walk 38) to Lake Agnes Teahouse. (Walkers bound directly for the Little Beehive may turn right after Mirror Lake for a shortcut that leads to Little Beehive.)

Otherwise, begin from the teahouse at the end of Lake Agnes. Behind the teahouse, take the trail that leads right up the hill away from the lake. Soon views open up back to Lake Louise with tiny Mirror Lake almost directly below. Keep straight at the trail junction at 0.2 km (0.1 mi) as the route works

Little Beehive

its way along the edge of the ridge. Directly across Lake Louise is Fairview Mountain, which strong hikers can climb without ropes from Saddle Pass (see Walk 37). Behind Fairview is the black, terrifying north face of Mt. Temple. The ridge to the right of Fairview leads to the glacier-hung peaks of Haddo, Aberdeen and, at the end of the valley, the imposing Lefroy.

The Little Beehive trail ascends through old slide areas over boulder-strewn fields vivid with wildflowers in summer. The trail soon reaches the edge of Little Beehive. Directly across the Bow Valley is the Lake Louise ski area and the Slate Range. Below is the village complex, and you can look down at all the activity around Chateau Lake Louise, grand dame of Rocky Mountain hotels.

To the left, the Trans-Canada Highway branches west and out of sight to climb the gentle slopes of Kicking Horse Pass. North is the Icefields Parkway (Hwy. 93) and Mt. Hector, its snowfields out of view on the other side. Beyond them, wave after wave of mountains lead up to Bow Summit and to the Columbia Icefield.

Spotted saxifrage

41. Dolomite Pass—*Dolomite and meadows*

Although long, the trail into Helen Lake and Dolomite Pass is extraordinary from start to finish. With only moderate climbing, it reaches one of the finest open alpine areas in Banff, revealing gentle, flower-covered meadows, small lakes, tarns and sparkling brooks under Cirque Peak. A little more effort takes you to a high ridge and panoramic views above Helen Lake.

access

From the Helen Lake parking area opposite Crowfoot Viewpoint on the Icefields Parkway (Hwy. 93), 32 km (20 mi) north of the Trans-Canada Highway.

Map: below
Distance: 19.2 km (12 mi) return
Time: Full day
Rating: Strenuous
Max. elevation: 2500 m (8200 ft)
Elevation gain: 550 m (1804 ft)
Footwear: Light hiking boots
Best season: June to early September

The route cuts east across the side of the long ridge that extends down from Cirque Peak, offering tantalizing views across to the Crowfoot Glacier. The trail finally cuts over the rounded shoulder of the ridge at treeline and turns north far above Helen Creek.

From this point on, the route remains open, very scenic and very exposed in bad weather. It leads through meadows busy with fat marmots, drops down to cross Helen Creek and then levels off in the vast ampitheatre around Helen Lake.

Fill up your water bottles at Helen Lake. You leave the meadows behind and ascend into ever more lofty terrain, switchbacking up to the high ridge between Dolomite Peak and Cirque Peak.

The area is wide and varied with several other small lakes and tarns amid meadows and small ridges, including Lake Katherine at the base of the crumbling, castellated cliffs of Dolomite Peak.

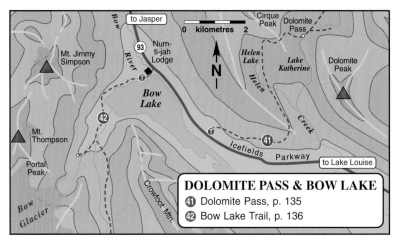

DOLOMITE PASS & BOW LAKE
41 Dolomite Pass, p. 135
42 Bow Lake Trail, p. 136

42. Bow Lake Trail

A lake, a glacier and a waterfall

Take a stroll along one of the most impressive lakes in the Canadian Rockies, then over braided gravel flats through a gorge, past a natural bridge to a vast, open alpine area topped by glaciers and a huge water-fall—a journey made without much exertion. Here is a trail among trails.

access

The turnoff to Num-ti-jah Lodge is 36 km (22 mi) north of the Trans-Canada Highway on the Icefields Parkway (Hwy. 93) or 40 km (25 mi) south of the David Thompson Highway. A parking area is situated on the entrance road. The trail begins just beyond the lodge building on the lake side.

Map: page 135
Distance: 6.8 km (4.2 mi) return
Time: 3 hours
Rating: Moderate
Max. elevation: 2042 m (6698 ft)
Elevation gain: 91 m (298 ft)
Footwear: Walking shoes/light hiking boots (trail can be wet)
Best season: Mid-July to October

The route leads across the grassy flats down to the lakeshore. The lake is glacial blue, reflecting the white glaciers of Crowfoot Mountain above. In season, the meadows are flush with flowers and the red-roofed lodge adds another vivid splash of colour.

The lodge was built by pioneer guide and outfitter, Jimmy

Bow Lake

Simpson, who first established a cabin here when the route from Lake Louise was nothing more than an arduous horse trail.

Ahead, the tongue of Bow Glacier dips down from the vast snowfields above, part of the Waputik Icefield, which straddles the Continental Divide. Out of sight, below the glacial tongue, is a small lake. Water from the lake plunges over the cliff in a brilliant white curtain. The massive rock walls on the right of the glacier belong to Mt. Thompson.

The trail passes under cliffs rising to a ridge of Mt. Thompson. Twenty minutes from the highway and it's a wild, rugged and quiet world. The trail soon reaches the gravel flats at the end of the lake. Even if you only make it this far, you'll be amply rewarded. This delta has been created by the boulders, pebbles and silt brought down from the glacier and falls above.

Cross the edge of the gravel and follow the inlet stream up the valley, climbing a series of old moraines before returning to the flats for the last time. The trail reaches a canyon that the creek has cut in the hillside

raccoon

and climbs very steeply for a short distance to get above it. There's a thunderous roar from below. You can peer over the edge and see the stream being forced through narrow cracks and under a natural bridge that was created when a huge rock fell across the gorge.

The trail comes out into the open atop an old moraine. Ahead is a vast open area of gravel, boulders, scree, streams and meadows leading up to the base of Bow Falls, which is the source of the Bow River and the South Saskatchewan River system. Less than 100 years ago, Bow Glacier extended right down into this valley. All glaciers of the divide area have been retreating because of a general warming of the climate.

Inversions Discourage Trees

Notice that the low-lying land close to Bow Lake is open meadow although the heights above remain forested. The lack of trees in the meadow is partly because of temperature inversions, in which cold air from the glacier and the alpine heights drains down into the valley bottom at night, creating a cool microclimate that is less receptive to trees.

biology

43. Peyto Lake Viewpoint—*Lake of liquid jade*

There are almost as many beautiful lakes in the Canadian Rockies as there are castles in England and pubs in Ireland. Peyto Lake, along with Louise and Moraine, is popular, often crowded—and one of the best. This short interpretive stroll gently ascends to a stunning viewpoint of the beautifully hued lake, set against high peaks and the forested Mistaya Valley. Signs along the way offer an excellent mini-lesson in alpine and subalpine terrain. A fine leg-stretcher for all. Combine it with the optional Bow Summit Loop for an enjoyable introduction to life at timberline, which is like life nowhere else.

access

Bow Summit is 42 km (26 mi) north of Lake Louise on the Icefields Parkway (Hwy. 93) or 37 km (23 mi) south of the Saskatchewan River Crossing. Parking, except for buses and the handicapped, is in the lower parking lot, where the trailhead begins.

Map: page 139
Distance: 1.2 km (0.7 mi) return
Time: 20 minutes
Rating: Easy
Max. elevation: 2133 m (6996 ft)
Elevation gain: 45 m (148 ft)
Footwear: Anything
Best season: July to October

As you start this walk, notice where the timberline appears on surrounding mountains. Note how it seems to be a firm line. When you get up close, as you will soon, you'll see that the transition is actually gradual, not sudden. This transitional band usually extends about 300 m (984 ft) from the edge of the forest to the lone remaining stunted trees. The walk ahead goes through just such a transition zone. If you choose to continue on the Bow Summit Loop, you'll see the transition line extend to an area of tree islands near the upper limit of treeline.

Peyto Lake

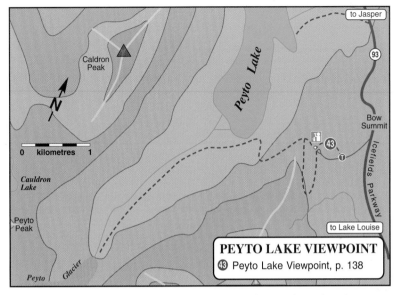

PEYTO LAKE VIEWPOINT
43 Peyto Lake Viewpoint, p. 138

On the way up, interpretive signs show how to distinguish Engelmann spruce, lodgepole pine and fir, which are among the toughest trees in the world. Here's a chance, as well, to view the phenomenon of 'krummholz,' German for 'crooked wood,' which is often seen at tree-line: the trees are twisted, gnarled and dwarfed by fierce winds.

You'll soon reach the viewpoint where Peyto Lake glistens far below the boardwalk and railings. The Mistaya Valley extends nearly 30 km (19 mi) north, and the forks of the North Saskatchewan River can be seen. Peyto Glacier is at the end of the lake and below it is a desolate area of rock and rubble that geologists say is the way Bow Summit must have looked 7000 years ago. At that time, the entire area, up to 500 m (1640 ft) above the viewpoint, was covered by Peyto Glacier, one tongue of the Wapta Icefield.

Peyto Peak is to the right of Peyto Glacier. Next to this peak, from left to right, are Mt. Mistaya, Mt. Barbette and Mt. Patterson. Continue left on the upper trail for the Bow Summit Loop, or return the way you came.

OPTION: This 1-km (0.6-mi) loop trail continues from the Peyto Lake Viewpoint, and illustrates how plants survive in this brutal habitat where snow can fall any day of the year. Take the upper trail to the left after the viewpoint.

This area is one of the newest and most fragile of the world's natural landscapes. Following glaciation, pioneer trees and plants required thousands of years to gain a foothold on these windswept ridges. Gradually, islands of spruce, pine and fir began to take root in protected locations.

A few minutes up the trail, views open onto a meadow with views of Mt. Thompson. Watch for hermit thrushes, Clark's nutcrackers and white-tailed ptarmigan. The latter live here year-round, feathers changing from brown in summer to white in winter. Note also the phenomenon of 'tree islands'—clumps of trees growing together to protect themselves from the dry winds and deep snow.

Wild Bill's Lake

One of the most colourful lakes in the Rockies is named after Bill Peyto, one of the most colourful of the early Banff guides. Peyto and alpinist-explorer Walter Wilcox passed through here in 1895 and paused at the sight of this exquisite lake. Who wouldn't?

Later, the story goes, Peyto began to find conditions becoming too crowded at his Bow Lake campsite. Usually a quiet, withdrawn man around strangers, he suddenly announced while sitting around a campfire at Bow Lake: 'There's too darn many people around here, I'm going where there's some peace and quiet.' He then retreated to a camp on Bow Pass above what people began to call Peyto Lake. What would he think today about the endless stream of traffic climbing Bow Summit?

history

hermit thrush

44. Mistaya Canyon—*A pot-holed gorge*

This is neither the longest nor the deepest canyon in the parks, but it is one of the loveliest: a pot-holed gorge delicately carved from limestone by the rushing waters of the Mistaya River. A good family leg-stretcher.

access

The trail starts at the Mistaya Canyon parking lot in Banff National Park, 13.6 km (8 mi) north of Waterfowl Campground or 3.2 km (2 mi) south of the Saskatchewan River Crossing on the Icefields Parkway (Hwy. 93). The trailhead is on the north side of the parking lot.

The trail descends on an old road and turns left away from the highway. To the southeast across the highway soars Mt. Murchison with its wide base and one of the few icefields on the east side of the Parkway.

Map: below
Distance: 1.5 km (0.9 mi) return
Time: 30–40 minutes
Rating: Easy
Max. elevation: 1525 m (5002 ft)
Elevation loss: Negligible
Footwear: Walking/running shoes
Best season: May to October

The Mistaya River, which originates on a glacier high above Peyto Lake, can be heard rumbling into the depths of the canyon from far up the trail. 'Mistaya' is a native people's word for 'grizzly.' The path descends through a fragrant sub-alpine forest to the remarkable nar-

Mistaya Canyon

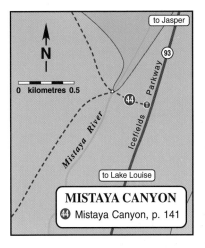

N

0   kilometres   0.5

Mistaya River

Icefields Parkway

93

to Jasper

44

to Lake Louise

MISTAYA CANYON
44 Mistaya Canyon, p. 141

row canyon. Small trails lead in either direction on the other side of the bridge.

Stop for a rest and contemplate the unusual sight of a flat-bottomed Mistaya River suddenly plunging over limestone canyon walls. It almost vanishes from sight, twisting and curving the soft rock into beautiful, smoothly scalloped formations.

Mistaya Canyon

45. Panther Falls and Bridal Veil Falls

Leap of a great cat

Panther Falls leaps 180 m (590 ft) out of a deep limestone canyon with the grace and beauty of a cat. On the other side of clear Nigel Creek, Bridal Veil Falls pushes over a cliff in a slim column. The trail that leads to a viewpoint for both these falls is short, although fairly steep on the return. No one should regret the small effort.

Map: page 144
Distance: 1.6 km (1 mi) return
Time: 30 minutes
Rating: Moderate
Max. elevation: 1813 m (5947 ft)
Elevation loss: 45 m (148 ft)
Footwear: Almost anything
Best season: July to October

access

The trail starts from the large paved area on the east side of the Icefields Parkway (Hwy. 93) on top of the Big Hill, 38 km (24 mi) north of the Saskatchewan River Crossing or 13 km (8 mi) south of the Icefields Centre. You want the uppermost of the two stunning viewpoints over the North Saskatchewan River Valley far below. The trail, which can be hard to find, descends steeply from the lower end of this parking lot, near the sign showing mountain profiles.

The trail is narrow and descends in a couple of switchbacks through a mossy, boulder-strewn forest, and then under a small cliff. You begin to see the impressive gorge below.

The path suddenly opens up. Panther Falls come into view high above. The whole force of Nigel Creek springs from the rock and over the cliff in a spectacular plunge. Mist from these falls is often picked up by the wind and carried well across the trail. To the right is the narrow plume of Bridal Veil Falls whose water originates in an icefield high above.

Panther Falls

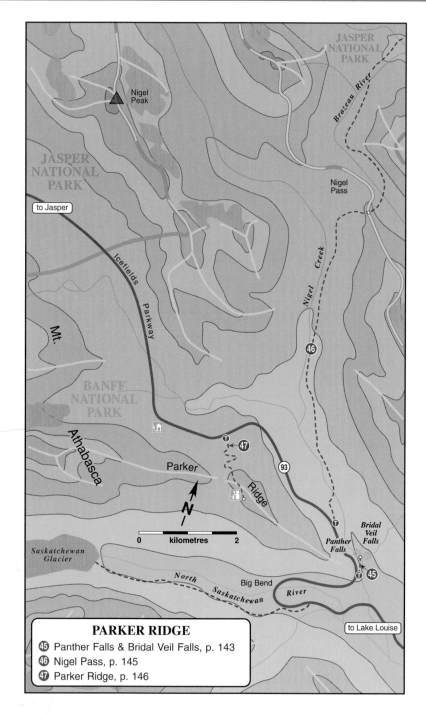

Nigel Peak

JASPER NATIONAL PARK

Brazeau River

JASPER NATIONAL PARK

Nigel Pass

to Jasper

Icefields Parkway

Nigel Creek

Mt.

BANFF NATIONAL PARK

46

Athabasca

Parker

47

93

Ridge

N

Saskatchewan Glacier

Bridal Veil Falls

Panther Falls

0 kilometres 2

45

North Saskatchewan River

Big Bend

to Lake Louise

PARKER RIDGE

45 Panther Falls & Bridal Veil Falls, p. 143
46 Nigel Pass, p. 145
47 Parker Ridge, p. 146

46. Nigel Pass—*Paradise at a price*

This trail shows you a beautiful valley with high peaks and cliffs above sub-alpine meadows, lush with wildflowers, a clear creek running through it. At the top, a rocky pass offers views back to the glacier-carved heights of Mt. Athabasca and over to the desolation of Upper Brazeau Valley. If there's a price for this paradise, it is 16 km (10 mi) of hiking.

Map: page 144
Distance: 16 km (10 mi) return
Time: 6 hours
Rating: Strenuous
Max. elevation: 2225 m (7298 ft)
Elevation gain: 365 m (1197 ft)
Footwear: Light hiking boots
Best season: Mid-July to October

access

The trailhead is 12 km (7.4 mi) south of the Icefields Centre and 38 km (24 mi) north of the Saskatchewan River Crossing. Turn off the Icefields Parkway (Hwy. 93) onto an old road just north of the Big Hill. The trail starts a few metres beyond the barrier across the road.

From the old road, once part of the main Banff-Jasper highway, turn right and cross Nigel Creek on a bridge. The trail climbs through trees and soon emerges on a wide avalanche track. The ascent is gradual with one open area following another, providing good views.

The forest gives way to upland meadow. From here on, the views are uninterrupted. The cliffs opposite, part of the ridge leading up to Nigel Peak, were named for Nigel Vavasour who assisted an 1898 climbing expedition in the region. You can see ahead to the pass, the low point at the end of the valley.

Much of the trail, which remains on the right side of sparkling Nigel Creek, is deeply eroded in these damp meadows, but passage isn't

difficult. If you walk beside the eroded trail, as most will, you'll create yet another erosion ditch and, before long, the meadow will be bisected by an ugly series of trenches. Please stay on the original trail.

The last kilometre is steeper, with an elevation gain of 275 m (902 ft), as you climb the final rocky ridge to the top of the pass, which marks the boundary between Banff and Jasper national parks. This pass is the home of the golden eagle (see page 336). On the far side of the pass, the trail descends towards Brazeau Flats. Behind you, bare Parker Ridge leads up to Mt. Athabasca.

Creek beyond Nigel Pass

47. Parker Ridge—*Tundra and glaciers*

In less than an hour, pass from the forest to a land of arctic tundra, ptarmigan, great glaciers, treeless ridges and bright wildflowers. This inauspicious-looking ridge offers one of the easiest and most rewarding opportunities to explore alpine terrain in the mountain parks. The huge Saskatchewan Glacier, out of sight from the highway, glistens on the other side of the ridge. Despite the large numbers of visitors, mountain goats can often be seen.

Map: page 144
Distance: 5 km (3 mi) return
Time: 2–4 hours
Rating: Strenuous
Max. elevation: 2255 m (7396 ft)
Elevation gain: 215 m (705 ft)
Footwear: Light hiking boots
Best season: Mid-July to mid-September

access

The trailhead parking lot is 117 km (73 mi) north of Lake Louise and 113 km (70 mi) south of Jasper townsite on the Icefields Parkway (Hwy. 93). It's 8.8 km (5.5 mi) south of the Icefield Centre.

Start up a wide path, with the dramatic horn of Mt. Athabasca to the northwest, its sides deeply cut by cirque glaciers. Parks Canada has worked diligently to restore this fragile area, which has been trampled by thousands of hikers. So slowly do plants grow here that the damage of a single boot may take years to recover.

About 350 million years ago, when a shallow inland sea covered this part of North America during the Devonian Age, a coral reef built up on the flat ocean bed. The ocean floor rose to become the Rocky Mountains and today, fossils of the primitive coral creatures can be found in the rocks.

The appetite-rousing path twists upwards, gaining elevation quickly, with ever-changing views back over Sunwapta Pass to Nigel Peak and Mt. Wilcox. The almost-level pass below Wilcox was once surveyed for the Banff-Jasper road, because the Athabasca Glacier then extended down to where the highway goes today.

Purple asters, arnicas and a multitude of other alpine flowers edge the trail at lower levels. Higher up, the vegetation is typical of upper subalpine terrain: feather mosses, heathers, grouseberries and stunted trees.

The walker enters the alpine zone, characterized by deep snow ranging from 100–150 cm (39–59 in) a year and winds that typically blow three times as hard as in the valley. Note how frost has churned up the soil. Mid-summer briefly sees these meadows starred with white mountain avens, alpine vetch, delicate blue alpine forget-me-not, red and white heather and moss campion. Frost may descend any day of summer.

At the top of the ridge is a tremendous panorama of the Saskatchewan Glacier, the largest

Saskatchewan Glacier from Parker Ridge

valley glacier in the Columbia Icefield system. This glacier, the source of the North Saskatchewan River, is nearly 2 km (1.2 mi) wide. Its surface is said to be unusually smooth because of the gentle underlying bedrock. Along with the other glaciers in the Rockies, the Saskatchewan has been receding for the last 150 years caused by a general warming of the climate. Beyond the glacier is Mt. Castleguard, known for its extensive cave system. To the south are Terrace Mountain, Mt. Saskatchewan and Mt. Coleman.

Watch for mountain goats. Also at home on the high ridge is the white-tailed ptarmigan, hard to spot even when you pass close by because of its clever camouflage of mottled brown in summer and white in winter.

Wheeler and Parker

A.O. Wheeler, an Irish-born land surveyor, and Elizabeth Parker, a writer for the *Winnipeg Free Press*, led the movement to establish the Alpine Club of Canada in 1906. Mountaineering, Wheeler maintained, is 'the sport of intellectuals' and 'requires some measure of poetic imagination.' In 1923, he and his crew completed the first accurate topographical maps of the Continental Divide area. Some of these maps are still in use.

history

Kootenay

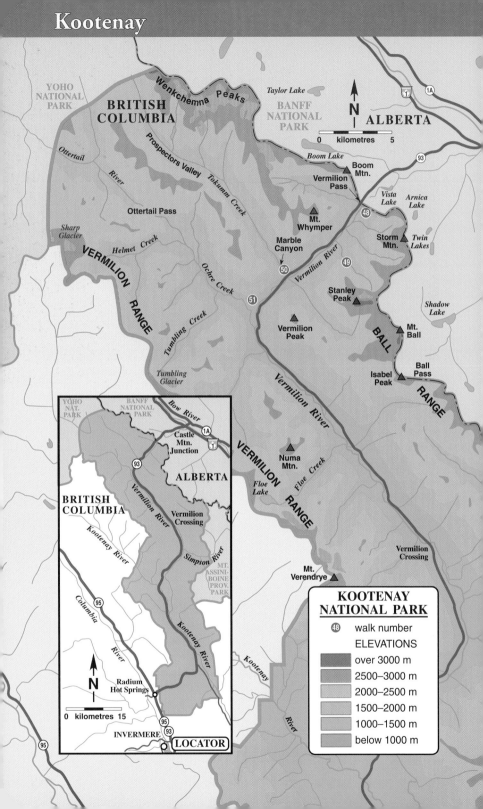

YOHO
NATIONAL
PARK

Wenckchemna Peaks

Taylor Lake

BANFF
NATIONAL
PARK

ALBERTA

BRITISH
COLUMBIA

Prospectors Valley

Ottertail

River

Tokumm Creek

Boom Lake

Boom
Mtn.

Vermilion
Pass

Vista
Lake

Arnica
Lake

93

N

0   kilometres   5

1

1A

Ottertail Pass

Sharp
Glacier

Helmet Creek

Mt.
Whymper

Marble
Canyon

48

Storm
Mtn.

Twin
Lakes

50

Vermilion River

49

Ochre Creek

Tumbling Creek

51

Stanley
Peak

Shadow
Lake

BALL

Vermilion
Peak

Mt.
Ball

VERMILION RANGE

Tumbling
Glacier

Isabel
Peak

Ball
Pass

RANGE

Vermilion River

Floe Creek

Numa
Mtn.

VERMILION RANGE

Floe
Lake

Vermilion
Crossing

Mt.
Verendrye

LOCATOR

YOHO
NAT.
PARK

BANFF
NATIONAL
PARK

Bow River

Castle
Mtn.
Junction

1A

1

93

ALBERTA

BRITISH
COLUMBIA

Vermilion
Crossing

Vermilion River

Kootenay River

Simpson River

MT.
ASSINI-
BOINE
PROV.
PARK

95

Columbia

River

Kootenay River

Kootenay

River

N

0   kilometres   15

Radium
Hot Springs

95
93

INVERMERE

95

KOOTENAY
NATIONAL PARK

48 walk number

ELEVATIONS

over 3000 m

2500–3000 m

2000–2500 m

1500–2000 m

1000–1500 m

below 1000 m

Continental Divide, Banff/Kootenay

CHAPTER 2

KOOTENAY NATIONAL PARK

Kootenay National Park, situated in British Columbia across the Continental Divide from Banff National Park, was actually established in 1920 to border the scenic Banff-Windermere Highway (Hwy. 93). The park, which has its headquarters in Radium, is 96 km (60 mi) long but only averages 30 km (19 mi) in width. The federal government wanted another national park, but could only persuade British Columbia to cede the land if a highway was built through it.

Much of the backcountry is therefore more accessible than in Banff or Jasper on 200 km (124 mi) of hiking trails. Its boundaries encompass 1406 sq. km (562 sq. mi).

Kootenay is less crowded than neighbouring Banff, and feels more removed from urban pressures. About 1.2 million people visit annually. Although smaller and quieter than Banff and Jasper national parks, Kootenay is rich in heart-stopping scenery and natural attractions. It's a splendid park for the casual hiker and sightseer, as

149

well as for cyclists who flock to the park for the Golden Triangle Loop each spring. The possibilities for backcountry hikes are more limited in this park than in some, but those found here are memorable. (See chapter 7 for details on backpacking trips.)

Since most attractions are fairly near the highway, Kootenay is an excellent destination for short sightseeing trips with small children or with those who have trouble walking long distances. The Radium Hot Springs Pools, at the south end of the park, make an intriguing destination for all ages. Here, subterranean heat keeps the water at a comfortable 39° C (102° F) in the hot soaking pool. Other sightseeing opportunities include Marble Canyon (Walk 50), with its deep gorge and waterfalls; the Paint Pots (Walk 51), a sacred place for native peoples, who once obtained vermilion there for rock paintings; and Vermilion Pass, which vividly depicts the aftermath of a devastating 1968 forest fire.

Accommodation and other facilities are plentiful in the town of Radium Hot Springs. There are several cabins and a lodge across from the hot pools complex. There are also cabins and other accommodations at Kootenay Park Lodge in rather isolated Vermilion Crossing; the hosts enjoy a good reputation for hospitality. See 'Sources' for where to obtain more information on accommodation and commercial facilities.

Neighbouring Parks Canada visitor centres in Banff, Lake Louise and Yoho supply information on Kootenay National Park on request. There are also two visitor information centres in the park. The West Gate Information Centre in Radium Hot Springs, in the hot pools complex, is open from 9 a.m. to 7 p.m. in July and August and 9 a.m. to 5 p.m. in May, June, September and October. Call (250) 347-9505. The information centre is closed from November through April, but you can call (250) 347-9615. In the centre, you'll find Parks Canada information and a Friends of Kootenay gift shop. The Vermilion Crossing Visitor Centre, which is 63 km (39 mi) north of Radium, offers similar services and is open in summer from 9 a.m. to 5 p.m., Sunday to Thursday, and 9 a.m. to 8 p.m., Saturday; no telephone; reduced hours in winter.

Outdoor Adventures and Indoor and Rainy-Day Guide

BICYCLING: The Banff-Windermere Highway (Hwy. 93), with its wide shoulders, varied grades and wonderful scenery, is excellent for road biking. Each spring it forms a major arm of the famed Golden Triangle bicycle ride, a three-day loop that attracts thousands of cyclists. The ride is organized by Calgary's Elbow Valley Cycle Club; call (403) 295-1261. See 'Sources' for web site.

Mountain biking is permitted on designated trails. See chapter 7 (page 351).

Radium Hot Springs

BOATING: Only experienced canoeists enjoy the challenge of the Vermilion-Kootenay river system, which provides almost 200 km (124 mi) of scenic boating, some of it in whitewater. (Definitely not for novices.) Non-motorized boats and canoes are permitted on all park lakes and rivers. Note that the lakes in the park are accessible by foot only. Lake Windermere, a 15-minute drive away from Radium Hot Springs, is a boater's mecca. Also see 'Rafting' listing (page 372).

CHILDREN'S PROGRAMS: Check at the nearest visitor centre or with your campground attendant for information on interpretive programs.

DINING OUT: Kootenay Park Lodge, (250) 762-9196, at Vermilion Crossing serves home-style meals in a licensed restaurant. There are many wonderful restaurants in the towns of Radium Hot Springs and Invermere and other parts of the Windermere Valley. They range from cappuccino bars to haute cuisine. Note that historic Storm Mountain Lodge was closed in 1997; check on its current status at a visitor centre.

DRIVES: Driving through Kootenay on the 94-km (58-mi) Banff-Windermere Highway (Hwy. 93) is itself a scenic drive with numerous viewpoints and stops of interest, plus the attraction of the hot springs pools at the end (if approaching from the north). For an enjoyable all-day expedition, drive the Golden Triangle from Castle Mountain Junction to Radium Hot Springs, then up through the Columbia Valley, a birder's delight, to Golden, B.C., and through Yoho National Park with its fascinating waterfalls and the Spiral Tunnels. The entire loop is 313 km (194 mi). Also see the following listings for Fort Steele, Panorama and Wetlands.

EVENING CAMPGROUND PROGRAMS: Enjoyable interpretive programs for the whole family, and you don't need to be staying at the campground to attend. Check at the nearest visitor centre or with your campground attendant. Subject to change.

FIREWEED AND CONTINENTAL DIVIDE: Don't miss the short looped walks through the site of the Vermilion Pass burn of 1968. Interpretive panels tell how the vegetation is recovering from the devastating fire. (See Walk 50.)

FORT STEELE EXCURSION: A great destination, rain or shine, for those who don't mind the drive of about 100 km (62 mi) south from Radium. Fort Steele is a meticulously restored fur-trading fort with dozens of buildings that bring the era of early B.C. vividly to life. Call Super Natural British Columbia, 1-800-663-6000.

GLACIER GAZING: The Stanley Glacier is a magnificent sight, and can be easily reached on a morning hike (see Walk 49).

GOLF: The area around Radium Hot Springs is a golfer's mecca, with golfing from April until October. The Springs at Radium Golf Resort is the site of two fine 18-hole courses. The Resort Course is geared for intermediates, but has enough challenge for experts; the Springs is one of the premier courses in B.C. Call (250) 347-9311 or 1-800-667-6444. Also contact the Radium Hot Springs Chamber of Commerce for information on other courses; (250) 347-9331.

HORSEBACK RIDING: The Running Horse Ranch at Radium Hot Springs offers trail rides. Inquire at (250) 347-9311 or 1-800-667-6444.

Rocky facts

HOT SPRINGS: A must-do. Radium Hot Springs Pools, the largest hot springs pools in the Canadian Rockies, is nicely situated beneath cliffs where mountain sheep can often be seen. The hot soaking pool has an average temperature of 39° C (102° F), and is adjacent to a full-size outdoor heated swimming pool. Open year-round; 9 a.m. to 10:30 p.m. in summer; 12 p.m. to 10 p.m. in winter; $5 for adults and $4.50 for children in summer; $4.50 for adults and $4 for children in winter. You can also enjoy a cappuccino in the Poolside Cafe, open in summer. Massage and reflexology are also available, (250) 347-9495 or 1-800-767-1611. As well, you can visit the Friends of Kootenay National Park bookstore or obtain park information at the West Gate Information Centre in the hot pools complex.

MARBLE CANYON MEANDER: Don't miss this dramatic gorge (see Walk 50).

MT. WARDLE: Mountain goats think Mt. Wardle is wonderful, and frequent the mineral cliffs at its base.

PAINT POTS: These cold mineral springs have a fascinating natural and human history. There's a 1.5-km (0.9-mi) hike to the Paint Pots, where interpretive panels tell their story (see Walk 51).

Why Radium?

Radium Hot Springs is named for radon, which is found in small traces in the water. The first scientific analysis, conducted in 1914 by McGill University, found that the water was more radio-active than the famous springs in Bath, England. The amount of radio-activity is much less than that given off by an ordinary watch dial, and is not considered harmful.

The first recorded European visit to the hot springs was made in 1841 by Sir George Simpson, the governor of the Hudson's Bay Company. He is said to have soaked away his explorer's tension in a small hot pool dug in the gravel.

PANORAMA RESORT: A favourite winter destination, Panorama is situated 20 km (12.4 mi) from Invermere, B.C., only a short drive from Radium Hot Springs. Summer and winter attractions include tennis, horseback riding, nearby golf, downhill and cross-country skiing and snowboarding. Call (250) 342-6941.

RAFTING: The Kootenay River Runners, (250) 347-9210, offers a variety of trips, including one on—what else?—the Kootenay River.

SINCLAIR CANYON: This deep canyon, with its red walls, forms a breath-taking entrance (or exit) from the park, and is worth a closer look. Situated 1.5 km (0.9 mi) north of Radium.

SKIING: There are no downhill skiing facilities in the park. See chapter 7 (page 363) for cross-country skiing information. Also see 'Panorama Resort' listing.

WETLANDS: The Columbia River wetlands west of Kootenay National Park are the longest continuous series of wetlands remaining in North America. They provide habitat for over 250 bird species, including the osprey, blue grouse and Lewis's woodpecker. Ask at a visitor centre if any special birding events are scheduled during your stay.

Indoor activities are limited in Kootenay National Park. Please refer to the Banff section (page 40).

Kootenay River near McLeod Meadows

facing page: Mt. Whymper

48. Fireweed Trail—Life returns to the high forest

Life from ashes and blossoms from blazing forest fires—that's the vivid lesson in forest ecology provided by the unusual Fireweed Trail. The little path wanders through the devastation left by a huge forest fire in 1968 at Vermilion Pass, right on the Continental Divide. Surprisingly, the walk is anything but depressing, with bright magenta fireweed, lodgepole pine and other new growth surging everywhere.

Map: below
Distance: 0.8-km (0.5-mi) loop
Time: 20 minutes
Rating: Easy (wheelchair accessible)
Max. elevation: 1640 m (5379 ft)
Elevation gain: Negligible
Footwear: Walking/running shoes
Best season: June to October

access

From Banff townsite, drive 28 km (17 mi) north on the Trans-Canada Highway and turn left onto the Banff-Windermere Highway (Hwy. 93) at Castle Mountain Junction. Vermilion Pass is 9 km (6 mi) from the junction. The trail starts on the right of the prominent Continental Divide sign, which marks the division between Banff and Kootenay national parks, as well as the Atlantic and Pacific watersheds. Walkers have a choice of two loops: a lower interpretive trail and a higher circle with a more away-from-it-all feeling and views down the Vermilion Valley. Both depart from the right side of the large parking area.

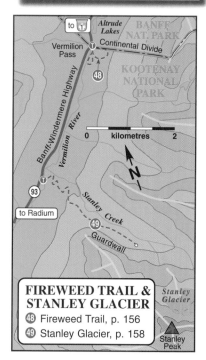

FIREWEED TRAIL & STANLEY GLACIER
48 Fireweed Trail, p. 156
49 Stanley Glacier, p. 158

O n July 9, 1968, lightning struck the Vermilion Pass area and burned 2464 ha (6160 acres). Since 1969, scientists have been studying the effects of fire on this mountain environment. The Fireweed Trail is a glimpse into that living laboratory.

The walk, through young pine and fir and the skeletons of devastated trees, illustrates how the burnt area is regenerating itself. New plants and animals have taken hold to such an extent that Parks Canada calls the result 'a more dynamic community than previously existed here.'

The first 'pioneer' species to colonize a burn area are light-loving trees such as trembling aspen or lodge-pole pine. Lodgepole pine cones are resin-sealed, and some only open in the extreme heat of a forest fire.

These pioneering trees begin to shade each other, blocking the growth of new aspens or lodgepoles that require sunshine. But spruce or subalpine fir can grow in these shady surroundings, so they begin to invade the forest and gradually the pioneer trees die out. What you see now are the beginnings of this process, which can take 200 years.

A good path leads through trees that are devastated but still standing. The lower loop trail heads off right while the higher loop continues straight under the shadow of Storm Mountain to the east.

This habitat is ideal for many animals, including moose, because it provides both food and shelter. The moose usually can't find enough to eat in the dense coniferous forest and depend on the clear areas produced by forest fires for the twigs and broad-leaved plants that they need.

Fireweed Trail

Blue grouse and northern hawk-owls nest here and small animals and rodents abound. Few places in the Rockies offer a richer sight than the renewing forest decorated with magenta fireweed (or great willow herb) in summer. This plant is easily recognized by its long spike, its brilliant blossoms and an affinity for forest clearings and burns. Watch also for yellow columbine and various mosses and berries.

New Light on Fire Management

Before the Rockies became parks, fires crackled through the Kootenay and Vermilion river valleys every 20 or 30 years.

At the beginning of the 20th century, however, park wardens began a rigorous program of fire suppression. But years of human intrusion took a toll on forest ecology. Because regular fires no longer thinned the forest, the stands became dense, wildlife dwindled, and dead wood accumulated on the ground, creating the danger of fuelling larger-than-ever fires.

Now, natural fires in remote areas are allowed to burn, although fires that threaten people or facilities are fought.

biology

49. Stanley Glacier—*Waterfall-clad cliffs*

A deservedly popular trail that offers almost everything for the hiker in just 4.8 km (3 mi): a brilliant carpet of alpine flowers, an awesome, waterfall-clad limestone cliff that soars 500 m (1640 ft) from a subalpine valley, the crevassed snout of a glacier and several hanging glaciers. Just don't expect solitude.

Map: page 156
Distance: 9.6 km (6 mi) return
Time: 4 hours
Rating: Strenuous
Max. elevation: 1960 m (6429 ft)
Elevation gain: 375 m (1230 ft)
Footwear: Light hiking boots
Best season: July to mid-September

access

From Banff townsite, drive 28 km (17 mi) north on the Trans-Canada Highway and turn left onto the Banff-Windermere Highway (Hwy. 93) at Castle Mountain Junction. The trail begins from the Stanley Glacier parking area, which is 12.2 km (8 mi) from the junction, on the east side of the Banff-Windermere Highway.

The trail crosses the Vermilion River on a bridge and switchbacks up through the Vermilion Pass burn of 1968, with the fresh greens of lodgepole pines emerging alongside bare, blackened trunks. The forest remains open enough to provide impressive views across the valley and to allow for a splendid cover of wildflowers, including yellow columbine, heart-leaved arnica and the distinctive magenta fireweed.

After about 2 km (1.2 mi), the trail emerges under the black limestone cliffs of the forbidding-looking Guardwall and follows Stanley Creek through the subalpine forest of the upper valley. This gently inclined section of trail is worth all the effort of the steep portion below. In spring, waterfalls cascade off the 500-m (1640-ft) cliff to your right. Ahead looms the crevassed snout of Stanley Glacier and several hanging glaciers above, which continue the work of carving Stanley Cirque.

The trail climbs the side of a lateral moraine deposited when the glacier extended further down the valley and terminates at a sign in a boulder field with a good view of the glacier and Stanley Peak beyond. (Lord Frederick Stanley was governor general of Canada from 1888–93 and is best known today for his donation of hockey's Stanley Cup.) Although the sign is the end of the official trail, cairns on both the right and left sides of the valley tempt determined rock hoppers on for a closer inspection of the desolate cirque under the glacier. The left side tends to provide somewhat easier travelling although the rocks are large, irregular and tiresome to traverse, whichever route you take. It's an awesome setting for a lunch break—wherever you stop.

facing page: Approach to Stanley Glacier

50. Marble Canyon—*Marble salad bowl*

The scalloped limestone walls of Marble Canyon, hewn from the rushing water of Tokumm Creek, are almost an art exhibit. This popular walk along the rim of this narrow chasm, ending at a striking outlook at the head of the falls, can be enjoyed by all ages.

You could also loll away a pleasant couple of hours by combining this walk with a visit to the nearby Paint Pots (Walk 51) and the Fireweed Trail (Walk 48).

Map: page 161
Distance: 1.6 km (1 mi) return
Time: 30–40 minutes
Rating: Easy (a few steep sections)
Max. elevation: 1432 m (4697 ft)
Elevation gain: Negligible
Footwear: Anything
Best season: May to October

access

From Banff townsite, drive north on the Trans-Canada Highway for 28 km (17 mi) to Castle Mountain Junction. Turn left here onto the Banff Windermere Highway (Hwy. 93), and climb Vermilion Pass, crossing into Kootenay National Park. The Marble Canyon parking lot is 16 km (10 mi) from the junction.

The gravel path dips down towards the junction of the Vermilion River and Tokumm Creek, and then ascends above the narrow canyon. The creek is an unforgettable milky turquoise. In summer, the trail is fringed with wildflowers—purple asters, daisies and arnicas.

Cross First Bridge, where the canyon is widest. You can see the river disappearing ahead into the limestone rock, which has been chiselled and carved over the centuries by the rushing waters of Tokumm Creek, which drains Prospectors Valley.

The canyon walls contain a strata of white and grey dolomite running through the predominantly grey limestone. When explorer James Hector and his party passed this way in 1858, some of the soft, white stone was taken to manufacture pipes.

At Second Bridge, the canyon is narrow and 17 m (56 ft) deep. Peer down at the ferns and mosses growing in the 'salad bowl' scooped out by eons of pounding water. The rising mist creates a lush, damp environment. The steepest portions of the canyon are at Sixth Bridge and Seventh Bridge, both at a dizzying 36 m (118 ft).

If the railings seem overly cautious along parts of the canyon edge, consider that at least three people have fallen to their deaths here, two because they backed too close to the edge when having their pictures taken.

Seventh Bridge is an impressive spot, with dramatic views of the rumbling, 21-m (69-ft) waterfall plunging into a foaming, turquoise pool at the very start of the canyon.

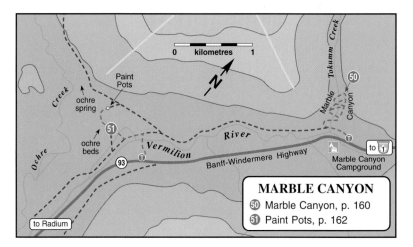

MARBLE CANYON
50 Marble Canyon, p. 160
51 Paint Pots, p. 162

51. The Paint Pots—*Place of the Red Clay Spirit*

This short, fascinating trail crosses the Vermilion River on a suspension bridge, leads past ochre-coloured meadows, and heads up an ochre-coloured stream to the Paint Pots, which are 'cones' formed by mineral deposits in the spring water. The stroll has historic and cultural significance and is a unique sort of walk to boot.

Map: page 161
Distance: 1.6 km (1 mi) return
Time: 30 minutes
Rating: Easy (wheelchair accessible)
Max. elevation: 1432 m (4697 ft)
Elevation gain: Negligible
Footwear: Anything
Best season: May to October

access

From Banff townsite, drive north on the Trans-Canada Highway for 28 km (17 mi) to Castle Mountain Junction. Turn left here onto the Banff-Windermere Highway (Hwy. 93), and climb Vermilion Pass, crossing into Kootenay National Park. The large parking area for the Paint Pots is 19 km (12 mi) west of Castle Mountain Junction. The trail leaves from the far side of the lot.

The path to the suspension bridge is paved and easy. The Vermilion River is fast moving, and its banks provide good views of the surrounding peaks.

The trail soon heads past flat, low-lying ochre beds, coloured red-brown by the mineral deposits. Around 1900, entrepreneurs dug up the ochre by hand and hauled it in sacks to the nearest railway, which was across Vermilion Pass at Castle Mountain Junction. Then, it was

Ochre beds

shipped to Calgary for use as a pigment in paints. Later, machinery was used to increase production. Horse-drawn scoops replaced the shovels while other machines ground up the ochre. Ochre production stopped in 1920 when Kootenay became a national park.

Continue up the ochre-coloured stream to a 'choked cone,' a dried-up mound of iron oxide, formed by what used to be a 'paint pot' until it was blocked by its own mineral deposits. Ahead are the Paint Pots themselves.

The pots are formed because the heavy concentration of iron in the water from underground springs forms a natural ring around the outlet. The iron oxide rim gets higher and higher until the water, always seeking the easiest route, forms another easier-running outlet elsewhere.

The Paint Pots

A Spiritual and Practical Place

To the native peoples, the Paint Pots are a place of great spiritual significance—the Place Where the Red Clay Spirit Is Taken.

Native peoples travelled here from both sides of the Continental Divide to obtain 'red earth,' which was used to decorate tipis, clothing and bodies and for the creation of rock paintings. They mixed the ochre with water, kneaded it and shaped it into flat cakes. These were baked in a fire. The hardened cakes were ground into powder and mixed with fish oil or animal grease for use as paint.

history

Yoho

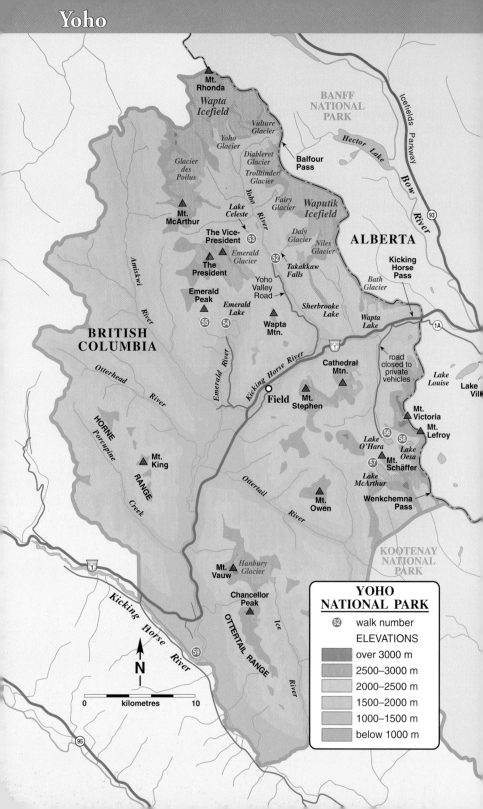

Mt. Rhonda

Wapta Icefield

BANFF NATIONAL PARK

Icefields Parkway

Vulture Glacier

Yoho Glacier

Diableret Glacier

Trolltinder Glacier

Balfour Pass

Hector Lake

Glacier des Poilus

Mt. McArthur

Lake Celeste

Yoho River

Fairy Glacier

Waputik Icefield

ALBERTA

Bow River

93

The Vice-President   53

Emerald Glacier

52

Daly Glacier

Niles Glacier

Kicking Horse Pass

The President

Yoho Valley Road

Takakkaw Falls

Bath Glacier

1A

Emerald Peak

Emerald Lake

55   54

Wapta Mtn.

Sherbrooke Lake

Wapta Lake

Amiskwi

BRITISH COLUMBIA

Emerald River

Kicking Horse River

Field

Mt. Stephen

Cathedral Mtn.

road closed to private vehicles

Lake Louise

Lake Vil...

Mt. Victoria

Otterhead

River

HORNE

Porcupine

Mt. King

RANGE

Creek

Ottertail

River

Mt. Owen

Mt. Schäffer

57

Lake O'Hara

56   58

Lake Oesa

Mt. Lefroy

Lake McArthur

Wenkchemna Pass

KOOTENAY NATIONAL PARK

1

Kicking Horse River

Mt. Vauw

Hanbury Glacier

Chancellor Peak

Ice

OTTERTAIL RANGE

River

95

59

N

0   kilometres   10

YOHO NATIONAL PARK

52 walk number

ELEVATIONS

over 3000 m

2500–3000 m

2000–2500 m

1500–2000 m

1000–1500 m

below 1000 m

CHAPTER 3

YOHO NATIONAL PARK

'Yoho,' the Cree word for 'awe,' is an apt name for the second smallest of the Canadian Rocky Mountain parks. It encompasses 1313 sq. km (525 sq. mi) of British Columbia, bounded by Banff National Park to the east and Kootenay National Park to the south. About 700,000 people visit annually.

In Yoho, the Trans-Canada Highway (Hwy. 1) cuts under spectacular peaks and dozens of lacy waterfalls are visible in spring and summer. The park is famous for the Burgess Shale fossils, a World Heritage Site that preserves marine life from more than five million years ago. (Expeditions to the shale beds can be arranged and must be guided. See page 170.) Yoho's recent history is also notable. The park contains the most famous stretch of railway track in Canada. The Spiral Tunnels were built to solve the problem of the sharp gradient of Kicking Horse Pass.

The park also encompasses two splendid hiking areas: Lake O'Hara and the Yoho Valley. Both offer transcendent walking in summer and fall. Access to the historic and outstanding Lake O'Hara is restricted, but it is definitely worth the

Mt. Burgess and Emerald Lake

Natural Bridge, Kicking Horse River

other outdoor pursuits.

The small town of Field is the service centre for Yoho. Until recently, the park had very limited accommodation, but this lack of accommodation is changing with the construction of some new inns and also more bed and breakfast facilities. (There is also a grocery store near the Kicking Horse Campground.) Both Lake O'Hara Lodge and Emerald Lake Lodge are considered among the finest places to stay in the mountain parks. Twin Falls Chalet, high in the Yoho Valley, offers a backcountry experience complete with prepared meals and a dry bed, and is a beloved Yoho destination of discriminating hikers (see Walk 53). See 'Sources,' page 386, for where to find more information on accommodation.

The best place to begin your visit is to stop at the visitor centre on the Trans-Canada Highway at Field, where Parks Canada has a wealth of information on exploring the park. Travel Alberta and Tourism British Columbia also have information booths at the centre, and the Friends of Yoho National Park operates a gift shop with proceeds going towards the park. The centre, (403) 343-6783, is open from 9 a.m. to 7 p.m., June 27 to August 30; 9 a.m. to 5 p.m., May 16 to June 26 and September 1 to 28.

Note: Many first-time visitors fail to realize how accessible Yoho is to Lake Louise, and how easily a trip to this beautiful park would fit into other trip plans. Although most of B.C. is in the Pacific timezone,

hassle to get there (see page 184).

In the Yoho area, there is prime whitewater rafting on the Kicking Horse River near Golden, B.C., which is outside the park. There's limited mountain biking on fireroads. Less well-known, but equally satisfying, are the park's cold-weather attractions. In winter, because of the heavy snowfall, Yoho is a magical place for cross-country skiing. The park is also popular with ice climbers. See chapter 7 for more information on these and

Yoho is in the mountain timezone like the rest of the mountain parks. You do not enter the Pacific timezone until you reach Glacier National Park in B.C.

Outdoor Adventures and Indoor and Rainy-Day Guide

BICYCLING: The big event is the Golden Triangle, an annual 314-km (195-mi) van-supported road-touring loop held each spring. The scenic and at times challenging route goes through Banff, Kootenay and Yoho in three days. For information, call (403) 295-1261. See 'Sources' for web site (page 394).

BOATING: Portions of the Kicking Horse River are navigable by canoe and kayak. Check at the Field Visitor Centre. Canoes and boats can also be rented at Emerald Lake Lodge.

BURGESS SHALE EXHIBIT: Be sure to take the time to view the Parks Canada exhibit on the Burgess Shale in the visitor centre in Field. It's an excellent introduction to the 515-million-year-old fossils that are among the most important in the world. Some displays are also provided at the Lake Louise Visitor Centre and at Emerald Lake.

BURGESS SHALE FIELD TRIP: The only way to see the famous shale beds is on a guided trip. It's a good idea to reserve in advance (see page 170).

CLIMBING: Yoho is popular with both rock and ice climbers. Contact the Association of Mountain Guides, (403) 678-2885, to hire a guide. Also see chapter 7 (page 374).

DINING OUT: For the budget-minded, the Siding General Store, (250) 343-6462, in Field offers soup and half a sandwich for $5.75; the Yoho Brothers Trading Post, (250) 343-6030, does box lunches for $7.50; buffalo burger, chicken breast and Pacific salmon are also on the menu. If you're in the mood for something fancier, the new Kicking Horse Lodge, (250) 343-6303, in Field serves dinner offerings such as chicken picatta and grilled salmon steak with strawberry salsa. For dessert, try a golden crepe with ice cream topped with chocolate sauce. At luxurious Emerald Lake Lodge, (250) 343-6321, chefs cook up such delicacies as seared pheasant breast with wild rice risotto ($27) and pecan-crusted lamb rack. For more casual fare, have a light snack on the terrace at Cilantro's-on-the-Lake, Emerald Lake Lodge. (Work up an appetite first by walking around the lake, rain or shine.)

DRIVES: The drive up to Takakkaw Falls is a must for most. The 13-km (8-mi) Yoho Valley Road has one very steep set of switchbacks (trailers can be left at the start). Other popular destinations are to the Spiral Tunnels (see following listing); Wapta Falls (Walk 59); Emerald Lake (Walk 54); Lake Louise (Walks 28 to 40); and the historic railway town of Golden, B.C. Those wanting a longer excursion could drive the Trans-Canada Highway to Golden, and then turn south through pastoral valleys along the Columbia River. Enjoy a soak in the hot springs pools at Radium and drive the Banff-Windermere Highway (Hwy. 93) over Sinclair Pass to Castle Mountain Junction. Return to Lake Louise or Field.

EVENING CAMPGROUND PROGRAMS: Enjoyable interpretive programs for the whole family, and you don't need to be staying at the campground to attend. Check at the Field Visitor Centre and with campground attendants. Subject to change.

FALLS FLING: If you love waterfalls, Yoho is a wondrous place to be. Check out Takakkaw Falls (Walk 52), Wapta Falls (Walk 59) and Hamilton Falls (seen on Walk 55) for starters.

FIELD EXCURSION: The tiny village of Field, with its vine-covered cottages, pottery shops and many historic buildings, is a pleasant place to stroll and stop for a snack.

GOLDEN EXCURSION: The town of Golden, 55 km (34 mi) from Field, is situated between the Selkirk Range to the west and the Rockies to the east. It has a rip-roaring railroad history, and was once optimistically named 'Golden City.' It's the largest centre close to Yoho.

GOLF: The closest course is in Golden. See previous listing.

GUIDED HIKES: A number of excellent interpretive walks are frequently offered in the park, but are subject to seasonal change. Check at the Field Visitor Centre and with campground attendants. Also see 'Summer Institute' listing.

HOT SPRINGS: If it's been raining for days and you need a break, consider visiting Radium Hot Springs for a change of pace. See Kootenay listings (page 153).

Burgess Shale guided hike

HORSEBACK RIDING: If you don't want to do your own walking, horses can be rented by the hour or the day at Emerald Lake, (250) 343-6000.

LAKE O'HARA EXCURSION: A magnificent backcountry hiking area, Lake O'Hara is also home to Lake O'Hara Lodge. You can arrange to go into the area by bus and return the same day (see page 184).

RAFTING: See chapter 7 (page 372).

MOUNTAIN BIKING: Mountain bikes are permitted in some designated areas. See chapter 7 (page 351).

SPIRAL TUNNELS: The display at the Lower Spiral Tunnel Viewpoint, 8 km (5 mi) east of Field on the Trans-Canada Highway, explains a railway marvel. At this interpretive display, you'll learn how looped tracks were devised to solve the problem of the sharp gradient on the Canadian Pacific Railway's (CPR) line between Field and Lake Louise. The result, completed in 1909, reduced the grade from 4.5 percent, the steepest of any North American railway, to 2.2 percent.

SKIING (DOWNHILL AND CROSS-COUNTRY): The closest downhill skiing is at Lake Louise. Note that Emerald Lake Lodge offers a free ski shuttle to Lake Louise. Yoho receives ample snow and has several tracked cross-country trails. Advanced back-country skiers will find challenging terrain in this park. See chapter 7 (pages 363–72).

SUMMER INSTITUTE: The Friends of Yoho National Park offers a terrific selection of educational field trips in summer months. Leaders are usually well-known authors, historians or naturalists. Recent offerings included 'Wild-flowers of Yoho National Park,' 'Prisoners in the Park,' a history of prisoners-of-war who were held in the parks during the two World Wars, and 'The History of the CPR between Lake Louise and Field.' Prices are reasonable and profits go towards park conservation. Call (250) 343-6393 to reserve.

SWIMMING: On a hot day, kids would enjoy a dip in the pond by the Field Visitor Centre. There's a picnic area, playground and pond beside the centre, so adults could enjoy a mid-day break from sight-seeing there as well.

TEAHOUSE TRIPPING: If you are truly adventurous, hike up to Twin Falls (Walk 53) in the Yoho Valley for hot lunch and tea. Complete your teahouse ramblings in two additional days by visiting the Plain of Six Glaciers Teahouse (Walk 35) and the Lake Agnes Teahouse (Walk 38) in nearby Lake Louise in Banff National Park. *Also see 'Tea Time' listing (page 56) in the Banff section.*

The Surprising Burgess Shale Beds

Renowned American paleontologist Stephen Jay Gould called the fossil beds in Yoho National Park 'the world's most significant fossil discovery.'

These fossils are so rich, diversified and intricate that the Burgess Shale Quarry on Wapta Mountain was declared a UNESCO World Heritage Site in 1981. It preserves the remains of an incredible variety of marine creatures, and suggests that the basic body structures found in the animal kingdom today evolved from the Middle Cambrian period, about 530 million years ago.

The Burgess Shale bonanza was started by Charles Walcott, an American paleontologist on a geological field trip in the Yoho Valley in 1909. A slab of shale he saw on the trail intrigued him so much that he split it open, to find the most amazing fossil impressions he'd ever laid eyes on.

For the next eight years, Walcott returned to the Yoho Valley and took back thousands of fossils to the Smithsonian Institution for further study. Unlike most other fossils, these ones had preserved exquisitely detailed impressions of soft body parts, which provided a far more complete view of the evolutionary process.

It wasn't until the late 1960s and '70s that scientists took renewed interest in the Burgess Shale. New research methods provided the technology required to remove outer layers of the impressions, yielding new discoveries in the anatomy of the 150 or more species so far found here and at nearby sites. Scientists return each summer to conduct further research.

Access to the fossil beds is restricted to those participating in special guided expeditions. At the time of writing, these expeditions were provided by the Yoho-Burgess Shale Foundation, established in 1994 to increase the exposure of the general public to earth sciences, especially geology and paleontology.

The foundation conducts Earth Sciences Educational Hikes in the Yoho area in summer, usually from July 1 to September 30. The Burgess Shale (Walcott Quarry) Walk is a 20-km (12.4-mi) return walk, with an altitude gain of 880 m (2886 ft). The fee is $40. The Mt. Stephen Fossil Beds Walk is shorter but steeper: 6 km (3.7 mi) return, an elevation gain of 520 m (1706 ft). These fossil beds are about the same age as the Burgess Shale at the Walcott Quarry. The fee is $25. Both are all-day hikes on maintained park trails.

Reservations are required. After April 1, call 1-800-343-3006 and in winter call (250) 343-6480. Procedures for booking hikes are subject to change; check at the Field Visitor Centre for more information. Phone the 1-800 number the day prior to your hike for possible changes.

Recommended reading: *Wonderful Life*, by Stephen Jay Gould.

facing page: At Emerald Lake

52. Takakkaw Falls—*The highest falls*

Takakkaw Falls in the striking Yoho Valley is among the highest in North America. Although the trail to the falls is little more than a short amble, getting there by car is half the fun. Yoho Valley Road provides great views and passes the Meeting of the Waters exhibit, where the Kicking Horse and Yoho rivers meet. Mountain goats can sometimes be seen along the road.

Map: below
Distance: 1 km (0.6 mi) return
Time: 25 minutes
Rating: Easy
Max. elevation: 1524 m (4999 ft)
Elevation gain: Negligible
Footwear: Anything
Best season: June through October

access

From Banff townsite, drive 56 km (35 mi) west on the Trans-Canada Highway to the junction with the Icefields Parkway (Hwy. 93). Continue straight on the Trans-Canada Highway 22.5 km (14 mi) into Yoho National Park or 3 km (1.9 mi) east of Field. Turn right at the sign for Yoho Valley at the bottom of the long hill down from Kicking Horse Pass. The 14-km (8.7-mi) paved access road, which becomes a ski route in winter, has one set of switchbacks that are extremely steep and narrow. (A drop-off area near the information bureau is provided for trailers at the beginning of the access road.) The trail begins at the parking and picinic area for Takakkaw Falls.

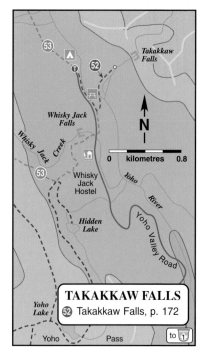

TAKAKKAW FALLS
52 Takakkaw Falls, p. 172

'Takakkaw' means 'magnificent' in Cree, and the 380-m (1246-ft) falls, named by Sir William Van Horne, do not disappoint. Although lacy streamers of spray can be seen from the parking lot, everybody must get closer. Picnic tables are nicely situated by the Yoho River.

The falls originate from the meltwaters of the Daly Glacier, out of sight beyond the cliffs. This glacier is fed by the vast Waputik Icefield that straddles the Continental Divide.

As you cross a bridge over the milky, glacier-fed Yoho River, the

roaring of the falls begins to dominate. The majestic peak of Mt.
Ogden at 2684 m (8804 ft) is
prominent on the right (to the
south). Looking north, you can see
the Yoho Glacier, another arm of
the Waputik Icefield.

For a view of the icefields above
the falls and a wide perspective on
the Yoho Valley, ascend to the
Iceline trail (see Walk 53), which is
on the other side of the valley. The
trail starts just up the road at
Whisky Jack Hostel.

Takakkaw Falls

53. Yoho Valley and Iceline

Valleys and moonscapes

These trails are deservedly the most popular in the Yoho Valley. They make possible a spectacular loop that combines soft walking on the lush valley bottom with a traverse through an alpine moonscape of moraines, snow patches and meltwater channels just below the blue ice of Emerald Glacier. The loop is only for strong hikers who get an early start in good weather. Otherwise, content yourself with the lower-level hike to graceful Twin Falls and the nearby chalet.

access

From Banff townsite, drive 56 km (35 mi) west on the Trans-Canada Highway to the junction with the Icefields Parkway (Hwy. 93). Continue straight on the Trans-Canada Highway 22.5 km (14 mi) into Yoho National Park or 3 km (1.9 mi) east of Field. Turn right at the sign for Yoho Valley at the bottom of the long hill down from Kicking Horse Pass. The 14-km (8.7-mi) paved access road, which becomes a ski route in winter, has one set of switchbacks that are extremely steep and narrow. (A drop-off area near the information bureau is provided for trailers at the beginning of the access road.) The hike starts at a walk-in campground.

Map: page 175
Distance: 14.2 km (8.8 mi) return to Twin Falls via Yoho Valley; 14.3-km (8.9-mi) loop via Yoho Valley, Lake Celeste and Iceline; 18.9-km (12-mi) loop via Yoho Valley, Twin Falls Chalet, Marpole Lake, Lake Celeste and Iceline
Time: Long day trip
Rating: Strenuous (very strenuous if Iceline options taken)
Max. elevation: 1800 m (5904 ft) at Twin Falls; 2225 m (7298 ft) at Iceline
Elevation gain: 300 m (984 ft) at Twin Falls; 700 m (2296 ft) at Iceline
Footwear: Hiking boots
Best season: July to early September

The campground is a good place to stay the night and get the early start you'll need if taking the high route. The hiking along the Yoho Valley is almost level on an excellent trail under a panorama of peaks, dominated by Yoho Peak on the north and Whaleback to its left.

Laughing Falls, a pluming, lacy cascade, is reached at 4.8 km (3 mi). Hikers planning to return via the high-level route should turn left up the Little Yoho Valley to join the Lake Celeste Trail in 2.2 km (1.4 mi) and then ascend to the Iceline. Be warned, however, that in bad weather, the high route ahead is one of the most exposed and potentially dangerous established routes in the Canadian Rockies.

If continuing to Twin Falls, keep straight on the Yoho Valley Trail to the junction with the Yoho Glacier Trail. Go left and switchback up to Twin Falls Chalet.

This cozy log cabin hut offers meals and snacks. Hikers who stay overnight can best sample the alpine delights of this rich region, including the spectacular Whaleback Trail, with some of the best glacier viewing anywhere in the mountains, or the alpine meadows far up the Little

Yoho Valley. The chalet is usually open from July 1 to September 15 and hikers should make their reservations by the end of May, because the popular chalet only has 14 beds in four bedrooms. Write to Box 23009, Connaught PO, Calgary, AB, T2S 3B1 or phone (403) 228-7079.

From the chalet, continue across the bridge on the Marpole Lake Trail for views of Twin Falls, which leaps 80 m (262 ft) in two branches. Valley hikers can either return the way they came or continue past

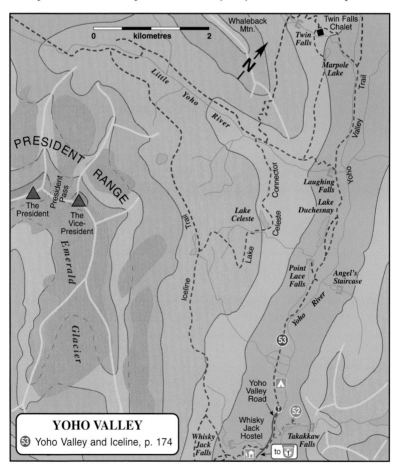

YOHO VALLEY
53 Yoho Valley and Iceline, p. 174

Iceline Trail and the President Range

pretty Marpole Lake and then descend under steep cliffs to the Little Yoho Valley Trail. Turn left on the Little Yoho Valley Trail and descend to the main Yoho Valley Trail that you started on.

ICELINE OPTION: If you want to return via the Iceline Trail instead of the Yoho Valley Trail, head west up the Little Yoho Valley Trail for 0.8 km (0.5 mi) from the Marpole Lake intersection to the Lake Celeste Connector, which climbs to join the Iceline.

The Iceline, built in 1987 to replace the environmentally damaged Highline Trail, ascends through flower-filled meadows and across a moonscape of boulders and scree high under Emerald Glacier on the slopes of the Vice-President. You can gaze across the valley to what valley-floor visitors to Takakkaw Falls always miss: the Waputik Icefield above the falls.

The lofty trail crosses a confusion of moraines and meltwater streams, and hikers may encounter snow-fields throughout summer. Take the cutoff at the sign for Takakkaw Falls and descend endlessly on switch-backs to the Whisky Jack Hostel. The parking lot where you started is a short distance to the left down the road.

54. Emerald Lake Circuit—*The $10 lake*

For many years, the image of Emerald Lake adorned the back of the $10 bill, and hikers who take this popular and easy stroll certainly get their money's worth. Although the shoreline is deeply forested, the lake is a stunning blue-green and the many clearings offer views of rugged Mt. Burgess to the south and Emerald Glacier to the north.

Map: page 178
Distance: 5.2 km (3.2 mi)
Time: 2 hours
Rating: Moderate
Max. elevation: 1312 m (4303 ft)
Elevation gain: Negligible
Footwear: Walking/running shoes/light hiking boots
Best season: June to October

access

Four km (2.5 mi) past the Field townsite turnoff, turn right off the Trans-Canada Highway, 30 km (19 mi) west of Lake Louise. Drive 10 km (6.2 mi) to the end of the road.

Head down the left-hand side of the lake on a popular nature trail past some of the best-situated picnic tables anywhere. The grassy area overlooks the lake and the great walls of Mt. Burgess (behind the lodge) and to its left, Wapta Mountain. Michael Peak is straight ahead.

The pavement turns to soft spruce needles and you cross open winter avalanche slopes bright with asters and fireweed. Benches close to the lake invite you to meditate on this lovely scene. The lake gets its colour as a result of suspended glacial silt washed into it from the heights of the President Range.

The trail leads across an old alluvial fan at the end of the lake and enters a lush, damp forest on the other side under the shadow of Mt. Burgess. This side gets more rain than the opposite shore, creating a world of thick moss, jungle-like undergrowth, massive trees and muddy trails, a good place to spot moose early in the morning. You can always dry off at the Emerald Lake day lodge.

Emerald Lake and Michael Peak

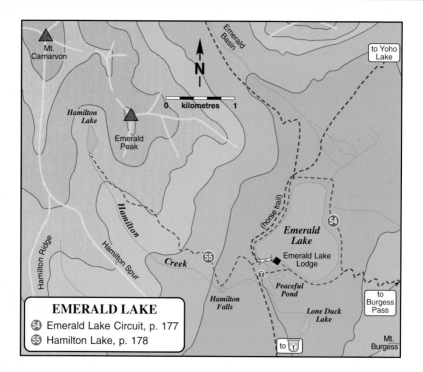

EMERALD LAKE

54 Emerald Lake Circuit, p. 177
55 Hamilton Lake, p. 178

55. Hamilton Lake—*Escape to a hanging valley*

Definitely a trail for those willing to delay gratification, the little-known Hamilton Lake route is relentlessly steep and almost entirely enclosed by forest until the very end. But the reward is a classic alpine lake with excellent views down the Kicking Horse Valley and an opportunity for further exploration.

access

Four km (2.5 mi) past the Field townsite turnoff, turn right off the Trans-Canada Highway, 30 km (19 mi) west of Lake Louise. The trail starts on the left near the entrance to the parking area.

Map: above
Distance: 11 km (6.8 mi) return
Time: 5 hours
Rating: Strenuous
Max. elevation: 2164 m (7098 ft)
Elevation gain: 850 m (2788 ft)
Footwear: Light hiking boots
Best season: July to early September

The trail climbs past Hamilton Falls and then switchbacks up steeply above Hamilton Creek. The ascent is relentless and views extremely limited until the trail reaches an open slide area. The trail finally tops a rise to reveal Hamilton Lake

Hamilton Falls

and the magnificent cirque behind it—a fitting reward for all that toil. (The lake is named for R.A. Hamilton, a Canadian Pacific Railway engineer who supervised the building of many Yoho trails early in the 20th century.)

Here is a classic alpine lake and cirque in a hanging valley, with the crumbling slopes and multi-coloured rock of Mt. Carnarvon behind it and smaller Emerald Peak to the right.

Hikers can continue down the left side of the lake to a grassy knoll that provides a spectacular lunch spot and views down the Kicking Horse Valley. From there, strong hikers could pick their way up past twisted rock formations to the fantastic moonscape in the col between Carnarvon on the left and Emerald Peak on the right. The route is littered with loose rock, however, and no real trail exists.

179

56. Lake O'Hara Circuit

Finest lakeshore circuit

This short stroll may simply be the finest lakeshore circuit in the Canadian Rockies. 'In all the mountain wilderness, the most complete picture of mountain beauty is realized at O'Hara Lake,' said explorer Walter Wilcox—and it hasn't really changed since his day. The only difficulty is getting to Lake O'Hara in the first place.

Map: page 181
Distance: 2.9-km (1.8-mi) loop
Time: 1 hour
Rating: Easy
Max. elevation: 2035 m (6675 ft)
Elevation gain: Negligible
Footwear: Light hiking boots
Best season: July to early September

access

Start from the Le Relais day shelter at the end of the restricted Lake O'Hara access road. See page 184 for access details.

Take the circuit in either direction. A clockwise circuit is described here. The route is a favourite evening or early morning stroll for those staying at the lodge or campground but remains superb at any hour for day visitors who still have to catch a bus.

Walk down to the lakeside next to the warden cabin across the road from Le Relais for a preview of the splendours to come. This spot is

Sargent's Point, named for the well-known American artist J.S. Sargent who painted a number of landscapes from this location. Keep left for the bridge over Cataract Brook, the lake's outlet and home to grey dippers that can walk along the bottom to feed.

You are walking on the Adeline Link Circuit, named for the wife of Dr. George Link, who worked with her husband on the trail in 1943 only to die of a stroke a year later.

Seven Veils Falls is visible at the end of the lake, the water appearing suddenly from cracks and boulders at the top of the cliff. The Wiwaxy Gap alpine route heads off to higher terrain while the lakeshore route

Lake O'Hara

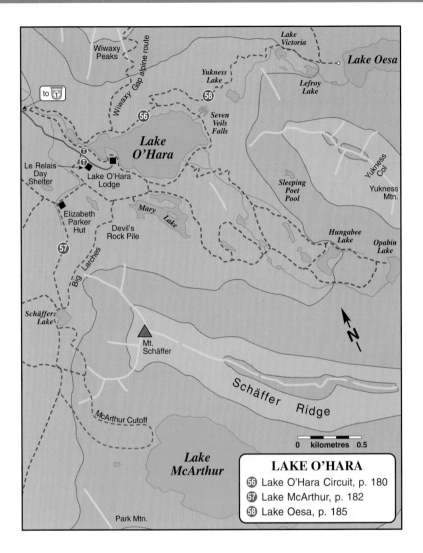

Wiwaxy Peaks
Wiwaxy Gap alpine route
to 🛣
56
58
Lake O'Hara
Yukness Lake
Seven Veils Falls
Lake Victoria
Lake Oesa
Lefroy Lake
Le Relais Day Shelter
Lake O'Hara Lodge
Mary Lake
Elizabeth Parker Hut
Devil's Rock Pile
57
Big Larches
Sleeping Poet Pool
Yukness Col
Yukness Mtn.
Hungabee Lake
Opabin Lake
Schäffer Lake
Mt. Schäffer
N
Schäffer Ridge
McArthur Cutoff
Lake McArthur
Park Mtn.

0   kilometres   0.5

LAKE O'HARA
56 Lake O'Hara Circuit, p. 180
57 Lake McArthur, p. 182
58 Lake Oesa, p. 185

rambles on under the steep slopes of the Wiwaxy Peaks.

At 0.8 km (0.5 mi), the Lake Oesa trail (Walk 58) branches off to the left while the lakeshore circuit passes under the falls, sometimes called the Seven Veils, sometimes the Seven Sisters. The latter name supposedly comes from a legend about seven sisters who were frightened by a hunter and begged the mountain to protect them. The mountain was a little overzealous in this task and turned them into seven falls.

The route passes trails leading to the Opabin Plateau and follows the lake more closely, before bypassing Lake O'Hara Lodge and ending at the fireroad just above Le Relais.

57. Lake McArthur—*Classic hike to classic lake*

In good weather, the astonishing deep blue of Lake McArthur, largest in the region, contrasts vividly with the white of Biddle Glacier at the far end. Getting there is just as scenic: a classic hike through alpine meadows dotted with delicate larches, with a well-engineered traverse over ledges and rock slides on steps laid down by legendary trail builder Lawrence Grassi.

Map: page 181
Distance: 7 km (4.3 mi) return
Time: 4 hours
Rating: Strenuous
Max. elevation: 2355 m (7724 ft)
Elevation gain: 320 m (1050 ft)
Footwear: Light hiking boots
Best season: Mid-July to early September

access

Start from the Le Relais day shelter at the end of the restricted Lake O'Hara access road. See Page 184 for details.

Mountain goats

The trail ascends gradually to a beautiful meadow and the Elizabeth Parker Hut operated by the Alpine Club of Canada. Keep left and climb through a high subalpine forest of Engelmann spruce and subalpine fir to Schäffer Lake, a striking scene of meadows and larches. The trail circles the north side of the lake to a junction.

Later in summer when the snow has disappeared from the high meadows, hikers can reach the lake on the high-level route, which heads off to the left. (Keep right for the lower, mostly wooded route to Lake McArthur via McArthur Pass.)

The high-level route (called McArthur Cutoff) climbs steeply above the lake onto the open, rocky slopes of Mt. Schäffer on a good trail that winds smoothly around huge boulders and climbs on stone stairs over ledges. It contours around a broad shoulder to reach windswept meadows overlooking Lake McArthur.

The deep lake, which often remains ice-covered until mid-July, is set in a barren cirque under the

Lake McArthur

steep cliffs of Mt. Biddle at the far end. The brilliant blue of the lake, whose depths reach 85 m (279 ft), contrasts with the white of the Biddle Glacier and the snowfields that linger through summer. Watch for goats on the crags above the lake.

The trail gradually descends to the lake through the meadows and loops back on the Lower McArthur trail, which rejoins the approach route at Schäffer Lake.

From Schäffer Lake, an alternate route returns to Lake O'Hara via the Big Larches Route. It branches right at the north end of Schäffer Lake and stays close to the bottom of a steep rockslide, descending steeply at times through the Devil's Rock Pile before looping back to rejoin the original route above Le Relais.

How to Get to Lake O'Hara

Getting to Lake O'Hara by bus and camping there or just staying for the day takes considerable planning. Although you can walk to Lake O'Hara on the 13-km (8-mi) Cataract Brook trail, why not save your energy for all the glorious hiking beyond the lake by taking the bus?

You need a reservation to take the bus to Lake O'Hara for day use and camping. The bus operates from June 19 to October 1. The campground has 30 sites and is a 'backcountry experience,' with limited facilities. To reserve the bus and/or campsite, call the Lake O'Hara office at Parks Canada in Yoho at (250) 343-6433. Reservations may be made three months in advance and only by phone (with the exception noted below).

Reservations for the coming season are accepted from late March until the end of September. The reservation desk is open 8 a.m. to 12 p.m. late March to mid-April; 8 a.m to 4 p.m., Monday to Friday, mid-April to mid-June; 8 a.m. to 4 p.m. daily, mid-June to the end of August; and reduced hours until September 30. Be prepared to give your first and second choice for preferred bus time. Return bus fare is $12 for adults; camping is $6 per person. If you have an annual Wilderness Pass, it will cover the camping fee. Present the pass when boarding the bus.

At the time of writing, buses went into Lake O'Hara at 8:30 a.m., 10:30 a.m., 4:30 p.m. and 7:30 p.m. Only morning buses can be reserved for day use. Outgoing buses returned at 7:30 a.m., 9:30 a.m., 3:30 p.m. and 6:30 p.m. Check for updated schedules.

It is possible to visit Lake O'Hara without making reservations in advance. If you show up at the Field Visitor Centre the day before you want to go, you might be able to reserve a day-use place on the bus and, if desired, a campsite. The visitor centre opens at 9 a.m. each day, and the Lake O'Hara office in the centre closes at 4 p.m. Parks recommends that you show up early, because a line-up usually forms before the doors open. Only six day-use places and three to five campsites are set aside for in-person reservations. (Not available by telephone.) The maximum party size for day-users is six.

If you are camping, be prepared for fairly crowded sites and limited common facilities. Lock-up boxes are available for valuable items; bring your own medium-sized padlock. You can warm up, take shelter or buy a snack at a day shelter, Le Relais. Lectures and films are sometimes held in the evenings.

Can't obtain a reservation? Remember that there are no restrictions on the number of people who hike the Cataract Brook trail into Lake O'Hara. Cycling is not permitted on the trail or on the Lake O'Hara fireroad. Pets aren't allowed on the bus, but can be walked into the valley.

The Lake O'Hara parking lot is situated just off the Trans-Canada, 15 km (9.3 mi) east of Field, B.C. and 11 km (7 mi) west of Lake Louise. Turn onto Hwy. 1A to access the parking lot. All park users require a valid National Park Pass.

58. Lake Oesa—*Ice lake*

Although this trail is the busiest in the Lake O'Hara region, it well deserves its popularity. The approach trail is one of the most interesting anywhere in the Rockies, offering superb views, cascades, waterfalls, ponds and a mixture of meadows and rocky ledges. It ends at a barren, turquoise lake (often frozen well into summer) set in a barren but spectacular cirque under the Continental Divide.

Map:	page 181
Distance:	7.2 km (4.5 mi) return
Time:	4 hours
Rating:	Moderate
Max. elevation:	2275 m (7462 ft)
Elevation gain:	257 m (843 ft)
Footwear:	Light hiking boots
Best season:	Mid-July to early September

access

Start from Le Relais cabin at the end of the restricted Lake O'Hara access road. See page 184 for details.

Follow the first part of the Lake O'Hara Circuit (Walk 56) and take the Oesa turnoff two-thirds of the way down the north shore of the lake. The trail switchbacks up through the forest and emerges atop a cliff that offers great views back over Lake O'Hara.

The route levels off amid rock piles and the trail is paved with large stones laid down by earlier trail makers, including guide Lawrence Grassi who served as warden at Lake O'Hara from 1956–60. It is a spectacular open region, with many small ponds and waterfalls.

A trail to the Yukness Ledges branches off at tiny Lake Victoria while the main route descends slightly to Lake Oesa. 'Oesa' is the Stoney name for 'ice.'

The milky-blue tarn is set in a huge, barren cirque under the great sculpted headwalls of the Continental Divide peaks (from left, Mt. Lefroy, Glacier Peak and Ringrose Peak). On the left side of the lake, a rough trail continues over boulders to a steep gully full of loose scree. The trail ascends to a historic hut at 2922-m (9584-ft) Abbot Pass, which overlooks Victoria Glacier and the 'Death Trap.' Not recommended for the casual hiker.

Lake Oesa

59. Wapta Falls—*Yoho's largest falls*

In a park known for its waterfalls, Wapta Falls is Yoho's largest (by volume). The entire Kicking Horse River thunders 30 m (98 ft) over a broad cliff into torrents of foam and clouds of mist. Since the access trail is almost level and takes less than 45 minutes, Wapta Falls makes an excellent family destination. The grassy shoreline below the falls is a good spot for a picnic or to get out your paint box.

Map: below
Distance: 4.8 km (3 mi) return
Time: 2 hours
Rating: Easy
Max. elevation: 1125 m (3690 ft)
Elevation gain: Nearly level
Footwear: Walking/running shoes/light hiking boots
Best season: May to late September

access

At the sign to Wapta Falls, turn off onto a gravel road on the south side of the Trans-Canada Highway, 3 km (1.9 mi) east of Yoho National Park's west entrance. Drive 1.6 km (1 mi) to the parking area at the end of the road. Westbound travellers from Field should note that there is no sign or turning lane on their side of the highway onto the access road, 25 km (16 mi) west of Field. Parks Canada asks westbound travellers to continue to the west gate—where they can turn around safely—and come back 3 km (1.9 mi) to the access road.

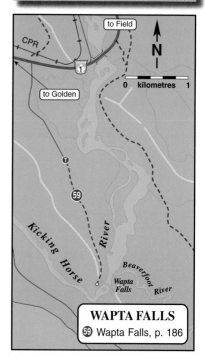

WAPTA FALLS
59 Wapta Falls, p. 186

The first kilometre is straight and flat, following an overgrown road through semi-open montane terrain of trembling aspen, balsam poplar, lodgepole pine and the occasional Douglas-fir. It is a good location to spot white-tailed deer. The trail narrows, climbs slightly, and enters a denser forest. You begin to hear the great roar of the falls.

The trail descends slightly to a fenced viewpoint overlooking the mighty falls—the Niagara of the Rockies. This torrent contains almost all the water runoff from across the entire 1313-sq.-km (525-sq.-mi) park—from the Wapta and Waputik icefields, Yoho River, Takakkaw Falls, Lake O'Hara, Amiskwi River, Ottertail River, Beaverfoot River and hundreds of vigorous creeks.

The Kicking Horse plunges over a cliff of impervious rock at a volume of up to 255 cubic metres (334 cubic yards) a second. Just below the falls is a second rib of resistant rock. The river gradually wore away the softer rock surrounding this rib and migrated upstream to its present location.

For an alternate and non-fenced view of the falls, return to the main trail and descend to the river bank downstream from the torrent. The Kicking Horse River returns to a more placid demeanor, although you can still admire the falls, the rainbows and the shifting clouds of mist upstream. The riverside is a fine and safe place for a picnic lunch. It's always tempting to approach the falls behind the second rock rib for a closer view. Be aware that the rocks and logs close to the falls are extremely treacherous because they are invariably slick from the clouds of spray and mist.

Unhappy Times on the Wapta

In August, 1858, part of the Palliser Expedition led by 23-year-old James Hector was camped just north of Wapta Falls where the Beaverfoot River joins the main channel. It was not a happy time. Led by their two guides, Nimrod and Erasmus, the exploration party had struggled in wet, cold weather through the Vermilion and Kootenay valleys to a third major river, named the 'Wapta' by native peoples.

The expedition's supplies of moose meat were rotting, and they couldn't catch any fish because the torrential rivers were choked with glacial silt. The valleys were a tangle of wet logs and thick brush.

A pack horse slipped off the steep bank above the river and the men scrambled down to rescue it. The other horses wandered away. James Hector finally found his own horse, but the animal kicked him hard in the chest and he fell to the ground unconscious. The other men thought he was dead and began preparations for a burial. Fortunately, before they could do so, James let out a groan.

Although in great pain, James managed to ride his horse the next day and the expedition continued up the pass following what the men now referred to as 'the Kicking Horse River.' The young explorer soon concluded that the pass was too steep for a transportation route.

James, later Sir James, was probably right, but the politicians overruled him. The difficult pass was finally used by the Canadian Pacific Railway (CPR) for its transcontinental route as opposed to the more gentle Yellowhead Pass to the north. The politicians were concerned that the Americans might try to take over the land in what is now southern British Columbia if it lacked a transportation link and settlement. The Kicking Horse Pass, meanwhile, remained a railway bottleneck until the Spiral Tunnels were built at great cost.

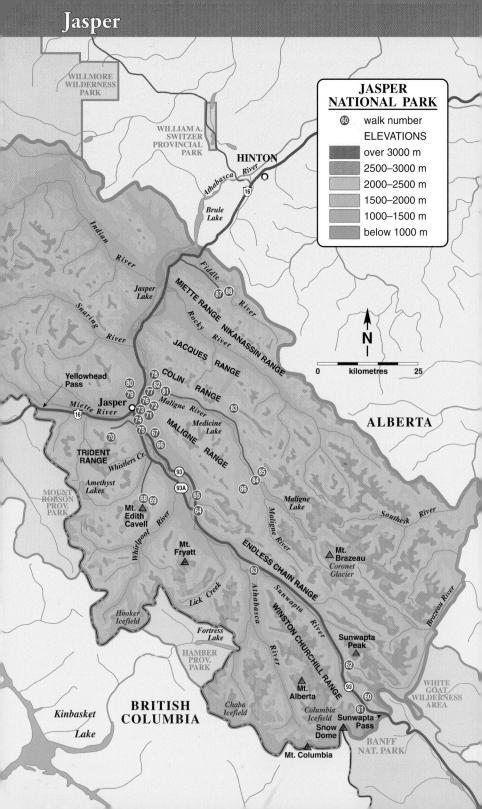

Medicine Lake and Colin Range

CHAPTER 4

JASPER NATIONAL PARK

Jasper National Park is the largest and most northerly of the Canadian Rocky Mountain national parks, a vast wilderness of peaks, glaciers, deep forests, clear lakes and the largest ice cap south of the Arctic Circle. Mammals ranging from grizzlies and cougars to elk, deer, mountain goats and bighorn sheep inhabit the park, along with more than 250 bird species, from the white ptarmigan to the ubiquitous grey jay.

The park covers more than 10,800 sq. km (4320 sq. mi), and is dominated by two mountain ranges—the Front and the Main ranges. Here are more than 1000 km (620 mi) of hiking trails, where walkers can observe three vegetation zones—montane, subalpine and alpine. New hikers will find the network of trails around the townsite especially friendly, owing to extensive new signage instituted in 1997 by the Friends of Jasper National Park in co-operation with Parks Canada.

The fur traders of the early 19th century were the first to explore much of what is now Jasper National Park. It was named after a nearby trading post operated by

189

Jasper Hawse and known as 'Jasper's House.' In 1907, the federal government established the Jasper Park Reserve, the predecessor of the national park.

Jasper is visited by about 2.2 million people annually and retains a lower-key atmosphere than Banff, its busy southern sister. The two are connected by the famous Icefields Parkway (Hwy. 93). Although less crowded and superb for backpacking, Jasper does not offer the same rich menu of day walks as Banff. Nor does Jasper, with 4000 permanent residents, offer the same variety of restaurants, cultural activities, nightlife or stores.

Jasper is situated 362 km (224 mi) west of Edmonton on Hwy. 16 or 426 km (264 mi) northwest of Calgary on the Icefields Parkway (Hwy. 93). Edmonton is the major gateway city to Jasper, although many visitors start in Calgary, visit Banff and then reach Jasper by travelling the Icefields Parkway

(Hwy. 93), one of the world's most scenic highways. Direct and one-stop flights connect Edmonton with most major North American and European cities.

Between Toronto and Vancouver, VIA Rail operates passenger service through Jasper in both directions (1-800-561-3949). Rocky Mountain Railtours also runs passenger service between Jasper and Vancouver in both directions (1-800-665-7245). Train service between Jasper and Prince Rupert is also offered. Frequent daily bus service is available from Edmonton to Jasper and between Calgary, Banff, Lake Louise and Jasper. Brewster Transport has daily bus service between Banff and Jasper from April 1 until the end of October.

Most accommodation is in the townsite or nearby in cabins along the Athabasca River. At the high end pricewise is Jasper Park Lodge; at the other end of the scale are the hostels in the townsite and along

Marmot Basin ski area

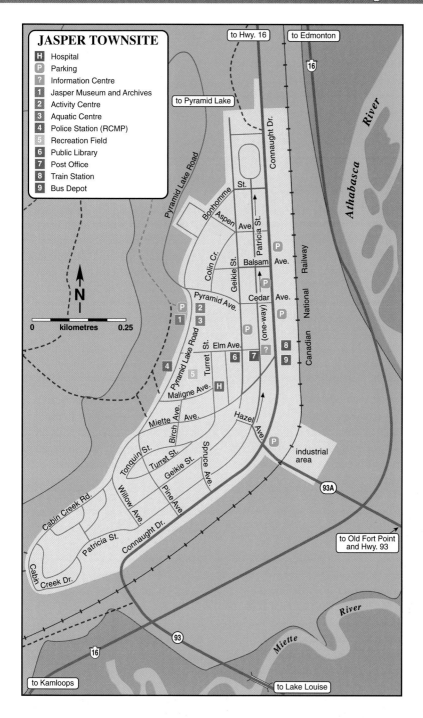

JASPER TOWNSITE

H Hospital
P Parking
? Information Centre
1 Jasper Museum and Archives
2 Activity Centre
3 Aquatic Centre
4 Police Station (RCMP)
5 Recreation Field
6 Public Library
7 Post Office
8 Train Station
9 Bus Depot

N

0   kilometres   0.25

to Hwy. 16
to Edmonton
to Pyramid Lake
Connaught Dr.
Pyramid Lake Road
Bonhomme St.
Aspen Ave.
Patricia St.
Colin Cr.
Geikie St.
Balsam Ave.
Cedar Ave.
Pyramid Ave.
(one-way)
Canadian National Railway
Athabasca River
Elm Ave.
Turret St.
Maligne Ave.
Miette Ave.
Birch Ave.
Tonquin St.
Turret St.
Geikie St.
Pine Ave.
Spruce Ave.
Willow Ave.
Hazel Ave.
industrial area
93A
Cabin Creek Rd.
Patricia St.
Connaught Dr.
Cabin Creek Dr.
to Old Fort Point and Hwy. 93
Miette River
93
16
to Kamloops
to Lake Louise

the Icefields Parkway (Hwy. 93). Patricia Lake Bungalows on Pyramid Bench offers comfortable, no-frills accommodation in a quiet setting away from the town. Be warned that some of the newer accommodation available in the area is both crowded and pricey. In winter, cabin accommodation is disappointingly limited.

An enjoyable alternative is the bed-and-breakfast route. The Jasper Home Accommodation Association publishes a pamphlet, *Private Home Accommodation Listings*, with dozens of B & Bs in the townsite and area. See 'Sources.'

The recently opened Icefield Centre at the Columbia Icefield includes the Glacier Gallery, an excellent interpretive gallery. The Jasper Museum and Archives is also a treat.

Start your visit at the Jasper Information Centre, 500 Connaught Drive, (403) 852-6176. Open daily: 8 a.m. to 7 p.m., June 14 to September 1; 9 a.m. to 5 p.m. weekdays, 8 a.m. to 5 p.m. Saturday and Sunday, September 2 to May 15; 8 a.m. to 5 p.m., May 16 to June 13. It has park information, maps, brochures, permits, etc. If you plan to hike around the town, ask for free maps of the surrounding trail network, provided by the Friends of Jasper National Park. The Friends also operates a gift shop in the information centre, and the Jasper Chamber of Commerce provides information on commercial facilities in the park.

Outdoor Adventures

ACTIVITY PLANNERS: If you would like to plan your adventure travel activities and accommodation through the Internet, in North America and abroad, CAN*travel*, 'Western Canada's Travel Directory,' is a good source: www.cantravel.ab.ca.

ALPINE COURSES AND GUIDED CLIMBS: Guide Peter Amann will introduce you to the joys of rock, snow and ice climbing. For a memorable experience, book a three-day course and ascend Mt. Athabasca on the third day. A two-day climbing course on the Columbia Icefield is also offered; $175 for two days, $250 for three days, (403) 852-3237.

ATHABASCA GLACIER ICE-WALKS: Former park naturalist Peter Lemieux offers guided walks on the amazing Athabasca Glacier at the Columbia Icefield. Choose between a three- to four-hour hike and a five- to six-hour hike, from mid-June to the end of September. Average group size is 15; prices are from $28 to $32 for adults, $12 to $14 for children. Book through the Jasper Adventure Centre, 1-800-565-7547 or (403) 852-5595. (Also see sidebar, page 195.)

BACKPACKING: See chapter 7 (page 334) for recommendations on some of the best overnight trips.

BICYCLING: See chapter 7 (page 348) for bicycle rental locations and a guide to the best road and mountain biking day trips.

BOATING AND CANOEING: See chapter 7 (pages 340 and 344) for boat and canoe rentals and a guide to travelling lakes and rivers.

BOAT CRUISES, MALIGNE LAKE: One of the most photographed scenes in the Rockies, Spirit Island on Maligne Lake, can be reached comfortably by boat. Indeed, many feel the full grandeur of the lake—surrounded by wide glaciers and high mountain peaks—is not revealed any other way. That's why a 1¹/₂-hour guided tour down Maligne Lake in a covered power boat is perennially popular. Choose a fine day if possible, because the lake is higher than Jasper townsite and can easily be socked in on rainy days. And be prepared for the hefty price: $31, adults; $15.50, children. Cruises operate hourly, 9 a.m. to 9 p.m., in summer (shorter hours until Thanksgiving). Call (403) 852-3370.

CANYON ICEWALK: The Maligne Canyon icewalk is an unusual and popular winter expedition. The three-hour walk takes you to the deepest part of the canyon, where you walk on the frozen 'floor,' stopping for photos at Angel and Queen of the Maligne icefalls. The tours are conducted by the Jasper Adventure Centre, which provides transportation, crampons

Maligne Canyon crawl

and a certified guide; $25 for adults, $13 for children, (403) 852-5595 or 1-800-565-7547. The tours are also offered by Maligne Tours, (403) 852-3370.

CARRIAGE RIDE: Tour Jasper townsite in an elegant horse carriage, or use one for a taxi. Call Horseback Riding, (403) 852-3562.

CHILDREN'S PROGRAMS: The Friends of Jasper National Park offers a Junior Naturalist Program at Whistler's Campground, and also makes special hiking kits available for families hiking at Old Fort Point. Check at the Jasper Information Centre. There are also hikes designed for families with young children through the Jasper Institute (see listing). Also see 'Children's Programs' in indoor listings.

COLUMBIA ICEFIELD EXCURSION: Everybody in North America could stand on this vast icefield, and there would still be room for others to join a rather chilly party. The 103-km (64-mi) drive up to this climatic and geological wonder is a must. Be aware that it's also crowded, rather desolate and almost always cold. Most people choose to 'explore' the Icefield via huge mechanized 'snocoaches,' but you can also go on guided hikes. At the new Icefield Centre, there's a hotel and cafeteria as well as the Glacier Gallery, with its stunning interpretive displays. If you haven't been to the Icefield Centre for a while, the gallery alone is worth the trip. Stay away during peak periods, between 11 a.m. and 3 p.m. in July and August, when the centre handles as many as 6000 people a day.

Columbia Icefield excursion

The Columbia Icefield

'The view that lay before us in the evening light was one that does not often fall to the lot of modern mountaineers. A new world was spread out at our feet; to the westward stretched a vast icefield probably never before seen by human eye, surrounded by entirely unknown, unnamed, unclimbed peaks.'

So wrote Scottish chemistry professor Norman Collie in August, 1898, after overlooking the Columbia Icefield from the summit of Mt. Athabasca.

The largest ice cap south of the Arctic Circle, it covers 325 sq. km (130 sq. mi) or about the area of Vancouver. Wilcox Pass (Walk 60) has the most dramatic views of the Icefield. Three of the six major glaciers—Dome, Stutfield and Athabasca—can be seen from the Parkway. The massive Saskatchewan Glacier can be seen from Parker Ridge (Walk 47). By far the most accessible is the Athabasca Glacier.

A stroll to the toe of the Athabasca Glacier (Walk 61) is a must. Don't attempt to walk on it yourself without an expert guide—it is estimated to have more than 30,000 crevasses. Instead, take a walk through Athabasca Glacier Icewalks with former park naturalist Peter Lemieux. The walks are three- to four- and five- to six-hours long, and are offered from mid-June to the end of September; $28 to $32 for adults; $12 to $14 for kids. Group size averages 15. 'We provide people with everything—crampons (spikes), rain gear, hats, sun-screen,' says Lemieux. Book through the Jasper Adventure Centre, 1-800-565-7547 or (403) 852-5595.

The Columbia Icefield Snowmobile Tours Ltd., (403) 762-6735, offers 'sno-coach' tours from 9 a.m. to 5 p.m., April 15 through September, and 10 a.m. to 4 p.m. until (usually) mid-October. Rates are $22.50 for adults; $5 for children. The excursions are 1¹/₂ hours long and are offered in many different languages. Reservations are not required for individuals. Dress warmly.

The $7.2-million Icefield Centre, which opened in 1996, incorporates a splendid Parks Canada interpretive centre, the Glacier Gallery, Parks administration, ticketing offices for Brewster snocoach tours, accommodation for 180, parking for 102 buses, 560 cars and 170 RVs, a dining room and a 300-seat cafeteria and terrace with fabulous views of the Athabasca Glacier. The centre is wheelchair accessible and designed to meet the needs of seniors and the disabled arriving by the busloads.

The Glacier Gallery opens at 9 a.m. The fascinating displays tell of the area's natural and human history. You'll find out what caused the mysterious 'baffle-ment of butterflies' on the Icefield and why glaciers can help us understand global warming.

Book in advance for lunch buffets if you want to eat upstairs in the Glacier Dining Room, (403) 852-3226. The snack bar serves cups of noodles and hot dogs, and the cafeteria has cold sandwiches, pizza by the slice, etc. Be warned that the crowds can be overwhelming. The best seats are the high tables for two by the window.

visitor tips

195

Ice fishing

DRIVES: The most popular drive is up the 48-km (30-mi) road to gorgeous Maligne Lake south of Jasper townsite, passing Maligne Canyon and 'disappearing' Medicine Lake along the way. This sparkling route features steep limestone mountains and fast-moving rivers. Another popular drive is up the dead-end road to Mt. Edith Cavell, a narrow, twisting route with good views over the Astoria Valley and a glacier at the end. Hwy. 93A south from Jasper townsite is a slower-lane alternative to the Icefields Parkway (Hwy. 93). The Fiddle River Road to Miette Hot Springs south of Hwy. 16 has been widened and improved. You can also drive west on Hwy. 16, 83 km (51 mi) to Mt.

Robson, which is the highest mountain in the Canadian Rockies, though it is often obscured by cloud. (If you do this drive in late August, carry on past Mt. Robson for Rearguard Falls to see the Kokanee salmon leaping up the falls, a truly memorable sight.) The world-renowned drive, of course, is the 226-km (140-mi) tour of awe-inspiring alpine scenery between Jasper and Lake Louise on the Icefields Parkway (Hwy. 93).

FISHING AND GUIDED FISH-ING: See chapter 7 for where to fish, where to find fishing guides and which lakes have which fish.

GOLFING: Designed by the famous golf architect Stanley Thompson, it took 200 men and 50 teams of horses a whole summer in the 1920s to clear the ground of huge boulders and timber for the Jasper Park Lodge golf course. The 18-hole course has recently won two awards as one of the top resort golf courses in the world (and was the only Gold Medal winner in Canada). Open late April to late October. Green fees from July to September, $69. Equipment rental and professional instruction are available, (403) 852-6090. The Hinton Golf Club, on Hwy. 16, also offers golfing with mountain views, at less cost. It's a scenic hour's drive east of Jasper townsite, (403) 865-2904.

GONDOLA: The Jasper Tramway whisks visitors up 2500 m (8200 ft) to the alpine zone below the summit of Whistler's Mountain, just west of Jasper townsite, for a panoramic view of the entire Athabasca Valley. The tramway takes about seven minutes to reach the top. On clear days, Mt. Robson can be seen 62 km (38 mi) to the west. A scenic hiking trail to the barren summit leads from the upper terminal (Walk 70). Some might enjoy taking the tram up and walking down. The renovated Treeline Restaurant at the top serves a sunrise breakfast for $4.95 (scrambled eggs, bacon, sausage, hash browns), lunch and a sunset dinner package ($34.30 for prime Alberta beef, Pacific Coast salmon or orange-brandy glazed chicken). The tramway operates from March until the end of October, (403) 852-3093.

GUIDED HIKES: Ben Gadd, the author of the excellent *Handbook of the Canadian Rockies*, and his wife, Cia, live in Jasper and conduct guided tours, day hikes and multi-day expeditions on request. They don't provide a van, but will accompany you in your vehicle. Call (403) 852-4012. The Jasper Adventure Centre (JAC) and the Jasper Institute are great places to find out about a variety of guided hikes with certified Parks Canada interpretive guides. Popular offerings from JAC are a three-hour 'Path of the Glacier' walk at Edith Cavell, a 'watchable wildlife tour' of Miette Hot Springs and a 'breakfast, birding and beavers' walk around ideal beaver

and bird habitats. Call (403) 852-5595. See a separate listing (page 199) for the Jasper Institute's excellent offerings.

Wendy Smith and Kirsten Schmitten, two Parks Canada interpretive guides, will take you on half- and full-day custom-tailored outings and interpretive talks. Some French, German and Japanese spoken, (403) 852-5193. Terri Hunter, of Backpacking Adventures, also a certified guide, offers day hikes, multi-day hikes and women's trips. If you want to travel without a guide, but need someone to do the planning, find your maps, plan the food and attend to all the other details, Backpacking Adventures will also step in. Call (403) 852-5301. Pyramid Mountain Interpretive Guided Hikes conducts walks on Pyramid Bench and through Cottonwood Slough, above the townsite. The Pyramid Bench hike provides fine views of the Athabasca Valley; the Cottonwood Slough hike takes you through Douglas-fir forest and wetlands with good opportunities to view wildlife. Call (403) 852-4944 to reserve.

Beyond the Beaten Path Sightseeing Tours also conducts guided hikes to Mt. Edith Cavell, wildlife searches and a 'picnic tour' where a gourmet lunch is added. Call (403) 852-5650. Maligne Tours, (403) 852-3405, operates guided interpretive hikes of between one and four hours at Maligne Lake. This trail is especially well-suited to children. Edge Control Outdoors, (403) 852-4945, also

Riding in the Tonquin Valley

conducts walks and talks in Jasper, in English and French. Raven Adventures, (403) 852-4292, conducts sunset 'photo safaris' with interpretive guides, as well as 'early bird' morning walks at 7:30 a.m.

Guided hikes are offered on the Athasbasca Glacier (see the beginning of this section). Also see following listings for Historic Walking Tours, the Jasper Institute and Naturalists' Evening Programs.

HIKERS' AND SIGHTSEERS' SHUTTLE: The Maligne Lake Shuttle Service, (403) 852-3370, stops at Maligne Canyon and the Skyline Trail trailhead. Also try Jasper Taxi Ltd., (403) 852-3600, for service to trailheads, lakes, beaches or other attractions within park boundaries.

HISTORIC WALKING TOUR: The Jasper Information Centre, built in 1913, is one of the finest and most influential examples of the rustic design tradition of the Canadian Rockies. Find out more about this heritage building and many others a short walk away. The Friends of Jasper National Park offers a 'Walk in the Past' nightly from June to September, starting at 7:30 p.m. at the Jasper Information Centre, (403) 852-4767. (You can register or just show up.) The Jasper Adventure Centre also conducts a three-hour van tour for $35. Call (403) 852-5595 or 1-800-565-7547.

HORSEBACK RIDING: At Jasper Park Lodge, horses can be rented by the hour. Explore Lake Annette for a short ride; a 4$^{1}/_{2}$-hour canyon tour is also offered. You can also rent a horse for a private ride of up to six hours or book riding lessons. Another well-established equestrian spot is Pyramid Stables, 4 km (2.5 mi) up Pyramid Lake Road from Jasper townsite, operated by Horseback Riding. One-, two- and three-hour rides are offered, as well as day rides, with special early-morning rates. The three-hour ride that takes you up the high ridges overlooking the Athabasca Valley is particularly enjoyable. The last ride leaves at 3:30 p.m. For reservations and information, call (403) 852-3562. In recent years, horseback excursions have been offered from Maligne Lake to near the summit of Bald Hills. There are twice-daily departures, at 10 a.m. and 2 p.m., for $55. Call Maligne Tours at (403) 852-3370.

If you have a longer expedition in mind, consider a three- or four-day trip based at Shovel Pass Lodge, the park's oldest backcountry camp. You'll stay in a newly renovated, private cabin, and enjoy home cooking that includes fresh salads. Contact Skyline Trail Rides Ltd., (403) 852-4215. Amethyst Lakes Pack Trips Ltd., operated by Wald and Lavone Olson, conducts three- to five-day trips to the beautiful Tonquin Valley. Call (403) 865-4417.

HOT SPRINGS SOAK: It's the best way to get soaked in Jasper. Soothe your cares and aches away at Miette Hot Springs, high up in the Fiddle Valley, with good views along the way and a chance to see Punchbowl Falls. Wheelchair accessible. As well, a number of excellent hiking trails radiate from the hot springs (see Walks 87 and 88). The Miette Hot Springs are the hottest in the Canadian Rockies, reaching a maximum temperature of 53.9° C (129° F). The water is cooled for bathers to a comfortable 39° C (102° F). There are two hot pools and a deeper cool pool with a diving board. You can spend your whole day at Miette, first hiking and then finishing with a hot springs soak and a meal. The Ashlar Ridge Cafe serves muffins and sandwiches, and has a popular afternoon grill featuring bison burgers. Bathing suits are permitted in snack area. To reach the hot springs, drive 42 km (26 mi) east of Jasper townsite on Hwy. 16 and turn south on Miette road. Punchbowl Falls is 0.5 km (0.3 mi) up the road. Drive 16.5 km (10 mi) further to reach the pool. Open daily mid-May to mid-October; 8:30 a.m. to 10:30 p.m. in summer; 10:30 a.m. to 9 p.m. in spring and fall. Call (403) 866-3939.

JASPER INSTITUTE: The Jasper Institute, (403) 852-4152, offers an outstanding array of natural history and education courses and field trips at reasonable rates. Many feature some of Jasper's most renowned naturalists, such as Ben Gadd (*Handbook of the Canadian Rockies*) and noted grizzly bear biologist Brian Horejsi. Courses and trips constantly change. Recent offerings include a weekend exploring Jasper's woodlands for spring wildflowers ($120), a five-day backpacking adventure with Ben Gadd ($325) and a family weekend learning about Jasper's cultural heritage with Cleone Todgham ($80 adults, $50 kids). Reasonably priced lodging is available at the Palisades Environmental Sciences Centre, located away from the town in natural surroundings. The Jasper Institute is operated by the Friends of Jasper National Park, a non-profit co-operative venture with Parks Canada. The Friends also loans free hiking kits for families heading to Old Fort Point (Walk 71). The kits include a hiking pack, guidebooks and crayons. Ask at the sales outlet in the Jasper Information Centre.

JAPANESE LANGUAGE TOURS: Ryuichi Abe at Magnex International, (403) 852-4771, offers Japanese language tours of the Jasper area and will also make cross-Canada travel arrangements.

JASPER PARK LODGE: Spend a pleasant afternoon at Jasper Park Lodge, being as energetic or lazy as you want. At the lodge, enjoy the short stroll around Lac Beauvert (Walk 72), golf, or rent a canoe, paddle boat or horse. You can always just enjoy the scenic views of Mt. Edith Cavell over the green lake from one of the sun platforms on the edge of the water. Call (403) 852-3301. See 'Indoor and Rainy-Day Guide' for historical background and other information about the lodge.

MOTORCOACH TOURS: In the outdoor-adventure-through-glass category, Brewster runs a number of popular excursions from the Jasper townsite. They include
 • a three-hour guided motorcoach tour of Jasper and the surrounding area. Prices start at $37 for adults and $18.50 for children.
 • a five-hour trip to Maligne Lake

Bicycle waiters at Jasper Park Lodge

that includes a 1½-hour cruise on the lake; $56 for adults and $28 for children.

• a nine-hour one-way tour along the Icefields Parkway (Hwy. 93) to the Banff townsite, including a stop at the Columbia Icefield for a ride on the Athabasca Glacier; also to Lake Louise; $79 for adults and $29.50 for children.

Tours start at the Brewster Transport office at the train station, (403) 852-3332.

MOUNTAIN BIKING: See chapter 7 (page 351).

NATURALISTS' EVENING PROGRAMS: Practise wolf calls on a summer evening, and listen for a real wolf to call back. Or stroll along the Athabasca River watching for wildlife. These and many other evening nature strolls are available through Jasper Nature Experiences, (403) 852-5933. Walks can be tailored to group interests. Parks Canada has not been offering naturalists' evening programs in campgrounds, but it might change in the future. Check at your campground or the Information Centre.

RAFT TOURS: See chapter 7 (page 372) for information on seeing this region as the fur traders did, more or less.

ROLLERBLADING: Rent 'em at Beauvert Boat & Cycle, at the Jasper Park Lodge marina, and blast along paved lakeside trails. Call (403) 852-5708.

SCRAMBLING: See chapter 7 for off-trail, non-climbing exploration.

SKATING: At Pyramid Lake, snow is ploughed off the lake and night lighting is provided. In February and March, the best skating might be east of town where chinook winds often sweep away the snow. Try Talbot Lake and Snaring Pond. Ask at the Information Centre for details.

SKIING (CROSS-COUNTRY): See chapter 7 (page 363) for the best trails for all levels, tips on what to take and warnings about avalanches.

SKIING (DOWNHILL): See chapter 7 (page 370).

SLEIGH RIDES: One of the more romantic ways to see Jasper in winter. Contact Skyline Trail Rides at (403) 852-4215 or (403) 852-3301 (ext. 6189).

SNOWBOARDING: Marmot Basin has a good reputation. See chapter 7 (page 372).

SWIMMING: Jasper is not a place where visitors usually think of swimming. Those glacial lakes are chilly! Hardy residents and visitors, especially those under 10, swear the water's fine at Pyramid Lake, Lake Annette and Lake Edith, which all have beaches. The beaches are at the north end of Lake Annette and at two locations on Lake Edith, where a number of beautiful cabins are located. Buses run regularly from Brewster's (in the train station at Jasper) to Jasper Park Lodge. Pyramid Lake, which is 7 km (4.3 mi) up Pyramid Lake Road, has a beach and picnic area on the south side with a fine view of Pyramid Mountain. A swim could be combined with a picnic on Pyramid Lake Island (see Walk 79). The pool in the Jasper Aquatic Centre is open daily to the public. See 'Indoor and Rainy-Day Guide.'

Indoor and Rainy-Day Guide

What can you do in Jasper National Park when the forecast calls for rain and more rain—your tent is awash, it's so cold you can see your breath and the kids keep whining about going home and playing Nintendo?

Of course, you could head 362 km (224 mi) east to West Edmonton Mall. Yet many who know Jasper would rather be soaked to their skins in that park any day. Jasper townsite, to be sure, is smaller and more low-key than Banff. You won't find the variety of museums and cultural events that make a rainy day almost welcome in that teeming town. Jasper in the rain is a place to relax, gear down, and psyche yourself back to small-town sensibilities. And that can be challenging.

The good news is that a lot of fine walks in Jasper National Park can be travelled despite a little rain. One strategy is to use an umbrella, which turns into a walking stick if the sun comes out. Some hikers even use umbrellas backpacking, despite supercilious stares from the minimalist crowd.

Stay off of narrow trails where you'll soon be soaked from the wet leaves and grass despite raincoat and boots. An ideal, non-muddy trail to wash away the rainy-day blues is the 2.4-km (1.5-mi) Lake Annette Loop (Walk 76), all on asphalt. Or walk part of the 3.5-km (2.2-mi) Lac Beauvert Loop in rubber boots (Walk 72), and then end up with a hot drink at the Jasper Park Lodge. The first part of Maligne Canyon (see Walk 81) is just as impressive in rain as in sunshine, and you can retreat afterwards to the teahouse for tea, chili or brownies.

ARTS JASPER: In winter, enjoy performances of the Alberta Ballet, Foothills Brass or a variety of other cultural groups held by Arts Jasper. This local arts council sponsors performances between October and March at the Jasper Activity Centre, 303 Pyramid Avenue, (403) 852-3381.

BILLIARDS: Jasper Pizza Place, 402 Connaught Drive, and Mountain Foods & Cafe, 606 Connaught Drive, have billiard tables.

BOOKSTORES: The best place for book-browsing is the gift store in the Jasper Museum and Archives, 400 Pyramid Lake Road. There's an excellent selection of books about Rocky Mountain history, flora and fauna. Open 10 a.m. to 9 p.m. daily, mid-May to Labour Day;

10 a.m. to 5 p.m. until mid-October. (Also see the Friends of Jasper Park sales outlet in the Jasper Information Centre.) Feel like putting your feet up and watching the rain come down? Settle down at Fred's Book Nook, a cozy window-side area in the museum, with donated books and mags to while away the hours. See the 'Museum Musing' listing.

CEMETERY CREEPING: An interesting time can be had at the Jasper cemetery, for people interested in local history. Early headstones tell of deaths by grizzly maulings, and give other evocative hints of what life was like for early settlers. The cemetery is just up the hill on the north side of Hwy. 16 just east of the townsite.

CHILDREN'S PROGRAMS: The Jasper Museum has a discovery nook for children, with a tent featuring Jasper animals, a dress-up area, books and more. See 'Museum Musing' listing. There's also a wading pool for kids and drop-in day-care at the Jasper Aquatic Centre, 401 Pyramid Lake Road, (403) 852-3663.

THE DEN: This museum houses more than 100 stuffed specimens of Rocky Mountain wildlife, from raccoons and golden eagles to grizzlies, set in dioramas depicting their natural habitat. Downstairs in the Whistlers Hotel, 105 Miette Avenue, admission $3. Open daily, 9 a.m. to 10 p.m., (403) 853-3361.

DINING: The L & W Restaurant, on the corner of Hazel Avenue and Patricia Street, (403) 852-4114, is deservedly popular for a tasty lunch or dinner in pleasant, leafy, glassed-in surroundings. The menu includes beef vegetable stew ($6.95), home-made Greek cabbage rolls ($11.25) and lamb souvlaki ($12.95); the pizzas are great. We also like the popular

The Great Hall, Jasper Park Lodge

and reasonably priced fare at Mountain Foods & Cafe, 606 Connaught Drive, (403) 852-4050. Includes yellow split-pea soup and cornbread ($3.25) and the Salmon Rushdie (smoked salmon, lettuce, cream cheese for $5.95). There's also a takeout deli with low-fat crackers, turkey sandwiches, etc. A good place to stock up for a picnic. Scoops and Loops, 504 Patricia Street, (403) 852-4333, has a decade-long following for ice cream, fresh fruit frozen yogurt, flurries, sundaes and milkshakes. There's been an addition in recent years: sushi. The Bear's Paw Bakery, 4 Cedar Avenue, has pleasant wooden tables, fresh baguettes and multigrain breads. Jasper residents swear by Tokyo Tom's, 410 Connaught Drive, (403) 852-3780, for such delicacies as salmon teriyaki ($12.95), sashimi and sushi. Truffles & Trout in the Marketplace on Patricia Street has a following, too. Also see 'Jasper Park Lodge' listing.

FITNESS CENTRE: You can drop in to use the racquetball/squash courts, universal gym and public skating rink for a flat fee at the Jasper Activity Centre, 303 Pyramid Avenue, (403) 852-3663. Weekdays from 8:30 a.m. to 11 p.m.; weekends from 9 a.m. to 11 p.m.

GYM: Try the Jasper Activity Centre, 303 Pyramid Avenue, (403) 852-3381.

HOT SPRINGS: The colder, gloomier and wetter the day, the better for soaking in a natural hot springs! See 'Hot Springs Soak' in 'Outdoor Adventures.' If you don't have your own transportation, call Raven Adventures at (403) 852-4292. They offer a 'rainy-day tour' to Miette.

ICEFIELD CENTRE: The crowds might be smaller on a rainy day, but postpone your trip if it's totally socked in. See 'Outdoor Adventures' and sidebar (page 195).

JASPER PARK LODGE: Lounge where the Guggenheims and Princess Margaret have lounged. Fine hotels are always splendid places to wait out the rain. Drive 7 km (4 mi) east of Jasper townsite to the lodge, or hike via Old Fort Point (Walk 71). A shuttle bus runs at least three times a day in summer months between the lodge and the bus depot downtown in the train station. Call (403) 852-3332. Jasper Park Lodge is not nearly as grand as its baronial counterpart, the Banff Springs Hotel, but it is beautifully set on green Lac Beauvert. The lake has a fine view of Mt. Edith Cavell over the water and is a holder of the hospitality industry's prestigious and rare Five Diamond award. Try people-watching in the main lobby. In Joe Clark's brief tenure as prime minister (1979–80), this hotel seemed on its way to becoming Parliament West. Watch for bellhops carrying drinks on bicycles, a lodge tradition.

The original lodge of felled logs was built by the Canadian National Railway (CNR) in June, 1922. That building burned down in 1952, and

Jasper

most of the original log cabins have been replaced with cedar chalets. Nine are still in use, and are much sought after. The hotel's lobby features carvings, a bison head and huge fireplaces to warm up by on cool evenings. The lower floor is devoted mainly to lavish stores. Have a drink in the Emerald Lounge, with its plush chairs, fireplace and gorgeous lake and mountain views. You can build your own pizza ($12.95) at the Meadows Alpine Cafe in the lodge, or tuck into an Italian buffet. Other eateries include the elegant Edith Cavell Dining Room, a sushi bar and Tent City, which has billiards, pizza and snacks. Call (403) 852-6052 for all lodge dining reservations.

LAUNDRY: What else are rainy days for? Head for Coin Clean, 607 Patricia Street, (403) 852-3852. There are also showers. If you can't stand that musty sleeping bag one more day, the laundromat has washers large enough to handle this challenge.

LIBRARY LOAFING: Occasional author prose and poetry readings are held, usually in winter, in the Jasper Library, 500 Robson Street, (403) 852-3652. Watch the *Jasper Booster* for details. Library hours are Saturday, 10 a.m. to 3 p.m.; Monday to Friday, 12 p.m. to 5 p.m.; evenings, Monday to Thursday, 7 p.m. to 9 p.m. Closed Sundays.

MOTORCOACH TOURS: Although the scenery won't be as fine in the rain, at least you'll be

dry. Brewster runs a number of bus excursions from Jasper townsite. See 'Outdoor Adventures.'

MOVIES: Regular Hollywood fare is screened at the Chaba Theatre at 604 Connaught Drive, (403) 852-4749.

MUSEUM MUSING: The Jasper Museum and Archives, one of the most delightful museums in the Canadian Rockies, houses an array of intriguing memorabilia, a cozy book nook, a discovery room for kids and a mini-amphitheatre with excellent ongoing videos about the park. The main museum is a fascinating collection of such memorabilia as Mt. Alberta's legendary ice axe and 'Sousie the Sousaphone,' which survived the 1952 fire at the Jasper Park Lodge. Cultural displays depict the history of native peoples in the area, immigration patterns, railway history and even Jasper's Hollywood connection. (Yes, Marilyn M. stopped 'em dead here, too.) The archives holds a library of 300 historical books and much more. The adjoining gift shop has offerings that range from Edward Goddal mountain prints for under $10 to fine sterling silver and metal jewelry by Alberta artists ($49 for a bearspaw necklace) to handmade lap quilts by Evelyn Reynar, of Edmonton ($115). Admission by donation. Located at 400 Pyramid Lake Road, (403) 852-3013. Open daily 10 a.m. to 9 p.m. from mid-May to Labour Day; 10 a.m. to 5 p.m. to mid-October; winter hours, Thursday to Sunday, 10 a.m. to 5 p.m.

Miette Hot Springs

RACQUET SPORTS: See 'Fitness Centre' listing.

SHOWERS: When it's showering outside, gritty campers might take the opportunity for a shower inside. Showers provided at Coin Clean, 607 Patricia Street.

SPAS: If you've overdone it on the hiking trail or ski slope, consider pampering yourself at the Jasper Wellness Centre, where registered therapists offer massage, acupressure, reflexology and more. A full spa is available. Open daily in the Sawridge Hotel, (403) 852-3252.

SWIMMING: The Jasper Aquatic Centre, 401 Pyramid Lake Road, (403) 852-3663, has daily public swimming in a 25-m (82-ft) pool, as well as a waterslide, steam room, whirlpool and wading pool for kids.

The whirlpool is popular among skiers on winter weekends and with sore-muscled hikers in summer. Check for times.

TEAHOUSE TRIPPING: Unlike Banff National Park, Jasper has no survivors of the rustic teahouses that were built at the turn of the century by the railway companies. But it can still be cozy to idle away part of a rainy day at the new, cafeteria-style teahouse at Maligne Lake. This better-than-average cafeteria features attractive wood tables, glass windows with splendid views looking out on the lake, and a satisfying menu that includes such fare as green split-pea soup ($3.50), chili ($3.75) and a good assortment of muffins and pastries. Open 8:30 a.m. to 7 p.m. in summer; 9 a.m. to 7 p.m. in spring and fall. Closed in winter.

facing page: Bridge to Pyramid Island

60. Wilcox Pass—*Best Icefields view*

The Wilcox Pass trail provides the most spectacular views around the awesome Columbia Icefield. The trail has almost no tedious stretches and no unrewarding slogging. Although fairly long and containing some steep stretches, it is open and exposed for virtually the entire distance, providing probably the best views of the Athabasca Glacier and elegant, lofty Mt. Athabasca that can be had anywhere, at least from a trail. It's also one of the most rewarding open places to see wildlife such as marmots, moose, bighorn sheep and golden eagles. You also have a slight chance of seeing a grizzly, most likely (and fortunately) at some distance. Bring binoculars.

Map: page 209
Distance: 12 km (7.4 mi) return
Time: 5 hours
Rating: Moderate
Max. elevation: 2377 m (7797 ft)
Elevation gain: 335 m (1099 ft)
Footwear: Light hiking boots
Best season: Mid-July to late September

access

Drive to the Icefield Information Centre, 104 km (64 mi) south of Jasper townsite on the Icefields Parkway (Hwy. 93). The trailhead is 2.5 km (1.6 mi) south of the centre at the entrance to Wilcox Pass Campground, the second campground after the centre. Coming from Lake Louise, the trailhead is 2 km (1.2 mi) north of the Banff-Jasper boundary. The trail starts on the left only a few metres up the road from the highway and campground gates.

The trail climbs steeply at first through an open forest with occasional views back towards Sunwapta Pass as you edge up the slope above the highway. You soon come out on the bare edge of the hillside. From here on up, the views are continuous and always changing.

Directly across the valley is the inspiring pyramid of glacier-clad Mt. Athabasca at 3491 m (11,450 ft), a favourite of experienced mountaineers. Its sides are cut deeply by glacial cirques. Climbers usually ascend from the creek that crosses the glacier tour access road above the Icefield Centre. They travel up over the moraine to the glacier, then right towards the northwest ridge, and then behind the lower peak to the main summit.

Down the valley on your left are yellow-green meadows leading up to Sunwapta Pass and bare Parker Ridge. Below right is the Icefield Centre, amidst a landscape of rock, glaciers and rubble. Above is the Athabasca Glacier itself, and you can see all its famous features from here: the glacial melt lake at the bottom of the toe, the icefall above rising to the snowy heights of the vast Columbia Icefield and Snow Dome behind and to the right. From the cliffs under Snow Dome, the steep Dome Glacier plunges to the barren valley below.

The trail now leads up through delightful alpine meadows, dotted with only a few stunted Engelmann spruce, below the steep ridge of Nigel Peak. Even if strollers go no further, they will have been amply rewarded. A grassy knoll overlooking the valley is a fine spot for a picnic.

The trail moves away from the valley's edge and into the pass, which was named for pioneer explorer Walter Wilcox, who may have been the first non-native person to traverse it. The rock exposed on the hillsides is sandy limestone of the early Paleozoic age. Some of the beds contain marine fossils, such as brachiopods.

You leave behind even the scattered islands of trees. (If you're experiencing any difficulty with the weather, especially with the visibility, turn back now.) Climb to a low rise marked by a cairn and some larger boulders, looking like a

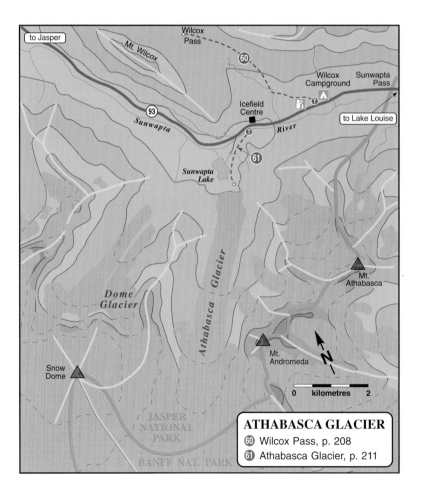

ATHABASCA GLACIER
60 Wilcox Pass, p. 208
61 Athabasca Glacier, p. 211

miniature Stonehenge. This high point, between the ridge of Wilcox Peak on the left and Nigel Peak on the right, might be as far as many strollers wish to go.

From here, the valley ahead is mostly flat for more than 1 km (0.6 mi), dotted with ponds and slow-moving streams. Among them are many distinctive round patches of moss campion, looking like a light green pincushion. The dominant vegetation is closely cropped 'sheep grass.' This valley was once used as the main horse trail between Banff and Jasper, and it was surveyed for the Banff-Jasper highway.

Wilcox Pass terrain

Beyond the high point, the trail is often indistinct in this grassy alpine meadow, although the way is clear in good weather. Ambitious hikers could continue to the end of the pass and follow the cairns down to the trees and the trail that descends Tangle Creek back to the Icefields Parkway (Hwy. 93), for a total distance of about 11.2 km (6.9 mi). If you want to take this option, arrange ahead of time for transportation back to your vehicle.

Most visitors will want to linger in the pass, one of the best places to spot moose, bighorn sheep and ptarmigan in the area, and then return the way they came. This windswept, bare valley seems so remote, such a different world from the teaming Icefield Centre area only a short distance below, where hundreds of thousands of visitors pass by every year. Most will never know the splendours above.

An Alternate Route

Some 90 years ago, the Athabasca Glacier extended right across the valley where the highway now runs. To avoid it and the difficult passage along a deep gully cut by the Sunwapta River, outfitters took the low-level Wilcox Pass and descended again by Tangle Creek on the far side into the Sunwapta Valley from the end of the pass.

history

61. Athabasca Glacier—*An icy approach*

The Athabasca Glacier creeps out of the Columbia Icefield in a dark and gloomy landscape almost overpowering in its immensity. The glacier is a crevasse-ridden river of ice, with mighty wedges at its toe. It is the most accessible glacier in North America. The winds can be cold, so be prepared to bundle up—even in July.

Map: page 209
Distance: 3 km (1.9 mi) return
Time: 1¹/₂ hours
Rating: Moderate
Max. elevation: 1981 m (6498 ft)
Elevation gain: Negligible
Footwear: Light hiking boots
Best season: June to September

access

The Columbia Icefield is 125 km (78 mi) north of Lake Louise and 105 km (65 mi) south of Jasper townsite. Turn west opposite the Icefields Centre. A parking area with an orientation sign is situated just off the highway.

The route follows a paved road through a landscape that looks almost lunar because of the glacial debris created by the Athabasca Glacier. The glacier has been shrinking since the late 1800s; in recent years, the glacier has retreated by at least 5 m (16.4 ft) a year.

Fireweed, purple vetch, small spruce and willow struggle to grow on the outer edges here—these plants are hardy pioneers beginning to establish themselves in inhospitable post-glacial terrain. The growing season is so short that even tiny plants may take years to grow and flower.

Pause to contemplate the stupendous proportions of the landscape. On the far left is the noble head of Mt. Athabasca at 3491 m (11,450 ft). To its right, on the same side of the Athabasca Glacier, Mt. Andromeda soars at 3444 m (11,296 ft). Note the icefall draping down from Andromeda in the foreground. The great tongue of the Athabasca, one of many glaciers emanating from the Columbia Icefield, is flanked on the right by a peaked spur, and behind it is Snow Dome.

The insignificant-looking hump of Snow Dome is actually what is called the 'hydrographic apex' of the continent. Water from it drains three ways: to the Athabasca River, which flows north and northeast to the Mackenzie River and then the Arctic Ocean; to the North Saskatchewan River, which flows to Hudson Bay; and to the Columbia River, which flows to the Pacific. The Dome Glacier spills out below Snow Dome; to its right is Mt. Kitchener.

Just below the Athabasca Glacier is Sunwapta Lake, a meltwater pond created by the glacier. Its levels can change daily, depending on the ice melt.

At a former parking area, the trail crosses a glacial stream and ascends steeply for a short distance through

211

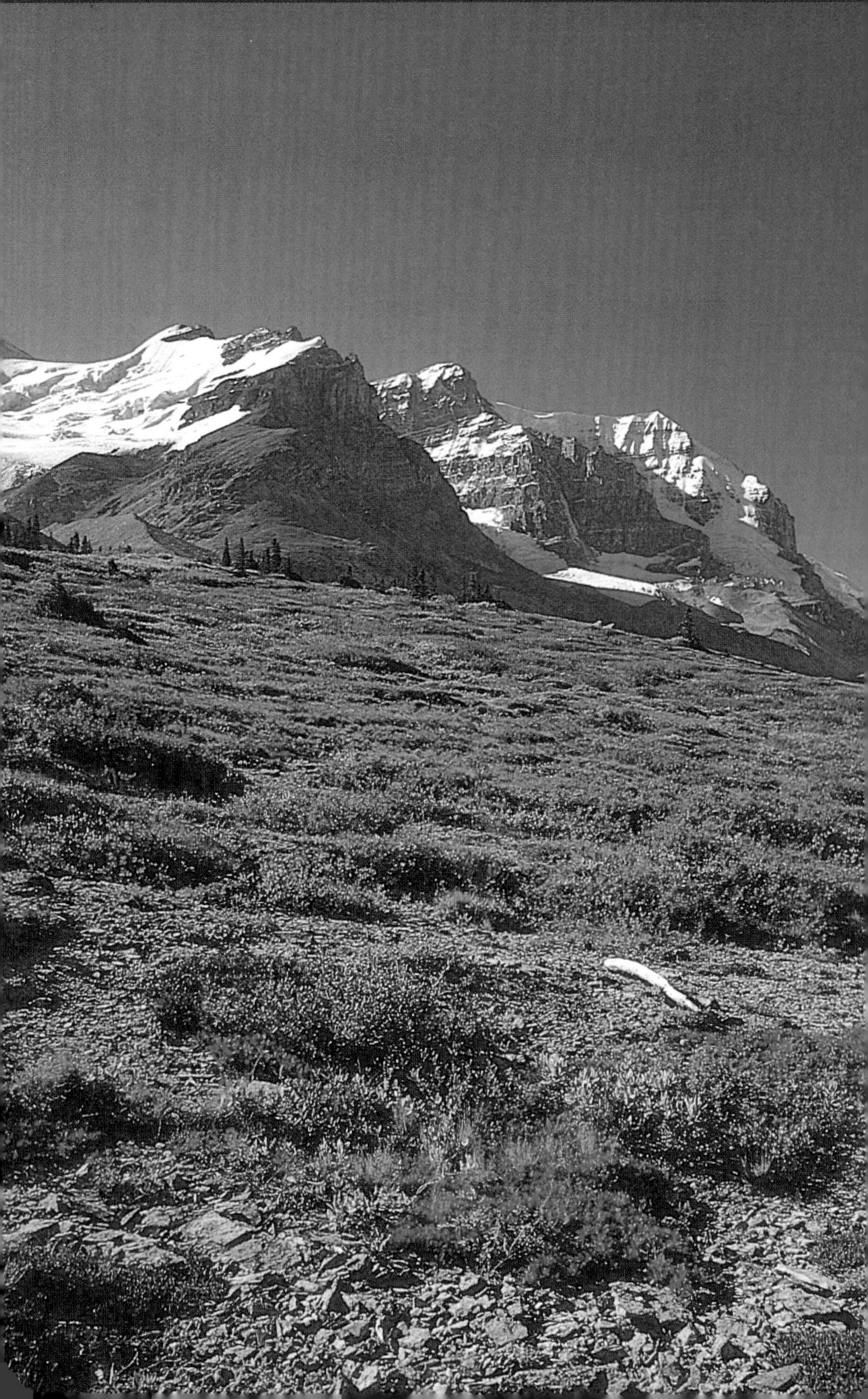

a confusion of moraines deposited as the glacier retreated. A fence—designed to discourage visitors from endangering themselves on the glacier—marks the end of the trail. It has taken the ice about 150 years to move down the Athabasca Glacier to this meltpoint.

This spot is an excellent place to see 'mill wells,' where surface water has cut into fractures on the surface, funnelling water down into the ice. Watch out for 'glacial goop,' which is powdered rock and ice water mixed into quicksand-like patches along the trail.

Look for bits of snow that in summer might be bright red, from red snow algae. The glacier's surface usually appears a dirty-white close up; it's laden with dust particles, not surprising considering its age. But when deep ice is exposed, it glows a beautiful pastel blue. The colour is caused by ice particles in the deep layers, which reflect only blue light.

Danger Ahead

Although you can clamber around on the moraines below the Athabasca Glacier toe for the best vantage point, visitors should absolutely stay off the glacier itself. Some people have died within sight of the trail-end because they climbed up onto the toe, which is laced with deep crevasses. Crevasses might be hidden by a soft layer of snow that gives way when a hiker steps on it. Even experienced climbers sometimes take a wrong step and end up in a crevasse.

Crevasse rescue—assuming that you and your companions are roped, properly equipped and trained—can be difficult, especially if the climber is injured by the fall. Rescuers use a difficult makeshift system involving the climbing rope and 'pulleys' consisting of carabiners anchored by ice screws. Some trapped climbers die of hypothermia before they can be hauled out. If you're not trained and equipped for the required emergency action, stay off.

Frosty Facts

- The average snowfall at the Columbia Icefield is 7 m (23 ft).
- The Columbia Icefield is 325 sq. km (130 sq. mi).
- The whole population of North America could stand on the Columbia Icefield and there would still be room for uninvited guests.
- The original icefield chalet was opened in 1939 by Jack Brewster.
- The ice behind the 'snocoach' turnaround area at the Icefield Centre is deep enough to cover a building 100 storeys high.
- Snowmelt from the Columbia Icefield goes to three oceans: the Atlantic, the Pacific and the Arctic.

facing page: Mt. Athabasca

62. Stanley Falls—*A beauty of a creek*

It is a beauty, a little-known trail that passes eight waterfalls within a couple of kilometres, ending at impressive Stanley Falls. This route is best in late spring or early summer when the water volume in the creek is heaviest.

Map: below
Distance: 6.4 km (4 mi) return
Time: 2 hours
Rating: Moderate
Max. elevation: 1680 m (5510 ft)
Elevation gain: 110 m (361 ft)
Footwear: Walking/running shoes
Best season: June to October

access

If travelling north, look for the trailhead 15.2 km (9.4 mi) north of the Icefields Centre or 5.8 km (3.6 mi) beyond the Stutfield Glacier Viewpoint. If approaching from Jasper townsite, it's 88.5 km (55 mi) south on the Icefields Parkway (Hwy. 93). On the braided, gravel flats of the Sunwapta River, watch carefully on the east side of the highway for two large culverts beside a dike—a man-made strip of land across the flat, wet ground—about 200 m (656 ft) long. A pulloff is beside the dike.

Walk down the dike towards the trees at the far end. This spot is inspiring, with ice-crowned Diadem Peak on Mt. Woolley rising across the valley. Ahead is the steep length of Tangle Ridge and down the valley begins the long, symmetrical slopes of the Endless Chain Ridge. The Sunwapta River has slowed on these valley flats and dumped the gravel and silt it carries, forming numerous braided channels.

At the end of the dike, a path leads through the trees to the former Banff-Jasper highway, its pavement now in ruins, a striking example of what happens when a road is left unmaintained. Turn right along this road to fast-moving Beauty Creek, where a narrow trail leads up the bank.

The trail ascends Beauty Creek, which begins to turn into a limestone gorge. Soon, you come to the first waterfall, the water disappearing through a narrow crack. Although not far from the highway, this area feels wild and remote.

The next falls is more of a cataract, while No. 3 flows impressively into a deep pool that you can walk down to. Along here are a number of potholes in the rock created by the scouring action of the water. The trail leads past No. 4, which drops into a round pool, and

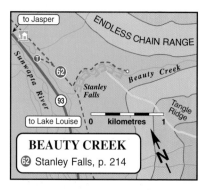

BEAUTY CREEK
62 Stanley Falls, p. 214

No. 5, which has a cascade about 7 m (23 ft) long in a narrow gorge. No. 6 and No. 7 are close together, two waterfalls plunging down into a deep, aquamarine pool.

No. 8 is Stanley Falls, the tallest and most impressive. All the water from Tangle Ridge and the icefields high on the Banff-Jasper boundary plunges through a narrow opening in the rock and thunders down into a large pool.

Beauty Creek

63. Lower Sunwapta Falls

Beyond the turbulent tourists

All summer, tourists by the busload converge daily on Upper Sunwapta Falls, walking only a few metres from the parking lot to the footbridge over the Sunwapta River. Only a minority take the scenic hike down to the lower series of falls. Although these falls may not be any more spectacular than the upper set, they are truly off the beaten path and feel more exciting. Strollers savour them because they have walked a little on a pleasant path to get there. The walker becomes part of the scene, an explorer in a small sense, not just another tourist crowded behind a chain-link fence.

access The turnoff road to Sunwapta Falls is 55 km (34 mi) south of Jasper townsite on the Icefields Parkway (Hwy. 93) and 175 km (109 mi) north of Lake Louise. Drive to the end of the short side road and take the busy trail to the upper falls.

After exploring the upper falls, with its deep canyon and dark roar of water where the river makes an abrupt change of direction, take the well-marked route to the lower falls on the right (north) side of Sunwapta River. Don't confuse this route with the long trail to Fortress Lake across the bridge on the far side of the river.

The trail to the lower falls is soft and wide as it gradually descends within earshot of the river through

Map: below
Distance: 4 km (2.5 mi) return
Time: 1¹/₂ hours
Rating: Moderate
Max. elevation: 1400 m (4592 ft)
Elevation loss: 80 m (262 ft)
Footwear: Walking/running shoes
Best season: May to October

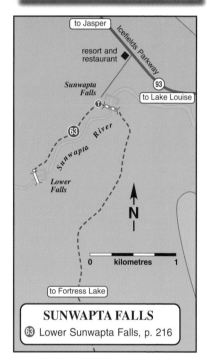

SUNWAPTA FALLS
63 Lower Sunwapta Falls, p. 216

a pleasant forest of lodgepole pine. A view opens up across the river.

Within 30 minutes or so, at about the 2-km (1.2-mi) mark, you reach the lower falls. The water plunges through a narrow gap and over a ledge, creating deep potholes in the rock, and works its way

Lower Sunwapta Falls

down to the more level Athabasca Valley, 1 km (0.6 mi) beyond. A short distance below is another equally impressive falls.

You can truly understand how the river got its name—'Sunwapta' is a native peoples' word meaning 'turbulent water.'

64. Athabasca Falls—*Thunder and mist*

Few visitors to Jasper National Park miss the fabulous sight of Athabasca Falls boiling and foaming, the water plunging 25 m (82 ft) into a narrow gorge. Instead of being content with the first viewpoint, take this short saunter, visit a now-abandoned river channel where the falls used to be, and escape the crowds.

Map: page 219
Length: 1.4 km (0.9 mi) return
Time: 45 minutes
Rating: Easy
Max. elevation: 1173 m (3847 ft)
Elevation gain: Negligible
Footwear: Anything for the first part, sturdy shoes beyond
Best season: May to October

access

Athabasca Falls is 32 km (20 mi) south of Jasper townsite and 198 km (123 mi) north of Lake Louise. It is also the point where Hwy. 93A rejoins the Icefields Parkway (Hwy. 93). Just follow the usually crowded asphalt path to the falls.

Lower canyon at Athabasca Falls

Stop at the first viewpoint, a dramatic spot to enjoy the spectacle of the river plunging into the deep gorge. The river eats away at the underlying quartz sandstone cliffs, gradually moving the falls further upstream. Each year the pounding water cuts the lip back a few millimetres.

Go over the pedestrian bridge and turn left to a second viewpoint on the other side of the falls. Here, you are close to the mouth of the steep canyon. Mist from the thundering falls rises above your head.

Towering Mt. Kerkeslin dominates the landscape to the southeast, and Mt. Fryatt and Mt. Christie are to the south. Look for the unusual angle of Mt. Edith Cavell, to the west.

Turn back to the pedestrian bridge, and continue straight past it through a narrow, abandoned gorge from the days when the water extended much higher than it does today. It can be muddy. In a few minutes, the walker reaches an excellent viewpoint of the canyon, honed and streaked with orange rock. Below is the milky Athabasca

River, its opaque colour a result of the fall's churning action, which stirs up the glacial rock flour in the water.

At the sign, you can descend to the rubble-strewn river. Watch your step here. This dramatic setting is a popular launching place for kayakers shooting Grade III rapids between here and Old Fort Point.

grey jay (whiskey jack)

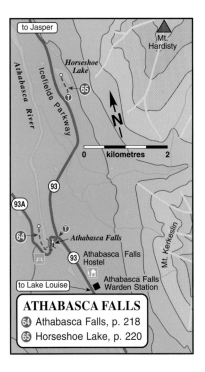

ATHABASCA FALLS

64 Athabasca Falls, p. 218
65 Horseshoe Lake, p. 220

A Cure for Blackflies

Sir James Hector travelled to Athabasca Falls in February, 1859, looking for a way across the mountains. But he had to turn back after his guide, Tekarra, hurt his foot. In 1893, A.P. Coleman, a professor of geology from Toronto, passed through the area looking for Mt. Brown and Mt. Hooker, which were erroneously believed to be the highest in the Rockies. Coleman's journey opened the trail between Sunwapta River and Jasper. At Athabasca Falls, the party sat on a rock overlooking the torrent and 'for a while forgot about slimy muskegs, tormenting blackflies, burnt trees and stifling heat.'

history

65. Horseshoe Lake—*Echoes and ecology*

The short trail to rockbound Horseshoe Lake offers a mini-outing, especially for those who want to stretch their legs after the rigours of parkway driving. The lake is somewhat unusual for this area, a valley-floor basin fringed with rocky outcroppings reminiscent of the Canadian Shield. A mellow afternoon could be lazed away on its rocky shoreline—picnicking, sketching, fishing, taking pictures, or bouncing echoes off Mt. Hardisty.

Map: page 219
Length: 2 km (1.2 mi) return
Time: 45 minutes
Rating: Easy
Max. elevation: 1250 m (4100 ft)
Elevation gain: Negligible
Footwear: Walking/running shoes
Best season: June to September

access

The Horseshoe Lake parking lot is 29 km (18 mi) south of Jasper townsite and 204 km (126 mi) north of Lake Louise, on the east side of the Icefields Parkway (Hwy. 93).

Follow the wide trail, fringed with wildflowers, to the tip of the lake's 'horseshoe.' A network of trails all lead from here to the lake. Perhaps the most scenic approach is to continue across the middle of the 'horseshoe,' and then make your way left to the lake, where the banks drop steeply off into deep water, a good place for casting from shore.

Across Horseshoe Lake are the reddish quartz sandstone slopes of Mt. Hardisty, which was named for Richard Hardisty, chief factor of the Hudson's Bay Company for Edmonton district between 1857–58. The flat, rocky ledges along the lake invite wandering and picnicking—on the rocks, that is. There are no picnic tables. Fishermen report catches of rainbow trout here.

On the return, you might head right along the shore to where the trail curves back into the woods past a huge boulder, where kids could have a good time. You can even walk through it, if you're not the claustrophobic type.

Horseshoe Lake and Mt. Kerkeslin

66. Wabasso Lake—*A modest piece of tranquillity*

Wabasso Lake is no big deal. All you get is tranquillity, meadows filled with flowers, a pretty stream and a green, placid lake, set under the Maligne Range. The access trail is appealing and doesn't involve much climbing.

access

From the Jasper Information Centre, drive 15 km (9.3 mi) south on the Icefields Parkway (Hwy. 93), to a parking area on the left (east) side of the highway.

Map: below
Distance: 6 km (3.7 mi) return
Time: 2 hours
Rating: Moderate
Max. elevation: 1250 m (4100 ft)
Elevation gain: 50 m (164 ft)
Footwear: Walking/running shoes/light hiking boots
Best season: May to October

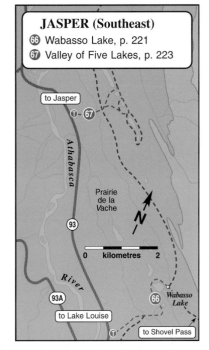

JASPER (Southeast)
66 Wabasso Lake, p. 221
67 Valley of Five Lakes, p. 223

The wide trail, which parallels the highway for a short distance, provides a view of the Athabasca River snaking below, and then turns into the trees, passing rock slabs and climbing over a series of ledges. These woods are the typical, dry montane forest—a retreat for deer, elk and sheep during winter when the subalpine snows become too deep and the climate too harsh.

The lodgepole pine and aspen forest opens up into meadows called Prairie de la Vache (Cow Meadows). The trail crosses a stream that it follows upwards, climbing to a scenic ridge. The footing becomes somewhat rocky, but the trail quickly reaches the lake at about the 3-km (1.9-mi) mark and follows along the west side of this peaceful retreat.

There's a picnic area with fire box (no camping) half-way along. The lake, named for a native peoples' word for 'rabbit,' is reputed to have rainbow and brook trout. Beyond the lake, the trail begins a long

ascent of the ridge to the Skyline Trail, one of the few places in the park where caribou are sometimes seen. Another branch leads to the Valley of the Five Lakes and back to the Jasper townsite.

Most strollers will be content to stay in the valley.

Wabasso Lake

wildlife

The Coyote and His Choir

If you see an animal that looks like an intelligent wild dog, it's likely a coyote. It's not uncommon to see a coyote slinking across a road in the Canadian Rockies, or even, in some places, standing and staring boldly at a parked car. Unlike wolves, they are scavengers and small-animal predators. Capable of running at speeds of up to 50 km (31 mi) an hour, they sometimes group together and adopt complex hunting strategies, such as having one coyote investigate a thicket for hares while the other stands outside, ready to pounce.

Even if you don't see coyotes during your stay in the Rockies, you'll likely hear them howling in the distance at dusk. It's thought that these 'community howling' binges help to reinforce bonds between adult coyotes.

67. Valley of the Five Lakes

Five lakes in one jaunt

For an easy family outing, a tranquil picnic by a woodland lake or fishing, this low-key walk is a gem. It's one of the most accessible near the Jasper townsite. The mostly level trail loops by all five lakes. There are agreeable glades beside the lakes. The first and last lakes can be good for fishing, and rowboats are available for rental. Pick up a key at any Jasper sporting goods store to unlock one of the padlocked boats.

Map: page 221
Length: 6 km (3.7 mi) return
Time: 2¹/₂ hours
Rating: Moderate
Max. elevation: 1100 m (3608 ft)
Elevation gain: 30 m (98 ft)
Footwear: Walking/running shoes/light hiking boots
Best season: May to October

access Drive 11 km (6.8 mi) south of Jasper townsite on the Icefields Parkway (Hwy. 93) to the sign for the Valley of the Five Lakes trail, and turn into the parking area on the left (east) side.

The wide, well-maintained trail winds through an open forest of lodgepole pine with a few aspen trees and scattered patches of wildflowers. There's a boardwalk across a shallow stream dammed by beavers. After a short climb, you reach open meadows (keep straight at the junction) with views back towards the snows of Mt. Edith Cavell and down the wooded Athabasca Valley.

Enter the woods again through a grove of aspen, bright with Micklemas daisies, Indian paintbrushes and goldenrods. Turn left at the junction (follow the sign to the first and second lakes). The route descends steeply to pass between the first and second lakes. The first is the largest, and there are picnic areas along its far side.

After crossing between the two lakes, turn right (the left fork leads back to the Jasper townsite) on a well-graded trail that leads through meadows above the second lake, and then on towards the third and fourth lakes. There's a picnic area and viewpoint on a little peninsula that you'll share with asters, flea-banes, dwarf dogwoods, everlastings and heart-leaved arnicas.

With little gain in elevation, the trail reaches the fifth and last lake where there's a scenic clearing, picnic area and locked rowboats. From the fifth lake, which contains rainbow and brook trout, the trail loops back to pass above the fourth and third lakes with a few ups and downs over rocky knolls. It then rejoins the original route.

Indian paintbrush

68. Path of the Angel Glacier Trail

The splendour of an angel

Few walks in the Canadian Rockies offer such grandeur right from the parking lot. Even a leisurely stroll of a few hundred metres rewards the visitor with a panorama of Mt. Edith Cavell, the devastation of a retreating glacier and the bluish-green splendour of Angel Glacier.

Map: page 226
Distance: 1.6-km (1-mi) loop
Time: 45 minutes
Rating: Easy
Max. elevation: 1768 m (5799 ft)
Elevation gain: 30 m (98 ft)
Footwear: Walking/running shoes
Best season: July to September

access

From the Information Centre in Jasper townsite, drive west on the main street (Connaught), which turns onto the Icefields Parkway (Hwy. 93). Keep going south on 93 for 8.5 km (5.3 mi); then turn right onto 93A. The Edith Cavell Road begins just after a bridge over the Astoria River. The 28 km (17.4 mi) to the trailhead is steep and contains a number of sharp, 180-degree turns at switchbacks. Although it's not difficult to drive in a car, leave trailers at a parking area where the Cavell road begins.

Start climbing up the asphalt path, with views of Mt. Edith Cavell becoming more impressive. The trail leads beside a brook, over a little wooden bridge and across the tumbled boulders of an old moraine. Benches are conveniently placed along the way.

Four hundred years ago, a worldwide cooling trend started a 'little Ice Age' in mountain regions. Glacial ice advanced to the site of the present-day parking lot. More recently, warm weather has caused a retreat. The rubble and debris before you is its legacy.

Glacial melt pond and Angel Glacier

Continue straight at the trail junction (the left turn here leads to the Cavell Meadows [Walk 69]). As the walker progresses over the moraine, Cavell looms ever more imposing above. Photographs are best taken in the morning when the low-angle light gives depth and detail to the glacier and rock wall.

The Angel Glacier—bluish-green with a layer of debris on top—spreads its wings on Cavell's inhospitable face, with waterfalls tumbling below. The forbidding north face, above Angel Glacier, was first climbed in July, 1961, by a party including Yvon Chouinard, the California climber who founded the Patagonia line of outdoor gear. Constantly falling rock inspired Chouinard to call the face 'a shooting gallery.' Thankfully, this walk isn't nearly so hazardous.

The trail leads down past massive boulders to a glacial melt pond, where the air is usually chilly, even in summer. It is an incredible place, the closest and most awesome vantage point to Angel Glacier, a magnificent cirque glacier. Ice breaks over the cliffs to create its 40-m (131-ft) thick wings. The remaining ice plunges down the steep valley, completing its white skirt.

Right across the pond is Cavell Glacier, whose ice feeds the lake. Sometimes ice is shorn away in flat sections, allowing you to see the vertical crevasses of its interior. Each summer, a little more of its toe is nibbled away by a slightly warmer lake, forming icebergs and ice caves.

Follow the trail down along Cavell Creek back towards the parking lot, through an area covered with glacial ice as recently as the 1950s. Life is slowly returning here after the devastation of the glacier. Patches of purple mountain heather and willow shrubs struggle to gain a foothold. Moose find the willow shoots irresistible during the long, cold subalpine winter. Scientists say it will take several hundred years before the valley is completely reforested.

Who Was Edith Cavell?

Edith Louisa Cavell, born December 4, 1865, in Norfolk, England, began her nursing career in a London hospital in 1895. In 1907, she became the first matron of the Berkendael Medical Institute in Brussels, which was later turned into a Red Cross hospital at the outbreak of the First World War.

She began to help wounded French and English soldiers who were first hidden at a chateau near Mons by Prince Reginald de Croy. The soldiers were conveyed to Cavell's house and those of her friends and given supplies to reach the Dutch border. About 200 soldiers found assistance this way.

Cavell was arrested and imprisoned on August 5, 1915, by German forces. She was shot on October 12, despite the efforts of a U.S. government representative in Brussels. 'Patriotism is not enough,' she said as the final sacrament was administered. She never saw the mountain that was named after her.

69. Angel Glacier–Cavell Meadows Loop

Angel spreads its wings

Deep rumbles and sharp cracks break the stillness of spruce and fir as the walker ascends the switched-back trail opposite the cliffs of Mt. Edith Cavell, which might be called the Mt. Fujiyama of Jasper. The sounds are the Angel Glacier 'spreading its wings,' its snow and ice cracking and avalanching down from the heights. From a safe vantage point across the Cavell valley, you can watch these avalanches—terror of climbers—for most of summer, particularly on warm afternoons. In an hour or so, walkers can reach rolling subalpine meadows where stunted, twisted spruce and fir give way to the tundra country and a riot of wildflowers blossom, for a few weeks each summer.

access

From the Information Centre in Jasper townsite, drive west on the main street (Connaught), which turns onto the Icefields Parkway (Hwy. 93). Keep going south on 93 for 8.5 km (5.3 mi); then turn right onto 93A. The Edith Cavell Road begins just after a bridge over the Astoria River. The 28 km (17.4 mi) to the trailhead is steep and contains a number of sharp, 180-degree turns at switchbacks. Although it's not difficult to drive in a car, leave trailers at a parking area where the Cavell road begins. Note that because of lingering snows

Map: below
Distance: 8 km (5 mi) return
Time: 4 hours
Rating: Moderate to strenuous
Max. elevation: 2103 m (6918 ft)
Elevation gain: 335 m (1099 ft)
Footwear: Sturdy shoes/light hiking boots
Best season: Mid-July to September

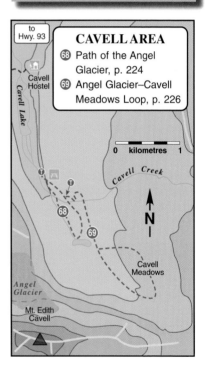

CAVELL AREA

68 Path of the Angel Glacier, p. 224
69 Angel Glacier–Cavell Meadows Loop, p. 226

and wet footing, the high portion of the route in the meadows is usually in poorer condition until at least mid-July.

From the parking area at the end of the road, take the asphalt trail, which leads a few steps up to a ridge that affords views of the Angel Glacier, the forbidding, 1500-m (4920-ft) north wall of Edith Cavell and the desolation of tumbled rock and ice below.

The trail leads along the top of a lateral moraine, the debris pushed to the side—as a plough pushes snow into two lateral ridges—by the glacier that covered this area as recently as 1950. Strengthened by a cooling trend, the ice pushed down the valley as far as the present-day parking lot, carrying with it rock from higher up the mountain. The warming trend since then has reduced the glacier severely.

As you ascend, the glacier views begin to improve. Here are benches

Angel Glacier and Mt. Edith Cavell

for peaceful contemplation of the rocky desolation, punctuated by the blue-green glacial melt pond below. The wings of Angel Glacier come into view.

At a junction and the end of the pavement, take the left branch that switchbacks up the moraine, then climbs slowly behind it, tumbled rocks on one side, deep forest on the other. The route leads up into fragrant, tangled woods of spruce and fir, climbing steadily, at times steeply.

The trees soon begin to open into meadows filled with Indian paintbrush, yellow arnica, golden fleabane and a multi-coloured carpet of heather. The flowers bloom bravely in a growing season that might not last more than a month—not much time to reproduce.

Mt. Edith Cavell is the dominant peak of the area at 3363 m (11,031 ft), and consists of Lower Cambrian and Precambrian quartz sandstone. It was named for the heroic British nurse who was executed for helping prisoners of war escape from the Germans in the First World War (see page 225).

From a viewpoint, the walkers' humble and safer route winds up into timberline meadows of heather where snow lingers into early summer. Across the valley, waterfalls plunge from the black-brown cliffs. On a warm, sunny day, there's no finer place to picnic.

Heed the warning signs, however, and keep to the trails. The damp alpine carpet of flowers, mosses, lichens and small shrubs is far too fragile to stand the footprints of the many who pass this way. In the short growing season, the damage of a single bootprint can take years to disappear.

history

Climbing Edith Cavell

Although the relatively easy west ridge of Mt. Edith Cavell was climbed in 1915, the great north face before you wasn't ascended until July, 1961, when the well-known climbers Yvon Chouinard and Fred Beckey, and cinematographer Dan Doody, established a route. They climbed the ice-covered rocks to the left of the Angel Glacier tongue, besieged by falling ice. Then the three climbed up over the centre portion of the glacier to the rounded buttress just above, and continued more or less straight up. The rock became more difficult as they went, the bombardment of rock fall never letting up. They bivouacked on a small ledge 300 m (984 ft) below the summit and made the top on the second day. 'Never have I felt so happy as that day on the summit with my friends,' said Chouinard.

70. Tramway to Whistlers Summit

Jasper from the summit

The easiest way to reach a barren, fascinating alpine area in the national parks is on the Jasper Tramway, which ascends 973 m (3191 ft) in a few minutes to a tramway building above timberline. The summit of The Whistlers is only a short, although fairly steep, walk from this building, through a vast area of arctic tundra, wildflowers and natural rock gardens. The views open in all directions.

Map: page 230
Distance: 3 km (1.9 mi) return from upper terminal
Time: 1½ hours
Rating: Moderate
Max. elevation: 2464 m (8082 ft)
Elevation gain: 199 m (653 ft)
Footwear: Walking/running shoes/light hiking boots
Best season: July to September

access

From the Information Centre in Jasper townsite, drive west and south for 4 km (2.5 mi) on the Icefields Parkway (Hwy. 93) to The Whistlers Mountain Road. Drive another 4 km (2.5 mi) to the end of the road and the parking lot for the lower terminal. Bus service is also available from Jasper. The tramway is usually open from March until the end of October, although the lofty trail to the summit itself might not be pleasant until the warmer days of summer. Call (403) 852-3093 for gondola schedules.

Many visitors, having passed from the montane through the subalpine to the high alpine zone in seven minutes, will understandably be tempted to go no further than the upper terminal. They're missing a lot; it's almost like the difference between watching a travelogue on television as opposed to travelling yourself. The views improve immensely as

you ascend The Whistlers. What's more, the relatively easy trail allows the walker to experience a true alpine area, something you can't get from a balcony at the terminal's restaurant and gift shop.

The trail to the rounded dome of the summit is well marked, and there are rock stairs in some of the steep places. Although some people will find the ascent steep, every step is worth the effort, even if you don't make it to the top.

Up here, only miniature plants a few centimetres tall can grow. Some take 25 years to flower, so don't spoil it for others by picking them or trampling on them. The most prominent alpine flowers include yellow alpine cinquefoil, white dryas and round moss campion, the last looking like a green pincushion with pink and lavender flowers growing through it.

In several spots, side trails afford closer views in each direction. Be warned that fat ground squirrels and marmots patrol these trails,

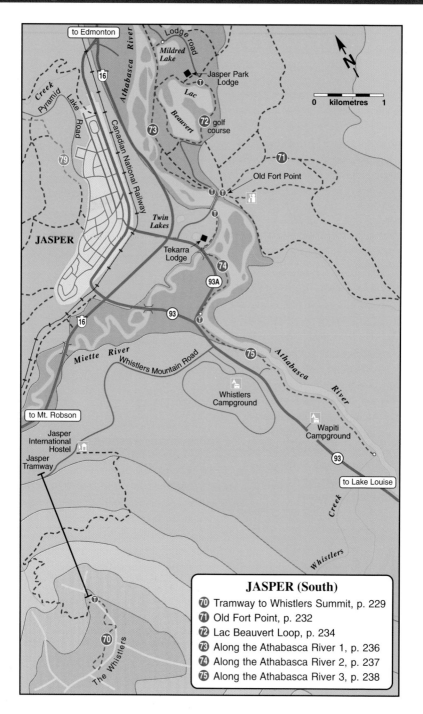

to Edmonton

Mildred Lake

Jasper Park Lodge

Lac Beauvert

golf course

Old Fort Point

Pyramid Lake Road

Creek

Athabasca River

Canadian National Railway

Lodge road

72

73

79

71

16

Twin Lakes

JASPER

Tekarra Lodge

74

93A

16

93

Miette River

Whistlers Mountain Road

75

Athabasca River

Whistlers Campground

Wapiti Campground

93

to Mt. Robson

Jasper International Hostel

Jasper Tramway

to Lake Louise

Whistlers Creek

The Whistlers

70

0 kilometres 1

JASPER (South)
70 Tramway to Whistlers Summit, p. 229
71 Old Fort Point, p. 232
72 Lac Beauvert Loop, p. 234
73 Along the Athabasca River 1, p. 236
74 Along the Athabasca River 2, p. 237
75 Along the Athabasca River 3, p. 238

experts at begging food from the visitor. Don't give in.

The trail climbs steeply, and then levels off briefly before turning right for the final push to the summit of The Whistlers, which was named for the whistling of marmots. (Marmots are much easier to find than the smaller pika. They love to sit upright on rocks when they're not eating, building up a thick layer of fat to carry them through winter hibernation.)

The large summit area is level. There's a log book and direction finder. To the north is Morro Peak, marking the beginning of a long ridge called the Colin Range, which stretches back towards Jasper townsite and culminates in the sawtooth peaks of Hawk and Colin. Closer at hand, to the northeast, is the rounded mass of Signal Mountain, the beginning of the long Maligne Range on which a splendid back-packing trail winds.

South in the direction of the Columbia Icefield are Mt. Kerkeslin, Mt. Christie and Brussels Peak. Turning southwest, you see the imposing mass of Mt. Edith Cavell with its spectacular glacier. In the distance to the west is the white pyramid of Mt. Robson, monarch of the Canadian Rockies at 3953 m (12,966 ft), and usually enveloped in clouds of its own making. Northwest is Monarch Mountain, Snaring Mountain and Pyramid Mountain, the latter built, the locals joke, thousands of years ago by the ancient Egyptians.

Closer at hand, the complexities of the Athabasca and Miette valleys are revealed, and you should be able to spot most of the 50 lakes in the region. Once, two mighty glaciers met near the site of the present-day Jasper townsite, one coming down the valley from the Columbia Icefield, the other from what is now Yellowhead Pass. When the glaciers began to melt, large chunks of ice remained. When this ice melted, it left water-filled depressions in the gravel.

The especially energetic could really experience the mountain by hiking all the way down to the road in a few hours. The 4.5-km (2.8-mi) trail (marked as Trail No. 5) heads down to the upper terminal, and then left to loop down towards the trees, under the tramway, ending near the hostel, 0.9 km (0.6 mi) down the road from the lower terminal. Now that's experiencing a mountain.

Above Jasper townsite and Athabasca River

71. Old Fort Point Trail—*A knobby knoll*

A grassy, glacier-carved knoll, sweeping views of the Athabasca Valley, a pinch of history and a peck of scenery combine to make Old Fort Point a super outing. This stroll is for those who don't care to venture far from the Jasper townsite. The trailhead can be reached by foot from the townsite in about 30 minutes. It's especially appealing in fall, when brilliant yellow aspens are set against deep, green-forested valleys.

Map: page 230
Distance: 6.4 km (4 mi) return
Time: 1 1/2–2 hours
Rating: Moderate
Max. elevation: 1160 m (3805 ft)
Elevation gain: 130 m (426 ft)
Footwear: Walking/running shoes
Best season: June to October

access

From the Jasper Information Centre, turn west on the main street (Connaught). At Hazel Avenue, turn left (south), cross the tracks and Hwy. 16, and continue about 0.7 km (0.4 mi) until the sign for Lac Beauvert Road. Follow the road to the parking lot just beyond the bridge over the Athabasca River. The trail starts up steep wooden stairs to the right of a water kiosk.

The stairs lead to a cairn commemorating fur trader and geographer David Thompson. He and 10 men passed through the area on a hard and wintry trek in 1810–11, which resulted in the discovery of Athabasca Pass and the Columbia River.

Scenic rewards come early—the turquoise Athabasca River bends and oxbows to the south; on a clear day Mt. Edith Cavell gleams prominently to the west. Behind the townsite is distinctive Pyramid Mountain, reddish-orange from its quartz sandstone cliffs.

Follow the trail (signed as Trail No. 1) up a bedrock ridge, with excellent views back to Jasper townsite, to reach a grassy meadow. Nearby shrubs and aspen and spruce groves are excellent grazing terrain for bighorn sheep. The males sport impressive curling horns with distinct rings that indicate their age. Each ring marks one year's growth.

The dirt path, marked with cairns, leads into groves of aspen and pine. Just before the third cairn, climb a high shale bluff for fine views of Jasper Park

ruffed grouse

Trident Range and Athabasca River from Old Fort Point

Lodge, aqua-green Lac Beauvert, Pyramid Mountain and Jasper townsite.

It's said that Mary Schäffer, an early explorer to the Rockies, passed by here in 1908 en route from Maligne Lake. The story goes that she astonished early Jasper resident John Moberly, who hadn't seen a non-native woman around this area for 15 years.

Descend the bluff among juniper, aspen and bearberry. Thrushes and grouse inhabit the aspen groves.

Even off the rib, the woodland walk is delightful. Almost 1 km (0.6 mi) away from the summit, the trail comes to a junction with the route to Valley of the Five Lakes (Walk 67). Keep left for the trail that circles back to the starting point. The trail descends steeply at first and leads back through pleasant woodland.

Of Forts and Fords

No one is really certain how Old Fort Point got its name, because it is unlikely that a structure would have been built on the ridge, which is off the main east/west route for fur traders and has no water. The name might be a corruption of 'Old Ford Point' because there might have been a ford on the river below.

Rocky facts

233

72. Lac Beauvert Loop—*A civilized stroll*

From the elegant, groomed grounds of Jasper Park Lodge, to the tranquil green lake and cool forest around it, to the velvet golf course by the water, this stroll is serene, leisurely and pleasant in almost all weather. The footing is good, grades are minimal, and you can relax afterwards in front of a huge fireplace at the lodge.

Map: page 230
Distance: 3.5-km (2.2-mi) loop
Time: 1 hour
Rating: Moderate
Max. elevation: 1020 m (3346 ft)
Elevation gain: Negligible
Footwear: Walking/running shoes
Best season: May to October

access

From the Information Centre, drive east to Hwy. 16, turn left and continue to the Maligne Lake Road turnoff and bridge at 4 km (2.5 mi) from the centre; then follow the signs right to Jasper Park Lodge. Leave your car in the visitor's parking lot on the left and walk down to the lake. Turn right towards the main lodge building.

The lakeside trail (signed as Trail 4A) leads past the lavish lodge. Right by the water is a concession with boat and bicycle rentals. Continue on an asphalt path with views across the water to The Whistlers and the snowy-layered pyramid of Mt. Edith Cavell. This spot is one of the best places in the evening to photograph the 'alpenglow' effect on Edith Cavell.

Lac Beauvert, which means 'beautiful green lake' in French, is shaped like a horseshoe. The pavement ends just past the lodge, and the trail continues close to the lake through appealing groves of spruce and pine. There are several log rest areas on the edge of the lake with tables and chairs, at once both elegant and rustic, for contemplation of these surroundings. The water is remarkably clear and changes quickly, depending on the sun, cloud and wind, to a variety of peacock-

snowshoe hare

Jasper Park Lodge

greens and green-blues.

The route curves into a cove, briefly rejoins the lodge buildings, then descends to the lake again and crosses the outlet on a wooden bridge. From here, the route becomes a forest path, usually close to the lake, providing views back towards the lodge—a tranquil setting indeed, among patches of Indian paintbrushes, dwarf dogwoods, asters and fleabanes. There are benches close to the shore.

At the end of the lake, the trail connects with the paved road to Old Fort Point (see Walk 71). This end of the lake is a favourite spot for scuba divers, who enjoy the lake's clear waters, although they wear wet suits for protection from the cold.

Stay close to the lake until the trail leads up through the golf course, past an elegant wooden gazebo, and then turns back towards the lodge. Follow the signs and descend again to the lake and a delightful needle-carpeted trail leading back to the lodge.

73. Along the Athabasca River (1)

Sandbars to picnics

This walk leads along the banks of the Athabasca River, past riverside sandbars ideal for picnics or children's play. It connects with the elegant Lac Beauvert route (see Walk 72). It can be made as long or short as the walker wishes—and you never have to retrace your steps.

access

From the Jasper Information Centre, turn west on the main street (Connaught); turn left (south) on Hazel Avenue and continue over the railway tracks. After crossing Hwy. 16, take the first left, heading downhill to the old bridge across the river at Old Fort Point. A parking area is just across the bridge, and the trail starts down by the river.

Map: page 230
Distance: Maximum 5 km (3.1 mi) return
Time: 1¹/₂–2¹/₂ hours
Rating: Moderate
Max. elevation: 1030 m (3378 ft)
Elevation gain: Negligible
Footwear: Walking/running shoes
Best season: May to October

The route (signed as No. 4) is a horse trail that remains close to the river. There are numerous side trails leading off, but you can't go wrong by taking the left riverside branch. Not much grows close to the river, except hardy shrub willow in the sandy soil of the flood plain. The forest further back is typical of the fairly dry montane zone. This trail becomes free of snow earlier in spring than the shaded paths in the forest.

The trail crosses a couple of stream beds that are usually dry, and passes areas along the river where long sandbars have formed. Although the river is fast moving here, it's still considerably slower than the other side of the bridge.

From here to the east end of the park, the valley is wide and almost flat.

Walkers who continue along the riverside trail for about 2.5 km (1.6 mi) will end up on Jasper Park Lodge road by Mildred Lake east of the luxury resort. Return by following the road to the lodge, then take the lakeside trail (Walk 72) and the road back to Old Fort Point.

Athabasca River and the Colin Range

74. Along the Athabasca River (2)

Riverside walk

This unofficial trail along the banks of the Athabasca River is a handy route from Old Fort Point to the cabins and motels south of Jasper townsite along Hwy. 93A. There are views along the fast-moving river and down the Athabasca Valley. The route connects with river trails and scenic hikes on both ends.

Map: page 230
Distance: 2.5 km (1.6 mi) one-way
Time: 45 minutes
Rating: Moderate
Max. elevation: 1040 m (3411 ft)
Elevation gain: Negligible
Footwear: Walking/running shoes
Best season: May to October

access

From the Jasper Information Centre, turn west on the main street (Connaught); turn left (south) on Hazel Avenue and continue over the railway tracks. After crossing Hwy. 16, take the first left, heading downhill to the old bridge across the river at Old Fort Point. A parking area is just across the bridge. The trail, however, starts on the Jasper side of the river, just before the crossing of an old stream bed. The route heads off on the west side of the road.

The trail enters the woods, turns towards the Athabasca River, and then climbs a short, steep ridge with views ahead to The Whistlers and back towards Signal Mountain and rocky Mt. Tekarra. The route crosses a beautiful, high bluff behind Tekarra Lodge, where a sign shows the location of prominent peaks. The view down the forested Athabasca Valley to the pyramid of Mt. Hardisty is especially impressive. Below the bluff, the river steepens into rapids, the last on the Athabasca until it

leaves the park en route to the Arctic Ocean. On the river gravel bars, you'll sometimes see Harlequin ducks, along with more common waterfowl. Moose, elk and mule deer are often seen below, especially in the early morning and evening.

The trail turns onto paved Hwy. 93A, crosses a bridge over the clear Miette River and resumes again 50 m (164 ft) further on the left, leading back to the silt-laden Athabasca. Thousands of years ago, this area was the junction point for two huge glaciers, one coming down what is now the Miette Valley from Yellowhead Pass, the other from the Athabasca Valley to the south. They brought with them huge accumulations of rocks and gravel that make up the 'benches' on which Jasper townsite is situated.

Beyond the bridge, the trail follows the top of an old embankment, 1 m (3.3 ft) or so above water level, finally ending at Hwy. 93A again, opposite Alpine Village near the junction with the Icefields Parkway (Hwy. 93).

75. Along the Athabasca River (3)

A short evening stroll

This little-known trail follows the high banks of the scenic Athabasca River and connects with the vast Wapiti Campground. It is accessible from the larger Whistlers Campground across the highway, plus several commercial bungalow resorts. It's a thoroughly enjoyable early morning, afternoon or evening stroll. There's even a sandy beach, most years at least.

Map: page 230
Distance: 3.5 km (2.2 mi) one-way
Time: 1 hour
Rating: Moderate
Max. elevation: 1060 m (3477 ft)
Elevation gain: 30 m (98 ft)
Footwear: Walking/running shoes
Best season: May to October

access

The trail starts near the intersection of the Icefields Parkway (Hwy. 93) and Hwy. 93A, 3.5 km (2.2 mi) south of the Information Centre in Jasper townsite. The trailhead is just east of Hwy. 93 near the edge of the river. Visitors staying at Wapiti Campground can simply walk down to the river, turn left and follow the route in reverse.

Don't follow the power line, but keep left on the soft trail close to the river. Views are good up the valley towards majestic-looking Mt. Hardisty. The river moves fast here,

with occasional rapids. The trail enters a forest of mostly lodgepole pines, passes a couple of picnic tables at a scenic location overlooking the river, and then runs behind Jasper Bungalows. From there, it descends to what in some years—depending on the shifting sands—is a beautiful sandy area close to the river, perfect for a picnic. Deer and elk can often be seen in these semi-open woods.

The trail climbs the river bank again and passes close to the outdoor theatre at Wapiti Campground. Then it runs more or less straight on the high bank above the fast-moving river, which is laden with glacial silt. To the right are the loops of the vast Wapiti Campground. Whistlers Campground is across the highway, a little closer to Jasper townsite.

After a few ups and downs, the trail reaches a stream at the edge of Wapiti. Most walkers don't bother to go further since the trail gets rough from here on and is blocked not far ahead by Whistlers Creek.

Rafting on the Athabasca River

76. Lake Annette Loop—*Lazy lakeside amble*

The leisurely loop goes around a pretty green lake on an asphalt path that's good in any weather. It's a loop that's almost level, accessible to wheelchairs and easy for all ages. This walk, although not spectacular, offers mountain vistas, a sandy beach with swimming and changing areas, a chance to see elk, coyotes, ravens and grey jays, and even a quicksand bog. Anglers report brook trout here, and the clear lake is popular with scuba divers. The path is off-limits to bicycles.

Map: page 240
Distance: 2.4-km (1.5-mi) loop
Time: 30 minutes to 1 hour
Rating: Easy (wheelchair accessible)
Max. elevation: 1019 m (3342 ft)
Elevation gain: Negligible
Footwear: Anything
Best season: May to October

access From the Jasper Information Centre, drive east on the main street (Connaught) to Hwy. 16, turn left and follow it to the Maligne Lake Road turnoff at 4 km (2.5 mi) from the centre. Cross the bridge over the Athabasca River and turn right to Jasper Park Lodge. The Lake Annette road soon heads off left. The parking lot is about 2.5 km (1.6 mi) further on the right.

You may see red flags on the water indicating scuba-divers below. Divers like the clarity of Lake Annette's water. Visibility in early fall can be as much as 30 m (98 ft), comparable to what you'd expect underwater at a tropical coral reef.

The lake is spring-fed. Close to the shore, the lake bottom is silt-covered and the water is light in colour. Parts of the lake bottom are littered with medium-sized boulders.

Lake Annette

Deeper water looks black because of the heavy vegetation on the bottom.

If you follow the loop trail

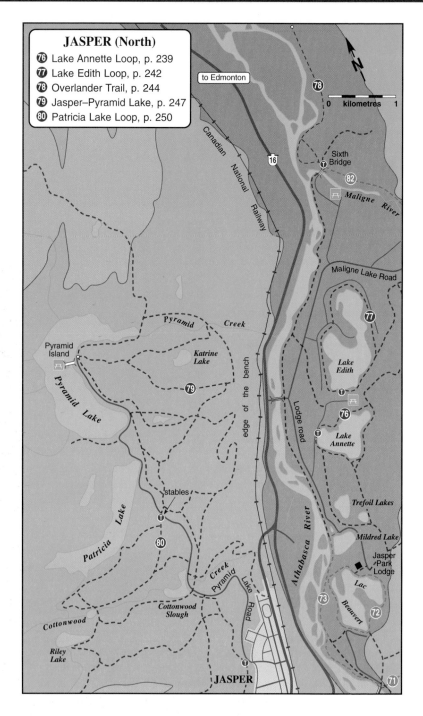

JASPER (North)
76 Lake Annette Loop, p. 239
77 Lake Edith Loop, p. 242
78 Overlander Trail, p. 244
79 Jasper–Pyramid Lake, p. 247
80 Patricia Lake Loop, p. 250

to Edmonton

N

0   kilometres   1

(signed as No. 4D) in a clockwise direction, you soon approach a marshy area on the right, fringed with clusters of goldenrod and rosebushes. Here are well-situated picnic tables and views of the lake.

The trail then opens onto a small, sandy beach. Lake Annette is one of the warmest swimming holes around, although it's still chilly by swimming pool standards. The trail goes by a fenced area of quicksand, which is actually loose silt caused by the constant motion of water flowing out of a spring into light sediment. Park naturalists warn that although the quicksand is not deep, it is deep enough to cause real problems for the unwary.

After the beach, the path ascends slightly and leads through a dry, open montane forest, dominated by white spruce and Douglas-fir, back to the parking lot where you started.

Bull elk

77. Lake Edith Loop

Cabinside and lakeside loop

The loop around Lake Edith near the Jasper townsite is an anomaly among national park routes—it is partly residential. But what residences! Gorgeous old log homes with large stone fireplaces are right on the lake. The trail is a mix of lakeside strolling and woodland walking. It can be done either as a loop around the lake or a short jaunt for a kilometre or two on either side. Lake Edith is also one of the warmest swimming lakes around Jasper. There's a beach at the start and swimming areas at a couple of other spots. The lake is a fairly long walk from the townsite, but it can be reached easily from Jasper Park Lodge. Dogs are not permitted on the beaches and lakeside trails.

Map: page 240
Distance: 4.5-km (2.8-mi) loop
Time: 1½ hours
Rating: Moderate
Max. elevation: 1020 m (3346 ft)
Elevation gain: Negligible
Footwear: Walking/running shoes
Best season: May to October

Lake Edith (left) and Lake Annette

access

From the Information Centre in Jasper townsite, drive east to Hwy. 16. Turn left and continue to the Maligne Lake Road turnoff and bridge at 4 km (2.5 mi) from the centre. Across the bridge, keep right and take the next left. This side road leads past Lake Annette (Walk 76) and ends at a parking lot and well-situated picnic area at the south end of Lake Edith. Walk down to the lake and turn right.

Walk past the swimming area around the end of the lake. There are good views across the lake to the sharp peak of Mt. Colin and the rest of the Colin Range. The lake water is strikingly clear for those accustomed to muddy prairie ponds. You soon reach a paved bike path, and there are more picnic tables on the right.

The route leads onto a traffic-free road that gradually moves away from the lakeside, although there are rough trails closer to the water. Many strollers will want to follow the lake for some distance, and then cut back to the road. Pick your own way; you can't get lost.

The limited-access road soon reaches the first of many graceful, old log homes, which predate park policy restricting such buildings outside of the townsites.

Lake Edith

The stroller can continue around the end of the lake following the road in front of the houses or by staying close to the lake itself. The lakeside route is a public right-of-way. The north end of the lake offers a striking view of snowy Mt. Edith Cavell.

The road on the other side of the lake carries a little residential traffic. A side road leads down to another beach area. Walk down to the lake and follow a trail next to the water. The trail passes a few more homes, crosses the outlet stream on a wooden bridge, and lands you back at the beach area where you started.

78. Overlander Trail
Route of the gold seekers

This modest route, which follows the Maligne and Athabasca rivers downstream for a little way, is used by fishermen seeking rainbow trout, brook trout and pike, by mountain bikers seeking an almost level single-track and by occasional hikers. There's a sense of history along here because this route constituted part of the old Overlander Trail. The trail was used in 1862 by gold seekers from the east searching for their personal El Dorado across the divide in the Cariboo country of British Columbia. The route is pleasant, but not especially scenic.

Map: page 240
Distance: 6 km (3.7 mi) return
Time: 3 hours
Rating: Moderate
Max. elevation: 1030 m (3378 ft)
Elevation gain: Negligible
Footwear: Walking/running shoes/light hiking boots
Best season: May to October

access From the Information Centre in Jasper townsite, drive east to Hwy. 16, turn left and continue until the Maligne Lake Road turnoff and bridge at 4 km (2.5 mi) from the centre. Keep left after the bridge and turn left on the Sixth Bridge road at 6.3 km (3.9 km). Follow the signs for the picnic area. The trail starts at the bridge over the Maligne River.

Beyond the bridge, turn left and follow the narrow river, which moves like an express train. Much of this water came through limestone underground passages from Medicine Lake high in the Maligne Valley. Open meadows and shady groves by the river offer places to linger amid asters, bunchberries and wild roses.

When the Maligne River meets the Athabasca, the trail turns downstream along the bigger river, and then heads more inland, following an old river channel. Strollers who venture further should be aware that some Jasper residents tend to shun this area because it has gained a reputation as a route for grizzly bears.

The route follows meadows and crosses a stream on an old wooden bridge, entering the woods on the far side. You reach a T-junction. The right fork leads back towards Sixth Bridge, passing the wardens' horse corrals.

The left fork continues above the Athabasca to the old farmstead where John Moberly's cabin, built in 1889, was once situated. He was the son of Henry Moberly, factor at Jasper House until 1861. John, like his brother Ewan, homesteaded in the valley until the national park was established. Then they sold their holdings to the government and moved to Grande Cache. From the farmstead, the trail continues higher above the Athabasca past

Athabasca River

Mt. Colin, Mt. Hawk and Mt. Morro, ending at Hwy. 16 just beyond the Athabasca River bridge. The total distance from the Maligne River to the highway is 15 km (9.3 mi).

The trail represents more or less the route of the gold-seeking Overlanders in the 1860s. Gold was discovered in the Fraser River, and as a result some people came west on a long, arduous trail from Fort Garry, near Winnipeg, through Edmonton to finally reach Jasper House, ragged and worn, on their way over the Continental Divide.

OPTION: The far end of the Overlander Trail is also enjoyable for a short stroll underneath grey, steep-walled Mt. Morro. From a parking area 21 km (13 mi) east of Jasper townsite, just past the Athabasca bridge, ascend to an excellent rocky viewpoint above the river and continue for a short distance around the base of Morro, a favourite 'practice' mountain for climbers. You might see mountain goats, but bighorn sheep are more common.

wildlife

The Overlander Bears

Bears have long frequented the area near the Maligne and Athabasca rivers because of natural food sources. For years, garbage from Jasper townsite was dumped into an open landfill across the river, and it became an attraction for the bears. Now the landfill is bear-proof behind an electrified fence, but the bears still remain in the area. Some return to the landfill and poke their black noses through the fence, sniffing the heady aroma. Although the chances of meeting a bear on the trail are slim, it's recommended that hikers make noise, leave their dogs behind and be aware of the bear precautions explained in the book (see page 58). These precautions apply particularly to mountain bikers, who have a greater chance of surprising a bear because of a bike's speedy, silent approach.

grizzly bear

79. Jasper–Pyramid Lake Trail

A bench above the valley

Among all the tangled networks of trails on the wooded bench behind the Jasper townsite, this trail is a favourite. Some of the bench trails, while handy to Jasper, are little more than secluded woodland routes with few views to speak of, except for a pleasant pond at the end. But the Pyramid trail begins right from the townsite and follows the edge of the bench, providing fine views across the Athabasca Valley and down to the townsite. It leads through semi-open meadows and up a rocky ridge, ending at one of the most beautiful picnic areas in Jasper, on an island.

Map: page 240
Distance: 7.2 km (4.5 mi) one-way
Time: 3 hours
Rating: Moderate
Max. elevation: 1320 m (4330 ft)
Elevation gain: 300 m (984 ft)
Footwear: Sturdy shoes/light hiking boots
Best season: May to October

The trail (marked No. 2) edges gradually up the side of the steep hill, climbing above the town. As close as you are to Jasper, this site can be an excellent place to see deer, elk and other game. Views across the valley to Mt.

access

From the Information Centre in Jasper townsite, drive one block east to Cedar Avenue, turn left and keep straight as Cedar turns into Pyramid Avenue. At Pyramid Lake Road, on the upper edge of town, turn left and park opposite the recreation centre. The trail begins on the steep slope.

visitor tips

One-way option

Hikers planning on walking all the way to Pyramid Lake could make arrangements for a ride back to the Jasper townsite. Otherwise, the return trip is long and tiring. A bicycle secured in the woods at the end of Pyramid Lake Road would make for a nearly effortless return. Or get a ride to the end of the road and do the route in reverse.

Pyramid Lake

Hardisty and east to the Colin Range improve as you climb the needle-covered path.

The trail enters the woods, levels off and in 1.8 km (1.1 mi) returns to Pyramid Lake Road at a parking area, an alternate place to begin the route. The trail resumes on the other side, crosses Cottonwood Creek on a footbridge and parallels Pyramid Lake Road for a while—a good area to spot birds such as the northern waterthrush, the Wilson's warbler and the rufous hummingbird.

The trail, here an old road churned up by horses, gradually veers right. At a junction, take Trail No. 2B. Views open up over the whole valley and townsite. Across the valley is rounded Signal Mountain. Behind it is the more craggy Tekarra Mountain, named after an early native guide. To the west is The Whistlers with its aerial tramway.

This route continues along the edge of the bench through beautiful open forest and meadow, offering excellent picnic spots. Ancient Douglas-firs guard the path, survivors of fires that devastated lesser trees. Now you can see right down the Athabasca Valley and up to the snowy heights of Mt. Edith Cavell, the Fujiyama of the Jasper area.

Close at hand, the somewhat confusing terrain in the townsite area comes into focus: Lac Beauvert with Jasper Park Lodge at one end; to its left are Lake Annette and Lake Edith and beyond them the Maligne Valley and the steep Colin Range. The dry, open montane forest below and on the bench constitutes an important winter range for deer, elk and moose. The snowcover is lighter than in the higher subalpine forest so it's easier for grazing animals to dig through the snow for grass and plants.

The trail turns left to skirt a ravine that cuts into the bench, then resumes on the other side without loss of elevation. Eventually, it turns left and plunges into the trees again, reaching a junction. Trail No. 2E will take you more directly back to Trail No. 2 and the Pyramid Lake Road.

Continue on 2B, if you have time. It leads right, into the open again, and then begins to climb a rocky ridge to the left. The way ahead is

Group of Seven Picnic

Pyramid Island, which is reached by a footbridge at the end of the road above Jasper townsite, is an irresistible spot, looking more like a scene from a Tom Thomson painting of the Canadian Shield than part of the Rockies. The island has shady groves, a rustic gazebo-picnic shelter and lots of picnic tables, all of them with stunning views over Pyramid Lake or to the heights of Pyramid Mountain

visitor tips

open, providing views over the wooded bench. At the top is a good viewpoint for Pyramid and Patricia lakes, the latter shaped somewhat like a human foot. Behind is the distinctive quartz sandstone peak of Pyramid Mountain with its microwave tower.

If you are turning back to the Jasper townsite, now is the time to do it. For those going on to Pyramid Lake, the trail descends steeply, ending at the Pyramid look-out fireroad. Turn left on the fireroad and in a few metres you come to the parking area at the end of the Pyramid Lake Road. Below the parking area is the bridge to the picnic area at Pyramid Island.

Moose

Where to See Moose in Jasper

Try Cottonwood Slough just up Pyramid Lake Road on the bench above Jasper townsite. Watch for a stream-crossing, just past the first parking area, and find the slough on the north side of the road. Other moose-watching areas: around Pyramid and Patricia lakes above Cottonwood Slough and on the road into Snaring Campground east of the townsite.

wildlife

80. Patricia Lake Loop
Woodlands and warblers

Here is a woodland stroll near the Jasper townsite to gladden the eye and delight a closet naturalist. The trail loops past Patricia Lake on the wooded bench above Jasper townsite, where moose and elk are sometimes seen and marshes are rich with waterfowl and beavers. The walk is a particular treat in fall when the aspens turn to gold.

Map: page 240
Distance: 4.8 km (3 mi) return
Time: 1–1½ hours
Rating: Moderate
Max. elevation: 1220 m (4002 ft)
Elevation gain: 70 m (230 ft)
Footwear: Walking/running shoes/light hiking boots
Best season: June to October

access

From the Jasper Information Centre, drive east one block to Cedar Avenue. Turn left. Keep straight on Cedar, which turns into Pyramid Avenue and then into Pyramid Lake Road. Follow it for 3.5 km (2.2 mi) to the Pyramid Stables. The parking lot is on the right side of the road. The trail starts at a kiosk in the parking lot.

Begin by ascending a gentle knoll through a mixed forest of jackpine, aspen and occasional isolated Douglas-fir on the trail signed as No. 6. After about 10 minutes, you reach a junction. Keep right and descend to Patricia Lake, which was named for Princess Patricia, the daughter of a former Canadian governor general, the Duke of Connaught. You can walk down to the opaque-green lake for

Patricia Lake and the Trident Range

facing page: Patricia Lake with Pyramid Mountain

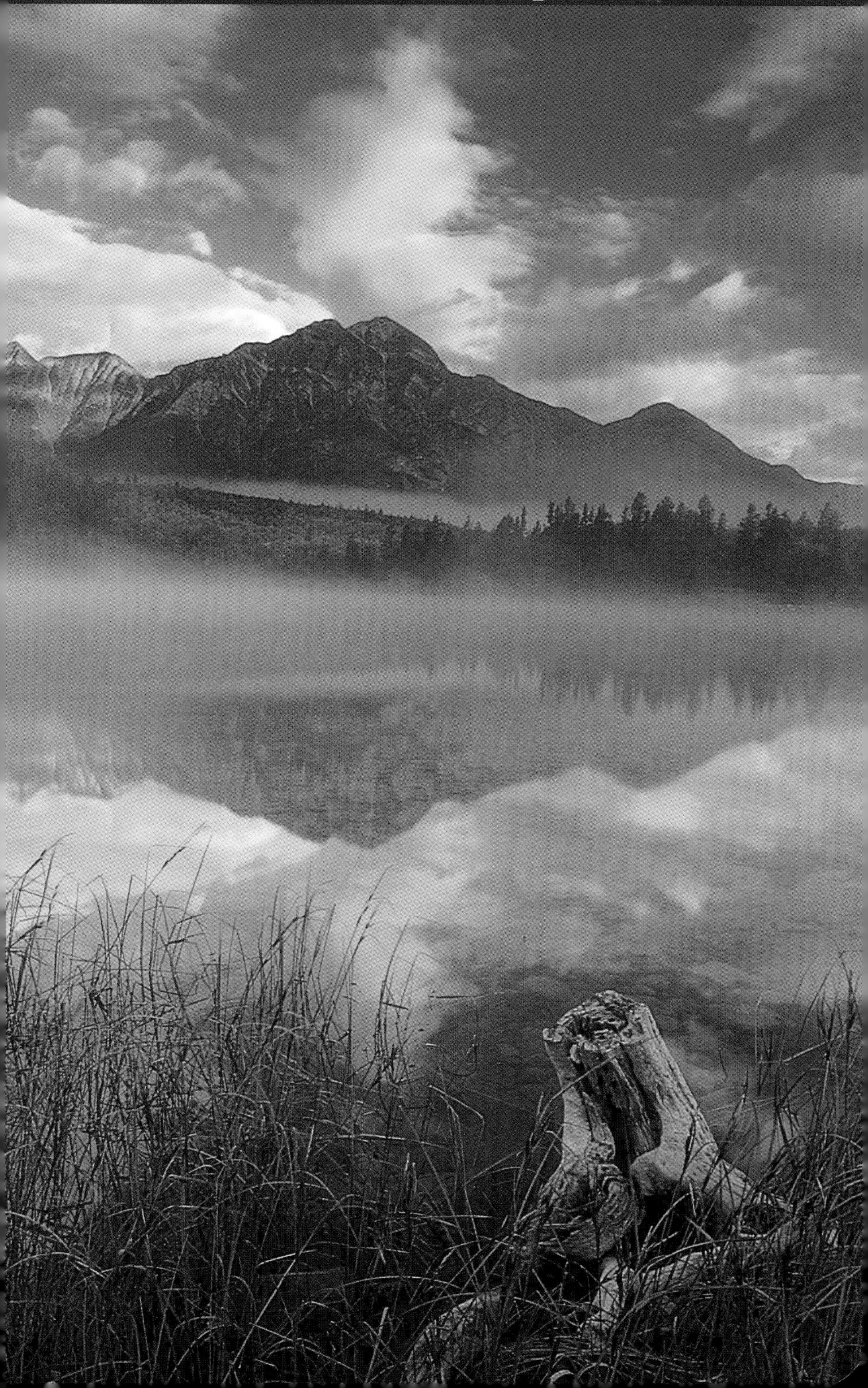

common yellowthroats

views of Pyramid Mountain, a colourful spectacle of mulberry and reddish-quartz sandstone. This 2766-m (9072-ft) mountain was first climbed in 1911 by Conrad Kain, conqueror of Mt. Robson, and George Kinney. Both were early climbers in this area. It isn't a difficult ascent.

A shoreline path leads to the end of the lake, past a green cove. The trail then veers left, away from the lake, over a rustic bridge and down into a small valley along Cottonwood Creek and Cottonwood Slough. This area is popular for birdwatching, with hummingbirds, warblers, yellowthroats and thrushes among summer sightings. Moose can sometimes be seen in the marshy areas in early morning or evening.

Keep left at a junction. The trail continues along the side of a bare bluff with pretty vistas and flat rocks convenient for resting. Stay left at another trail junction, while enjoying the panoramas, before heading into the woods briefly and back to the trailhead.

Dumb Ideas Department

Patricia Lake was used by scientists during the Second World War for some strange schemes indeed. One, called Operation Halakkuk, involved the use of ice for a ship's hull. The ultimate aim was to use ice to construct airfields in the North Atlantic. In Jasper, one structure was built, composed of an ice hull and a wooden superstructure. Before the research could be put to use, however, the war ended.

Conrad Kain

'Ye Gods, Mr. MacCarthy, just look at that; they will never believe we climbed it.' These were the words of the Austrian guide Conrad Kain, upon climbing Mt. Robson in 1913. He conquered the highest peak in the Canadian Rockies in the company of Albert MacCarthy and Bill Foster, an accomplishment deemed especially remarkable because his companions were not experienced alpinists. Kain went on to make dozens of first ascents in the Canadian Rockies. His memoirs are published in his autobiography, *Where the Clouds Can Go*.

history

81. Maligne Canyon Loop

Quick look at the canyon

Pounding water swirls, pummels and shapes Maligne Canyon into a narrow, potholed gorge, as delicate and powerful as a fine work of art. This short loop takes you over and alongside the limestone canyon from its deepest point—where the vertical walls are 30 times the height of a person—to its shallowest point, all in 20 minutes. Although the longer, one-way walk to Fifth Bridge or Sixth Bridge is recommended for those with more time, this walk is short and easy enough for everyone, and no visitor to Jasper should miss it.

Map: below
Distance: 0.8-km (0.5-mi) loop
Time: 20 minutes
Rating: Easy
Max. elevation: 1160 m (3805 ft)
Elevation loss: Negligible
Footwear: Anything
Best season: May to October

access

From the Jasper Information Centre, it's 11.2 km (6.9 mi) to Maligne Canyon. Drive east on the main street (Connaught), and turn left (east) onto Hwy. 16. After 4 km (2.5 mi) from the centre, turn right across the bridge to Maligne Lake Road, which heads up to Maligne Canyon. Begin at the exhibit at the lower end of the vast parking lot.

The walk descends through an open forest on a wide trail, giving little hint of the drama ahead. Suddenly, you reach Second Bridge. Here, the narrow gorge drops 50 m (164 ft)—the deepest part of the canyon. Water-bearing sand and silt swirl against the rock walls. The limestone walls are being worn down by water 0.5 cm (0.2 in) a year, slow by human standards, but a breakneck pace in mountain time.

The steep escarpments provide homes for small creatures, such as bushy-tailed woodrats and field mice. The canyon is also one of the

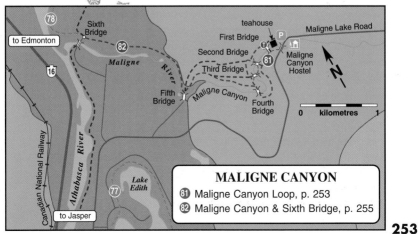

MALIGNE CANYON

81 Maligne Canyon Loop, p. 253
82 Maligne Canyon & Sixth Bridge, p. 255

253

Maligne Canyon from Second Bridge

few places in Alberta where black swifts nest.

At the other end of the bridge, you could turn right and explore further down the canyon (Walk 82). Otherwise, turn left and head gradually uphill along the canyon's edge, which has been securely fenced. A few unfortunates have met their end along here. One visitor apparently tried to jump the canyon—and failed.

Fine views continue up the slope as the steep canyon becomes smaller. Below, ferns and mosses live in the potholes, an ideal damp environment. The trail stays close to the canyon edge to First Bridge, where the drop is 38 m (125 ft). Just above the bridge is a dramatic waterfall. As you near the teahouse, the canyon is only a few feet deep. The rocks contain fossilized remains of marine creatures that lived 350 million years ago. The walk ends at the large teahouse/cafeteria/gift shop.

82. Maligne Canyon to Sixth Bridge

The awesome canyon

Of all the canyon walks in the Rockies, Maligne is the longest and perhaps the most interesting. You could, of course, view the deepest part of the canyon in a short, interpretive loop (Walk 81). But you would miss the wilder lower canyon, which shows how the gorge interacts with plants and animals and provides outlets for a large underground river.

Map: page 253
Distance: 3 km (1.9 mi) one-way
Time: 1¹/₂ hours
Rating: Easy
Max. elevation: 1160 m (3805 ft)
Elevation loss: 130 m (426 ft)
Footwear: Walking/running shoes/light hiking boots
Best season: June to September

access

From the Jasper Information Centre, it's 11.2 km (6.9 mi) to Maligne Canyon. Drive east on the main street (Connaught), and then turn left (east) onto Hwy. 16. After 4 km (2.5 mi) from the centre, turn right across the bridge to Maligne Lake Road, which heads up to Maligne Canyon. Begin this walk by the Maligne Teahouse.

The name 'Maligne' comes from a French word meaning 'bad,' an apparent reference to a wicked ford near the mouth of the Maligne River. On this walk, you need not worry about fords; you have your choice of six bridges.

At the start of this walk, the canyon is only a couple of feet deep, with water flowing over smooth limestone. The rocks contain fossilized remains of marine creatures that lived 350 million years ago. The scalloped canyon quickly deepens. What you are seeing is a continuous sculpturing process that began more than 10,000 years ago, wearing down the limestone 0.5 cm (0.2 in) a year.

At First Bridge, where the canyon is 38 m (125 ft) deep, a thundering 23-m (75-ft) waterfall plumes and boils into the gorge. With this view, you begin to understand the water's force. The water has worn away the softer rock to leave the harder layers

bushy-tailed woodrat

in the shape of a bulb.

In a few minutes, the stroller reaches Second Bridge. The steep escarpments provide homes for small rodents, such as bushy-tailed woodrats and field mice. Ravens have built nests here to escape egg-stealers. At Third Bridge, cross into a damp, misty environment on the right side of the canyon. After this point, there are no more safety barriers or asphalt, and the walk feels more adventurous. The path (signed as No. 7) continues close to the canyon, by a waterfall, to Fourth Bridge.

You soon approach one of the large seepages of Medicine Lake. Water takes at least 70 minutes, and often several days, to flow 15 km (9.3 mi) through a series of underground channels in the limestone from Medicine Lake to the lower canyon. The increase in water volume as you go from the top of the canyon to Fifth and Sixth bridges is a direct result of the springs. It is the most obvious early in the season and in fall.

At a junction, walkers who have had enough can turn left and cross the Maligne River at Fifth Bridge. A road leads from the bridge back to Maligne Lake Road. Otherwise, continue straight for Sixth Bridge, where the path suddenly veers into a shady, dewy forest that can be boggy. The trail ends at Sixth Bridge where there are nicely situated picnic tables by the Maligne River.

geology

A Wicked River and a Bad Lake

Where did all that water come from? That's a natural question for walkers along Maligne Canyon who see the river swell from a few feet at the mouth of the canyon to a wide river at its lower end.

The answer won't meet the eye, but it's one of Jasper's most fascinating geological phenomena. Medicine Lake, 15 km (9.3 mi) above the bottom of the canyon, acts like a sink without a plug, draining water into what is believed to be one of the biggest inaccessible cave networks anywhere.

In fall and winter, Medicine Lake literally disappears, leaving a soggy clay basin. Native peoples called the vanishing lake 'Bad Medicine.'

The lake has long fascinated residents. One park warden once went so far as to dump two truckloads of *Saturday Evening Posts* into Medicine Lake to see where the water went. The results were messy and inconclusive. It wasn't until 1956 that a French scientist, Jean Corbel, first identified a sinking river. Later, researchers from McMaster University used fluorescent dyes to determine where the water went and to prove the physical characteristics of the underground complex.

If the underground passages keep enlarging, scientists say that one day the underground system could handle all the water flowing into the Medicine Lake basin.

83. Summit Lakes—*Limestone valley*

A wide path leads gently up a narrow valley between steep limestone ranges, reaching two lakes within a few kilometres. Although the name Summit Lakes has the sound of alpine grandeur, the reality is more modest. For casual walkers, it should be enough.

Map: below
Distance: 9.6 km (6 mi) return
Time: 4 hours
Rating: Moderate
Max. elevation: 1530 m (5018 ft)
Elevation gain: 90 m (295 ft)
Footwear: Light hiking boots
Best season: June to September

access | From the Jasper Information Centre, drive east to Hwy. 16. Turn left and follow the highway to Maligne Lake Road at 4 km (2.5 mi) from the centre. Keep left towards Maligne Lake. The trailhead is at 31.7 km (19.7 mi), at the far end of Medicine Lake, by the parking lot for a picnic area.

From the parking area, the trail parallels Beaver Creek on a dirt road, and passes a vehicle barrier, a cabin and corral before starting a gradual climb up the gentle, wooded valley. Beaver Lake, a secluded woodland pond, is reached in 1.5 km (0.9 mi).

The trail continues past the lake and soon begins to level off as you attain the first Summit Lake, nestled between the grey, steeply tilted Queen Elizabeth (right) and Colin (left) ranges. These rocks contain traces of marine life from 600 million years ago, when seas covered everything and the mountains were not yet formed.

There's a grassy clearing at the lake's end. Note that although this clearing is at the lower end, there's no outlet into Beaver Creek. Like

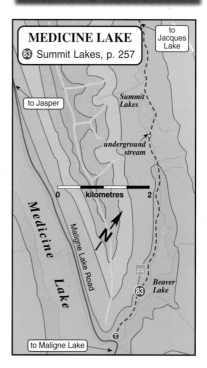

Medicine Lake below, Summit Lake has underground passages in the limestone that connect its drainage to the vast subterranean system hereabouts.

The main path leads through the forest to the right of the lake. The second Summit Lake is not far ahead. The trail continues for about 6 km (3.7 mi) to Jacques Lake. That makes for a long day hike, however, and most will find the Summit Lakes just as interesting.

First Summit Lake

84. Maligne Lakeside Loop

Trail of the legendary lake

This short, popular loop goes down the shore of Maligne Lake, largest in the Canadian Rockies and surely one of the most beautiful. An excellent family stroll. Finish up with a snack at the adjacent teahouse, which has one of the Rockies' best cafeterias.

Map: below
Distance: 3.2-km (2-mi) loop
Time: 1–1½ hours
Rating: Easy
Max. elevation: 1700 m (5576 ft)
Elevation gain: Negligible
Footwear: Walking/running shoes/light hiking boots
Best season: June to September

access

Maligne Lake is 48 km (30 mi) from Jasper townsite. From the Jasper Information Centre, drive east on the main street (Connaught), turn left onto Hwy. 16 and then cross the Maligne Lake Road bridge at 4 km (2.5 mi) from the centre. Turn left after the bridge and continue up the valley to the lake. Park on the east side of the lake and teahouse. The trail begins by the lake, just in front of the boathouse.

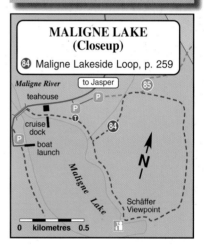

MALIGNE LAKE
(Closeup)

84 Maligne Lakeside Loop, p. 259

Maligne River   to Jasper   85
teahouse   P
P
cruise   T
dock   84
P
boat launch
N
Maligne Lake
Schäffer Viewpoint
0   kilometres   0.5

Walk down the asphalt trail along the lake, keeping on the lower path, past a rustic boathouse built in 1926. Rowboats, canoes and motorboats may be rented here. Or you can take a guided cruise down the lake to the Narrows and Spirit Island, one of the most photographed sights in the Rockies. Mt. Charlton, at 3209 m (10,526 ft), and Mt. Unwin, at 3270 m (10,726 ft), soar in the south, both part of the Queen Elizabeth Range. H.R. Charlton was the general advertising agent for the Grand Trunk Pacific Railway. Locally, these two mountains are called 'the sweater girl.'

To the left is a forest of lodgepole pine, identified by their long needles, mixed with a few short-needled Engelmann spruce. Lodgepole pine covers most of the lower Maligne Valley.

The easy asphalt path leads past some of the most beautifully situated picnic tables in Jasper. It then narrows to dirt, offering only glimpses of the lake through the trees. Moose, elk and mule deer are frequently seen, and the upper alpine meadows of the Maligne Valley are the southern-most grazing grounds in the Canadian Rockies for caribou. The Maligne Valley is said to be home to more than 60 species of birds, including American dippers.

Walkers who are tempted to wade in the lake on a hot day will quickly discover that even in summer it never warms up—the surface temperature rarely exceeds 11° C (52° F). At a stunning overlook with benches, you could retrace your steps back along the lake, or continue on the loop trail.

The loop trail continues past a peaceful, clear green cove popular with fly fishermen after trout. The record rainbow trout for Alberta was caught in Maligne in 1980 and weighed just over 9 kg (20 lb). At the end of the cove, keep straight, heading inland from the lake, traversing an area of meadows and small pines with views of reddish-brown Opal Peak, named by Mary Schäffer.

Ascending through an open forest of lodgepole pine, the trail reaches an open meadow filled with low mounds. These are 'kames,' formed by rock and gravel that were washed into depressions in the glaciers that once covered this area. When the ice melted, the debris was deposited in

Mt. Charlton and Mt. Unwin from Maligne Lake

these mounds. They are the opposite of kettles.

The trail soon leads past a 'kettle.' These bowl-shaped holes in the earth were caused by huge blocks of ice breaking off from a glacier. When the ice melted, it left a kettle-shaped hole.

American dipper

Mary Schäffer's Magnificent Lake

Early in this century, when non-native women were a rarity in this part of the Canadian Rockies, Mary Schäffer, a feisty Philadelphia widow who spent her summers in the Rockies, heard Stoney natives speak of a mysterious lake.

Schäffer—whose Quaker background emphasized equality between the sexes—resolved to find it. She set off in 1908 from what is now Lake Louise with 22 horses, six riders and a dog named Muggins.

The party searched for three weeks before discovering beautiful Maligne Lake. Schäffer, who named several of the peaks in this area after members of her party, thus became the first non-native woman to set eyes on the legendary lake. She returned for further explorations in 1911.

'There burst upon us that which all in our little company agreed was the finest view any of us had ever beheld in the Rockies,' she wrote of her approach on the south side. The successful expedition even had a romantic ending—Schäffer later married her guide, Billy Warren.

history

85. Opal Hills Loop—*A hidden alpine valley*

You round a corner and there, hidden from sight until the very end, is an open valley of lush alpine meadows, bright flowers and deep gullies high above Maligne Lake. All you have to do to reach this Shangri-La is ... sweat. The access trail is relentlessly steep.

access

From the Jasper Information Centre, drive east to Hwy. 16. Turn left and follow the highway to the turnoff for Maligne Lake Road at 4 km (2.5 mi) from the centre. Keep left after crossing the bridge and follow the road to Maligne Lake at 48 km (30 mi). The trail begins from the upper side of the upper parking lot.

Map: below
Distance: 8-km (5-mi) loop
Time: 4 hours
Rating: Strenuous
Max. elevation: 1985 m (6511 ft)
Elevation gain: 305 m (1000 ft)
Footwear: Light hiking boots
Best season: July to September

The trail connects with a path from the lake and leads through a meadow filled with 'kames.' These are low mounds formed by rock and gravel that were washed into depressions in the glaciers that once covered this area. When the ice melted, the debris was deposited in these mounds. The

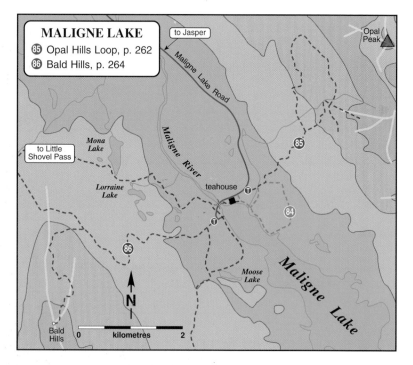

MALIGNE LAKE
85 Opal Hills Loop, p. 262
86 Bald Hills, p. 264

to Jasper

Opal Peak

Maligne Lake Road

to Little Shovel Pass

Mona Lake

Maligne River

85

Lorraine Lake

teahouse

84

86

Moose Lake

Maligne Lake

N

Bald Hills

0   kilometres   2

meadows are a good place to spot moose or caribou.

The trail then climbs steeply through a lodgepole pine forest, levels off slightly and passes a trail junction. Follow the sign and keep left, because this route represents the easier ascent.

The climbing grows easier as the route edges along the hillside, and the forest opens up into meadows filled with wildflowers and shrubs. Views begin to appear back across the valley to Bald Hills and the Maligne Range, and you can just make out the end of Maligne Lake.

The best is yet to come as you go round a corner with the Bald Hills opening up before you, green at the base and brown along the top of the ridge. Below, only a few scattered islands of Engelmann spruce and subalpine fir survive. Only by growing together in clumps can these trees withstand the wind. The hills are cut by deep gullies and to the right is Opal Peak, so named because of its pink patches. Up there, snow patches usually linger into August.

The trail turns right to wind back through a delightful valley, home of ground squirrels and marmots. This open country is an excellent place to spot elk and moose or even an occasional wolverine, a solitary, frightening-looking member of the weasel family about the size of a bear cub and notorious as a vicious fighter. It eats almost everything, from roots and berries to small mammals and birds. But it will stay clear of hikers.

At the end of the valley, the trail crosses a gully and climbs the other side. Here, an unofficial trail leads left farther up the hills for those inclined to exploration. The main trail turns right along the top of the gully. Views open to Maligne Lake and its surrounding peaks. Down the lake, on the far side, the dominating peaks are Mt. Unwin and Mt. Charlton.

Closer to this end of the lake, the Maligne Range is more gently rounded, hospitable enough to allow a fine backpacking trail—the Skyline—to traverse much of its length back towards Jasper townsite. Take the first descending trail leading back into the trees. The descent is steep until you reach the trail junction (sign) where you began the loop.

Opal Peak above Maligne Lake boathouse

86. Bald Hills—*Fireroad walk to stunning views*

This fireroad walk leads to what is probably the finest view of Maligne Lake. Although views are limited on the way up, wildflowers fringe the path in summer. Pick a clear day and plan to ramble on the subalpine meadows.

Map: page 262
Distance: 10 km (6.2 mi) return
Time: 3¹/₂–4 hours
Rating: Moderate
Max. elevation: 2170 m (7118 ft)
Elevation gain: 490 m (1607 ft)
Footwear: Walking/running shoes
Best season: June to September

access

Maligne Lake is 48 km (30 mi) from Jasper townsite. From the Jasper Information Centre, drive east to Hwy. 16, turn left and proceed to the Maligne Lake Road bridge at 4 km (2.5 mi) from the centre. Cross the bridge and continue up the valley to the lake. At Maligne Lake, follow the main road over the Maligne River to a parking lot. The signed trailhead starts just right of the sign for the warden station.

The road winds gently upwards, and then, in the quirky way of mountain routes, alternately levels off and becomes steep. To the northeast, the light grey limestone Queen Elizabeth Range rises against the skyline. The range is composed of Devonian limestone more than 300 million years old.

After about 30 minutes, views open to the east to reveal the Opal Hills. Mt. Unwin, named by Mary Schäffer for one of her guides, soars dramatically on the right side of the lake at 3270 m (10,726 ft). You soon leave lower subalpine terrain for the peak-rimmed, open meadows of timberline. Watch for feather

mosses, grouseberries and heathers.

The trail ends at a high viewpoint, once the site of a forest lookout tower. If the weather cooperates, this area can be a fine place to picnic, to explore the alpine meadows above or just to enjoy the panorama.

Maligne Lake, 22.4 km (14 mi) long, is dazzling in the distance, a milky emerald-and-aqua gem surrounded by jagged peaks. Prominent across the lake is Leah Peak on the left and Samson Peak on the right. The latter is named after the Stoney man whom Schäffer met in what is now Banff National Park. He drew a map showing her how to reach the lake. She became the first non-native woman to see it.

caribou

Bald Hills above Maligne Lake

The Caribou Connection

Caribou are like some people we know: they like to be on the move. The subspecies of caribou found in the Rockies is usually seen in open alpine areas in summer and in the woods in winter. These graceful members of the deer family, with their distinctive creamy throats, are rarely sedentary. They are excellent swimmers and climbers. They also possess hooves that can act like snow shovels in winter, when they have to dig for food, and like snowshoes when they have to traverse large areas. The Columbia Icefield area, Maligne Lake, Medicine Lake and some parts of the Icefields Parkway (Hwy. 93) are possible places to see caribou. They are fairly rare, so consider yourself lucky if you do spot these lovely creatures.

wildlife

87. Miette Hot Springs Trail

Source of the sulphur

The stroll takes only about 30 minutes, but this little trail behind the old Miette hot pool takes you up a narrow, interesting valley past unique rocks that look like huge, grey sponges and are formed only in areas of hot springs. Beyond the rocks, the paved path crosses to where one of the hot springs issues from the side of the mountain. Most of the route is wheelchair accessible.

Map: below
Distance: 1.5 km (0.9 mi) return
Time: 30 minutes
Rating: Easy
Max. elevation: 1378 m (4520 ft)
Elevation gain: Negligible
Footwear: Anything
Best season: May to October

access

The Miette Hot Springs road is 42 km (26 mi) east of Jasper townsite on Hwy. 16. Drive the Miette road for 17 km (11 mi) to the end. The route starts at the end of the parking area below the hot pools.

Follow the paved road, now closed to vehicles, up Sulphur Creek, past large rocks of tufa (pronounced TOO-fa), composed mostly of calcium precipitates and found primarily at the outlets to hot springs. This spring water has a high calcium content, about 366 parts per million, while sulphur

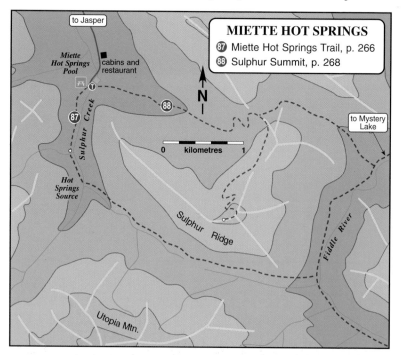

to Jasper

Miette
Hot Springs
Pool

cabins and
restaurant

Sulphur Creek

87

88

N

MIETTE HOT SPRINGS
87 Miette Hot Springs Trail, p. 266
88 Sulphur Summit, p. 268

to Mystery
Lake

0   kilometres   1

Hot
Springs
Source

Sulphur Ridge

Fiddle River

Utopia Mtn.

Miette Hot Springs

runs up to about 1085 part per million, enough to create a considerable odour.

Centuries ago, the outlet to these springs was much higher on the mountainside. As the hot, calcium-laden water cooled at the surface, it no longer could retain all the minerals. So the calcium precipitated and built up as the solid, Swiss-cheese sort of rock called tufa. Eventually, some of this tufa broke off and tumbled down into the creek bed.

The route climbs a ramp and enters the evocative ruins of the original Miette Aquacourt, which was open from 1938–84. Ahead is the source of one of Miette's four hot springs, rushing from a hole in the rock wall. The sulphur smell of rotten eggs is strong, but everybody lingers long enough to put their hand into the water to feel its temperature. There are four springs with a flow of about 568,000 L (124,960 gal) a day. The average temperature of this water is 53° C (127° F), making the Miette hot springs among the warmest in Canada.

Sometimes, when earthquakes have occurred elsewhere in North America, these hot springs have gushed black, murky water into the pools. Trappers and fur traders ventured up this creek in the late 1800s and apparently built circular bath pools along here to relieve their tired muscles.

What is Tufa?

Tufa is a form of limestone found near the outlets of hot springs. Water from rain and snowmelt is drawn by gravity down through the folded and funnelled rock layers. Underground, it dissolves calcite from the limestone it passes through. Where the water emerges from the ground again, some of the calcite is released and deposited in nearby plants and rocks, creating new limestone from old.

geology

88. Sulphur Summit—*Summit of adventure*

The Sulphur Summit hike is the outstanding route in the Miette area. From the barren summit of Sulphur Mountain, the wild peaks stretch back to the horizon like ocean waves. Although the climb to the rounded top of Sulphur Ridge is steep and fairly long, the reward for your exertions is great indeed. Walkers also have the treat of soaking in the hot springs at the bottom of the trail after their toil.

Map: page 266
Distance: 9.5 km (5.9 mi) return
Time: 5 hours
Rating: Strenuous
Max. elevation: 2062 m (6763 ft)
Elevation gain: 692 m (2270 ft)
Footwear: Light hiking boots
Best season: July to September

access

The Miette Hot Springs road is 42 km (26 mi) east of Jasper on Hwy. 16. Drive the Miette road for 17 km (11 mi) to the end. The trail starts on an old road to the right of the hot springs pool.

The road enters the trees and climbs gradually, passing a horse trail on the left. Ahead to the left are the steep rock slabs of an unnamed ridge, where goats are often seen, while the less dramatic Sulphur Ridge rises on the right. At 2.4 km (1.5 mi), turn right at a junction. The trail straight ahead follows the Fiddle River for 8 km (5 mi) to Mystery Lake. To the right, the Sulphur Mountain trail switchbacks steeply up the ridge into the subalpine zone through stunted firs and Engelmann spruce and then into a world of steep rock and scree.

The trail levels off briefly in a col that offers the trees and hikers protection from the wind. It then climbs the steep ridge to the right. Now you can begin to see over the other side to the steep, remote Fiddle River Valley where few hikers ever venture. You pass the treeline and, partway up the ridge, come across a large, white quartz rock, which looks like an imposing tombstone. This rock is probably a glacial erratic, carried here long ago by the ice and deposited far from its place of origin.

The trail climbs steeply to the cairn marking the top of the ridge, a few steps from the bare, rocky Sulphur Summit. Views are spectacular over to Utopia Mountain to the south and to the craggy tops of Ashlar Ridge above the Miette access road.

This ridge is part of the true alpine zone. Notice how almost all the vegetation in this zone of high winds and loose rocks has anchored itself in cracks or in the shelter of boulders. An exception is moss campion, which has such a low profile and wide base that it can hold on where other plants are blown away. Up here, the growing season for plants may be less than 60 days a year and frost may descend any day of summer.

Sulphur Summit

Rocks of the Fiddle Valley

The rocks of the Fiddle Valley are formed from layers of sediments 135 million to 570 million years old. During that time, shorelines and sea levels shifted frequently, and so did the nature of the sediments being deposited. Limestone formed from the remains of plants and animals that accumulated on the bottom of the warm, shallow seas.

geology

Kananaskis

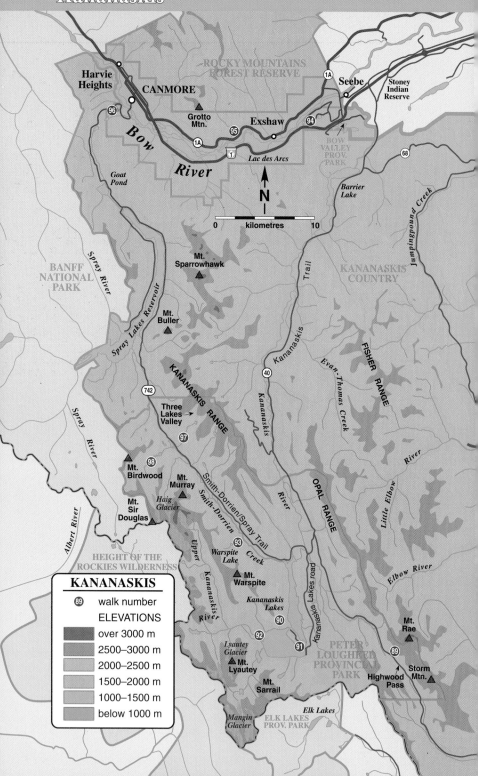

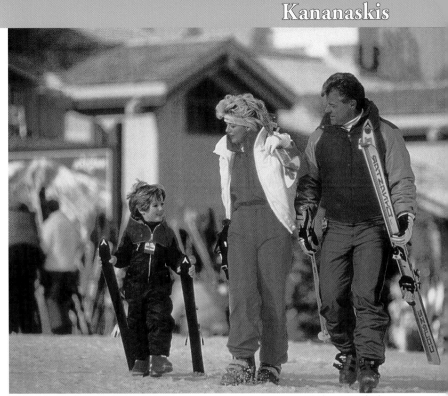

Skiers at Nakiska

CHAPTER 5

KANANASKIS COUNTRY

Kananaskis Country is a huge Rocky Mountain recreation area that encompasses breathtaking alpine scenery, rolling foothills and montane forests, the beautiful Kananaskis Valley and well-designed facilities, which rarely get in the way of the natural beauty. This land of peaks and foothills, 90 km (56 mi) southwest of Calgary and only 60 km (37 mi) southeast of Banff National Park, has something memorable to offer almost everyone.

We're puzzled by the lukewarm attention this area receives in many other guides to the Canadian Rockies. Some books suggest that the scenery is less spectacular (arguable); others focus on the lack of facilities (we think that the ones provided are excellent and sufficient—we certainly don't miss the fudgeries and T-shirt shops). It's true that Kananaskis Country is not set up as a major tour bus destination, that accommodation is limited, and that if your 'sport' is shopping,

271

Kananaskis Village

you'll be disappointed. The general pace of Kananaskis Country is more relaxed than in adjoining Banff, the camping facilities are varied and luxurious by comparison, and accommodation is not a problem for those who plan ahead. The range of recreational opportunities is outstanding for all ages and abilities, including for the elderly and the handicapped. Many Albertans prefer to holiday in this area instead of the national parks because of its less frenzied and less commercial atmosphere. Kananaskis Country is visited by one to two million people annually. The majority of visitors are from Calgary, although people do visit from around the world.

Kananaskis Country is composed of 4250 sq. km (1700 sq. mi) divided into eight zones, with various uses permitted. These zones mean that the term 'multi-use' doesn't have to strike terror into the heart of the fervent hiker or cross-country skier—for example, mechanized vehicles such as trail bikes are confined to selected areas. The boundaries of the area include four provincial parks: Bow Valley, Bragg Creek, Elbow/Sheep Wildland and Peter Lougheed. The latter is the largest provincial park in Alberta and is spectacularly situated high in the Kananaskis Valley.

Because Kananaskis Country was developed during the oil boom of the 1970s, more recently than the national parks in the Canadian Rockies, it is better designed in some ways. (In fairness, it is also under fewer growth and visitation pressures.) The Kananaskis Valley area is the site of most visitor facilities, including Mt. Kidd, a 229-site campground complete with hot tubs; Kananaskis Village, with world-class facilities, including a range of accommodation and dining; a 36-hole golf course; and William Watson Lodge in Peter Lougheed Provincial Park, which offers accommodation and many recreational/educational opportunities for the handicapped.

Wildlife viewing in Kananaskis Country is superb, owing partly to the high elevations in Peter Lougheed Provincial Park. You may see moose, mountain goats and even flying squirrels. These high elevations also mean that you can often reach the alpine area easily in a day hike. With 41 trout-stocked lakes, hundreds of kilometres of hiking and biking trails and abundant lakes and whitewater, Kananaskis Country offers a wide variety of choices in outdoor pursuits. If auto-touring is your preference, the Kananaskis Trail (Hwy. 40) cuts through the stunning Kananaskis Valley and climbs over Highwood Pass, the highest paved road in Canada.

Most visitors either stay in the campgrounds (be warned that campground facilities fill up early in summer months) or in Canmore, a thriving sports- and arts-oriented community of 9000. Bed and breakfast accommodation is a popular choice for many visitors. Mt. Engadine Lodge, a European-style lodge, also gets good reviews. Two budget options are the Alpine Club of Canada Clubhouse near Canmore and the Ribbon Creek Hostel near Kananaskis Village. See 'Sources' (page 386). South of the Trans-Canada Highway, groceries are available at several places,

including Kananaskis Village, Mt. Kidd, Fortress Junction and the Boulton Creek Trading Post in Peter Lougheed Provincial Park.

To explore Kananaskis, you'll need your own vehicle, or you could rent one. Note that the Kananaskis Trail (Hwy. 40) is closed beyond the Kananaskis Lakes turnoff to Highwood Junction from December 1 until June 15.

The Barrier Lake Visitor Centre, located at the entrance to Kananaskis Country on Hwy. 40, is a good stop to orient yourself and pick up maps, brochures and books. (If you time your visit right, you might be able to get Ruth Oltmann, the author of several books on Kananaskis and Rocky Mountain history, to sign one of her books. She works as a travel advisor here.) In Peter Lougheed Provincial Park, there is also a visitor centre, 4 km (2.5 mi) from the Hwy. 40 turnoff.

Outdoor Adventures

ALPINE COURSES AND ROCK CLIMBING: Yamnuska Inc. Mountain School offers a complete package of skiing, mountain leadership skills and survival courses, with accommodation, meals and technical equipment provided. The school, (403) 678-4164, has a well-established reputation for safety and excellent instruction, often from climbers who have scaled the world's highest peaks. The M & W Guides Office, (403) 678-2642, also offers a variety of courses, including 'Rock Tots,' an alpine course for children as young as four years who love to climb.

BICYCLING: Kananaskis is extremely popular with mountain bikers. For those on road bikes, the extra-wide Kananaskis Trail (Hwy. 40) is superb for bicycle travel. Families will enjoy a network of asphalt trails that weave between campgrounds in Peter Lougheed Provincial Park; a pleasant path also leads from Kananaskis Village to Wedge Pond. See chapter 7 (page 348).

BIRDWATCHING: The Bow Valley and the Kananaskis Valley are the site of twice-yearly, mass migrations of golden eagles. As many as 6000 fly through the valleys around mid-March and mid-October.

CANMORE NORDIC CENTRE: The Canmore Nordic Centre is Alberta's most comprehensive cross-country facility. The site of Nordic skiing and biathlon events during the 1988 Winter Olympics, it offers more than 27 km (17 mi) of challenging new trails and a cedar-beamed lodge with skylights, a fireplace and a buffet-style cafe, with a salad bar, snacks, BBQ chicken, etc. The centre is also a major hub for mountain biking. See chapter 7 for more details on skiing and mountain biking. The Nordic Centre, about 100 km (62 mi) west of Calgary, is 1.8 km (1.1 mi) south of Canmore on the Smith-Dorrien/Spray Trail (Hwy. 742). Open daily year-round; a fee is charged for skiing. Call (403) 678-2400.

The carefully designed network of ski trails allows racers to reach speeds of over 80 km/h (50 mph) on downhill sections. Recreational skiers can choose their own more comfortable pace. Another 10 km (6.2 mi) of scenic trails link the Nordic Centre with the town of Canmore and lead west to the Banff National Park boundary. In summer, you can hike, ride a mountain bike or picnic along these same trails.

CHILDREN'S PROGRAMS: Ask at the visitor centres for information on children's programs, or check with your campground attendant.

COVERED WAGON RIDES: Step back in time on a covered wagon trip through Kananaskis Country. You'll travel on roads closed to motorized vehicles, and enjoy a chance to fish and hike. The trips are family-oriented. Call (403) 933-3599.

DRIVES: The drive on the Kananaskis Trail (Hwy. 40) up the Kananaskis Valley from the Barrier Lake Visitor Centre to Highwood Pass makes a fine excursion, with plenty of spots of interest along the way. At the pass, stretch your legs on Walk 89, Ptarmigan Cirque. (Kananaskis Trail is closed above Peter Lougheed Provincial Park from December 1 to June 15.) Another classic loop is to drive on the Kananaskis Trail (Hwy. 40) to

Peter Lougheed Provincial Park, then turn right onto Kananaskis Lakes road and then right again on the Smith-Dorrien/Spray Trail (Hwy. 742) at the bottom of the hill. It takes you through some fine valleys and along Spray Lakes before descending steeply to Canmore. Return to Hwy. 40 on 1A, which is slower-paced than the Trans-Canada.

FISHING: See chapter 7 (page 358).

GOLF: The Kananaskis Country Golf Course, planned by world-renowned golf course designer Robert Trent Jones, offers 36 holes of golf under the towering mass of Mt. Kidd. Jones is said to have called it 'the finest location I have ever seen for a golf course.' There's also a large clubhouse, lounge, spike bar, Pro Shop, club and power-cart rentals. For easy handicapping, each hole can be played from four different tees. *Golf Digest* called the Mt. Kidd and Mt. Lorette courses two of North America's top five. Call (403) 591-7272; Calgary direct, (403) 261-4653; Edmonton direct, (403) 463-4653. Canmore also has an 18-hole course, (403) 678-4784, and the new Silver Tip course is scheduled to open in 1999 near Canmore, on the north side of the Trans-Canada Highway.

GUIDED HIKES: Inquire at the Barrier Lake or Peter Lougheed visitor centres about interpretive hikes that are offered most weekends in July and August (usually Sunday at

Upper Kananaskis Lake

2 p.m.). Back of Beyond, (403) 678-6606, also offers interpretive day hikes and mountain-hut adventures in summer and cross-country ski (including moonlit) and snowshoe trips in winter.

HANDICAPPED FACILITIES: William Watson Lodge in Peter Lougheed Provincial Park offers outstanding facilities for the physically disabled and for seniors. There are wheelchair-accessible trails; Mt. Lorette Fishing Ponds is also wheelchair accessible. See 'William Watson Lodge' listing.

HISTORIC WALKING TOUR: Ask at the Canmore/Kananaskis Chamber of Commerce, #12, 801 8th Street, for the booklet, *Historic*

Walking Tour of Canmore. This excellent brochure will guide you past 12 historic buildings, including the Ralph Connor United Church, the Canmore Hotel (the second oldest operating hotel in Alberta) and the home of the former manager of Canmore Mines.

HORSEBACK RIDING: Numerous guest ranches in the region offer organized trail rides on 200 km (124 mi) of equestrian trails. Boundary Ranch, (403) 591-7171, offers a one-hour lodgepole loop as well as ridge rides with BBQ steak and rafting. Brewster Mountain Pack Trains operates pack trips of varying lengths in scenic foothills and mountain terrain. Brewster's well-known Kananaskis Guest Ranch, (403) 673-3737, is the base for the trips.

IN-LINE SKATING: You can rent in-line skates and other sports equipment at Kananaskis Village. The paved bike trails at Ribbon Creek and Peter Lougheed Provincial Park have short hills and thrills.

MOUNTAIN BIKING: See chapter 7 (page 351).

RAFTING: Kananaskis Country is a popular spot for whitewater rafting. See chapter 7 (page 372).

SKATING: There's skating on ponds at Kananaskis Village and at Allen Bill Pond in the Elbow Valley.

SKIING (CROSS-COUNTRY AND DOWNHILL): The cross-country skiing in Kananaskis is unbelievable and can last into April. Downhillers, note there is on-hill accommodation at Fortress Mountain. See chapter 7 (pages 363–372) for more information on both downhill and cross-country skiing.

SPORTS EQUIPMENT: You can rent sports equipment from in-line skates to croquet sets at Kananaskis Village (Village Centre).

SWIMMING: Kids and tough adults swim in the Barrier Lake reservoir. There's a wading pool for children at Mt. Kidd.

On the trail in Kananaskis Country

TEEPEE TIME: For a different kind of camping experience, consider Sundance Lodges, which offers accommodation in heated teepees and trappers' tents. The tents and teepees have wooden floors and wood-framed beds with foam mattresses. Call (403) 591-7122.

TENNIS: There are courts at Mt. Kidd and at Kananaskis Village. See listings.

TOBOGGANING: Enjoy thrills and spills on a banked run, right next to Kananaskis Village. Night lighting. Rentals are available.

Indoor and Rainy-Day Guide

BOOKS: The Alpine Club of Canada and the Kananaskis visitor centres now sell books. See 'Sources.' Mountainside Books, #106, 721 8th Street, Canmore, has a good selection of mountain history and other books. Call (403) 678-4482.

CANMORE EXCURSION: The historic coal-mining town of Canmore, 25 km (15.5 mi) east of Banff townsite, is the commercial hub for Kananaskis Country, even though it is situated on its northwest corner. In recent years, the community has flourished as a kind of 'Alberta Aspen,' with more resident potters, artists and writers per square block than probably any other community in the province. Head here for historic walking tours, gallery viewing, pub crawling and a choice of eateries, described in the following listings.

CHILDREN'S PROGRAMS: Ask at the visitor centres for information on children's programs, or check with your campground attendant.

COLONEL'S CABIN: This provincial historic site on the Kananaskis Trail (Hwy. 40) in the Kananaskis Valley dates back to the Second World War when it was part of a prisoners-of-war camp. The guard tower has also been preserved. Open 10 a.m. to 4 p.m. on summer weekends.

DINING OUT: Boulton Creek Trading Post in Peter Lougheed Provincial Park offers full meals, pizza, a children's menu, homemade desserts, cappuccino, etc., in a glassed-in licensed restaurant and patio. Breakfast fare ranges from a toasted bagel and cheese ($3.29) to a cheddar cheese omelet ($5.99); dinners include sautéed veggie stir-fry ($7.99) or chicken mushroom alfredo ($8.90). (Some hikers like to stroll up Mt. Indefatigable before breakfasting here.) There's also ice cream plus a gourmet pantry with smoked salmon, jellies, etc., for improving on that picnic; open May to mid-October. Call (403) 591-7678.

For fancier dining, Mt. Engadine Lodge on the Smith-Dorrien/Spray Trail (Hwy. 742) serves a set-menu dinner with European cuisine at

6 p.m.; reservations are required 48 hours in advance, (403) 678-4080.

Kananaskis Village has a variety of restaurants: L'Escapade with its trademark flaming desserts and the Peaks Dining Room with its Sunday brunch; call (403) 591-7711, ext. 52 for reservations for either restaurant. There is also dining at Rafter Six Ranch Resort, (403) 673-3622, and the Kananaskis Guest Ranch, (403) 678-0755, on Hwy. 1X.

Being budget-minded, we've been happy with pizza and salad at Obsessions; the total bill, for two with coffee, was about $20. Fortress Mountain, 30 minutes from Kananaskis Village, has a restaurant that is open daily; Sunday brunch is served in July and August, (403) 591-7108. At Deadman's Flats, the Grizzly Bar & Restaurant serves a traditional special breakfast ($3.99). In Canmore, there's a buffet-style cafeteria at the Canmore Nordic Centre, (403) 678-2400. A long-time favourite is the popular Canmore Hotel, with its cafe, patio and bar, 738 Main Street, (403) 678-5181. The Sherwood House, 838 8th Street, (403) 678-5211, also has a long and devoted following; pizza by the slice and beer by the jug is sold downstairs daily from 12 p.m. to midnight. The Canmore Rose & Crown, 749 Railway Avenue, (403) 678-5168, serves traditional English meals, including steak, kidney pie and shepherd's pie.

For lighter fare, try the Rocky Mountain Bagel Co., 830 8th Street, (403) 678-9968. A hiker's/skier's lunch is $5.95. For picnic fare, head for The Railway Cafe (formerly Nutters), a bulk and natural foods store that also serves 100 plus varieties of vegetarian sandwiches; corner of Main Street and Railway Avenue, (403) 678-3335. See 'Night Life' listing for pubs.

DINNER THEATRE: Chateau Canmore offers gourmet dinner and theatre packages in summer; reservations are required, (403) 678-0801.

ELDERHOSTEL PROGRAMS: Elderhostel Canada operates a wide range of educational experiences and adventure programs, based in the Kananaskis Inn at Kananaskis Village. A typical package includes five nights at the inn; subjects range from the history of the Kananaskis Valley to art in the Rockies. Call (403) 591-7500; see 'Sources' for Internet listing.

GALLERY GAZING: Canmore is beloved by artists and craftspersons. One of the best galleries is the Stonecrop Studio, located at 8th Street and 8th Avenue. Call (403) 678-4151. The Mountain Avens Galley, 709 Main Street, features a variety of local crafts. Call (403) 678-4471. In Kananaskis, the shops in the Lodge in Kananaskis Village offer good gallery gazing.

HOT TUB IT: In luxurious Mt. Kidd RV Park, you can soak in a jacuzzi while looking through huge windows at the mountain scenery. Cost of the hot tub is included in camping fees; if you are not camping, you can still soak in the tubs by paying a small fee. Saunas, whirlpools and showers at Village Centre in Kananaskis Village are also open to the public; $2 per person/shower, $3 includes lock/towel.

KANANASKIS VILLAGE: Billed as a resort for all seasons, Kananaskis Village features three resort lodges, from deluxe to mid-range. The Village is conveniently located by Naskiska, site of the 1988 Winter Olympic downhill skiing events. The Lodge at Kananaskis Village has modern alpine architecture, 255 guest suites and luxuries ranging from an aerobics room to saunas and a 'shabu shabu' bar. The 70-room Hotel Kananaskis is a luxurious manor-style hotel. The Kananaskis Inn contains 96 guest suites, many with sleeping lofts and kitchenettes.

You'll find a variety of eateries here, from deli to French cuisine. The central reservation number is 1-800-332-1013 (toll-free in Alberta only); toll-free in Canada, 1-800-661-1064.

LAUNDRY: Head for the Mt. Kidd RV Park, where your laundry can churn as you walk along a river trail.

MT. KIDD RV PARK: The amenities at the Camper's Centre include tennis courts, a large, glassed-in hot tub area with mountain views, saunas, lots of hot showers (no quarter is required), satellite hookups, a games room, lounge and fast-food counter. If the evening is

cool or rainy, you can retreat to a large lounge with a fireplace and have your sandwiches or burgers there. Open year-round; 229 campsites. Reservations are recommended in July and August, (403) 591-7700.

MOUNTAIN LECTURES, LORE, READINGS: St. Michael's Hall, 709 7th Street in Canmore, is the site of occasional lectures on summer nights, with high-profile speakers such as Brian Patton, author of *The Canadian Rockies Trail Guide.* Call the Canmore/Kananaskis Chamber of Commerce at (403) 678-4094.

MUSEUMS:

The Canmore Centennial Museum, 907 7th Avenue, depicts Canmore's history through its coal-mining days; it also houses one of Alberta's largest collections of historical dolls. Open daily from 12 p.m. to 4 p.m. Admission by donation. Call (403) 678-2462.

The North-West Mounted Police Barracks, 8th Street and 5th Avenue, Canmore. This refurbished 1893 building is enhanced with circa 1920s furniture and police artifacts. There is also a tea room with home baking and a gift shop. Open Thursday to Tuesday from 10 a.m. to 5 p.m., (403) 678-1955.

NATURE PROGRAMS: How did Kananaskis get its name? Why do some parts of Peter Lougheed

Provincial Park receive so much snow and others so little? Inquire at the Barrier Lake or the Peter Lougheed visitor centres about interpretive programs, or ask your campground attendant. Some guided hikes are also available. (Interpretive programs are also held in the Mt. Kidd amphitheatre; the one-hour programs start at 8 p.m.)

NIGHT LIFE: For upscale entertainment, head for Kananaskis Village with its well-appointed lounges, etc. At Fortress Mountain Resort, the restaurant doubles as a freestyle lounge in the evenings, with a pool table, drinks and a big-screen TV with nightly movies. Call (403) 591-7108. In Canmore, check out the popular Rose & Crown pub, 749 Railway Avenue, and The Sherwood House, 838 8th Street. The Grizzly Pub, 622 Main Street, (403) 678-9983, calls itself the only brew pub in the Canadian Rockies; try Rutting Elk Red Ale and Beaver Tail Raspberry Ale.

PETER LOUGHEED VISITOR CENTRE: You'll find displays about the geological, natural and human history of Kananaskis. Park information staff are on hand to answer questions. There's a pleasant lounge for shelter on a cold day or for relaxation after a hike or ski. The centre is located in Peter Lougheed Provincial Park, 4 km (2.5 mi) from the Kananaskis Trail (Hwy. 40) turnoff.

SHOWERS: Non-guests can use the coin-operated showers in the campgrounds. There are also showers available at Bighorn Store & Hotel in Deadman's Flats (you can rent a towel, and purchase soap and conditioner).

TEAHOUSE TRIPPING: Mt. Engadine Lodge, on the Smith-Dorrien/Spray Trail (Hwy. 742) at the Mt. Shark turnoff, serves afternoon tea from 12 p.m. to 5 p.m. daily, from mid-June to Canadian Thanksgiving; Thursday to Sunday only, December to mid-April. Call (403) 678-4080.

WILLIAM WATSON LODGE: The purpose of this lodge is to ensure that Kananaskis Country is accessible to persons with disabilities. Overlooking Lower Kananaskis Lake, the well-designed lodge and cabins minimize natural and structural hindrances to people who need barrier-free access. There's a huge deck, fireplace, dining area and library in the main lodge, which is available for day-use groups by advance reservation. There are also eight cabins, some with fireplaces, and a barrier-free campground. The facility is intended for the disabled and also for Albertans over 65. Open year-round; there is also accommodation available for friends or family members. Rates are from $25 a night for a one-bedroom with a fireplace. Call (403) 591-7227.

facing page: Chester Lake

89. Ptarmigan Cirque—*Easy route to alpine*

Because this steep but relatively short interpretive trail starts right at Highwood Pass just below treeline at 2206 m (7236 ft), it is one of the easiest routes in the Rockies to spectacular alpine glories. Take a wildflower book and a camera.

access

The trail starts from the Highwood Meadows parking area at Highwood Pass, 17 km (11 mi) south of the north winter gates in Peter Lougheed Provincial Park on the Kananaskis Trail (Hwy. 40). The highway through Highwood Pass is only open between June 15 and December 1.

Map: below
Distance: 5 km (3.1 mi) return
Time: 1¹/₂–3 hours
Rating: Short but strenuous
Max. elevation: 2438 m (7997 ft)
Elevation gain: 230 m (754 ft)
Footwear: Light hiking boots
Best season: Early July to early August (when most wildflowers are blooming)

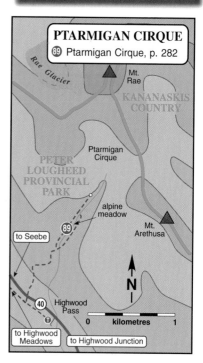

PTARMIGAN CIRQUE
89 Ptarmigan Cirque, p. 282

The route parallels the highway and then crosses the road and switchbacks up steeply through a semi-open forest of larch, Engelmann spruce and subalpine fir. It crosses winter avalanche tracks that are filled with glacier lilies and quickly reaches stunning meadows where the trail divides. Keep left.

These meadows, which can look so inviting in summer, are often covered in snow for almost nine months. During the remaining three months, the plants are buffeted by strong winds, searing sunlight and changeable temperatures—from nighttime freezing to more than 30° C (86° F) in the daytime—that would quickly shrivel less-adaptable species. The hardy inhabitants bloom quickly, as soon as the snow recedes, and form a brilliant carpet of reds, whites and yellows that contrast with the grey limestone in the cirque above.

The trail quickly leaves the last stands of fir and spruce behind, crosses a brook and loops around between Mt. Rae and Mt.

Ptarmigan Cirque

Arethusa. The route skirts rock rubble containing horn coral fossils.

This rocky area is home to countless numbers of Columbian ground squirrels, which are busy trying to eat enough to survive the nine-month winter ahead. You'd be lucky to see the white-tailed ptarmigan, after whom the trail is named.

Survival Strategies of an Awkward Bird

If you find white-tailed ptarmigan hard to spot when somebody else points to one, it means that their survival strategy is working. (Or almost working. Someone in your group did see it, didn't she?)

In summer, ptarmigan are a mottled brown and blend in almost perfectly with the alpine vegetation that they feed on. In winter, they molt to pure white, with only their dark eyes and bill to give them away in the snowy landscape.

Ptarmigan are fortunate that they have this one survival strategy because otherwise they are 'sitting ducks,' you might say, and give themselves away. They are slow moving, almost lethargic at times. They coo, cluck, flap their wings but seldom fly—and made many an easy dinner for early travellers in the mountains. They are still a favourite food of hawks and owls.

wildlife

90. Mt. Indefatigable—*Superb valley views*

You quickly ascend a classic semi-open ridge to superb viewpoints that overlook Upper and Lower Kananaskis lakes and most of the Kananaskis Valley. The price is a steep grind on a trail littered with small, loose pebbles that can roll your feet around ominously with every step. It's even worse on the descent. Hiking boots are essential.

access

In Peter Lougheed Provincial Park, turn right off the Kananaskis Trail (Hwy. 40) onto the Kananaskis Lakes road. The trail starts from the North Interlakes picnic area/parking lot at the end of the road.

Map: below
Distance: 8.6 km (5.3 mi) return
Time: 4 hours
Rating: Strenuous
Max. elevation: 2160 m (7085 ft)
Elevation gain: 460 m (1509 ft)
Footwear: Light hiking boots
Best season: June through September

Cross the North Interlakes Dam between Upper and Lower Kananaskis lakes following the Upper Lake trail. The views across the water to Mt. Sarrail and Mt. Lyautey are superb. Within 500 m (1640 ft), the Indefatigable trail branches off right and climbs gradually to the foot of the ridge.

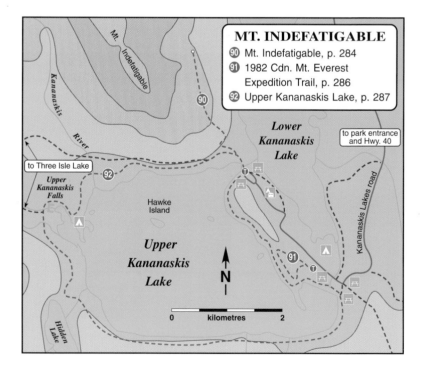

MT. INDEFATIGABLE
90 Mt. Indefatigable, p. 284
91 1982 Cdn. Mt. Everest Expedition Trail, p. 286
92 Upper Kananaskis Lake, p. 287

Lower Kananaskis Lake

to park entrance and Hwy. 40

to Three Isle Lake

Upper Kananaskis Falls

Hawke Island

Upper Kananaskis Lake

Kananaskis Lakes road

N

0   kilometres   2

Hidden Lake

Mt. Indefatigable from Upper Kananaskis Lake

The needle-covered path leads through a pleasant forest of spruce and pine.

That's the warm-up. The route quickly turns steep and stony as it climbs the ridge. It weaves around large boulders and patches of shale on a dusty carpet of rounded pea gravel that's nasty on the ascent and worse on the descent. If you don't take care, you'll land hard on your backside—but you won't fall off a cliff.

As compensation, however, the views quickly open up and you soon reach the Wendy Elekes memorial bench on a crag. This spot offers one of the best views of Upper Kananaskis Lake and across it to the glaciers and waterfalls below Mt. Sarrail and Mt. Foch. These peaks were named for French generals of the First World War. 'Indefatigable'

was the optimistic name given to a British battle cruiser that was blown up at the Battle of Jutland in 1916 with the loss of all but two of the 1000-man crew.

The ascent is somewhat easier above the viewpoint and from the edge of the escarpment, new vistas open up across Lower Kananaskis Lake and the serrated Opal Range beyond. The ridge levels off in a forest of spruce and larch. (Strong hikers can branch off to the left towards the summit of Mt. Indefatigable. It's a steep but not difficult ascent on shale and grass to the south ridge and outstanding views.)

The main route ends on another crag with a bench and an airy viewpoint overlooking the lower lake and the ridges of Mt. Invincible, named after another warship that went down at the Battle of Jutland.

91. 1982 Canadian Mt. Everest Expedition Trail—*Antithesis of Everest*

This pleasant, wooded family stroll is the antithesis of an Everest expedition. Instead of a treacherous icefall, avalanches, a death zone and impossible weather, you get stairs up the few steep parts and fenced viewpoints, with benches and good interpretive signs, overlooking Upper and Lower Kananaskis lakes.

Map: page 284
Distance: 2.1-km (1.3-mi) loop
Time: 1 hour or more
Rating: Easy family hike
Max. elevation: 1796 m (5891 ft)
Elevation gain: 122 m (400 ft)
Footwear: Walking/running shoes
Best season: June to late September

access

In Peter Lougheed Provincial Park, turn right off the Kananaskis Trail (Hwy. 40) onto the Kananaskis Lakes road. The trail begins from the White Spruce day use area, which is across from the Mt. Sarrail Campground near the end of the road. The trailhead is also at the end of a paved bicycle path connecting most of the Peter Lougheed campgrounds. Lock your bikes at the trailhead, however, because they aren't permitted on the trail.

On October 5, 1982, Laurie Skreslet, supported by 10 members of the Canadian Mt. Everest Expedition, became the first Canadian to set foot on the summit of the world's highest mountain. The trail is dedicated to this group's achievement.

Winding through a spruce forest, the trail leads past interpretive signs about the geology of the region and the Stoney peoples. Keep right. Stairs (with benches) surmount a few steep portions as the trail works its way out onto a ridge with good viewpoints over Upper Kananaskis Lake and the impressive skyline dominated by Mt. Foch, Mt. Sarrail and Mt. Lyautey.

The route loops back above the lake on rocky south-facing slopes with more good viewpoints before entering the spruce forest again. Turn right at the intersection.

92. Upper Kananaskis Lake

Long lakeside circuit

Although the circuit of Upper Kananaskis Lake is long, the route is mostly level and full of variety. You should never get tired of the views across the water to striking peaks such as Mt. Indefatigable. Hikers only out for a short jaunt might want to turn back at the Upper Lake campground.

access

In Peter Lougheed Provincial Park, turn right off the Kananaskis Trail (Hwy. 40) onto the Kananaskis Lakes road. The trail starts from the North Interlakes picnic area/parking lot at the end of the road.

Map: page 284
Distance: 15.3-km (9.5-mi) circuit
Time: 5 hours
Rating: Strenuous
Max. elevation: 1615 m (5297 ft)
Elevation gain: Negligible
Footwear: Light hiking boots
Best season: June through September

Upper Kananaskis Lake

Follow the signs for Three Isle Lake–Upper Lake trail across the dam at the end of the lake. In 1.1 km (0.7 mi), turn left and descend slightly to stay on the Upper Lakes trail, a softly carpeted path near the shoreline. There are good spots for picnics among the driftwood on the shore.

The trail soon enters a boulder field under the crumbling cliffs of Mt. Indefatigable and climbs gradually to the cutoff at 3.8 km (2.4 mi) for a well-situated campground on a peninsula.

The main trail crosses Upper Kananaskis River by a mossy fall. Now a narrow, forested path, the trail ascends out of sight of the lake and then slowly works its way back to the shoreline. From here, the path stays close to the water and views are stunning.

At the Upper Lake picnic area/parking lot, hikers can save time by walking back on the road to North Interlakes.

OPTION: The longer but more scenic option is to continue for another 3.8 km (2.4 mi), again close to the lakeshore, for a complete and rewarding circuit.

93. Black Prince Cirque—*Emerald-green tarn*

This interpretive loop follows an old logging road and trail up through a forest that's making a slow recovery from the extensive cutting that took place in the early 1970s. The reward is an inspiring view of Black Prince Cirque, a gigantic bowl carved by glaciers.

access

In Peter Lougheed Provincial Park, turn right off the Kananaskis Trail (Hwy. 40) onto the Kananaskis Lakes road. In about 2 km (1.2 mi), turn right opposite the Pocaterra day use area onto the Smith-Dorrien/Spray Trail (Hwy. 742), which soon becomes a gravel road. In about 9 km (6 mi), turn left into the Black Prince parking area.

Map: below
Distance: 7 km (4 mi) return
Time: 2 hours
Rating: Moderate
Max. elevation: 1828m (5996 ft)
Elevation gain: 90 m (295 ft)
Footwear: Light hiking boots
Best season: Late June to mid-September

Trees grow slowly at these relatively high elevations, especially on this north-facing slope where the snow-free season might be as short as four months. Logging has left so much slash or waste wood on the ground that the new growth has a hard time working up through it.

The road climbs fairly steeply for short pitches above Warspite Creek and approaches Warspite Lake, which turns green in mid-summer because of the growth of an aquatic algae on the submerged rocks. Although the lake appears to have no outlet, the water escapes underground and reappears in the creek lower down.

If you leave the trail and approach the lake more closely through a maze of huge boulders, you'll get an

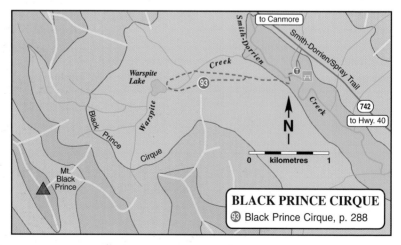

BLACK PRINCE CIRQUE
93 Black Prince Cirque, p. 288

inspiring view of Black Prince Cirque. Above you are hanging valleys, cascades and a collection of smaller cirques, arêtes and moraines.

The memorable name of 'Black Prince' refers, of course, to England's Edward, who was known for his striking black armour and skill as a fierce warrior in battle. (Edward lived in the 14th century and was the father of King Richard the Lionheart.) But the mountain was actually named after a ship (which was named after Edward).

The naming was done by A.O. Wheeler, of the Alpine Club of Canada, who passed through this part of the mountains in 1916 on a surveying expedition. He named this mountain and many of the surrounding peaks (Indefatigable, Invincible, Warspite) after ships engaged in the Battle of Jutland during the First World War.

The trail loops counter-clockwise through the subalpine forest and rejoins the original route for the return to the parking lot.

Black Prince Cirque

94. Many Springs—*Unusual wetland*

A level trail loops around a fascinating wetland that's home to orchids, warm springs and even flesh-eating plants.

access

From the Trans-Canada Highway, turn off onto Hwy. 1X and then turn west into Bow Valley Provincial Park. Keep left at Middle Lake and follow the road to the Many Springs parking area, where the trail begins.

Map: below
Distance: 1.6 km (1 mi)
Time: 1 hour or less
Rating: Easy
Max. elevation: 1310 m (4297 ft)
Elevation gain: Negligible
Footwear: Walking/running shoes
Best season: May to October

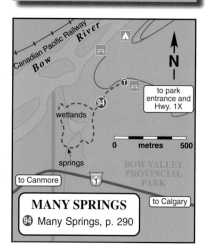

MANY SPRINGS
94 Many Springs, p. 290

The trail leads through a montane forest to a junction. Turn right and follow the edge of a wetland. You will cross Many Springs Creek, which remains at about 6° C (43° F) year-round because of the many warm springs that emerge along the McConnell Fault.

You'll notice plenty of animal tracks in the wet areas alongside the trail. Deer, elk and other mammals come down to drink the water for its high sodium content. It's also a good place to spot hummingbirds performing their courtship displays or defending their territory of flowers.

A viewpoint overlooks a lazy side channel of the Bow River. The trail loops back around the wetland and arrives at the route's highlight: a platform on the edge of the water where dozens of small springs boil up through the sand beside you.

The constant flow rate of these springs, the high mineral content of the water and the relatively warm temperatures create just the right conditions for abundant growth of orchids, such as the yellow lady's-slipper and round-leaved orchid.

Equally interesting, although harder to spot, is the butterwort with its purple, violet-like flowers. (The plant's common name comes from the traditional use of its leaves to curdle milk.) The butterwort uses a flypaper technique to trap insects on the hairy, greasy upper surface of its leaves, which then fold over to begin the three-day process of digestion. The leaves contain two types of glands: one secreting a sticky fluid and the second producing a digestive liquid.

These springs are also home to a blind insect known as an aquatic isopod (*Salmasellus steganothrix*), which has been found in only a few other places in western Canada. It lives under rocks, sustained by the constant flow of the springs and dining on plant debris.

Many Springs wetlands

95. Grotto Canyon—*Meditation on rock*

This popular family hike through a limestone canyon is a meditation on rock: curved, sculpted rock walls rising 60 m (197 ft) or more, hoodoos, a prehistoric rock painting and modern, lycra-clad rock climbers. Although the footing is stony throughout the canyon, the route only slopes gently and is easy to follow for just about any age. Be warned, however, that the official approach is marred by the industrial roar from the Baymag II plant that the trail passes.

Map: below
Distance: 5 km (3.1 mi) or more return (depending on how far you hike up the canyon)
Time: 2 hours or more
Rating: Moderate family hike
Max. elevation: 1525 m (5002 ft)
Elevation gain: 200 m (656 ft)
Footwear: Light hiking boots
Best season: May to October

access Take Hwy. 1A east from Canmore. The trail starts from the Grotto Mountain picnic area, which is 12 km (7.4 mi) east of Canmore on the north side of the highway.

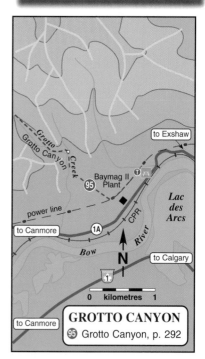

GROTTO CANYON
95 Grotto Canyon, p. 292

If you can get through the first half-hour, everything gets much, much better. Follow a cart track along a power line right-of-way, past a quarry. The roar from the Baymag plant (the world's largest magnesia fusing operation) gets increasingly louder. Just when you think you can't stand it anymore, the trail heads away from the power line right-of-way across the flats to join Grotto Creek. At last, the only sounds are the gentle gurgle of water and the occasional shouts of rock climbers high on the walls.

There's little actual trail up the canyon. Follow the stony canyon floor, crossing and re-crossing the small brook—it's an easy step across most of the time. Be aware that the canyon can be subject to flash floods in storms or during spring runoff and hikers could potentially be trapped.

The rock paintings, believed to have been painted by ancestors of the Kootenai perhaps 800 years ago, are difficult to spot, because they are low down on the left side near the start of the canyon. Don't touch them. Greasy fingers have already caused damage.

The rock walls grow steadily more impressive as you go deeper into the canyon. Watch for bolts and 'hangers' starting about 4 m (13 ft) up the rock faces. They have been placed by climbers for protection on many of the established routes. The climbers clip a carabiner (snaplink) onto the hangers and then clip their rope through the carabiner.

Along this portion of the trail, climbing routes bear such names as Cerebral Goretex, Falling from Heaven and Lunatic Madness.

About 1 km (0.6 mi) in, the canyon divides in front of a spectacular face called the Headwall. The right fork leads to a small triple waterfall and is blocked by a huge clockstone. The left fork makes for fascinating travel. Here, the canyon reaches its narrowest and highest point.

All too soon, the canyon opens and the walls fall back to create a more commonplace valley. On the left, the hillside has eroded and is beginning to create hoodoos—hoodoos in training, you might call them.

Grotto Canyon widens into a sunlit valley

96. Grassi Lakes—*Lakes like gemstones*

The rewards of this popular family trail are plentiful: two tiny lakes of gem-like beauty, and the opportunity to view an ancient pictograph and to watch climbers practise on steep rock faces. On a sunny day, pack a picnic and a book and enjoy a half-day overlooking the lakes.

Map: below
Distance: 3.5 km (2.1 mi) return
Time: 1¹/₂–2 hours
Rating: Moderate
Max. elevation: 1675 m (5494 ft)
Elevation gain: 300 m (984 ft)
Footwear: Walking/running shoes/light hiking boots
Best season: July to October

access

In Canmore, turn left at the end of the main street (8ᵗʰ Street), cross the Bow River and follow the signs for the Canmore Nordic Centre. Take the first left just past the centre. The sign says 'Grassi Lakes Recreation Area.' The trail starts at the parking area.

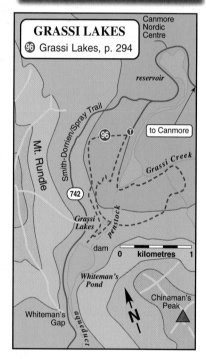

GRASSI LAKES
96 Grassi Lakes, p. 294

Canmore Nordic Centre
reservoir
Smith-Dorrien/Spray Trail
96
to Canmore
Grassi Creek
Mt. Rundle
742
Grassi Lakes
penstock
dam
0   kilometres   1
Whiteman's Pond
Whiteman's Gap
aqueduct
Chinaman's Peak
N

Lawrence Grassi, a Canmore coal-miner and renowned Canadian Rockies trail-builder, constructed this scenic trail in the 1920s as a gift to the people of Canmore. Ever since, it's provided an enjoyable and accessible walk for all ages. The two tiny lakes, which are the trail's destination, are extraordinary in their clarity and colour. Expect serendipity, but not solitude.

The trail begins as a pleasant forest walk, and climbs gently to the first viewpoint, which offers views of the Bow Valley and the waterfalls from Grassi Lakes. Interpretive panels illuminate the highlights of Canmore's history as an early coal-mining town.

A hydro-electric dam on the Upper Spray River diverts water along a canal at Whiteman's Gap and into the Bow River, achieving a drop of about 330 m (1082 ft). The next portion of the trail rises sharply as you climb steep steps.

When you reach an abandoned road, turn right. (Otherwise, you go up to a penstock.) Proceed a short way and then go left at the trail sign to arrive at the lower lake. Most

Upper Grassi Lake

people walk clockwise around the second lake, where benches are provided on the west side and sunny picnic spots on the east. The clarity of the two lakes and their intense aqua tones are truly remarkable.

Hikers interested in viewing the rock painting should head up the steep trail at the end of the lake. The pictograph is beside the trail, on the first large boulder on the left-hand side. A sign beneath the boulder warns visitors not to touch the painting. Archaeologists have determined that the Bow Valley has been used by humans for 11,000 years. The early inhabitants hunted mammoth, bison, sheep and caribou, and left teepee rings, stone cairns, bison kill sites, cobble quarries and a few rare rock paintings such as this one.

It's also worth taking a look at the spongy rock cliff that rises above the lake. The cliff was once a reef, formed in the Devonian Period 340 to 400 million years ago. You may enjoy exploring the small caves at its base. On weekends, the cliff resounds with climbers of all skill levels.

Picassos of the Past

Hundreds, perhaps thousands of years ago, some artist painted on a large boulder above Upper Grassi Lakes the stark figure of a human holding a hoop. The age of this rare painting isn't known, although archaeologists suspect that most rock art was produced in the last 1000 years.

There are two types of rock art: pictographs, paintings executed on rock with a mixture of red ochre, animal grease and water, and petroglyphs, figures cut or etched into rock. The Grassi Lakes painting is a pictograph. Grotto Canyon is also the site of several pictographs (Walk 95).

(Several dozen rock art sites have been identified in Alberta, the most outstanding at Writing-on-Stone Provincial Park in south-central Alberta.)

Who Was Lawrence Grassi?

Miner and trail-builder extraordinaire, Lawrence Grassi was an Italian woodcutter who came west to Canmore in 1916 and signed on as a coal-miner. He built the Grassi Lakes trail in the 1920s with a group of miners left idle by a strike. Originally named Twin Lakes, the lakes were renamed in Grassi's honour in 1938 by the people of Canmore.

Although some of the stone steps and wooden benches Grassi built have been replaced, his fine trail-building remains an enduring contribution to the hiking system of the Canadian Rockies. (He also worked for several summers building trails at Lake O'Hara.)

history

97. Chester Lake—*Lake of jade*

The hike to this jade-coloured lake under the grey cliffs of Mt. Chester is highly popular with families and fishermen. It's a idyllic place to spend a sunny afternoon. From Chester, a 4-km (2.5-mi) return side trip to the alpine meadows of Three Lakes Valley opens up terrain that's even more impressive.

Map: page 298
Distance: 9.6 km (6 mi) return
Time: 4 hours
Rating: Moderate
Max. elevation: 2220 m (7282 ft)
Elevation gain: 310 m (1017 ft)
Footwear: Light hiking boots
Best season: July to mid-September

access

From Canmore, drive the Smith-Dorrien/Spray Trail (Hwy. 742) to the Chester Lake parking area on the east side of the road opposite the Burstall Pass parking area. Alternately, from the Kananaskis Lakes road in Peter Lougheed Provincial Park, turn north on the Smith-Dorrien/Spray Trail (Hwy. 742) and drive 15 km (9.3 mi) to the parking area.

All the tedious stuff comes early. From the upper end of the huge parking lot, follow the old logging road that constitute the Smith-Dorrien bike-hike network. Bicycles are allowed only on the first 2.4 km (1.5 mi): a relentless grind up to a concrete bike stand and a 10-minute exaltation going down.

Although the network has many intersections, the route is well-signed and obvious and you even get a few views across the valley to Burstall Pass. The road turns into a trail past the bike locks, and the hiking quickly improves with a subalpine forest gradually opening onto a series of flower-filled meadows

Chester Lake

rimmed with larches.

Don't expect solitude at Chester Lake. It's very popular with fishermen, who lug up their belly boats, and with casual hikers. But the lake and its grassy shoreline opposite Mt. Chester is an idyllic spot on a sunny day. The dinosaur-backed peak behind the lake is The Fortress.

There's even more interesting terrain ahead for those with the time and energy for another 4 km (2.5 mi) of hiking. The most obvious way is to follow a rough trail from the far end of the lake over rocky ledges and patches of meadow. This trail leads to a gloomy tarn amid a tedious accumulation of scree and boulders.

The Three Lakes Valley is a much better option. Half-way down the lake past the fish station, turn left into the trees on an unmarked trail and climb gradually to a fascinating meadow of huge boulders called Elephant Rocks.

The trail works over into Three Lakes Valley. The first lake is a smaller version of Mt. Chester. The trail works its way up a grassy slope and reaches Lake No. 2, right on the edge of the headwall and rimmed by smooth rock slabs and meadows. You can simultaneously watch for goats and admire the lake, the ramparts of Mt. Galatea and the wide perspective down the valley and across to Commonwealth Peak and Mt. Burstall. Although you can explore further up the valley, Lake No. 3 is a sink hole that's usually ice-filled year-round.

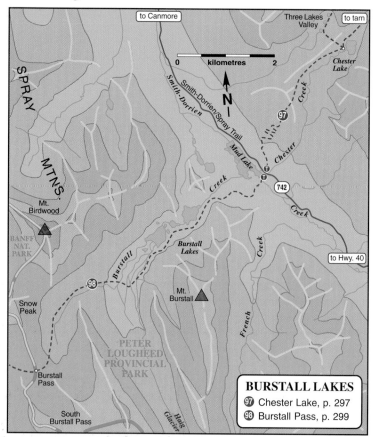

BURSTALL LAKES

97 Chester Lake, p. 297
98 Burstall Pass, p. 299

98. Burstall Pass—*Alpine meadows and karst ridges*

The Burstall Pass trail is one of the easiest and most popular routes to splendid alpine meadows and fascinating karst ridges in all of Peter Lougheed Provincial Park.

access

From Canmore, drive the Smith-Dorrien/Spray Trail (Hwy. 742) to the Burstall Pass parking area on the west side of the road opposite the Chester Lake parking area. Alternately, from the Kananaskis Lakes road in Peter Lougheed Provincial Park, turn north onto the Smith-Dorrien/Spray Trail (Hwy. 742) and drive 15 km (9.3 mi) to the parking area.

Map: page 298
Distance: 14.8 km (9.2 mi) return
Time: 8 hours
Rating: Strenuous
Max. elevation: 2346 m (7695 ft)
Elevation gain: 460 m (1509 ft)
Footwear: Water-resistant hiking boots
Best season: July to September

The trail rises gradually on a old logging road above three small lakes. These first few kilometres are routine walking and can be hastened by the use of a mountain bike. Bikes, however, aren't permitted beyond the concrete bike stand positioned just before the point where the trail narrows. Descend on foot to the dryas flats created by the stream draining Robertson Glacier.

The stream breaks into many constantly shifting channel in the flats. Many of the channels can be jumped or crossed on rocks and logs. Others might require foot-numbing wading, although the water shouldn't be more than ankle deep if you pick wide stretches to cross. (Some hikers bring sandals for the inevitable crossing; others simply take off their socks and shoes.)

Beyond the flats, the trail climbs steeply through forest to the meadows of the upper valley under Mt. Birdwood. The going is splendid from here on. The trail switchbacks up the right side of the final headwall over karst ledges and through occasional clumps of larches. It emerges on the flower-filled meadows of Burstall Pass, overlooking the Spray Valley in Banff National Park.

On a fine day, hikers should plan to leave early enough to give themselves time to explore this easily traversed alpine terrain. One fine option is to ramble south for about 1.5 km (1 mi) to South Burstall Pass, with its impressive close-up views of glacier-clad Mt. Sir Douglas.

Burstall Pass

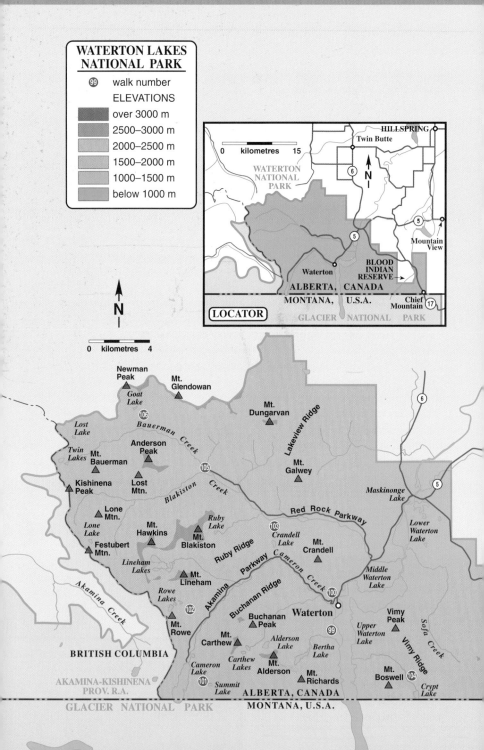

**WATERTON LAKES
NATIONAL PARK**

(99) walk number

ELEVATIONS

- over 3000 m
- 2500–3000 m
- 2000–2500 m
- 1500–2000 m
- 1000–1500 m
- below 1000 m

LOCATOR

HILLSPRING
Twin Butte
WATERTON
NATIONAL
PARK
0 kilometres 15
N
6
5
Mountain
View
Waterton
BLOOD
INDIAN
RESERVE →
ALBERTA, CANADA
MONTANA, U.S.A.
Chief
Mountain
17
GLACIER NATIONAL PARK

N

0 kilometres 4

Newman
Peak
Goat
Lake
Mt.
Glendowan
Mt.
Dungarvan
Lakeview Ridge
105
Lost
Lake
Bauerman Creek
Anderson
Peak
Twin
Lakes
Mt.
Bauerman
Lost
Mtn.
105
Blakiston Creek
Mt.
Galwey
Kishinena
Peak
Maskinonge
Lake
5
Lone
Mtn.
Lone
Lake
Mt.
Hawkins
Ruby
Lake
Red Rock Parkway
103
Crandell
Lake
Mt.
Crandell
Lower
Waterton
Lake
Festubert
Mtn.
Mt.
Blakiston
Ruby Ridge
Lineham
Lakes
Mt.
Lineham
Akamina
Parkway
Cameron Creek
Middle
Waterton
Lake
Rowe
Lakes
102
Buchanan Ridge
100
Akamina Creek
Mt.
Rowe
Buchanan
Peak
Waterton
Vimy
Peak
Mt.
Carthew
Alderson
Lake
99
Upper
Waterton
Lake
Vimy Ridge
Sofa Creek
BRITISH COLUMBIA
Cameron
Lake
Carthew
Lakes
Mt.
Alderson
Bertha
Lake
Mt.
Richards
Mt.
Boswell
104
Crypt
Lake
AKAMINA-KISHINENA
PROV. R.A.
101
Summit
Lake
ALBERTA, CANADA
GLACIER NATIONAL PARK
MONTANA, U.S.A.

Cameron Lake

CHAPTER 6

WATERTON LAKES NATIONAL PARK

Waterton Lakes National Park is the tiny jewel of the Canadian Rockies. The mountains rise abruptly from the prairies, creating a stunning landscape of jagged peaks, hanging valleys and colourful rock layers of red argillite, dramatically set against rolling grasslands.

Situated in the southwest corner of Alberta on the U.S. border, 264 km (164 mi) southwest of Calgary, Waterton Lakes was established in 1895. In 1932, Waterton was dedicated as an 'International Peace Park' with adjacent Glacier National Park in Montana.

At only 525 sq. km (210 sq. mi), it contains some of the oldest exposed bedrock in the Canadian Rockies; eons of geological activity have left a legacy of richly coloured mountains and canyons. Encompassing the transition zone between prairies and mountains, it is home to a rich variety of animal and plant life and offers some of the best wild-flower displays in North America. The grasslands on the eastern edge of the park, such as those at the beginning of the Red Rock Parkway, are among the best places in Alberta to see wild herds of elk. These herds are larger and less tame than the ones that frequent the road edges in other parks. They are a treat to see (please use binoculars and don't get close). These foothills also boast an incredible diversity of plants, with over 900 species identified. The wildflowers are outstanding in June.

The park is more remote and less well known than Banff and Jasper national parks. The majority of the 350,000 who visit annually are from Alberta or Montana. Many people from outside the region have never heard of this outstanding Rocky Mountain park.

That's a shame, because Waterton is a grand destination if you enjoy a low-key, outdoors-oriented holiday. The park is particularly well-suited for 'base camping,' because it offers many opportunities for interesting day trips (see page 338). Within park boundaries, you'll find more than 175 km (109 mi) of hiking trails, excellent fishing, the opportunity to cruise on a lake between two countries, and much more. Waterton is an excellent choice for short hikes, even one-way day trips or loops. The availability of one-way hiker's and biker's shuttles in recent years has increased the options for these activities. Every Saturday in summer, interpretive staff lead a day-long Peace Park hike across the border to the U.S.'s Glacier National Park.

Another Waterton attraction is its geographic location, with many cultural and historical attractions on both sides of the international border within a day's drive. Examples include the Crowsnest Pass Area, the Frank Slide Interpretive Centre, Cardston, with its Mormon temple and Remington-Alberta Carriage Centre, Logan Pass and Glacier National Park. (*The Alberta-Montana Discovery Guide: Museums, Parks & Historic Sites* is a helpful resource for trip planning. See further reading.)

Tiny Waterton townsite—with about 80 permanent residents—is the only commercial centre in the park. The downtown is quaint, sheltered and only steps away from the park's natural attractions. Full services are available May to October when the town's population grows by the thousands. Basic services are available year-round.

Although Waterton remains small and remote, there are changes afoot. In recent years, the range and sophistication of services have increased. Accommodation is still limited, with about 400 rooms in the park (compared with 900, 20 years ago). This situation is expected to ease somewhat with the opening of the new $8.1-million Lodge at Waterton Lakes in 1998 and Waterton-Glacier Suites, affiliated with the Bayshore Hotel. A pool and spa are also planned; a 20-bed hostel is to open under an agreement with the International

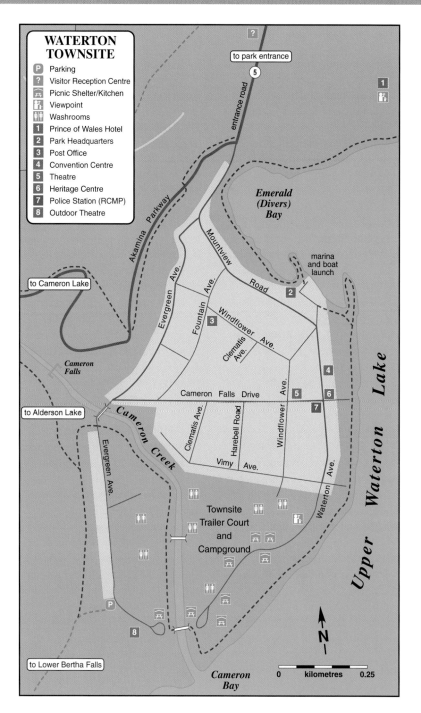

WATERTON TOWNSITE

P   Parking
?   Visitor Reception Centre
🏠   Picnic Shelter/Kitchen
🔭   Viewpoint
🚻   Washrooms
1   Prince of Wales Hotel
2   Park Headquarters
3   Post Office
4   Convention Centre
5   Theatre
6   Heritage Centre
7   Police Station (RCMP)
8   Outdoor Theatre

to park entrance

5

?

1

Emerald
(Divers)
Bay

marina
and boat
launch

2

to Cameron Lake

Akamina Parkway

entrance road

Evergreen Ave.

Mountview

Fountain Ave.

Windflower Ave.

3

Road

Clematis Ave.

Cameron
Falls

to Alderson Lake

Cameron Falls Drive

4

5   6

7

Clematis Ave.

Harebell Road

Windflower Ave.

Cameron Creek

Evergreen Ave.

Vimy Ave.

Waterton Ave.

Townsite
Trailer Court
and
Campground

Upper Waterton Lake

8

to Lower Bertha Falls

N

Cameron
Bay

0   kilometres   0.25

Hostelling Association. There's also increased focus on winter activities, with accommodation year-round at Kilmorey Lodge and at the new Lodge at Waterton Lakes. The venerable Prince of Wales Hotel is also looking at ambitious expansion plans, with convention facilities and possible year-round use, subject to final approval from Parks Canada.

If there are drawbacks to Waterton, one would be the difficulty of exploring the park without a car and the second would be frequent rainy weather (even in sunny Alberta). Shuttle buses or vans serve Waterton Lakes in summer via Pincher Creek; you can rent taxis in Pincher Creek to take you to the park. Sorry, we can't do anything about inclement weather; winds can be cruel in this part of the country, and snow can fly almost any time of year. The flip side is that if you hit the weather right, you'll think you're in paradise.

If you are visiting in July or August and aren't camping, reserve accommodation. If you are camping, try to arrive early in the day; it's not unusual for campgrounds to be booked by mid-afternoon. Commercial campgrounds are situated just outside the park.

Start your visit by dropping into the Visitor Reception Centre, on the right side of the main Waterton Road, opposite the Prince of Wales Hotel (before you reach the townsite). Here, you'll find general information and publications on park activities. Open 8 a.m. to 6 p.m., May 15 to June 19; 8 a.m. to 8 p.m., June 20 to September 1; variable September 2 to October 13. Call (403) 859-5133.

Outdoor Adventures

BACKPACKING: See chapter 7 (page 334).

BICYCLING: See chapter 7 (page 348) for cycling and mountain biking information. The townsite provides flat and gentle cycling for all fitness levels. There are also excellent and rewarding longer tours both within the park and into Montana's Glacier National Park. You can rent 18-speed mountain bikes, tandems and scooters at Pat's, behind the marina. Pat's, (403) 859-2266, is also open late in the evening for groceries. Tamarack Shuttle & Guide Services, (403) 859-2378, offers shuttle services for cyclists and hikers.

BOATING AND CRUISES: Upper Waterton Lake is the deepest in the Canadian Rockies and one of the most beautiful. Scenic cruises up the lake are available. Ask at the marina. Along the way, you'll have splendid views of rugged peaks and perhaps even see bears or moose. A descriptive commentary is provided. A stop in Montana at the end of the lake is usually included. Ask about sunset cruises. Boat service to the trailhead for Crypt Lake (Walk 104) can also be arranged through Waterton Inter-Nation Shoreline Cruise, (403) 859-2362. If you have your own boat, you'll find a launch site for Upper Waterton Lake opposite the park administration office. There's also a boat launch in Emerald Bay next to the Marina. (Strong winds can blow up without warning, creating dangerous conditions for small boats, especially on Upper Waterton Lake.)

You can also rent fishing rods, boats and canoes at Cameron Lake and learn about the area's unique ecosystem at the small but imaginative interpretive centre. Why does annual precipitation total 152 cm (58 in) at Cameron Lake, 107 cm (42 in) at the townsite and only 76 cm (30 in) at the park gate? Here's the place to find out.

CHILDREN'S PROGRAMS: The International Peace Park Hike and evening campground programs are oriented for the whole family. Ask at the Visitor Reception Centre. Kids' programs and a day camp are offered through the Heritage Education Program, (403) 859-2624. Also see 'Guided Hikes' and 'Evening Campground Programs.'

CLIMBING: Waterton is better known for its long ridge walks. See chapter 7 for information about the limited rock climbing possibilities.

DRIVES: Waterton is a fine base for numerous interesting auto tours. Aside from obvious ones in the park (to Cameron Lake and Red Rock Canyon), you can cross the international border and visit Glacier National Park in the U.S. (Hwy. 6 to the border is only open from June to September.) It's 74 km

(46 mi) to St. Mary, Montana and another 82 km (51 mi) over Logan Pass to West Glacier, Montana. Interesting Alberta excursions include visiting Crowsnest Pass, with a rich and dramatic history of mine disasters, labour unrest, train robberies, bootlegging and the Frank Slide, where you can see the 90 million tonnes (99 million tons) of rock that buried much of the town of Frank in 1903. Cardston, an easy drive northeast from Waterton townsite, is the site of a huge Mormon temple, restored a few years ago. The community was founded in 1887 by Utah Mormons. The town is also the site of the $14-million Remington-Alberta Carriage Centre, a stunning collection of 250 vehicles from stagecoaches to sulkies. See the 'Remington-Alberta Carriage Centre' listing.

EDUCATIONAL FIELD TRIPS: The Waterton Natural History Association, a non-profit organization, offers an outstanding selection of guided field trips. Recent outings include 'The Bears of Waterton' by world expert Dr. Charles Jonkel and 'Canoeing the Valley,' a one-day interpretive canoe trip. Prices are reasonable; profits go to the park. Reserve early, (403) 859-2642.

EVENING CAMPGROUND PROGRAMS: Lost your hat? Want to find what makes it so windy in Waterton? What kinds of animals live in the park? More about bears? If so, be sure to attend interpretive programs, held summer evenings at the Falls Theatre in the townsite (near Cameron Falls) and at Crandell Theatre at Crandell Campground. Check for programs at the Visitor Reception Centre.

FISHING: See chapter 7 (page 358).

GOLFING: The 18-hole Waterton Lakes Golf Course is situated about 2 km (1.2 mi) north of town, adjacent to the main entrance road.

Power cart and club rentals are available. Call (403) 859-2383.

GUIDED HIKES: Hike in two countries with the knowledgeable companionship of a park interpreter. The International Peace Park hike is offered every Saturday in summer. Participants hike down the lake to Goat Haunt and take a boat back. The hike is free, but there is a charge for the boat ride. Inquire at the Visitor Reception Centre. Ike

wildlife

Mighty Moose

Moose, the largest members of the deer family, are solitary animals, except for the female and her calves.

The mating season is mid-September to November when the bulls turn particularly aggressive. The calves are often twins and are born in May or early June, weighing about 9 kg (20 lbs). They put on weight fast and remain with the mother all through summer and the next winter for protection in the deep snow, which restricts movement. In spring, the mother drives her yearling offspring away before a new calf is born.

moose

Isaacson at Canadian Wilderness Tours offers a variety of interpretive and educational hikes, including full-day treks and bird-watching. Call (403) 859-2058 to book during summer and call (403) 627-3291 during winter. Tamarack Shuttle & Guide Services conducts a guided, 20-km (12.4-mi) hike of the Carthew–Alderson Trail and a two- to four-day 'High Alpine Tour'; reservations are advised, (403) 859-2378.

GUIDED (MOTORIZED) TOURS: For scenic drives, Canadian Wilderness Tours offers 'step-on' guides who will describe the area's natural history and wildlife to you. These guides will accompany you in your own vehicle. Call (403) 859-2058 to book during summer or (403) 627-3291 during winter. Mountain Sunset Tours offers scenic tours to a variety of Waterton's special attractions. Reservations are required. A townsite taxi and hiker shuttle service is also provided. Call (403) 859-2612.

HIKER'S SHUTTLE: Tamarack Shuttle & Guide Services, (403) 859-2378, in the Tamarack Mall offers shuttles to trailheads such as Cameron Lake, start of the famous Summit Lake–Carthew Summit trail (Walk 101). You finish back in Waterton townsite. You can also rent tents at Waterton Sports & Leisure in the mall and possibly guide services.

HORSEBACK RIDING: Alpine Stables, (403) 859-2462, offers horse rentals and guides from 9 a.m. to 6 p.m. daily; there are over 250 km (155 mi) of trails, including to Crypt Lake (Walk 104). Visitors can also board horses at the stables. Backcountry corrals are provided at Alderson Lake, Crypt Landing and Lone Lake.

ICE CLIMBING: As the sport expands, Waterton is becoming increasingly popular with ice climbers. Routes such as Hip Wader Gully and Fernie Pillar are situated near the end of the Red Rock Parkway, although the road is closed to vehicles around the end of October. The Akamina Parkway, which is usually open for access to ski trails, offers a few other routes a short distance above the town. Sullivan Falls and Crypt Falls offer outstanding climbing, but it's a long ski-in to reach the base. The Visitor Reception Centre or the Warden's Office has information on each climb. Be aware that the chinooks, which blast through Waterton, can quickly weaken the waterfall ice. This deterioration may not be readily apparent at the base of the climb.

KITE-FLYING: A popular Waterton activity in the often stormy winds. Pick up a kite and test the breezes on the Prince of Wales hill.

RED ROCK CANYON: Don't miss this unusual geological phenomenon. A short loop takes you through a rose-, red- and pink-hued canyon. The site has been occupied by humans for over 8000 years. It's a fine outing for families, and also a great place to see wildlife (see Walk 105).

REMINGTON-ALBERTA CAR-RIAGE CENTRE: Situated in Cardston, an easy drive northeast of Waterton, this $14-million centre houses one of the world's best displays of horse-drawn vehicles. More than 250 vehicles have been lovingly restored, some whose owners included royalty. There are also many special events and equestrian demonstrations. Free guided tours available. You can easily make a day of a visit to this centre. Pack a picnic and eat it in the adjoining park in the Lee Park valley. Open daily, May 15 to Labour Day, 9 a.m. to 8 p.m., and 9 a.m. to 5 p.m. for the rest of year. Call (403) 653-5139 and toll-free in Alberta 310-0000.

RIDGE WALKS: There are a number of outstanding ridge walks for experienced hikers in Waterton.

Ask at the Visitor Reception Centre or talk to Brian Baker at Tamarack Shuttle & Guide Services in Tamarack Village Square for information on these challenging ridge walks. Call Tamarack at (403) 859-2378.

SCUBA DIVING: Emerald Bay in the townsite is considered one of the best places in Alberta to scuba dive. That's because the wrecked hull of Gertrude, a 1920s stern paddle-wheeler, lies about 15 m (49 ft) under the surface. Some of the best visibility to see Gertrude is in early spring, late in fall or through the ice.

SKATING: Occasionally (but not often), the ice is cleared off for skaters in front of Kilmorey Lodge.

SKIING (CROSS-COUNTRY): See chapter 7 (page 363).

SNOWBOARDING: If there's enough snow, try the hill at the Bertha Falls trailhead (see Walk 99).

wildlife

The Chipper Chickadee

The black-capped chickadee, with its pert black bib, friendliness and cheery call, is a hardy little bird that lives in tree cavities and nestboxes. This snowbird is no wimp. It has a remarkable ability to withstand many weeks of a cold winter, a talent under study by biologists in Alberta. (We might have a few things to learn from this little bird.)

SNOWSHOEING: Favourite places for this activity are the Crandell Lake and Cameron Lake area.

SURREY RIDING: See Waterton townsite from the vantage of a surrey, with or without a fringe on top. You can rent them from Pat's, behind the marina. Call (403) 859-2266.

SWIMMING: Waterton Lake is too cold for all but the toughest. An indoor swimming pool and spa are to be opened at The Lodge at Waterton Lakes in 1998.

TENNIS, ANYONE?: A public tennis court is situated one block from Main Street on Cameron Falls Drive. Free.

Indoor and Rainy-Day Guide

'Do not leave because it rains. Hang on until the dismal time passes, then fly to the high places. The mountains will be at their best and appear, even though far distant, as polished gems. The shining mountains will then be understood.'
—Morton Elrod, 1924

Elrod's wise advise notwithstanding, even a rainy day needn't be a 'dismal time' in Waterton, although two bad days in a row can get tedious. This little park has some warm, cozy spots that are good for waiting out the inclement weather. Where could one find a friendlier atmosphere than at Pearl's Deli?

What could be more relaxing than lounging in the Prince of Wales Hotel, rumoured to have at least two ghosts? A rainy day is also a good time to view the exhibits, art gallery and bookstore at the Waterton Natural History Association's Heritage Centre.

The people and parks staff of Waterton always seem to have a little more time for visitors than they might in the busier parks to the north. So make time for the indoor side of Waterton on your travels, and be ready for a few surprises.

ART GALLERY: The Night Singer Art Gallery has hundreds of hand-crafted items from the people of the Blackfoot Confederacy; located on Hwy. 6 between Waterton Lakes and Glacier National Park or call (403) 737-3080.

BOOKSTORES: Many excellent books are available through the Waterton Natural History Association, which operates the Waterton Heritage Centre at 117 Waterton Avenue, near the campground. The association also sells books at the Visitor Reception Centre at the entrance to the townsite. There is also a bookstore in the Tamarack Mall with a good selection of outdoor books.

CARRIAGE HOUSE THEATRE: The community of Cardston offers lively summer theatre, including musicals such as 'Mountain Mischief' and 'Fabulous Fifties.' Box office, (403) 653-1000.

DINING OUT: Despite the small size of Waterton townsite, the variety that it offers diners is impressive. Try the Prince of Wales for lunch or dinner. The dining room, with its view over the lake, is reminiscent of an earlier, less hurried time. The luncheon specials may include delicious shepherd's pie or Canadian pea soup, fresh Canadian salmon glazed with lemon dill butter or English fish and chips. The Tea Room is open from 2 p.m. to 5 p.m.; a buffet is featured on Sunday. Call (403) 859-2231 for times. Another popular spot for sophisticated dining in Waterton is the Kootenai Brown Dining Room in the Bayshore Inn, where windows on one side of the room overlook the lake. For lunch, you might enjoy fish and chips, the pasta special or a fresh vegetable sandwich; the evening meal may offer such appetizers as French onion soup ($4.95) and main courses such as Dijon rack of lamb ($19.95) or rainbow trout amandine ($12.95). The award-winning Lamp Post Dining Room at Kilmorey Lodge is another well-liked gathering spot. Appetizers include wild boar pâté ($7.95) and slow-roasted caribou ($7.95); dinner offerings include Trout Kilmorey, rainbow trout in wine sauce with fresh basil, sun-dried tomatoes, crepes and shrimp ($16.95); the saskatoon pancakes at breakfast are to die for. In summer, you can sit in a gazebo overlooking the lake.

Where do the locals eat? Most likely, you'll find them at Pearl's Deli & Cafe on Windflower Avenue—and for good reason. Pearl's continues its tradition of tasty home-cooking that is reasonably priced. Its fare has warmed the hearts of many a homesick student! Menu items include bagels, muffins, sandwiches and burgers. Open for lunch and dinner. Tootsie's Ice Cream, at the corner of Windflower and Cameron Falls Drive (same doorway as the theatre), makes a refreshing stop on a hot day. It's known for its tropical shakes and frosts, which include strawberry daiquiri and mai-tai flavours. The Big Scoop Ice Cream Parlour, at 114 Waterton Avenue (part of Caribou Clothes), features old cartwheel tables and a good selection of flavours, including black forest and bubble gum. Zumis has Rocky Mountain rainbow trout ($14.95) and southwest chicken ($13.95).

HERITAGE CENTRE MUSEUM /BOOKSTORE: Puppet shows on the lawn? Music in the park? Video program on Waterton's history? Head for the Waterton Heritage Centre at 117 Waterton Avenue, in the centre of the townsite. This museum and bookstore is the home of the Waterton Natural History Association, which offers everything from information on park highlights to displays from various local artists. They have excellent outdoor posters for sale. The centre, (403) 859-2624, is open daily in summer. It provides a variety of exhibits on the natural and human history of Waterton. There's also a special children's outdoor program for kids 7 to 11. Funds go to help non-profit park ventures.

LAUNDRY: The Itussistukiopi Launderette, on Windflower Avenue, is open daily.

MASSAGE: Drop in or make an appointment at Bear Paw Massage Therapy, 2nd Floor, 309 Windflower Avenue, (403) 859-2070.

MOUNTAIN LORE AND LECTURES: The Waterton Natural History Association, a non-profit organization, provides guest speakers each Saturday in summer on a variety of park topics. Recent subjects were 'The Alpine in Bloom' and 'Wildlife's Wonders.' Call (403) 859-2624 for information.

MOVIES: The Waterton Lakes Opera House, on the corner of Windflower Avenue and Cameron Falls Drive, features movies every night.

NIGHT LIFE (BARS): The younger crowd congregates at The Thirsty Bear Saloon in the Bayshore Inn, 111 Waterton Avenue, (403) 859-2211. Check out the unusual art. Dancing nightly. The more sedate Bayshore Inn Fireside Lounge is the place for a quiet drink. For a special treat, head up to the Prince of Wales Hotel Lounge. The Kilmorey Lodge, 117 Evergreen Avenue, is open year-round and has a bar.

PRINCE OF WALES: Don't miss having a look at this magnificent wooden hotel, a designated national historic site known around Waterton as the 'POW.' It stands as a picturesque sentinel above Waterton Lake. The glassed-in lobby overlooks the lake and has a delicious feel. On a rainy day, this hotel would be a wonderful place to write a few postcards, or read a mystery. If you're hungry, drop in for high tea in the afternoon. Call (403) 859-2231.

SHOWERS: If you're staying at Crandell Lake Campground, which has no showers, or if you're just back from a long hike, drop into the townsite campground where the showers are free. There's parking along Waterton Avenue just south of the campground.

SWIMMING: There is an indoor pool available to the public at The Lodge at Waterton Lakes.

WINTER MURDER MYSTERIES, ETC.: Kilmorey Lodge, (403) 859-2334, offers a number of 'magical winter weekends,' including a Valentine weekend romance package ('imagine the possibilities,' states the brochure), murder mystery weekends, Celtic celebrations, etc.

history

The Prince of Wales: A Prince of a Hotel

The Prince of Wales, the magnificent seven-storeyed hotel at the north end of Waterton Lake, might have ended up looking quite different than it does today.

Louis Hill, president of the Great Northern Railway, chose the site for the building in 1913. At first, he thought that the design should be long and low, somewhat like the Many Glacier Hotel in Montana, or perhaps it should resemble a French or Swiss chalet.

Hill proved to be so indecisive that the building had to be changed four times before he was satisfied. The result is the steep-pitched building that opened the summer of 1927.

Builders also had to contend with Waterton's horrendous winds. High winds twice blew the building off its centre during construction; the second time, according to a leaflet published by the hotel, 'construction had gone too far for the building to be aligned absolutely.'

Today, the building still sways slightly under heavy winds, and guests on upper floors can feel it. No danger exists; the hotel has been constructed to withstand the fiercest gales.

The hotel is named after the Prince of Wales, who later became Edward VIII and abdicated the British throne for the love of Wallis Simpson, a divorced woman. Edward never visited the hotel, although he was invited to open it.

Wildlife are attracted by the hotel. Bighorn sheep, deer and coyotes have all been seen looking quizzically at their reflections in the windows at ground level. Occasionally, an aggressive sheep has even charged!

The hotel's official literature makes no mention of the ghosts rumoured to reside there. Staff whisper, however, of 'two friendly ghosts' that are occasionally heard locking and slamming doors and taking a shower in the cook's room.

There are plans to turn many of the rooms into suites and to build an addition on the side of the hill, pending negotiations with Parks Canada.

facing page: Red Rock Parkway

99. Lower Bertha Falls

Quiet walk to modest falls

This shady route to Lower Bertha Falls offers grand views down Waterton Lake and across the townsite to the prairies beyond. In its last stretch, the trail ascends gradually beside a vigorous brook that bubbles over rocky cascades. Ambitious hikers can travel beyond the lower falls, ascending to a steep-walled cirque that encloses Bertha Lake in the subalpine zone.

Map: page 315
Distance: 5.8 km (3.6 mi) return
Time: 1½ hours
Rating: Moderate
Max. elevation: 1479 m (4851 ft)
Elevation gain: 200 m (656 ft)
Footwear: Running/walking shoes/light hiking boots
Best season: June through September

access

In Waterton townsite, head south on Evergreen Avenue to Cameron Falls. Cross Cameron Creek and continue south on a dead-end road. The trail begins from a small parking area just before the turn-around.

The trail ascends gradually through an aspen forest that soon opens up to offer views across Waterton Lake. Note the tongue of milky water extending out into the lake from Cameron

Creek. The light colour is rock flour or glacial silt, ground up by the glaciers above Cameron Lake. The trees make a gradual transition to a montane forest of lodgepole pine. Southwards lie deep mountains; to the east beyond the Prince of Wales Hotel is bare, rolling prairie.

A short side trail leads to a rocky outcrop with even better views down the lake. Here is the hardy, scrub-like limber pine found only in isolated patches in the park. You can confirm its identity by the needles—clusters of five, which are stiff, slightly curved and from 4–7 cm (1.6–2.7 in) long.

The trail turns into the steep-walled Bertha Valley, crosses the creek and ascends gradually to Lower Bertha Falls, more of a long cascade than a waterfall.

OPTION: Hikers with more time and energy can continue 2.8 km (1.7 mi) further from the falls to Bertha Lake. The trail quickly steepens and climbs to the upper

Bertha Falls

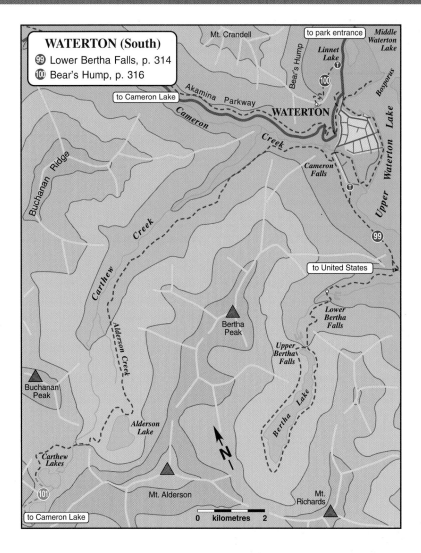

WATERTON (South)
99 Lower Bertha Falls, p. 314
100 Bear's Hump, p. 316

to Cameron Lake

Mt. Crandell

to park entrance

Middle
Waterton
Lake

Bear's Hump

Linnet
Lake

Akamina Parkway

Cameron

WATERTON

Bosporus

Creek

Cameron
Falls

Upper Waterton Lake

Buchanan Ridge

Creek

to United States

Carthew

Lower
Bertha
Falls

Bertha
Peak

Upper
Bertha
Falls

Alderson Creek

Buchanan
Peak

Bertha Lake

Alderson
Lake

Carthew
Lakes

N

101

Mt. Alderson

Mt.
Richards

to Cameron Lake

0   kilometres   2

floor of the valley, passing from the montane zone to the subalpine zone. The switchbacks are relentless through the spruce, fir and low alder as you attain the upper floor of the hanging valley. The creek plunges over the lip to form Upper Bertha Falls.

Bertha Lake is beautifully set against a glacier-carved cirque.

Much of the lakeshore is scoured by avalanches in winter. The trail descends to the lake, and the right branch leads to a small but nicely situated backcountry campground in about 0.6 km (0.4 mi). A rough trail circles the lake, ideal for fishermen after rainbow trout ... or anyone seeking tranquillity.

100. Bear's Hump—*Waterton panorama*

About 40 minutes of steep hiking alongside the limestone-dolomite cliffs of Bear's Hump, takes you to one of the most glorious panoramas in a park full of them. The summit makes a breathtaking picnic stop on a sunny day.

access

The trail begins behind the Visitor Reception Centre, just east of Waterton townsite on the entrance road.

Map: page 315
Distance: 2.8 km (1.7 mi) return
Time: 1¹/₂ hours
Rating: Strenuous
Max. elevation: 1560 m (5117 ft)
Elevation gain: 210 m (689 ft)
Footwear: Running/walking shoes/light hiking boots
Best season: June through September

The trail leads through an aspen grove, and then heads steeply up through a forest of lodgepole pine and Douglas-fir. You'll catch a few glimpses of Emerald Bay, the Prince of Wales Hotel and in the distance the prairies stretching to the east. Views are limited until the top of the cliff.

Parks Canada has a problem with hikers taking shortcuts between switchbacks on this trail. This practice causes serious erosion and rock-fall problems on the steep slope.

The last portion is particularly strenuous. At the top, sweeping views extend across the townsite, lake and prairies. Conditions can be exceedingly windy. Do refrain from tossing rocks off the top. Climbers may be using the cliffs below.

Bear's Hump

101. Summit Lake–Carthew Summit

Beargrass, mule deer and more

You begin at one stunning lake and hike to an equally beautiful and more secluded one, climbing steadily most of the way. On the ascent, you pass through a forest that includes 500-year-old spruce. In good weather, hikers can climb 3.7 km (2.3 mi) beyond the lake to the treeless, windswept heights of Carthew Summit, one of the most splendid alpine viewpoints in the park. Strong hikers who make transportation arrangements in advance can hike all the way back to Waterton townsite.

Map: page 318
Distance: 8 km (5 mi) return to Summit Lake; 15.4 km (9.6 mi) return to Carthew Summit
Time: 2 hours (Summit Lake); 5 hours (Carthew Summit)
Rating: Moderate
Max. elevation: 1906 m (6252 ft)
Elevation gain: 250 m (820 ft)
Footwear: Light hiking boots
Best season: July to mid-September

access

Drive 15.5 km (9.6 mi) to the end of the Akamina Parkway. The trail begins along the south shore of Cameron Lake, just left of the boat rental facilities.

The trails climbs steadily above Cameron Lake through a green, damp, ferny forest. The weather at Cameron Lake is often warmed by moist Pacific air from nearby mountains, which has made the area a sanctuary for some types of plants and animals usually found further west. Varied thrush and Steller's jay, uncommon in any other parts of the park, are often seen here.

The slope relents about two-thirds of the way up, and the trees become more stunted. Beargrass, which is actually a kind of lily, grows to great heights in this area in summer months. Bears, you'll probably be glad to know, have no particular attraction to the plant, despite the name. Take the usual precautions, however. Bears do tend to be found in similar habitats and grizzlies have been seen on this trail.

The trail descends slightly to the spruce-fringed lake, a great place to rest. The mountain that dominates across the lake is Chapman Peak in the U.S., at 2866 m (9400 ft).

OPTION: In good weather, hikers with more time and energy can climb 3.7 km (2.3 mi) further to Carthew Summit. Don't attempt this climb above the treeline if the weather is bad, because the open

Carthew Summit

ridge can be hazardous. The return trip from Cameron Lake to Carthew Summit takes about five hours.

From Summit Lake, the Carthew–Alderson trail quickly moves out into the open and begins the switchback above the stunted fir trees. Looking south, you can see the tiny subalpine lakes and imposing peaks of northern Glacier National Park. The trail crests the windswept ridge; the vistas in the other direction are equally impressive.

Below are the two tear-drops of Carthew Lakes surrounded by Waterton's distinctive red scree. In the far distance, the mountains drop away into open prairie.

You can make out the trail descending steeply to the lakes. It is a total of 19 km (12 mi) from Cameron Lake to the trail's end at Waterton townsite. The upper section of the route by the lakes (including Alderson Lake) is fascinating, although the last half is a more routine march along a tree-lined path with few views.

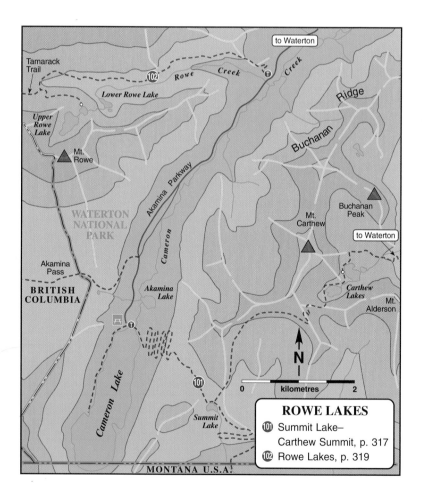

ROWE LAKES

101 Summit Lake–
Carthew Summit, p. 317
102 Rowe Lakes, p. 319

102. Rowe Lakes—*Invitation to subalpine wandering*

Set under cliffs amid snow patches that usually linger though summer, the green, larch-rimmed Rowe Lakes seem a magical place. Although it takes considerable effort to get there, hikers who make an early start might find the surrounding flower-filled meadows and knolls delightful to explore.

Map: page 318
Distance: 12.4 km (7.7 mi) return
Time: 5 hours
Rating: Strenuous
Max. elevation: 2200 m (7216 ft)
Elevation gain: 600 m (1968 ft)
Footwear: Light hiking boots
Best season: Late June to September

access

From Waterton townsite, drive west up the Akamina Parkway. At about 10 km (6.2 mi), or 2 km (1.2 mi) past the Oil City historic site, is a parking area for the Rowe Lakes trail on the right side of the road.

The trail heads gently up the north side of Rowe Creek through lodgepole pine. Under the steep, grey face of Mt. Lineham, it passes outcrops of Waterton's characteristic red rock. The pines soon give way to a denser forest of fir and spruce. The soft-carpeted path continues on a gentle grade as the valley narrows and you begin to cross slide areas bright with fireweed and aster for much of summer.

A short side trail leads across the stream to Lower Rowe Lake, a pleasant though unspectacular green pond set under cliffs. In spring and early summer, a 150-m (492-ft) waterfall descends from the hanging valley above, draining Upper Rowe Lakes.

The main trail ascends again beside the creek, and the valley gradually opens up into a grassy basin between Mt. Lineham (right) and Mt. Rowe (left). At 5 km (3.1 mi), you reach a beautifully situated picnic area in a flower-filled meadow under the red scree slopes. Some hikers will be content to go no further.

On the other side of a meadow, the Tamarack Trail branches right to begin the arduous switchback up Lineham Ridge. This more demanding, more rewarding option is intended for the energetic hiker— the views from the top, far above treeline, are outstanding. The price is a 3.5-km (2.2-mi), one-way grind up one of the most relentlessly steep trails in Waterton.

The easier and shorter 1.2-km (0.7-mi) trail to Upper Rowe Lakes heads off left and begins a steep ascent out of the amphitheatre. Small Engelmann spruce and alpine fir grow sparsely among the rocks. Views are outstanding. Near the top of the ridge, you enter the zone of the light green alpine larch.

The trail finally levels off, and then descends slightly through a fine open forest to meadows and the lake itself. It's a magical place on a fine day. (Don't bring your fishing gear, however. There are usually no fish.) Beaches of flat stones surround the vivid green waters that are set under cliffs and snow slopes, an invitation to subalpine wandering.

Upper Rowe Lake

103. Crandell Campground to Lake Crandell—*An undemanding lake*

A gentle trail leads up from Crandell Campground to Crandell Lake, a good family outing, after dinner leg-stretcher or even a leisurely destination for backpackers. Camping is allowed at Crandell Lake (a back-country permit is required). Some hikers may want to hike right across to the Akamina Parkway if they can get someone to pick them up on the other side.

Map: below
Distance: 4 km (2.5 mi) return
Time: 1½ hours
Rating: Moderate
Max. elevation: 1524 m (4999 ft)
Elevation gain: 120 m (394 ft)
Footwear: Walking/running shoes/light hiking boots
Best season: June to late September

access

Start at the Crandell Mountain Campground off the Red Rock Parkway. The trail begins near the northwest end of the campground on the access road opposite Loop K.

Cross a log bridge and then begin a gentle climb. Views of Mt. Galwey dominate the east horizon. The angle increases before long, and you reach an area of rocky outcroppings and more stunted alpine growth.

Watch for a sign pointing left to Crandell Lake, which you will probably reach before you know it. Linger in this lovely spot, if you have the time.

Hikers who have arranged for

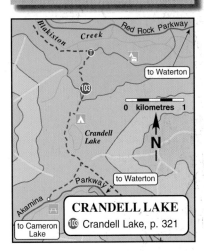

CRANDELL LAKE
103 Crandell Lake, p. 321

transportation on the other end can continue past the lake for only 1.6 km (1 mi) further to the Akamina Parkway, 7 km (4.3 mi) west of Waterton townsite.

Those Jabby Jays

wildlife

Both the grey jay (also known as the whiskey jack, see illustration on page 219) and the blue jay are common in the Rockies. A bird that's friendly to a fault, the grey jay is dark around the neck, with grey, fluffy plumage. Its natural diet is insects, but it's shameless about begging. Do the bird a favour and resist. The blue jay, with its conspicuous blue crest, is usually seen during the day in flocks of up to 50. Much less common is the Steller's jay (see illustration on page 82), a stunning bird with a dark crest and a raucous call.

104. Crypt Lake Trail—*A walk in a million*

One magazine voted the Crypt Lake Trail 'Canada's best hike.' It is simply among the most unusual, interesting and spectacular in Canada: hikers can visit two countries; the trailhead can only be reached by boat; and, not least, one short section of the route is underground. The price for this variety is a very steep, long and often hot ascent and some vertical exposure. Unfortunately, this hike has become hugely popular, attracting hundreds of hikers on some days.

Map: page 323
Distance: 17.2 km (10.7 mi) return
Time: 6 hours
Rating: Strenuous
Max. elevation: 1950 m (6396 ft)
Elevation gain: 670 m (2198 ft)
Footwear: Light hiking boots
Best season: July to early September

access

In July and August, shuttle boats leave the marina in Waterton townsite for Crypt Landing at 9 a.m. and 10 a.m. Boats return from Crypt Landing at 4 p.m. and 5:30 p.m. Contact the marina ticket office at (403) 859-2362 for the off-season schedule.

Crypt Landing is a pleasant place to linger whether you're waiting for your boat ride or camping overnight. The campground is right by the beach in a cove.

The trail initially heads off south along the lake, through a dense forest of spruce and fir, and begins to switchback. A short side trail leads to Hell Roaring Falls, beautifully set in a canyon of copper-coloured rock, although the falls itself really only roars in spring and early summer. The main trail continues up the valley past a good viewpoint for Twin Falls. The trees gradually open up after Burnt Rock Falls.

The trail leads past a swampy lower lake and heads up on a more strenuous set of switchbacks, finally levelling off in subalpine terrain and reaching the popular campground. Cross the creek and head up a steep talus slope. It is hot, dry work on this south-facing slope, especially when the sun is shining. Carry water. At the top, a short ladder takes you up the rock wall to the tunnel entrance. The passageway is about 25 m (82 ft) long and low enough that you'll have to crawl along one section.

At the end of the tunnel, the trail heads up and along an exposed rock wall, although a sturdy cable anchored to the rock provides reassurance. The route soon levels off.

Crypt Lake

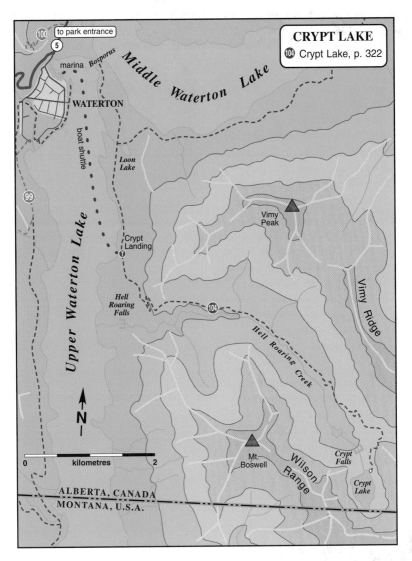

CRYPT LAKE

104 Crypt Lake, p. 322

(Map labels: to park entrance, 100, 5, marina, Bosporus, Middle Waterton Lake, WATERTON, boat shuttle, Loon Lake, 99, Vimy Peak, Crypt Landing, Upper Waterton Lake, Hell Roaring Falls, 104, Hell Roaring Creek, Vimy Ridge, N, kilometres, 0, 2, Mt. Boswell, Wilson Range, Crypt Falls, Crypt Lake, ALBERTA, CANADA, MONTANA, U.S.A.)

Nearby, a creek emerges from the limestone after a subterranean passage from Crypt Lake. The water drops over the edge to create the 175-m (574-ft) Crypt Falls.

Crypt Lake itself is just over the top of the ridge and is worth all the sweating and steep places that you traversed to get here. The deep green lake is set in a spectacular cirque. Snowfields can linger here all summer and icebergs usually dot the lake. The far end of the lake is on the U.S. border. You can walk down to it on a rough trail. Be sure to allow yourself plenty of time to return to the landing to catch the shuttle boat back to Waterton townsite.

105. Red Rock Canyon Loop

Walk in a rainbow canyon

The interpretive walk is short (but often crowded), the red-hued canyon is gorgeous, and you're almost guaranteed to come practically nose to nose with wildlife. You'll also receive an instant geological education. If the day is warm, explore Blakiston Falls as well, and then picnic overlooking Blakiston Valley.

Map: below
Distance: 0.7 km (0.4 mi)
Time: 20 minutes
Rating: Easy
Max. elevation: 1500 m (4920 ft)
Elevation gain: Negligible
Footwear: Walking/running shoes
Best season: June to October

access

Drive 14 km (9 mi) to the end of the Red Rock Parkway. The surprises can begin right at the Red Rock Canyon parking lot, one of the surest places in Waterton to spot wildlife. Deer and bighorn sheep are frequently seen.

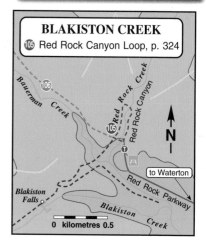

An asphalt path leads past an interpretive display and to the beginning of the trail. The horn of Anderson Peak, at 2683 m (8800 ft), dominates the skyline. Downstream is the floodplain of Blakiston Creek, which has rearranged gravel and glacial silts in the Blakiston Valley for thousands of years.

The canyon ahead is not large, but its rose, red and pink hues make up in beauty what it lacks in size. The canyon began as mud deposited in an ancient, shallow sea. As parts of the sea dried up, exposure oxidized the iron, forming a red mineral called 'hematite.' Unexposed layers formed green and white bands, causing a layer-cake effect in parts of the canyon. Take a moment to peer at the ripple marks that were caused by slow currents and waves in that ancient, shallow sea.

Head uphill to the wooden bridge at the deeper part of the canyon, taking a good look at the varied ribbons of colour in the canyon wall. It took 7000 to 10,000 years for water to carve this small gorge, and the process is continuing. Interpretive signs explain how erosion wears the canyon down by the thickness of a nickel or two a year. Continue descending on the other side of the canyon.

facing page: Red Rock Canyon

Note that archaeological sites dating back 8000 years have been found in Red Rock Canyon, which appears to have been used as a seasonal campsite by prehistoric native peoples. An ancient corridor to South Kootenay Pass existed along Blakiston Creek.

OPTION: Hikers with a little more time and energy could continue to walk southwards from the canyon on the wide, easy trail to South Kootenay Pass. It climbs gradually through lodgepole pine and in 15 minutes or so, you reach a good viewpoint overlooking Blakiston Falls.

The falls are especially impressive in spring and early summer. The water is forced through a cleft and down into a clear pool.

white-tailed deer

mule deer

wildlife

How to Tell Your Deer

You can tell the mule deer by its large, mule-like ears, black-tipped tail and a white rump patch. They are larger than the less common white-tailed deer and tend to migrate higher in summer.

White-tailed deer are more common to abandoned pastureland of the East, but can still be found in the parks. They can be smaller than mule deer and have long, brown tails that are held upright at any sign of danger. When the tail is up, you can see its white underside.

106. Goat Lake

Alpine meadows, waterfalls and a hanging valley

Green Goat Lake is set in a stunning hanging valley that is above a series of cascades and waterfalls. Near the lake are lush meadows filled with glacier lilies and other wildflowers. The area lives up to its name: an excellent place to spot mountain goats. This relatively quiet route is a good alternative to the busy Crypt Lake Trail.

Map: below
Distance: 14.2 km (8.8 mi) return
Time: 4 hours
Rating: Strenuous
Max. elevation: 2010 m (6593 ft)
Elevation gain: 515 m (1689 ft)
Footwear: Light hiking boots
Best season: July to early September

access

Start from the parking area at Red Rock Canyon at the end of the Red Rock Parkway, 14 km (9 mi) from the park entrance road.

Cross Red Rock Canyon on the bridge at the lower end of the parking lot and follow the Snowshoe Trail for the first 4.6 km (2.9 mi). The slightly overgrown fireroad follows Bauerman Creek along the wide valley floor. Although it's a pleasant rolling

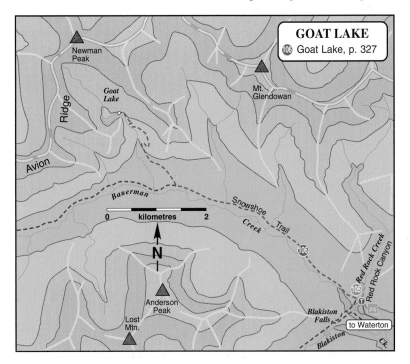

GOAT LAKE
106 Goat Lake, p. 327

Newman Peak

Goat Lake

Mt. Glendowan

Ridge

Avion

Bauerman

Snowshoe Trail

Creek

0 kilometres 2

N

106

105

Anderson Peak

Lost Mtn.

Blakiston Falls

Red Rock Creek

Red Rock Canyon

to Waterton

Blakiston Ck.

woodland trail, hikers bound for Goat Lake will have their minds on higher things and may resent the relatively long walk before they can start the ascent. Bikes can eliminate valley-hiking tedium. In fact, the Snowshoe route is one of Waterton's best mountain bike trails, and hikers can leave their iron steeds locked to a tree (out of sight) at the bottom of the Goat Lake trail.

From the valley floor, the Goat Lake trail climbs steeply and views soon open up across the valley to Lost Mountain and Bauerman Mountain. Like the Crypt Lake Trail (Walk 104), this south-facing slope can be a hot climb in sunny weather. Mountain goats can often be seen on the rocky ledges above the trail or on the trail itself.

The route turns up into a steep-sided valley above a long cascade and switchbacks in open terrain to the lip of the valley, beside a water-fall. Past the waterfall is green Goat Lake in a subalpine forest, set under a steep ridge running down from Newman Peak.

Hikers can continue past the lake and a backcountry campground to the open, flower-filled meadows just beyond that afford better views of the Avion Ridge above, which is capped by red argillite.

OPTION: In good weather, the ridge can be ascended in 1.6 km (1 mi) one-way by strong hikers who take a rough, unofficial path that follows the stream until diverting right to find passages through a couple of steep bands of rock. Above the ledges, the trail attacks an open slope of red argillite and works up a windswept pass.

Goat Lake

facing page: One of several waterfalls on the Crypt Lake hike (Walk 104).

Skoki Lodge in Banff National Park

CHAPTER 7

A DETAILED GUIDE TO OUTDOOR ACTIVITIES

Backcountry Huts

While alpine backcountry huts are used primarily by climbers, they can provide great overnight facilities for hikers and scramblers, and are especially welcome in cold or wet weather or at high elevations.

You don't have to be a member of the Alpine Club of Canada to stay in an ACC backcountry hut. Members with a 'Facilities Upgrade' get discounted rates and six-month advance bookings. Non-members can only book 30 days in advance. Bookings are made through the ACC's national office in the Canmore Clubhouse, (403) 678-3200.

For most of the backcountry huts, you pack in your sleeping bag and food, and can use the pots and pans and stoves provided. Bring your own white gas.

Although many of the huts are accessible only to those experienced in glacier travel or technical climbing, some huts can be reached by strong hikers. A few are easily accessible. For example, you can drive to the Canmore facility and the Elizabeth Parker Hut is only a 15-minute walk from the Lake O'Hara bus stop.

Selected Huts

Banff National Park

Bow Hut (ACC): A large facility just below the vast Wapta Icefield with outstanding views across the Bow Valley, Bow Hut is popular for glacier ski touring, but is also an excellent destination for hikers. You can reach it in several hours from Bow Lake (Walk 42). Look for a junction on the left at the top of the first slope beyond the lake. Scramble over the boulders (awkward and potentially dangerous for people with heavy packs) to the other side of the creek and follow the trail, staying on the left of the creek until the bottom of a headwall. The hut is visible atop the headwall, and is reached on a steep trail.

Yoho National Park

Abbot Pass Hut: This hut is a historic stone building at 2926 m (9598 ft) in the pass between Mt. Victoria and Mt. Lefroy, right on the Continental Divide between Lake Louise and Lake O'Hara. You approach via a long, gruelling scree gully above Lake Oesa (Walk 58). Allow a full day for bus access to Lake O'Hara (see page 184) and the walk/scramble to the hut.

Elizabeth Parker Hut: A rustic log cabin in a gorgeous meadow, the hut is a 15-minute walk from Le Relais where the shuttle bus stops at Lake O'Hara (see Walk 56, page 180, and sidebar about bus access, page 184). This highly popular hut is the second-best place to stay at Lake O'Hara and costs only a fraction of what you'd pay at Lake O'Hara Lodge. All of the splendid hiking at Lake O'Hara is before you. Book long in advance. The hut makes a great destination for ski touring, and good telemark runs can be found nearby.

Stanley Mitchell Hut: This comfortable log hut in a gorgeous meadow in the Little Yoho Valley is easily accessible in a few hours from the Yoho Valley trail (Walk 53). A good place for families. It makes a great base for hiking the Iceline (Walk 53) and Whaleback trails.

Jasper National Park

Fryatt Hut (ACC): This hut is a terrific destination, and is located in a meadow atop the easily climbed headwall in the upper Fryatt Valley. Reach it on the Fryatt Valley trail, which starts at the Geraldine Lake fireroad off Hwy. 93A. The first part is flat and tedious, and is best traversed by mountain bike. Then leave your bike hidden in the trees and ascend steeply to the hut. The hut is usually booked long in advance.

Wates-Gibson Hut: An excellent centre for exploring the spectacular Tonquin Valley, it is reached after an all-day hike by the Astoria River trail and the Chrome Lake turnoff. The route can be very muddy. Give yourself a couple of days to explore the terrain around the Ramparts and Amethyst Lakes.

Kananaskis Country

Canmore Clubhouse: The clubhouse, located above the Bow Valley Parkway (Hwy. 1A) just east of Canmore, is an inexpensive, convenient place to stay while exploring Banff and Kananaskis. Nonmembers pay $19 a night for bunks in rooms that hold four to six people. Bring your sleeping bag. There's a cozy lounge with a fireplace and a good selection of mountain books.

Mt. Assiniboine

Naiset Cabins: An ideal place to stay while exploring the historic, spectacular Mt. Assiniboine area. Located below the Mt. Assiniboine Lodge. Can be reached via helicopter from Canmore or on a long all-day hike or mountain bike trip on the Bryant Creek trail from Watridge Lake Road in Kananaskis Country. Operated by B.C. Parks in summer and Mt. Assiniboine Lodge in winter. Reservations, (403) 678-2883, are necessary in winter.

Backcountry Lodges

The backcountry lodges of the Canadian Rockies provide some of the most delightful accommodation in the national parks. Most lodges require that you hike or ski-in, and most combine a love for tradition with excellent food and service. Although prices may seem high, in our experience guests receive high value for their money. (The cost usually includes all meals, snacks, guiding services, etc.)

Banff National Park

Shadow Lake Lodge and Cabins: (403) 762-5454. A relatively easy, 13-km (8-mi) hike or ski-in from the trailhead at Red Earth Creek parking lot leads to this lodge. The restored lodge features home cooking; afternoon tea is served daily. Excellent hiking and ski-touring from the lodge.

Skoki Lodge: (403) 762-5454. To get to this lodge, follow an 11-km (6.8-mi) hike or ski trail that starts behind the Lake Louise ski area and ascends Boulder Pass and Deception Pass. This rustic log-cabin lodge was recently declared a national historic site. Skoki is an excellent base for hiking and ski-touring. Great food and ambiance; afternoon tea is served. (No electricity or indoor plumbing.) Reserve well in advance.

Sundance Lodge: (403) 762-4551. The lodge, situated on Brewster Creek south of Banff, is reached by a 16-km (10-mi) horseback ride or ski in the Sundance Valley—10 km (6.2 mi), if you approach from Healy Creek. Amenities include showers and solar-powered lighting.

Yoho National Park

Lake O'Hara Lodge: (250) 343-6418. Situated at the heart of one of the finest hiking areas in the

wildlife

Watch Your Marmots and Pikas

While hiking, watch rock piles closely for marmots and pikas (see photo, page 99). The marmot has a high-pitched whistle, while the smaller pika lets out a shrill 'eeeep!'

The marmot weighs between 4.5 kg and 13.6 kg (10 and 30 lbs), and has grizzled hair on its back, although the rest of its body may be fairly brown.

The chubby, small-eared pika is about the size of a hamster and is otherwise known as the 'rock rabbit.' Its grey colouring blends with the rocks it lives on.

hoary marmot

You can sometimes discover where pikas live by looking for the little 'haystack' they spend the summer gathering: a fine collection of grasses and other plants, even marmot droppings, often hidden in the shelter of an overhanging rock. Don't disturb it. The pika relies on this material for its winter meals, taken in peace under the snow.

Rockies, Lake O'Hara Lodge is open winter and summer. It's the most expensive backcountry lodge ($185 per person/night), but it also offers extraordinary comforts and front-door views, plus electricity, indoor plumbing and central heating. The ski-in is 11 km (7 mi); in summer, you can take a bus.

Twin Falls Chalet: (403) 228-7079. This cozy log chalet at Twin Falls in the Yoho Valley is usually open July 1 to September 15. Excellent base for day hikes; book early.

Jasper National Park

Dixon's Lodge: (403) 852-3909. Skiing in to Dixon's Lodge is more demanding than to other backcoun-

try lodges, because it involves a 23-km (14-mi) trek over Maccarib Pass into the Tonquin Valley. The reward is incredible scenery and a delicious sense of remoteness. Private cabins. Expect hearty food and down-home hospitality.

Mt. Assiniboine

Mt. Assiniboine Lodge: (403) 678-2883. Kananaskis Country is the jumping-off point for the famous Mt. Assiniboine Lodge in B.C.'s Mt. Assiniboine Provincial Park. It's expensive but provides outstanding food and atmosphere, plus guided hikes or skiing. Many guests from outside Alberta use Mt. Engadine Lodge, (403) 678-4080, as their base and then go into Mt.

Assiniboine by helicopter. It can also be reached by a fairly long hike or ski or by mountain bike.

Backpacking in the Canadian Rockies

Although day walkers travel light and fast and sleep in a comfortable bed at night, they may be missing something—the deep backcountry, for one thing. So much splendid country simply can't be reached and fully enjoyed in one day. By the time you get to that high backcountry lake or pass, you have to turn right around to be back by sundown. And maybe the true wilderness feeling is diminished by returning to a highway campground or motel at night rather than staying in the backcountry alongside a creek.

The downside is that backpacking can be plain hard work. You have to lug your house on your back, as backpacking guru Colin Fletcher described it. The journey is just

Backpacking in Mt. Assiniboine Provincial Park

about all uphill on the way in when your pack is heaviest. Unless you are a climber away from trails (with the proper permit), you have to stay in official backcountry campgrounds in most areas, which can mean forced togetherness with noisy strangers. (In fairness, we seem to get along with just about everybody we meet in the deep backcountry. There's usually a shared sense of environmental ethics and wilderness values and a feeling that we've all sweated hard to get there.) In some parks under minimal impact rules, random camping is permitted in designated remote areas.

Some backcountry campgrounds such as Paradise Valley (see Walk 33) and Egypt Lake in Banff are heavily used all summer. Quotas are imposed and park use permits are issued a maximum of only six days in advance. Now is the time to be flexible with your plans. Parks staff can suggest lesser-known alternatives, and you may end up having a better time with a greater sense of solitude and exploration.

Two concepts can substantially improve your backpacking experience: go light and/or basecamp.

New Concepts in Backpacking

'Backpacking Lite' is catching on among experienced travellers. Although newcomers tend to take too much 'just in case,' veterans of the backcountry are finding innovative ways to cut weight so they can walk all day without strain. Excellent lightweight tents and other equipment and freeze-dried food are available, of course. But some light travellers are experimenting with other notions such as backpacking without a stove or cooking pots, as one example.

The key might be not to make

First Rule of Backpacking: Bring Money

The backcountry can be expensive these days. Anyone staying overnight in the mountain national parks away from the road needs a Wilderness Pass.

The cost is $6 per night per person to a maximum of $30 per person per trip. Annual passes are available for $42 a person. Children 16 and under are free. There's an additional fee for use of shelters such as Bryant Creek and Egypt Lake in Banff. Add on a reservation fee of $10, and you'll understand why you need your credit cards in the great outdoors.

See 'Sources' at the end of the book for the numbers to call to reserve backcountry campsites and get further information.

The idea behind all of these fees is that the burden of paying for support and maintenance of backcountry trails and facilities, plus warden patrols and resource studies, should be borne more by the users than by taxpayers in general. Parks staff point out that the fees don't even begin to cover the costs of their backcountry work. Watch for further increases.

Visitor tips

wildlife

Eagle Mania

It pays to be eagle-eyed in the Canadian Rockies, where both bald eagles and their somewhat smaller counterparts, golden eagles can sometimes be seen soaring high above grassy meadows. Watch for the golden eagle above the meadows near the Columbia Icefield and in the eastern part of the Bow Valley. (You can only see the golden neck feathers at close range.) In recent years, huge migrations of golden eagles have been noted in spring and fall. Bald eagles can sometimes be seen on the tops of trees or flying above lakes and ponds in Jasper National Park. They are easy to distinguish from the golden eagle because of their white heads and larger bills.

golden eagle

bald eagle

radical changes in what you bring but to make a number of small, incremental improvements. Scrutinize everything and ask whether you can substitute something lighter (baking soda in a plastic bag instead of that tube of toothpaste), cut the weight of what you must bring (detach map portions of areas you won't reach), or simply eliminate (reject that extra shirt).

Despite the extra weight, we now backpack with pairs of collapsible ski/walking poles that substantially help the upper and lower body bear the extra strain of carrying a big pack. The poles provide an extra push on the ascent and take some of the strain off the knees on the descent.

The second helpful concept in backpacking is backcountry base camping. Instead of walking all day, every day and stopping at a new campsite each night, try hiking in to a diverse backcountry area, staying put for a few days and then taking day trips afield from your base. You only have to carry a heavy pack on the trip in and the trip out.

At Lake O'Hara, the backpacking is limited to loading your pack on the bus, if you can get a reservation. (See Walks 56–58 and the sidebar on page 184.)

Here are some of the major backpacking routes in the Rockies, although this book isn't the one to explore backpacking in detail. See the *Canadian Rockies Trail Guide,* by Brian Patton and Bart Robinson. For Kananaskis Country, see Gillean Daffern's *Kananaskis Country Trail Guide.*

Backpacking in Banff

Egypt Lake via Healy Pass (weekend or longer): Situated over a rounded pass into a high valley area of lakes and meadows under the Continental Divide. Highly popular. Starts from Bourgeau Lake parking lot below the Sunshine ski area.

Skoki Valley via Boulder Pass (weekend): Across lofty Deception Pass to the Skoki Valley where there are stunning lakes and a network of side trails. Popular. Starts from the base of the Lake Louise ski area.

Backpacking in Kootenay

Floe Lake–Numa Pass–Tumbling Pass (2–3 days): The trail parallels the crest of a steep, glaciated range, crossing several high passes. Routes can be tailored to your time and energy. Popular. Starts from the Banff-Windermere Highway (Hwy. 93) at Marble Canyon, Numa Creek or Floe Creek.

Backpacking in Yoho

Lake O'Hara (2–4 days): From a central camp, explore numerous high lakes and alpine areas (one of the most highly developed hiking regions in the parks). Extremely popular. Starts at the Lake O'Hara fireroad off the Trans-Canada on the Bow Valley Parkway (Hwy. 1A) near Kicking Horse Pass. Bus transportation is available to the lake at 8 a.m., 11 a.m. and 4 p.m. With the bus, extended carrying of your pack is unnecessary. Reservations are essential and difficult to obtain (see Walks 56–58).

Yoho Valley Circuit (2–3 days): Loop up the valley at one level and return on another. Splendid views, waterfalls, lakes and sidetrip options. Highly popular. Starts from Takakkaw Falls at the end of Yoho Valley Road, which leads off the Trans-Canada above Field (Walk 53). The Twin Falls chalet makes an excellent base for exploration. See 'Backcountry Lodges' in this chapter.

Backpacking in Jasper

Brazeau River–Poboktan Creek via Nigel Pass (3–4 days): This trail is an extended loop with different campsites every night and a variety of scenery from high passes to remote lakes and long valleys. Popular. Access is from the Icefields Parkway (Hwy. 93), 12 km (7.5 mi) south of the Icefields Centre, and at Poboktan Warden Station on the parkway, 72 km (45 mi) south of Jasper townsite.

Fryatt Creek (2–3 days): The trail terminates in an impressive valley, with a beautiful lake and an opportunity to scramble higher past cascades to the upper valley floor. Popular. Access from the Geraldine Lake fireroad near Athabasca Falls. You can bike the first portion.

Skyline Trail (2–3 days): It follows the crest of the rounded Maligne Range, with exceptional views and several passes. Highly popular. Hikers must plan to hitchhike back to their vehicle or arrange for shuttle transportation. Starts at Maligne Lake. Ends at the base of the old Signal Mountain fireroad near Maligne Canyon.

Tonquin Valley (2–3 days): On this hike, you visit a long lake under the towering Ramparts, one of the most stunning valleys in the mountains. Highly popular. Heavy use by horses. Starts from Mt. Edith Cavell Road near Cavell Lake or from Marmot Basin Road (a longer route via Maccarib Pass).

Backpacking in Mt. Robson Provincial Park

Berg Lake (weekend): This easy trail in Mt. Robson Provincial Park leads gently around the base of Robson, highest in the Canadian Rockies, past awesome rockwalls, waterfalls, cascades and ending at the impressive lake at the foot of Berg Glacier. Highly popular. Starts from the Robson River parking area, off Hwy. 16, 58 km (36 mi) west of Yellowhead Pass.

Backpacking in Mt. Assiniboine

Mt. Assiniboine via Citadel Pass (3–5 days): This classic trip to a classic mountain, along the Continental Divide, over a high pass, culminates in a beautiful subalpine area of lakes, meadows, passes and peaks. Highly popular. Begins at Sunshine Village—there are alter-

nate routes from the Spray Lakes reservoir south of Canmore. Can be reached from Spray Lakes on a mountain bike; you have to walk your bike on the final stretch. The Naiset Cabins at Lake Magog are available on a first-come, first-serve basis in summer. See 'Mt. Assiniboine Provincial Park' in 'Sources.'

Backpacking in Waterton Lakes National Park

Carthew–Alderson Trail (1½ days): Although strong hikers can do the 20-km (12-mi) route from Cameron Lake to Waterton townsite in a single day (Walk 101), backpackers have the advantage of being able to linger at some of the beautiful lakes, the flower-filled meadows and the high pass along the way. The only campsite is at Alderson Lake. Avoid a transportation hassle and use the hiker's shuttle.

Crypt Lake or Goat Lake (overnight): Expect hard, hot trudges up to pretty subalpine lakes, which make great basecamp areas for further exploration and ridge-walks (see Walks 104 and 106).

Tamarack Trail (2–3 days): The longest route in Waterton, this 36-km (22-mi) trek follows the Continental Divide, offering everything from windswept ridges to lonely lakes. Numerous steep ascents and descents. Solve the trailhead transportation hassles by taking a hiker's shuttle to the start.

Where to See Mountain Goats

Goats look best in winter when their coats are white and fluffy. In summer, they molt in great messy patches. Goats, like sheep, can climb to feed on remote, almost inaccessible mountain ledges high in the backcountry.

Banff: Watch for goats on Parker Ridge (Walk 47) near the Banff-Jasper boundary at Sunwapta Pass and on the steep slopes of Mt. Wilson and Mt. Coleman north of the Saskatchewan River Crossing.

Kootenay: The best spot to find them in the mountains is the Mt. Wardle Goat Lick, 51 km (32 mi) west of Castle Mountain Junction on the Banff-Windermere Highway (Hwy. 93).

Yoho: Look for mountain goats on the road into Takakkaw Falls (Walk 52).

Jasper: You might find goats around Disaster Point on Hwy. 16 East. The best spot is the goat lick viewpoint, on the Icefields Parkway (Hwy. 93), 38 km (24 mi) south of the townsite.

wildlife

mountain goat

Kayaking on the Athabasca River

Boating and Lake Canoeing

Banff National Park: Moraine Lake and Lake Louise are especially splendid from the water, and it's a good way to escape the camera-clicking crowds on the shore. While Lake Minnewanka is beautiful, it can be dangerous because huge waves and high winds build up suddenly. Two Jack Lake just south of Minnewanka is safer.

Canoeists, indeed all boaters, should be especially careful on mountain lakes. The water is usually extremely cold, perhaps only a few degrees above freezing. A capsize can be serious, because the unprotected body can't maintain strength for long in water that cold.

An excellent way to enjoy the Banff environs, away from the commercialization of Banff Avenue, is to rent a canoe. Banff Canoe Rentals, (403) 762-9205, on the corner of Wolf Street and Bow Avenue, is open May 15 to September 30. You can spend a delightful hour or day canoeing on the Bow River, Forty Mile Creek and Vermilion Lakes; one- to two-hour tours are also offered.

Boats are also available for rent at Lake Minnewanka, Two Jack Lake, Moraine Lake and Lake Louise.

Jasper National Park: A peaceful paddle on one of Jasper's glacial lakes might be as near to tranquillity as it's possible to come.

Pyramid Lake is the only lake in Jasper where motorboats are permitted. Pyramid Lake Boat Rentals,

(403) 852-4944, offers motorboats, rowboats, kayaks and sailboats.

Rowboats and canoes can be rented at the Jasper Park Lodge marina, (403) 852-5708, on Lac Beauvert. Rowboats, kayaks, canoes and fishing tackle are available at magnificent Maligne Lake, (403) 852-3370.

Maligne is subject to high winds and waves, however, and the water is extremely cold, even in late summer. Maligne has two backcountry campgrounds that are accessible by canoe.

Most of the lakes in the Jasper townsite area have rowboats and canoes for rent. Obtain keys beforehand from townsite fishing tackle stores. See 'Fishing,' page 361.

Waterton Lakes National Park:

Rowboats and canoes can be rented at the townsite marina or you can launch your own power boat at Emerald Bay. Waterton Lake is the deepest in the Canadian Rockies and one of the most beautiful. But the water remains ice-cold in summer, and winds can suddenly change the surface from dead calm to high waves. If you must cross the lake in a small boat, it's best to do so at a narrow point near the townsite and then stick to the shoreline.

A better place for small boats is Cameron Lake at the end of the Akamina Parkway, where rentals are available.

Camping

At their best, campgrounds bring people closer to the mountains and each other. A campsite is more than a parking stall and picnic table. People seem to enjoy the mountains as much for the camping as for the scenery: soothing air under lodgepole pines, campfires, steaks around the picnic table, stars of awesome clarity at night.

Of course, you might get noisy neighbours who want to party all night. Trailer owners could run their generators for hours. You might get rain, lots of rain, plus mud and creeping cold, even in July and August.

First, you must find space.

In summer, Tunnel Mountain Campground above Banff townsite is often filled by 12 p.m. Lake Louise and Kicking Horse campgrounds fill early, as do most others. Overflow sites for late arrivals are just big gravel parking lots.

Space is allocated on a first-come, first-serve basis, so come early. No reservations. Some campers spend their first night just outside the park and show up by 10 a.m. to claim a choice site as the campground begins to clear. Fees, which might change every year, depend on whether you stay at a campground with limited services, such as pit toilets, or one with flush toilets and hot water. You pay more for serviced sites with electrical hookups.

If your campground doesn't have showers, you can usually drop in at another one that's fully equipped. Some campgrounds will charge you $5 for your group to shower. Other campgrounds have coin showers.

Everybody who camps a lot has

favourite campgrounds and favourite sites in them. Here are some biased selections.

Banff National Park

Lake Louise: A big campground in a choice location with well-designed and usually well-spaced sites. It is situated within an easy stroll of Samson Mall along a pleasant riverside trail and handy for Lake Louise, Moraine Lake and the network of surrounding trails. Fills up fast in summer; when it is full, you'll get sent to the more primitive, less convenient Protection Mountain Campground, which is along the Bow Valley Parkway (Hwy. 1A).

Tunnel Mountain Village 1: On Tunnel Mountain Drive, 4 km (2.5 mi) east of Banff townsite. Not our favourite but not a horror story either. For its size, this campground on the heights above Banff can be surprisingly intimate. Sites are mostly well-spaced on the loops. Try for the sites on the outside of loops. The area is well-treed with good facilities, including showers and fine interpretive programs. You can walk to the Hoodoos viewpoint (Walk 9) or take Tunnel Mountain Drive (Walk 8) into Banff, although that's a considerable stroll. This campground tends to become noisier than some of the less-accessible ones because it's so close to the townsite—and to Calgary. People who are more interested in partying than in mountains tend to end up there.

Two Jack: Located north of Banff townsite on Lake Minnewanka Road. For anyone wishing to stay near Banff townsite, these campsites are usually quieter than the Tunnel Mountain metropolis. Two Jack Lakeside is more scenic and open and fills up faster. Be aware that some sites are uncomfortably close to the washrooms. Sites at Two Jack Main tend to be more secluded.

Waterfowl Lake: Located on the Icefields Parkway (Hwy. 93) north of the Trans-Canada Highway. It is a medium-sized campground with well-separated sites and facilities, plus a fantastic location at the end of the beautiful lake where the Mistaya River flows in.

Kootenay National Park

McLeod Meadows: Situated 26 km (16 mi) north of Radium Hot Springs in a flat, wooded area. Although it is not a beautiful campground, many of the sites are exceptionally private, and it is one of the best areas in the parks for observing big game such as moose, elk and deer. It doesn't fill up as fast as most of the Banff campgrounds.

Yoho National Park

Chancellor Peak: Situated 23.8 km (14.8 mi) west of Field. This slightly primitive campground is in a beautiful setting next to the Kicking Horse River, but it's not the place for light sleepers. The main

Canadian Pacific Railway (CPR) trans-continental route runs right behind the campground and heavy freights roar through at all hours of the night, shaking the ground. Try for a site close to the river and as far away from the tracks as possible.

Kicking Horse: Situated 5 km (3.1 mi) east of Field, it is the main Yoho campground and the busiest. Get there early. It has excellent facilities and a scenic location under Mt. Stephen. Try for sites close to the river.

Jasper National Park

Wabasso: Situated on Hwy. 93A, 20 km (12.4 mi) south of Jasper. It is far enough removed from the Jasper townsite area to escape some of the crowds. Beautifully situated along the shore of the fast-moving Athabasca. Handy to Athabasca Falls and Angel Glacier.

Wapiti: Situated on the Icefields Parkway (Hwy. 93) just south of Jasper townsite. Smaller than the massive Whistler's Campground across the highway, Wapiti has a more relaxed atmosphere, especially if you can get one of the sites close to the Athabasca River, a good place for a stroll in the evening (Walk 75).

Kanananaskis Country

All the campgrounds in Peter

Camping in the Rockies

Lougheed Provincial Park and many in surrounding areas are highly recommended. They tend to be newer and better designed than the national park campgrounds, with lots of space and trees between sites. Some accept reservations.

Campgrounds along Lower Kananaskis Lakes (Interlakes, Mt. Sarrail and Lower Lake) are especially scenic. Only Lower Lake and Boulton Creek across the road accept reservations in this area, (403) 591-7226. Mt. Kidd RV Park and campground has lavish facilities, including hot tubs, lounge, tennis courts, games room, snack bar and a good store, plus an outstanding location under the impressive bulk of Mt. Kidd. Reservations, (403) 591-7700. Bow Valley Provincial Park is beautifully set opposite Mt. Yamnuska. Try for sites close to the Bow River. Reservations, (403) 673-2163.

Waterton Lakes National Park

Crandell Mountain Campground: Wilder and more laid-back than the townsite campground, it offers well-spaced sites in mixed grassland and forest, with terrific views over the Blakiston Valley to Mt. Galwey. Situated 12 km (7.4 mi) from the townsite up the Red Rock Parkway, a route you should never tire of driving. No showers, but campers can use the townsite campground facilities for free.

Waterton Townsite Campground: In a lovely location on the edge of the townsite, this grassy, open area looks right down Upper Waterton Lake to some of the finest scenery in the Rockies. The townsite is small enough that you can walk everywhere right from your campsite. Exceedingly popular. Visitors often have to spend the night at a large commercial campground just outside the park and line up early in the morning for a place. The effort is worth it. The drawback is that because the campsites are open, there's no privacy and it can be very windy and cold in bad weather. You have to accept it as an open, almost urban scene, a place for people-watching as well as gazing upon the scenery—more like a European campground.

Canoeing the Easy Rivers

Even hikers get the blues. They begin to have non-walking fantasies that may go something like this: You're sitting on a padded seat in a canoe on a warm, sunny day, drifting down the Bow or Athabasca rivers. You're watching the clouds and the mountains, letting the river do most of the work, sipping a cold beer, maybe even dropping in a fishing line in a moment of high energy.

This fantasy can be a reality. Canoes can be rented. (See 'Boating and Lake Canoeing,' page 340.) For smaller lakes and some rivers, visitors don't need whitewater canoeing skills, just the ability to steer and manage their canoe safely. Canoeists with some experience could probably handle the easier trips on the

Canoeing on the Bow River, Banff National Park

Bow or Athabasca rivers. They should, nonetheless, wear life jackets and be reasonably strong swimmers.

The major obstacle might be road transportation. If your party has two vehicles, leave one at your destination and with the other take your canoes to the starting point. Reverse the procedure at the other end.

If canoeing from Lake Louise to Banff, take a bus back (leaving the canoe behind) to pick up your car. Do the same from Jasper to Hinton or Banff to Canmore. Be creative— the transportation hassle is only a small obstacle to one of the greatest pleasures in the parks.

Major Banff Canoe Routes—Bow River

Lake Louise to Castle Mountain Junction (1 short day, 27 km, 17 mi): Don't try to start above or at Lake Louise Village. The river can be difficult near the town and is impossible higher up. There is a small set of rapids right beside the Trans-Canada bridge, just south of Lake Louise. The canoeist can launch just below them. Beyond, there are small waves, but no real rapids until after the Castle Mountain Junction bridge. It is a great trip, with sand bars and a winding, glacial-fed river of incredible blue. The adjacent Trans-Canada Highway seems to be on another planet.

The river is fast moving and changes direction frequently. The canoeist must avoid sand and gravel bars, the occasional rock and 'sweepers' (logs jutting into the water). Not a route for beginners.

Castle Mountain Junction to Trans-Canada Highway Bridge (1 day, 32 km, 20 mi): This stretch of the Bow River is fascinating, with the craggy peaks of the Sawback Range rising on the left. The one difficulty is the Redearth Rapids, 11 km (7 mi) below the bridge. In June, July and perhaps early August of most years, the river is high enough to cover the boulders.

Below the rapids, the river starts to slow, and becomes braided and ox-bowed. Here is an excellent place to see big game, such as moose, which come to feed in the shallows. The take-out point is on the right side of the river at the picnic grounds, just before the double Trans-Canada Highway bridges that cross the Bow.

Trans-Canada Bridge to Banff Boathouse (half-day, 11 km, 7 mi): Start at the picnic area just beyond the double Trans-Canada Highway bridges over the Bow, about 7 km (4 mi) (by car) west of Banff townsite. This trip is fine for less experienced canoeists because there are no rapids or fast-moving water. The river has turned into lazy ox-bows and multiple channels. It's more like a long, thin lake than a river. That, however, does mean you have to paddle more to get anywhere. Fortunately, the route is short.

The river enters Banff townsite and canoeists take out at the boathouse on the left bank where there is a boat rental concession. Heed warning signs. On no account should canoeists go further. Once past the Bow Bridge, the placid river turns to rapids and could sweep a canoeist over the deadly Bow Falls.

Canoeing in Jasper National Park

Banff to Canmore (1 day, 21 km, 13 mi): Travelling on the Bow River east of Canmore involves portages, a couple of potentially treacherous lakes, a waterfall and four dams. But the short jaunt from Banff to Canmore has none of these difficulties. Although it isn't for the beginner canoeist, it is a lovely, fast-moving trip, with small waves and multiple channels but no rapids.

The start is below Bow Falls (you better believe it!), just across the Spray River Bridge beneath the Banff Springs Hotel. The river flows swiftly past the golf course with Tunnel Mountain and the hoodoos on the left and the great cliffs of Mt. Rundle sweeping up on the right.

The river leaves the national park and canoeists are advised to take out at the first bridge leading into Canmore.

Major Jasper Canoe Routes

Miette River to Old Fort Point (2 hours, 5 km, 3.1 mi): This canoe route is a calm, easy stretch along a relatively narrow but deep river that winds through lodgepole forest in the beautiful country just west of Jasper. It is an excellent place to see moose and elk, especially in the evening.

Start at the Hwy. 16 bridge over the Miette River, just west of Jasper townsite. The Miette winds through level forest, passes under the Icefields Parkway (Hwy. 93) bridge and eventually under the 93A bridge, just before entering the broad, faster-moving Athabasca. This spot is an alternate take-out point. The Athabasca carries you swiftly down to the old bridge at Old Fort Point, where there's a convenient, sandy take-out on the right, just past the bridge.

Athabasca River—Old Fort Point to Jasper Lake (1 day, 25 km, 15.5 mi): This route is an ideal mountain river trip. While the river is fast moving, there are no rapids or treacherous areas. The Athabasca flows through a historic valley, which was once the route of explorers, such as David Thompson, who were followed by the fur traders. Away from Hwy. 16, it seems unchanged from those early days. The mountains on both sides of the valley are steep and spectacular. Near the end are sand dunes. On a sunny day, there's no better place to be.

Start at the Old Fort Point Bridge just south of Jasper townsite. From there, the river flows gently past numerous islands. Take the channels that appear to have the most water. The river passes the Maligne Road Bridge and leads out past interesting rock formations. At 15 km (9.3 mi), canoeists can stop and climb the right bank through a few trees to an open field where the ruins of John Moberly's old cabin are situated. He was the son of Henry Moberly, factor at Jasper House until 1861.

The river passes the junction with the fast-moving Snaring River and goes under Hwy. 16. An alternate pull-out point is located here.

The grey mountain on the right is Morro, a favourite practice spot for climbers. The river slows and widens into Jasper Lake, and the paddler is in for some interesting going. The lake is so clogged with sandbars that only a couple of inches of water can sometimes be left under the keel. While the maps show deeper channels, you probably won't be able to follow one for long. You might even have to get out in places and pull the canoe along through the shallows. While the water is extremely cold, your feet do get used to it and the bottom is pleasantly sandy. This small area along the lake is in the rain shadow of nearby mountains and has a semi-arid climate.

From this point, paddlers could keep to the right, close to the highway, for the most direct route to a take-out point. Canoeist with more time will find it interesting to keep left and explore the sand dunes on the north bank. From there, you'll have to cut straight across the lake to the pullout point.

Take out along the right bank on Jasper Lake, where the highway runs close to the lake. Don't go too far down the lake or you'll have to portage to get back to the highway. And beyond the lake, there's only one, easy-to-miss access point close to the highway. After that, it's a long, overnight trip to the bridge near Hinton, a fine trip for those prepared to camp out, a nightmare for those who aren't. Note that camping out along any river requires a Wilderness Pass and overnighters will be asked to stay in designated areas within the national park.

Cycling and Mountain Biking

Road Biking

The roads and highways of the Canadian Rockies provide some of the most spectacular cycling in the world. Cyclists come from all over Canada and the U.S., even from Europe, to spend a few days on the Icefields Parkway (Hwy. 93) between Jasper and Banff. This route was rated by *Outside* magazine as 'one of the 10 best in North America' for cycling.

Walking is the best way to appreciate the backcountry and cycling the best way to appreciate the parkways. Something new appears every few kilometres: turquoise-coloured lakes, castellated mountains, snow-capped summits, glacial valleys, waterfalls, wildlife and tumbling rivers. More than 100 glaciers are visible from the highway, and cyclists are protected from traffic, more or less, by the wide, paved shoulder. The cyclist sees and feels what the motorist misses.

Seventeen campgrounds are located along the route between Banff and Jasper townsites. Eight hostels are conveniently spaced for cyclists. While you can buy meals, potato chips, chocolate bars and the like at several locations along the parkway between Lake Louise and Jasper, don't count on finding bread or even Kraft Dinner. You can usually

Stopping for a bicycle picnic

buy a few oranges, apples or bananas in the restaurants/cafeterias. You might be able to pick up a few groceries at Saskatchewan River Crossing.

Cyclists can bring boxed bicycles to Banff and Jasper by bus. The Brewster buses, which operate every day between Jasper and Banff, will take boxed bicycles.

Cyclists tend to average $3^1/_2$ to $4^1/_2$ days to travel the 290 km (180 mi) between Jasper and Banff townsites, although it could easily be stretched to a week or more with sidetrips and stops for day hikes.

The Bow Valley Parkway (Hwy. 1A), northwest of Banff, which is quieter and more scenic than the parallel Trans-Canada, makes a fine route for one- or two-day cycles and most of the roads in the Banff area are excellent for short trips.

The Banff-Windermere Highway (Hwy. 93) between Castle Mountain Junction and Radium is another superb cycling road. It can be turned into a 314-km (195-mi) loop: cyclists head north from Radium to Golden; then east again on the Trans-Canada (the hardest section of the trip) into Yoho; over the Kicking Horse Pass, where the Spiral Tunnels were dug, to Lake Louise; and then south to Castle Mountain. This route is known as the 'Golden Triangle.' It's the scene of a highly popular group ride each spring. See 'Sources,' page 394.

The cycling is splendid in Kananaskis Country on the eastern slopes of the Rockies, 60 km (37 mi) southeast of Banff townsite. The shoulders are wide on the Kananaskis Trail (Hwy. 40), grades are mostly gentle, and the riding surface is excellent. Camping and picnic facilities are perhaps more abundant than anywhere else in the country. Those cyclists who make the ascent of Highwood Pass can conquer Canada's highest paved road.

Waterton has only two roads besides the townsite access route— the Akamina Parkway and the Red Rock Parkway—but both are superb for shorter day trips. For long-distance routes from Waterton, head into the U.S. and attempt the awesome ascent of Logan Pass on the Going-to-the-Sun Road. Be warned that the road can be dangerous for cyclists because of the heavy traffic and blind curves. One-way restrictions apply for cyclists. Check at the park gates. All distances are one-way unless otherwise specified.

Cycling Routes—Banff Townsite Area:

Vermilion Lakes Drive
(12 km, 7.5 mi). Walk 6

Banff Golf Course Loop
(12 km, 7.5 mi).

Tunnel Mountain Drive Loop
(11.8 km, 7.3 mi). Walk 8

Banff–Lake Minnewanka Loop
(19 km, 12 mi).

Cave and Basin to Sundance Canyon
(10.4 km, 6.4 mi). Walks 1, 2, 3

Banff to Johnston Canyon
(48 km, 30 mi).

Cycling Routes—Lake Louise:

Lake Louise Village to Valley of the Ten Peaks
(28 km, 17 mi return).

Lake Louise Village–Lake Louise-Great Divide–Kicking Horse Pass Loop
(22 km, 14 mi).

Cycling Routes—Yoho:

Trans-Canada Highway to Takakkaw Falls
(28.4 km, 18 mi).

Cycling Routes—Jasper Townsite Area:

Jasper to Old Fort Point, Lac Beauvert, Lake Annette, Lake Edith
(19 km, 12 mi).

Jasper to Pyramid Lake
(14 km, 9 mi).

Jasper to Maligne Canyon
(23.5 km, 15 mi).

Jasper to Athabasca Falls via Hwy.
93A and the Icefield Parkway
(Hwy. 93)
(67 km, 42 mi).

**Cycling Routes—Kananaskis
Country:**

Ribbon Creek to Wedge Pond
*(19.6 km, 12 mi return). Bicycle
path.*

Peter Lougheed Visitor Centre (in
Peter Lougheed Provincial Park) to
Elkwood
(9.4 km, 6 mi return).

Elkwood to Boulton
(9.4 km, 6 mi return).

Boulton to Upper Kananaskis Lake
(10 km, 6 mi return).

Cycling Routes—Waterton:

Waterton townsite to Red Rock
Canyon
(31 km, 19 mi return).

Waterton townsite to Cameron Lake
(31 km, 19 mi return).

Mountain Biking

Single-track trails and even
fireroads can become magic on
mountain bikes. There's joy in the
technical challenge of manoeuvring
over and around rocks and logs, and
climbing and descending steep
pitches. There's the exhilaration of
speed on the descent, your reward
for the uphill puffing. There's your
enhanced ability to get deeper into

Fall mountain biking, Banff National Park

the backcountry in a single day than any hiker could. It's easy on the feet, although hard on the backside. The Rockies are what mountain bikes are made for.

If there's a downside, it's that many trails are just about all uphill going in. Cyclists should also be aware that they are even more susceptible to sudden bear encounters than hikers. Because of their speed and silent approach, cyclists have a greater chance of surprising a bear—and a surprised bear is a potentially dangerous bear. Take the precaution of using bear bells and making noise, especially when heading through shrubby areas or around corners. Parks wildlife experts now recommend that backcountry cyclists carry bear spray, one canister for each cyclist. Be sure to carry it in an accessible place (see page 58).

Many hikers also use mountain

Old Fort Point in Jasper National Park

bikes to quickly reach steep portions of the trail. Burstall Pass (Walk 98) in Kananaskis and Goat Lake in Waterton (Walk 106) are good examples of how bikes can be used to speed up (and make enjoyable) long stretches of fireroad. Bring a lock and cable to secure your bike before you start the hiking portion. It's also a smart idea to bring enough tools to make emergency repairs or fix a flat. Cyclists can travel so far into the backcountry in one day that they get into deep trouble if they have equipment problems and have to walk out.

Mountain biking is restricted in the parks. Check at the visitor information centres for changes and conditions. Although trails that are very muddy or snowy may be acceptable to hikers, there are probably best avoided by all but the most intrepid mountain bikers. See the following listing (page 356) for names of operators who provide mountain bike tours and stores that rent bikes.

The following lists some favourite mountain biking routes. It is not all-inclusive. Check at the visitor information centres for other routes. And try to match a trail to your strength and abilities. Distances are **one-way** (except for loops), because many cyclists turn back before the end of some trails.

Banff National Park

Healy Creek (4.8 km, 3 mi): A pleasant double-track that follows the Bow River from Sundance Canyon to the Sunshine Road. Good for families.

Lake Minnewanka (up to 30 km, 19 mi): One of Banff's best trails for intermediate-level cyclists, it heads uphill beyond the bridge at Stewart Canyon (Walk 16) and descends over slides to the lakeshore. From there, the going is easier on a single-track, with occasional rocky sections. Great lunch spots at campgrounds or on the rocky beaches. Turn back before you get tired.

Redearth Creek (12 km, 7.5 mi): There are more interesting options if cycling is all you want to do. But this former fireroad provides access to some great hiking country such as Egypt Lake and Shadow Lake. You have to leave your bike (bring a lock) at the end of the road and go on foot the rest of the way. You can go on to Shadow Lake Lodge for tea.

Rundle Riverside (14 km, 9 mi): A challenging technical ride on a narrow trail, with lots of roots, boulders and short, small, steep pitches along the Bow River from the Banff Springs golf course to the Canmore Nordic Centre. Wooded with limited views across the river.

Spray River Loop (12.5 km, 7.8 mi): An easy, almost level family loop on fireroads. The trail starts just past the first fairway on the Banff Springs golf course (Walk 13), and leads into the woods and up the Spray River for the first portion. Keep straight at the first bridge (the crossing for the shorter Spray River Loop) and continue to the second crossing (bridge) and a pleasant picnic area. Return on the west side (of the river) past the hostel, ending up at the Banff Springs Hotel.

Spray River/Goat Creek (19 km, 12 mi): One of the most popular routes in Banff, this double-track trail follows the Spray River fireroad for 10 km (6.2 mi) and then turns up at Goat Creek under Mt. Rundle, ending at the Smith-Dorrien/Spray Trail (Hwy. 742) above Canmore. A gradual ascent. The reverse route is popular with organized groups who can gently coast most of the way to Banff. A circle can be made by strong cyclists by descending the Smith-Dorrien/Spray Trail to the Canmore Nordic Centre and then following Rundle Riverside Trail to the Banff Springs golf course. Total distance is 48 km (30 mi).

Kootenay National Park

Mountain biking is permitted on fireroads only, principally the East and West Kootenay Trails from the Banff-Windermere Highway (Hwy. 93). They are mostly smooth gravel surfaces, with bridges over the creeks and many open areas, which provide views across the wide valley. Trips can be made in various combinations and loops, from short-day jaunts from McLeod Meadows Campground to overnight trips beyond the park boundary. Check at the Parks Information Office in Radium or at the Banff Information Centre for conditions and access.

Detailed Guide

Yoho National Park

Amiskwi Trail (24 km, 15 mi): Mountain biking is permitted from the end of the road that leads past Natural Bridges west of Field, through an extensive burn area along fireroads, which are frequently overgrown. Steady climbing. Great views of a seldom-visited valley.

Kicking Horse Trail (19.5 km, 12.1 mi): This trail is an easy, pleasant double-track as far as the Otterhead Trail (4.1 km, 2.5 mi), starting from the same place as the Amiskwi Trail. Rougher and more overgrown beyond. The Otterhead Trail climbs steadily on an old fireroad and provides access to Tocher Ridge Lookout. Leave your bike and hike the last steep section.

Ottertail Trail (14 km, 9 km): From the Trans-Canada Highway, 8.5 km (5.3 mi) west of Field, head up the generally smooth fireroad to the McArthur Creek Warden Cabin. From there, hiking trails lead to Ottertail Falls and Goodsir Pass.

Jasper National Park

Fortress Lake Trail (25 km, 16 mi): From Sunwapta Falls, follow an old fireroad to the Athabasa Crossing suspension bridge. This area has a real backcountry, 'away-from-it-all' feel.

Fryatt Trail (11.4 km, 7 mi): A pleasant, mostly smooth and level path along the Athabasca from the Geraldine fireroad. A good way to access the more scenic upper Fryatt Valley (on foot).

Milna–Riley Lake Loop (9 km, 6 mi): Mostly single-track with some steep portions.

Old Fort Point to Valley of the Five Lakes (11.2 km, 7 mi) and Wabasso Lakes (19.3 km, 12 mi): Through rolling terrain on a mixture of fireroads and single-track. Mostly in good condition with some more technical stretches that are covered with boulders or large roots. Return to Jasper on the Icefields Parkway (Hwy. 93). (See Walks 66 and 67.)

Overlander Trail (14 km, 9 mi): An outstanding trip offering the best of mountain biking (see Walk 78). Runs along the Athabasca River between Sixth Bridge and Hwy. 16 below Mt. Morro. Excellent single-track with some challenging stretches. Good views over the river and Athabasca Valley. Passes the historic Moberly farmstead. Beware of bears, especially close to Sixth Bridge in spring. Return on Hwy. 16.

Saturday Night Loop (27.4 km, 17 mi): A combination of easy fireroad and challenging single-track, with some steep portions and a few potentially wet sections. Wooded throughout. Not for the faint-of-heart.

Summit Lakes (5 km, 3.1 mi): One of the few easy family bicycling trails in Jasper, it heads from the far end of Medicine Lake to Summit Lakes, with little elevation gain on a smooth fireroad (Walk 83). The route beyond the Summit Lakes to Jacques Lakes is heavily laced with roots and has some muddy sections.

Kananaskis Country

Bow Valley Park (4.4 km, 2.7 mi): This route connects the visitor centre and the campground through forest and meadows. Easy family trail.

Burstall Pass (2.7 km, 1.7 mi): A mostly gentle fireroad ascent goes past three lakes to a bikestand that is just before the gravel flats below Robertson Glacier. Bring a lock and continue for an additional 4.7 km (2.9 mi) to Burstall Pass (Walk 98).

Pocaterra (9.8 km, 6 mi): A wide trail, with good surfaces and a relatively gentle ascent, that heads through meadows and forests above Kananaskis Lakes in Peter Lougheed Provincial Park. Connects with Lookout and Whisky Jack trails. Cyclists can loop back to the start by taking a short, steeper side trail at 7.9 km (5 mi) and returning on the Kananaskis Trail (Hwy. 40) and the Kananaskis Lakes road.

Ribbon Creek (4.9 km, 3 mi): From the Ribbon Creek parking area, off the Kananaskis Trail (Hwy. 40). Follows old roads up the creek, with a loop possible on Link, Kovach and Terrace trails.

Mountain biking at Lake Minnewanka

Smith-Dorrien Trail System (various distances in a vast network): Although these former logging roads with good colour-coded signage are open to mountain biking, they actually make better ski routes (no longer groomed). There isn't a lot to see in most places, except for a forest struggling to recover from extensive logging. Parking at the Chester and Sawmill areas on the Smith-Dorrien/Spray Trail (Hwy. 742) in Peter Lougheed Provincial Park.

Three Isle Lake Trail (3.6 km, 2.2 mi): A mostly level and very scenic family trail along Upper Kananaskis Lake from the North Interlakes parking area. One rocky area to cross. Bikes are not permitted past Point Campground.

Waterton Lakes National Park

Crandell Lake Loop (2 km, 1.2 mi): From Crandell Mountain Campground, climb on a moderate grade to Crandell Lake (Walk 103). Cyclists can make this route into a long loop by continuing past the lake and down to the Akamina Parkway, and then down to the townsite and up Red Rock Parkway to the campground, a distance of about 20 km (12.4 mi).

Snowshoe Trail (8.2 km, 5 mi): Waterton's best mountain bike route starts at Red Rock Canyon and follows an abandoned fireroad along Bauerman Creek to the Snowshoe Warden Cabin. There are small hills and some creek crossings, but it is possible for many families. Good access for hikes to Goat Lake (Walk 106), Castle Divide and other trails.

Wishbone Trail (10.5 km, 6.5 mi return): Starts at Chief Mountain Highway, just south of the junction between the road from the townsite and Hwy. 6. The first half is easy on an old wagon road, and you can see the transition from grassland to aspen forest to mountain terrain. The last half is narrow and often overgrown, a place to make noise and watch for bears. Ends at Wishbone backcountry campsite where bikes can be left for the hike to Crypt Landing and Crypt Lake (Walk 104).

Bike Rentals and Guided Tours

Banff National Park

The Ski Stop, (403) 762-5333, rents mountain bikes at the bus entrance to the Banff Springs Hotel. Baby carriages and panniers are also available. Adrenalin Descents/ Bactrax has one- to four-hour tours, (403) 762-8177.

Cycling the Rockies offers half-day and full-day bike rides, as well as a 'pedals and paddles' package, with guided cycling in the morning and a raft ride down the Kicking Horse River in the afternoon; departures from Banff and Lake Louise. Call (403) 522-2211; toll-free 1-888-771-9453.

Jasper National Park

Mountain bikes can be rented from On-Line Sport & Tackle, 600 Patricia Street, (403) 852-3630. The price includes a lock and trail maps. At the Jasper Park Lodge marina on Lac Beauvert, bicycles

Bike touring in the Rockies

can be rented at Beauvert Boat & Cycle, (403) 852-5708.

Wheel Fun Cycle Tours has a shuttle service to Maligne Lake followed by an interpretive cycling trip ending at Maligne Canyon (and yes, it's almost all downhill). The five-hour trips run daily, rain or shine, starting at Freewheel Cycle, 618 Patricia Street, at 9 a.m. Call (403) 852-3898.

Kananaskis Country

Bikes can be rented at the Canmore Nordic Centre, (403) 678-6764, Mt. Kidd RV Park, (403) 591-7700, and Boulton Trading Post, (403) 591-7678.

Waterton Lakes National Park

Pat's, (403) 859-2266, behind the marina in Waterton townsite, rents 18-speed mountain bikes and tandems.

Children's Programs

The Town of Banff sponsors a Summer Fun Program with eight weekly sessions from early July to late August. The program is open to school-age children and provides activities ranging from camping, hiking and canoeing to music and art. You can enroll your kids for just one day, if that suits your schedule. (This camp is popular, so it's a good idea to reserve.) Day care is also available at the Banff Child Care Centre, (403) 762-1229, for children from 19 months to kindergarten.

Day care is available at the Jasper Children's Centre, (403) 852-4666. There's also a wading pool at the adjoining facility.

The Jasper Institute has a limited number of free 'Family Adventure Packs' available for loan to help families enjoy the park. The kits include a pack, binoculars and a guide to a specific natural area.

Check under 'Outdoor Adventures.'

In Waterton, special day camps are offered one afternoon a week through the Waterton Natural History Association's Heritage Education Program, (403) 859-2624.

There are interpretive programs and guided hikes in all of the parks that are designed for all ages. Ask at the nearest visitor information centre, or inquire at your campground.

Don't be afraid to abandon conventional and highly commercialized activities for those that will allow the imagination freer rein. The remains of the coal-mining town of Bankhead (Walk 14), for example, could be far more entertaining and educational than yet another long drive in the car.

Museums and interpretive centres in most of the parks also have attractions sure to entertain children on rainy days. These activities vary from the scary pool at the Cave and Basin in Banff to the 'kid's forest' and dress-up area in the Jasper Museum and Archives. See the 'Indoor' sections for each of the parks.

For a useful guide on enjoying a holiday in the parks with young ones, see *Hiking the Rockies with Kids*, by Celia McLean.

Fishing

Fishermen who hike or mountain walkers who fish may have a considerable advantage. So many fishermen never venture far from the road, never fish lakes or streams that lack vehicle access. Obviously, if you spend an hour or two walking a steep trail to reach a backcountry lake, it's not as likely to be over-fished as one beside a road.

The legend of the almost undiscovered backcountry lake is true—to a point. One backcountry disadvantage is that many high-country lakes and rivers are clouded with glacial silt, not optimum conditions for fish or fishermen. Another problem is that because the water temperature in the high altitude lakes tends to be extremely low, only a few degrees above freezing in many cases, neither the aquatic plants nor the fish grow fast.

Some of the high lakes are blanketed most of the year under thick ice covered by heavy snow. This covering blocks sunlight and kills aquatic plants. Fish may die for lack of oxygen. Because of this winter kill, fishing on any particular lake may vary considerably from year to year. Fishermen should inquire at tackle stores in the townsites to discover what the best lakes and streams seem to be at that moment and what's bringing them in.

The fishing experience is changing in the national parks. In the past, the parks used to stock lakes with introduced varieties of rainbow, cutthroat and eastern brook trout, often making survival difficult for native species such as westslope cutthroat, Athabasca rainbow and bull trout. Sometimes the native fish were even poisoned before the exotic ones were introduced.

Now some native stocks are gone

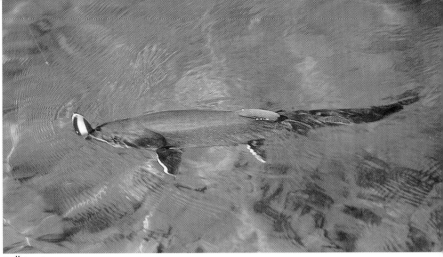

Bull trout

forever; others are recovering only slowly. That's one of the reasons why 'catch and release' is the preferred option for fishermen in the parks. After all, if you can't pick wildflowers or shoot a deer in the parks, why should you be able to harvest fish? (The traditional answer is that people have always caught fish and taken them home to eat.)

Parks Canada hasn't altogether banned traditional fishing, but they've greatly reduced catch and possession limits on native fish. Open seasons have been adjusted to protect stocks in spawning season. A few lakes and streams are now closed to fishing.

A national parks fishing permit is required and is available at the parks visitor information centres and sporting goods stores. Lead sinkers and jigs are absolutely banned in national parks because they are easily lost and are frequently eaten by loons and other water birds, which then die of lead poisoning.

The catch and possession limit is two each for northern pike, whitefish, trout, char and cutthroat (except in Banff where no cutthroat can be taken). The catch and possession limit is zero for bull trout, Kokanee salmon and all other species. No one is allowed to have in their possession more than two fish at any one time. For information on open seasons, closed waters and special restrictions, see the fishing regulations summary widely available at visitor information centres and fishing and sporting goods stores throughout the Rockie Mountain region.

Early in the 20th century, these regulations even caught up with the Duke of Connaught, who was advised by a park warden at Consolation Lakes of the 15-fish daily limit of the time.

'Per angler, per day, perdition,' the Duke sputtered. 'My good man, I ask you what is the sense of me being governor of this widespread, far-flung, sea-to-sea dominion if I cannot catch all the fish I have a mind to?' The warden was unmoved.

Banff National Park

Lake Minnewanka is the only lake on which power boats can be used. This beautiful lake, north of Banff townsite, can be treacherous in stormy weather. It contains some big specimens indeed, if you can find them: rainbow trout and lake trout, the last ranging up to 18 kg (40 lbs). Boat rentals are available.

Minnewanka Tours, (403) 762-3473, also offers guided fishing aboard 6.6-m (22-ft), sonar-equipped cabin cruisers.

The Upper Cascade River, which flows into Lake Minnewanka at Stewart Canyon (Walk 16), is a good place to find brook trout, rainbow trout and cutthroat.

For those who want to fish on their own, fishing equipment can be rented. The Banff tackle stores remain your best bet to find out the secrets of where the fish are biting and what is bringing them in.

In Banff, Don Reilly, of Alpine Anglers, offers a variety of guided fishing trips and fly-fishing instruction, including a full day on the Upper Bow River for $295 (one to two fishermen). Call (403) 762-8222.

Forget about Lake Louise. Although there are boats to rent, the lake, according to parks officials, has had it for fishing. That's the price of beauty and glacial silt, we suppose. Lake Louise is visited by millions. What chance does a fish have?

Fishing at nearby Moraine Lake (Walks 28, 29) is still possible, although the pressure of visitors is intense, too. Consolation Lakes (Walk 30) is a good place to escape the Moraine crowds and fish off the boulders that line the shore. Across from Lake Louise Village, a 2-km (1.2-mi) trail leads to unglamorous Mud Lake where the fishing for brook trout and cutthroat has often been good.

Closer to Banff townsite, Johnson Lake, off Minnewanka Road, has small rainbows and brookies that must be taken from shore. No boats are allowed. Two Jack Lake, also off Minnewanka Road, is close to campgrounds, but as a consequence gets heavy use from fishermen after its good-size rainbows and lake trout. Vermilion Lakes, which has boats for rent, is also popular and a wonderful spot to watch for moose and other game, even if you can't find fish. Its rainbows and brookies are reputed to run up to 4 kg (9 lbs).

North of Banff townsite, head for Bourgeau Lake if you're interested in small brook trout, although it's a considerable hike in (Walk 21). The same is true for Boom Lake (Walk 25). While the Bow River between Lake Louise and Banff townsite flows close to the Trans-Canada in many places, you'll need to leave your car at designated parking areas along the four-lane highway. You'd have better luck from the Bow Valley Parkway (Hwy. 1A). See the canoeing listing (page 345) for Bow River trips, which will take you to the less-frequented pools.

North of Lake Louise on the Icefields Parkway (Hwy. 93), Hector Lake looks inviting but the trail to it involves a major ford of the Bow River. Bow Lake, of course, is famous for its scenery, its lodge and its lake trout (Walk 42). Chephren and Cirque lakes, accessible on moderate walks from Waterfowl Lakes Campground, are worthwhile fishing destinations.

Jasper National Park

There's not much about fishing in Jasper National Park that the knowledgeable folks at Currie's Tackle, 416 Connaught Drive, (403) 852-5650, or Online Tackle, 600 Patricia Street, (403) 852-3630, can't tell you.

They can provide fishing guides, electric motors, rod and reels and most of all, give you advice. Both Currie's and Online offer guided fishing trips for $149 for a full day at Maligne Lake or alpine lakes, or they offer fly-fishing instruction. They also have boats available at many backcountry lakes: Talbot, Celestine, Marjorie, Hibernia, Dorothy, Yellowhead, Valley of the Five Lakes and others.

Boats and tackle are also available through Maligne Tours, 626 Conn-aught Drive, (403) 852-3370, or at

the boathouse at Maligne Lake. With its extremely cold water, Maligne has large brook trout and some rainbows and such scenery as to make fishing only an excuse for being there.

The Maligne River is open August 1 to October 1 for fly fishing, and you can easily reach portions of it alongside the Maligne Lake Road. The river is deep and fast moving, even ferocious in places, and it takes a lot of skill to catch rainbow and brook trout in this torrent. Medicine Lake has what's believed to be the longest underground drainage system in the western hemisphere. The lake empties into a single channel late in summer, concentrating all the fish

Chester Lake in Kananaskis Country

into a narrow area. A great place for dry fly fishing if you don't mind a lot of slogging through mud.

Talbot Lake near Jasper is shallow and clear, offering exciting fishing for pike at times. In winter, it's a popular ice-fishing location.

Although heavily fished, Pyramid Lake, on the wooded bench north of Jasper townsite, is one of the few in the national parks open to motorboats. Early in the season, you might try casting from shore for rainbow and lake trout. Later, trolling works best. Patricia Lake, just down Pyramid Lake Road, has rainbows, and it is easily accessible with a (non-motor) boat.

Horseshoe Lake has rainbows. The shore drops off steeply into the water, which is ideal for casting. Leach Lake on Hwy. 93A is known for its rainbow trout.

Lake Edith (Walk 77) has rainbow trout and Lake Annette (Walk 76) has brook trout. Away from the road, try Wabasso Lake (Walk 66) for smaller rainbows and Valley of the Five Lakes (Walk 67) for brook and rainbow trout. The first and last lakes are the best and have rental boats. Amethyst Lake in the Tonquin Valley is renowned for its rainbow trout as well as its scenery. Getting there is either by a major backpacking trip or a horseback trip organized by an outfitter. See 'Outdoor Adventures' in the Jasper chapter.

Kananaskis Country

The Kananaskis River is no longer a first-rate trout stream, because of daily water-level fluctuations caused by the upstream dams. The Bow River, downstream from Banff townsite to the dam at Seebe, is a beautiful place to go after brown trout, brook trout and whitefish. Float the river in a drift boat if you can (watch for fast-moving sections and 'sweepers' along the shore), or gain access from Hwy. 1A or from Bow Valley Provincial Park.

Fishing on Lower Kananaskis Lake is picking up, thanks to the excellent bull trout spawning runs on the Smith-Dorrien Creek. Nonetheless, the variable water levels on the lake (caused by fluctuating flows through the dams) still apparently cause problems. Watridge Lake is deservedly popular for cutthroats, and Chester Lake is a good scenic spot to go after dolly vardens.

On the other side of Highwood Pass, the Highwood River can provide outstanding fishing for rainbow, cutthroat and bull trout.

Mountain Fly Fishers, (403) 678-9522, in Canmore provides Bow River float trips ($325) and a number of walk and wade, or hike and wade trips ($300 for a full day throughout Kananaskis Country).

Waterton Lakes National Park

Waterton's backcountry lakes and trout streams can offer exceptional fishing. The three big lakes—Upper, Lower and Middle Waterton—provide brook trout of 7 kg (15 lbs) or more, plus smaller rainbows, brookies and cutthroats. You can rent boats at the marina. Beware of rapidly changing weather conditions on these lakes. Violent winds and big waves can strike without warning, making boating hazardous. Try the Waterton River between the lakes and the reservoir for brown trout, rainbow trout and cutthroat.

Because conditions can vary from year to year, it's a good idea to check with the Visitor Reception Centre and tackle stores in town, such as Pat's, (403) 859-2266. Some of the top lakes include Alderson for cutthroat (Walks 99, 100), Bertha for rainbows (Walk 99) and Maskinonge for northern pike. Cameron Lake has rainbows and brook trout, and boats can be rented.

High Crypt Lake (Walk 104) is a beautiful spot to fish, although the cutthroat are notoriously hard to catch. One of the best places to fish is, naturally, the least accessible. Lineham Lakes above the Akamina Parkway are crystal clear, and you might sometimes have the whole place to yourself. The drawback is that to reach Lineham, you have to continue from the end of the official trail and along a narrow, potentially hazardous ledge. Parks considers it a climb rather than a hike. Somewhat easier to reach is Goat Lake (Walk 106), a beautiful spot to pursue cutthroats.

Cross-Country Skiing

Winter can be the best season in the mountain parks. You can glide through a pristine landscape on skis either on a prepared track or on your own in the backcountry. Under the right conditions, you can cover more ground with less effort on skis. No mosquitoes, no boggy areas. Even wooded trails that might seem tedious in summer take on a fresh beauty and interest. You haven't totally experienced the mountains until you've skied them in winter or, better still, in early spring.

Be aware, however, that some safe and easy summer trails can be deadly in winter because of avalanche hazard. Untrained skiers without special equipment should try to keep clear of potential avalanche slopes. Check with park wardens or visitor information centres before venturing onto any trail or area not specifically designated for cross-country skiing by Parks Canada. And check every time. A trail that is safe one week can be deadly the next because of snow build-up. The Canadian Avalanche Awareness Association also provides avalanche bulletins from the Canadian Avalanche Centre and backcountry avalanche reports from Parks Canada, 1-800-667-1105.

Here are a few fairly short, not-too-difficult but enjoyable cross-country trails that, Parks Canada suggests, are usually safe from avalanches, except as noted. These trails are signed by Parks and will usually have set tracks, although drifting and fresh snowfall can obscure any trail. Also see *Ski Trails in the Canadian Rockies* by Chic Scott.

Banff National Park

Novice Trails

Banff Springs Golf Course (various lengths): In Banff townsite, start at the Bow Falls parking lot and cross the Spray River Bridge, following a network of trails and loops around the edge of gently rolling fairways.

Cascade Fireroad (13 km, 8 mi return): Start at the Upper Bankhead picnic area on Lake Minnewanka Road, north of Banff townsite.

Cave and Basin River Trail (1.5 km, 1 mi): In Banff townsite, start at the Cave and Basin parking lot and ski north towards the river, looping along the Bow and joining Sundance Canyon road.

Fairview Loop (7.5 km, 4.7 mi): Start at the highest Chateau Lake Louise parking lot, and follow the trail to the Moraine Lake Road. Turn left on the road. Near the gate, take the Tramline Trail left back to Lake Louise.

Johnson Lake Loop (8.2 km, 5 mi): Start from the dead-end road that leads off from the Lake Minnewanka Road–Two Jack Lake Road north of Banff townsite.

Lake Louise Shoreline (6 km, 3.7 mi return): From Chateau Lake Louise, follow the signs right, into the trees above the lake. The upper route is better than the summer

lakeshore trail. Use caution if you ski on the lake itself. An avalanche area begins beyond the end of the lake, and is considered extremely dangerous, even if you have the proper backcountry equipment.

Moraine Lake Road (16 km, 10 mi return): Drive 1.1 km (0.7 mi) up the hill on the Bow Valley Parkway (Hwy. 1A) from Lake Louise Village and park at the Fairview picnic area. Ski onto the unploughed Moraine Lake Road. An avalanche area starts at end of the signed trail.

Pipestone Loops (various lengths): From the parking area off the Trans-Canada Highway, opposite the west entrance to Lake Louise Village, take the 12.6-km (7.8-mi) loop or shorten the trip by returning on shortcuts.

Spray River Loop (2.2 km, 1.4 mi): In Banff townsite, start from the Bow Falls parking lot, cross the golf course close to the river, and ski up the Spray River Trail, crossing on the first bridge. Return on the fireroad on the other side.

Intermediate Trails

Forty Mile Creek Loop (9 km, 5.6 mi): From the Norquay ski road north of Banff townsite, the trail starts from the far end of Parking Lot No. 3. The trail passes the Wishbone T-bar and continues on a fireroad. Take the right fork (Elk Lake) at 1.1 km (0.7 mi), which is an avalanche zone, and loop around by Forty Mile Creek to return again to this point.

Spray River Loop (10.8 km, 6.7 mi): In Banff townsite, start from the Bow Falls parking lot, cross the golf course close to the river, and ski up the Spray River Trail to the second footbridge. Return on other side on the Spray River fireroad, crossing two avalanche zones and ending at the Banff Springs Hotel.

Yoho National Park

About 40 km (25 mi) of trails are track-set regularly for cross-country skiing.

Novice Trails

Emerald Lake Circuit: An easy, 5.2-km (3.2-mi) circuit that begins at the parking lot at Emerald Lake and continues around the lake (Walk 54). If you want a longer ski, there's another 3.5-km (2.2-mi) loop at the end of the lake.

Hwy 1A. to Great Divide: This 11-km (6.8-mi) return trip begins at the Lake O'Hara parking lot and goes along the road to the picnic shelter. You could also continue 22 km (14 mi) to Lake Louise along the road, or take a 1.3-km (0.8-mi) side trip to Ross Lake.

Wapta Falls: This trail is an easy, 8-km (5-mi) loop that starts from the Trans-Canada Highway in the park's west end. You ski along a logging road and then rolling hills to a spectacular view of Wapta Falls (see Walk 59).

Skiing on Lake Louise

Intermediate Trails

Lake O'Hara: This 23.4-km (14.5-mi) return trip starts at the Lake O'Hara parking lot near the junction of the Trans-Canada Highway and Hwy. 1A. It climbs moderately to Lake O'Hara. At the 10-km (6.2-mi) point, strong skiers have the option of going to Linda Lake (2 km or 1.2 mi one-way) or the Duchesnay Basin (5 km or 3.1 mi one-way). Light meals are available at the lodge on weekends from mid-January to mid-April. Check at the visitor centre for details.

Yoho Valley to Takakkaw Falls: To start this 26-km (16-mi) return trip, drive 3 km (1.9 mi) east of Field to Yoho Valley Road and continue 1 km (0.6 mi) to a parking area at the end of the ploughed section. It's mostly a moderate climb to the falls. Don't stop in avalanche zones! There is winter camping at Takakkaw Falls; permit required.

Other popular trails include the Natural Bridge, Amiskwi Firecircle and Monarch Campground. These trails are groomed by the Field Cross-Country Ski Club.

Jasper National Park

In Jasper, the best cross-country ski area is at Maligne Lake at the end of the Maligne Lake Road, 48 km (30 mi) southeast of the townsite. There is a variety of trails and terrain, and in spring, the snow stays in good condition longer than at the lower townsite area. The chalet at the lake is closed in winter. Also, in winter, there are no services at the lake.

The townsite area is the most convenient for cross-country skiing and has a wide and safe network of trails, both official and unofficial, on the wooded, lake-filled bench above Jasper.

Maligne Lake—Novice Trails

Maligne Lakeside Loop (3.5 km, 2.2 mi): An easy and level loop that starts from the Maligne Lake Chalet, goes past the boathouse on the left shoreline to a small bay, and then loops back through the woods.

Moose Lake Trails (various trails): From parking area P2, go a short distance up the Bald Hills fireroad and turn left at the Maligne Pass trailhead signs. Proceed on fairly level terrain to a junction, where you have your choice of
• Option A, Moose Lake Loop: An easy, 4.4-km (2.7-mi) loop. Turn sharply to the left to continue on the Moose Lake Trail, which has a moderate downhill grade and levels off beyond the lake back to the parking lot.
• Option B, Upper Moose Lake Loop: An easy, 7.6-km (4.7-mi) loop. Continue on this trail that heads up a short, steep hill. It turns left at the next junction and begins a gentle descent, terminating at the lakeshore. From there, it's a smooth glide back to the parking lot.

Of Chipmunks and Squirrels

yellow-pine chipmunk

When is a chipmunk not a chipmunk? Most probably, when it's a golden-mantled ground squirrel.

This appealing scamp is often mistaken for a large chipmunk because of its stripes. However, you can tell the two apart: if the stripes extend to the head, it is a chipmunk. If not, it's a squirrel. The mature squirrel is also larger than the mature chipmunk.

The golden-mantled ground squirrel can be found in many areas of the parks from valley to timberline, but it usually inhabits rocky areas. It is not gregarious and rarely appears in groups of more than two.

golden-mantled ground squirrel

wildlife

Maligne Lake—Intermediate Trails

Lorraine Lake Trail (7.3-km, 4.5-mi loop): From the chalet, ski across the bridge to the Bald Hills fireroad above the last parking lot. Climb the road until the Lorraine Lake Trail branches right, descends slightly and passes the lake. Turn right on the Skyline Trail, which has some interesting, curved descents.

Maligne Lake—Advanced Trails

Evelyn Creek Trail (13-km, 8-mi loop): From the chalet, ski across the bridge and up the Bald Hills fireroad. About two-thirds of the way to the top, the Evelyn Creek Trail branches right and continues around the side of the mountain, leading to a steep descent that should be walked by inexperienced skiers. Turn right at the bottom onto the Skyline Trail, which has some interesting, intermediate-class curved hills on the more gradual descent back to the lake.

Jasper Townsite Area—Novice Trails

Whistler's Campground Loop (4.5 km, 2.8 mi): Drive 3.2 km (1.9 mi) south of Jasper townsite and turn right on the Whistler Sky Tram Road, and left to the campground parking area. The trail follows the campground perimeter road loop, and is level and easily followed.

Detailed Guide

Jasper Townsite Area—Intermediate Trails

Mina–Riley Loop (9 km, 6 mi): Start at the first parking lot on the left, up Pyramid Lake Road from Jasper townsite. The trail (No. 8) loops past Mina and Riley lakes, with one long descent to the lakes. Return on the Cabin Lake Road.

Pyramid Bench Trails (various lengths): Start at the first parking lot on the left, up Pyramid Lake Road from Jasper townsite. Cross the road and find the wide path (marked as 2B) through the trees that leads to the edge of the bench and up to Pyramid Lake.

Jasper Townsite Area—Advanced

Patricia Lake Circle (5.9 km, 3.7 mi): Start from the riding stable parking lot up Pyramid Lake Road from Jasper townsite. The trail (No. 6) crosses the road and loops, sometimes steeply, through varied terrain south of Patricia Lake.

Kananaskis Country

The groomed trails in Peter Lougheed Provincial Park are among the best in the Rockies. The park has more than 90 km (56 mi) of groomed trails, most of them rated 'easy' or 'intermediate.' Pocaterra Hut and the Peter Lougheed Visitor Centre are open as ski information and warm-up centres.

Kananaskis—Novice Trails

Lodgepole Trail (4.7 km, 2.9 mi): A pleasant, forested route between Elkwood parking area and Pocaterra Ski Hut without much change in elevation. There is one short, steep section (which can be walked) near Pocaterra.

Pocaterra Trail (10 km, 6.2 mi): One of the most popular trails in the park, it rises gradually from Pocaterra Hut and links with several other trails in the park.

Kananaskis—Intermediate Trails

Elk Pass Trail (7 km, 4.3 mi): From the Elk Pass parking lot, climb gradually on the old fireroad to the Alberta-B.C. border. Great views and an opportunity to link up with several other trails for a grand loop.

Moraine Trail and Fox Creek Trail (3.8 km, 2.4 mi): From the Boulton Creek ski parking, these two trails offer good views of the Kananaskis Valley and a narrow, winding route along a creek. Makes a good loop combined with the Boulton Creek trail.

Ribbon Creek

The Ribbon Creek area off the Kananaskis Trail (Hwy. 40) has 47 km (29 mi) of trails. Because this area is subject to frequent chinook melting, it's advisable to check conditions first at the Barrier Lake Visitor Centre on Hwy. 40, 6 km

Loppets Take the Chill off Winter

In recent years, citizen cross-country races or 'loppets' have become increasingly popular in the mountain parks. The focus is on fun and events are arranged for all ages and fitness levels.

The Jasper Park Classic usually kicks off the season early in the New Year. Held at Jasper Park Lodge, the 'classic' is a bargain that includes accommodation and meals. It's followed by the Rocky Mountain Ski Marathon in Canmore, the Kananaskis Ski Marathon in Peter Lougheed Provincial Park, the Lake Louise Loppet and the Hinton Loppet. Contact Cross Country Alberta, (403) 453-8620.

(3.7 mi) south of the Trans-Canada Highway.

Smith-Dorrien

This network of trails varying from 3 km (1.9 mi) to 12.2 km (7.6 mi) is not groomed or patrolled. (Dogs are permitted on leashes.) Start at the Chester Lake parking lot or Sawmill picnic area. For information on trail conditions, call (403) 591-7222.

Canmore Nordic Centre

The Canmore Nordic Centre, a site for the 1988 Winter Olympic Games, is a competitive training facility with some recreational opportunities. It's best known for challenging trails with steep dips and sharp corners. The Banff Trail is the only one recommended for novice skiers. It crosses over the bridge at the end of the stadium and leads to the west boundary of the Nordic Centre at 6 km (3.7 mi). Four other trails are also recommended for recreational skiing.

They vary in length from 2.5 km (1.5 mi) to 15 km (9.3 mi) return. There's a day lodge at the centre and a cafeteria, (403) 678-2400. Fee for skiing.

Waterton Lakes National Park

Few of Waterton's trails are groomed for cross-country skiing. Many of the summer routes, such as Cameron Lake, Crandell Lake and the Lakeshore Trail, are suitable depending on snow and avalanche conditions. For these routes, it is important to check in advance with park staff. Detailed avalanche forecasts and information regarding backcountry skiing are available by contacting a warden at (403) 859-2224.

Depending on snow conditions, popular trails include Crandell Lake (easy-moderate), Akamina Pass, Summit Lake and Wall/Forum Lakes (all difficult). These trails are not marked or maintained, and may be subject to avalanche hazard. Designated ski trails are listed on the next page.

369

Skiing at Sunshine

Cameron Ski Trail: An easy, 5-km (3.1-mi) loop from Little Prairie Trailhead, which is on the Akamina Parkway, to Cameron Lake.

Dipper Ski Trail: A moderate, 6.5-km (4-mi) loop from Rowe Trailhead, which is on the Akamina Parkway, to Little Prairie Trailhead.

Downhill Skiing

Rocky Mountain ski areas have recently united to offer eight-area season passes all winter; call (403) 256-8473 for more information.

Banff National Park

Banff Mt. Norquay: This area just outside Banff townsite is known for its steep, challenging mogul runs, although there are good lower-angle slopes for novices and many inter-mediate runs. A local favourite.

There are two quad lifts and a new licensed day-use lodge that was added in 1996—includes pub and restaurant. Average snowfall is 300 cm (117 in) a year; the vertical drop is 497 m (1630 ft). Night skiing; snowboard school. Call (403) 762-4421.

Lake Louise: Situated 40 minutes from Banff townsite, Lake Louise is Canada's largest ski area, with four mountain faces and 105 named runs. Known for its great variety, Lake Louise has novice runs from every chair, so less experienced skiers aren't confined to the bottom slopes. Average snowfall is 360 cm (140 in); vertical drop is 1000 m (3280 ft). Voted one of the top five North American ski destinations by *Ski Magazine*. Call (403) 522-3555, toll-free 1-800-258-7669.

Wily Wolverine

This is one animal you're unlikely to see in the Canadian Rockies, and it's probably just as well. This bold scavenger has a bad reputation for breaking into deserted cabins and helping itself to anything it wants. Although not large, the wolverine has been known to bring down moose almost 30 times its weight. It appears to plan attacks cleverly, often waiting in a tree until it can jump on the back of a passing prey and sever the victim's jugular vein. Sometimes nicknamed 'skunk bear,' the wolverine resembles a small bear in the distance. Its fur is highly prized among trappers because it does not ice up in winter.

wildlife

wolverine

Sunshine Village: Located 20 minutes from Banff townsite, Sunshine Village is the highest ski resort in the Canadian Rockies at 3160 m (10,365 ft) on the Continental Divide. It's known for its abundant powder snow and the longest ski season in the region, which guarantees fine spring skiing. The season runs from mid-November to June, averaging 180 days. The 89 runs include those suitable for skiers of all abilities, from tightly treed runs at lower elevations to open bowls at top. A day lodge, full accommodation (including saunas and hot tubs) and dining lodge are provided. Goat's Eye Mountain opened in 1995 and the fourth high-speed lift opened in 1996—you can ski in both Alberta and B.C. on the same run. Average snowfall is 1020 cm (398 in); vertical drop is 1070 m (3510 ft). Call (403) 762-6500, toll-free 1-800-661-1676.

Jasper National Park

Marmot Basin: Never underestimate Marmot Basin, a favourite of many Albertans. This friendly ski area, southwest of Jasper townsite, offers outstanding scenery and a good mixture of tree-lined runs and alpine bowl skiing. The new Caribou Chalet is licensed with a full-service restaurant; the hill is more low-key than Banff. Average annual snowfall is 400 cm (156 in); vertical drop is 897 m (2942 ft). Call (403) 852-3816.

Kananaskis Country

Fortress Mountain: Situated up the valley from Nakiska, Fortress might be usually less crowded than other ski areas in the Rockies and has on-hill accommodation. Vertical drop is 340 m (1115 ft). Call (403) 591-7108 and from Calgary, (403) 264-5825.

Nakiska: Situated on Mt. Allan in Kananaskis Country, an hour's drive from Calgary and 45 minutes from Banff. Nakiska was developed for the 1988 Winter Olympics and has been plagued some winters by lack of natural snow, but there's no doubt that the facilities and runs are excellent. Vertical drop is 918 m (3011 ft). More than two-thirds of the runs at Nakiska are intermediate; average annual snowfall is 200–250 cm (78–98 in), which can disappear fast in a chinook. Two day lodges with lounge and dining services. Call (403) 591-7777.

Rafting

It's as wild and wet as you want it. Most companies offer family rafting excursions for beginners, as well as thrill-a-minute rides.

Rafting on the Bow River

sports

Jasper-Banff Relay

The mountain parks are the site of several well-known races. The most famous is the Jasper-Banff Relay, a 285-km (177-mi) race the length of the Icefields Parkway (Hwy. 93) between Jasper and Banff national parks. The relay, which winds through glacier-carved valleys and over mountain passes, attracts teams from all over the world. (It's limited to 120 teams.) It's usually held in late May or early June. Call (403) 436-0062.

The Canadian Rocky Marathon is usually scheduled in mid-September at the Canmore Nordic Centre. There's an 8-km (5-mi) race as well as a full marathon. Numerous other runs are held between April and October. Contact local chambers of commerce or running stores.

Banff, Lake Louise, Yoho and Kootenay Areas

Rocky Mountain Raft Tours, (403) 762-3632, offers peaceful three-hour trips down the Bow River and longer wilderness trips on the Kootenay River; tickets and transportation are available from the bus depot or Banff Springs Hotel.

Kootenay River Runners conducts excursions on the Kootenay and Kicking Horse rivers, ranging from a four-hour paddle from Radium Hot Springs to a full day down the Kootenay and a one-day whitewater adventure on the Kicking Horse River, in Banff through Summit Vacations. Call (403) 762-5561 and in B.C., (250) 347-9210.

Western River Runners' Rocky Mountain Raft Tours, established in 1972, was the first commercial rafting company in Canada and is still going strong. Call (403) 762-3632.

Wet 'n' Wild Adventures has half-day and full-day whitewater trips on the Kicking Horse River, with

departures from Banff, Lake Louise, Radium and Golden. Call (250) 344-6546 or 1-800-668-9119.

Wild Water Adventures conducts half-day raft trips on the Kicking Horse River, departing from Lake Louise, and a full-day bike and paddle trip from Banff. Call (403) 522-2211 or 1-888-771-9453.

Jasper National Park

Jasper Raft Tours, (403) 852-3613, runs 14-km (9-mi) round trips on the Athabasca River, suitable for everyone from toddlers to senior citizens; departures are three times daily, including 7 p.m.

Raven Adventures begins its 'canyon run' excursion on the Athabasca River from the base of Athabasca Falls. Other options include 2$^{1}/_{2}$-hour guided trips on the Athabasca and Whirlpool rivers. Call (403) 852-4292.

Rocky Mountain River Guides, (403) 852-3777, runs trips down the Maligne and Athabasca rivers.

Whitewater Rafting (Jasper) Ltd. offers a variety of outings including two-hour trips on the Athabasca, Maligne and Sunwapta rivers. Departures from Jasper townsite, Jasper Park Lodge, Maligne Lake and Sunwapta Falls Resort. Call 1-800-557-RAFT or (403) 852-RAFT.

Mt. Robson Area

If you venture further west to Mt. Robson Provincial Park in British Columbia, you'll have a wide choice of rafting options:

Sekani Mountain Tours runs nature float tours starting at the base of Mt. Robson: 14-km (8.6-mi) runs down the Fraser River are well suited for novices; a 'not for the faint of heart' trip down the Canoe River; and a two-day tour. Call (403) 852-5211 or 1-888-288-7238.

Mt. Robson Whitewater Rafting Co., (250) 566-4879, will take you on a three-hour trip down the Fraser, British Columbia's longest river. Along the way, you'll visit an historic gold panner's cabin, see Rearguard Falls, and view salmon returning to their spawning grounds in mid- to late summer.

Mt. Robson Adventure Holidays runs a gentle, two-hour 'salmon float trip' suitable for all ages. If you're staying in Jasper townsite, you can be picked up by van at any Jasper Hotel to join the raft trip. Call 1-800-882-9921 or (250) 566-4386.

Kananaskis Country

Kananaskis River Adventures Ltd., (403) 591-7773, conducts a 'whitewater thriller' for first-timers and families through Class I to Class III rapids on the Kananaskis River.

Manachaban River Tours of Canmore, (403) 678-6535, offers gentle raft floats on the Bow River, with an emphasis on wildlife viewing and natural history.

Rainbow Riders offers rafting tours on the Kananaskis River; start and finish at Rafter Six Ranch Resort. Call (403) 678-RAFT and in Calgary, (403) 850-3686.

Scrambling

Few trails in the mountain parks ever get to the summit of anything. There's little Tunnel Mountain in Banff townsite and the rounded slopes of Sulphur Ridge in Jasper, plus the peaks that have cable lifts.

But officially maintained trails usually stay in the wooded valleys, rising to cross a rounded pass or ending at a lake or cirque on the very edge of the open alpine terrain. Well, that's certainly adventure and beauty enough for most.

A few need to get to the top, or at least onto high ridges away from the trails. One solution is to hire a guide or take climbing courses, and we've listed where you can do that. See the 'Alpine Courses and Rock Climbing' listings for Banff and Jasper. Yet many of the peaks in the Canadian Rockies can be ascended without climbing technique or without a rope, an ice axe or the courage of a Mesmer attempting Everest solo. What you need is an early start, lots of stamina, a bit of map-reading and route-finding ability, common sense and the willingness to turn back, if prudent.

Many of the mountains can be climbed ropeless by climbers who seek out the easy side. Not all peaks have an easy side, of course. Scrambling is by no means as safe as following a trail: you can get lost, you can fall, you can be hit by rock fall or snow avalanches, you can get hypothermia—the list is long

On the other hand, you could get hit by a car while walking to the corner store.

The trick in scrambling is knowing when to retreat. Many ridges and other routes might quickly become too steep for ropeless climbing. When a slip could mean a fall of some distance, abandon the climb or find another route. Similarly, be prepared to turn back if

the weather becomes threatening.

As a ropeless scrambler, stay completely away from glaciers, even fairly steep snowfields, without an ice axe and the practised ability to do a self-arrest. It's not essential, but a very good idea to register your scramble at warden's offices or visitor information centres in both the national and provincial parks. At least let someone responsible know where you are going and when you will be back—and what to do if you don't return. The Warden Service has specific information, even photos, showing many off-trail routes.

It's a matter of examining the mountain, both on the map and from the road. Obviously, a mountain such as Rundle is deadly on the north side for inexperienced climbers and easier on the south side. Even Cascade has an easy ridge leading to the summit (on the right of the Cascade Amphitheatre), although there's a tricky portion near the end. And, unfortunately,

Castle Mountain is a technical climb from the west side (shown) and a scramble from the back side.

many peaks in the soft Canadian Rockies are little more than a summit sticking its head just above a depressing mound of rock debris. This rotten rock is strictly unreliable, and constant vigilance is needed not to knock it down on companions.

Try to use a trail wherever possible to get close to the area you'd like to explore. Seek a trail that leads to timberline to avoid a tiring bushwhack through the thick subalpine forest. Five km (3.1 mi) of trail walking can be much faster than just 1 km (0.6 mi) of bushwhacking. There are many unmarked and largely unmaintained mountain access trails not listed in the hiking books. Good sources of information are the climbers' guides to the Rockies, although you still need route-finding skills.

Examine 1:50,000 contour maps carefully for white (open) sides of mountains above timberline, where the lines are relatively far apart.

Even then, be prepared to turn back or find an alternative. Forty-m (131-ft) contour lines can hide an impassable 30-m (98-ft) cliff. Wear sturdy boots and long pants and be sure to bring a windproof jacket, gloves, perhaps a parka in a stuff bag, water and some high-energy food.

Classic scrambles include Rundle and Cascade near Banff townsite, Castle Mountain (from the easy backside) up the Bow Valley Parkway (Hwy. 1A), Mt. Temple above Moraine Lake, the easier Mt. Fairview above Lake Louise (from Walk 36), Mt. Yukness from Lake O'Hara and even historic Abbott Pass Hut, reached on a long scree gully above Lake Oesa (Walk 58) in the Lake O'Hara area.

Two excellent books cover Rockies scrambling in detail: *Scrambles in the Canadian Rockies* by Alan Kane and *Kananaskis Country Trail Guide* by Gillean Daffern.

Mt. Rundle is a good scramble from the Banff townsite side (shown).

Rock Isle Lake, best alpine meadows

CHAPTER 8

Best of the Rockies

Best of the Walks

Banff National Park

Banff Townsite Area:

Best Short Family Walk: Stewart
Canyon (Walk 16)
Best Interpretive Trail: Cave and
Basin Trail (Walk 1)
Best Views: Tunnel Mountain
(Walk 7)
Best Canyon Walk: Johnston
Canyon (Walk 22)
Best Historical Walk: Bankhead
Historical Loop (Walk 14)

Most Strenuous: Cory Pass
(Walk 19)
Easiest Way to Alpine: Sulphur
Mountain Vista (Walk 6)
Best Nature Walk: Fenland Nature
Trail (Walk 4)
Best Alpine Meadows: Rock Isle
Lake (Walk 20)

Lake Louise Area:

Best Short Family Walk: Lakeshore
Trail (Walk 34)
Best Views: Big Beehive; Lake Agnes
(Walks 38, 39)

Maligne Canyon

Best Glacier Views: Plain of Six
Glaciers (Walk 35)

Moraine Lake Area:

Best Short Family Walk: Moraine
Lake Viewpoint (Walk 28)
Best Views: Sentinel Pass and
Paradise Valley (Walk 33)

Icefields Parkway (Hwy. 93):

Best Short Family Walk: Panther
Falls and Bridal Veil Falls
(Walk 45)
Best Scenic Lake Walk: Bow Lake
(Walk 42)

Most Dazzling View: Peyto Lake
Viewpoint (Walk 43)
Best Waterfalls: Panther Falls and
Bridal Veil Falls (Walk 45)
Best Walk on Alpine Tundra:
Parker Ridge (Walk 47)

Kootenay National Park

Best Short Family Walk: Marble
Canyon (Walk 50)
Best Interpretive Trail: Paint Pots
(Walk 51)
Best Glacier Views: Stanley Glacier
(Walk 49)

Jasper National Park

Columbia Icefield:

Best Short Family Walk: Athabasca
Glacier (Walk 61)
Best Glacier Views: Wilcox Pass
Trail (Walk 60)

Icefields Parkway (Hwy. 93):

Best Short Family Walk: Lower
Sunwapta Falls (Walk 63)
Best Waterfall: Athabasca Falls
(Walk 64)
Best Glacier Views: Path of the
Angel Glacier Trail (Walk 68)
Easiest Way to Alpine: Tramway to
Whistlers Summit (Walk 70)

Maligne Area:

Best Short Family Walk: Maligne
Canyon Loop (Walk 81)
Most Elegant Walk: Lac Beauvert
Loop (Walk 72)
Most Scenic Walk: Opal Hills Loop
(Walk 85)

Best Lake Walk: Maligne Lakeside Loop (Walk 84)

Kananaskis Country

Best Short Family Walk: Grotto Canyon (Walk 95)
Best Historical Walk: Grassi Lakes (Walk 96)
Easiest Way to Alpine: Ptarmigan Cirque (Walk 89)
Best Interpretive Trail: Many Springs (Walk 94)

Waterton Lakes National Park

Best Short Family Walk: Red Rock Canyon Loop (Walk 105)
Best Views: Bear's Hump (Walk 100)
Best Alpine Walk: Summit Lake–Carthew Summit (Walk 101)

Best Spring and Fall Hikes

Banff National Park

Banff: townsite trails (Walks 1–13); Bankhead Historical Loop (Walk 14); Johnston Canyon (Walk 22)
Lake Louise: Lake Agnes (Walk 38)

Kootenay National Park

Fireweed Trail (Walk 48)
Marble Canyon (Walk 50)

Yoho National Park

Emerald Lake Circuit (Walk 54)
Wapta Falls (Walk 59)

Jasper National Park

Old Fort Point (Walk 71)
Lac Beauvert Loop (Walk 72)
Maligne Canyon and Sixth Bridge (Walk 82)

Best Fall-Colour Hikes

Banff National Park
Larch Valley (Walk 32)

Jasper National Park
Angel Glacier–Cavell Meadows Loop (Walk 69)

Kananaskis Country
Ptarmigan Cirque (Walk 89)

Waterton Lakes National Park
Summit Lake–Carthew Summit (Walk 101)

Best Itineraries

Banff National Park

Banff Townsite:

Day 1: If visibility is good, start early with a ride up Sulphur Mountain Gondola Lift. From the teahouse at the top, stroll up the easy trail to the old meteorological station (Walk 6) and Sanson Peak and enjoy the splendid views. In the afternoon, you might like to catch the scenic cruise down Lake Minnewanka or picnic by the lake and stroll to Stewart Canyon (Walk 16). On the way back to Banff townsite, consider stopping at the fascinating Bankhead historical exhibit (Walk 14). The best way to end the day is surely with a soak at the hot springs.

Day 2: Explore the lavishly done interpretive trails at the Cave and Basin: the Marsh Trail (Walk 1) and the Discovery Trail (Walk 2) show how the hot sulphur water not only changed the environment but led to the creation of Canada's national parks. Later, consider a stroll from Banff Bridge to Bow Falls (Walk 12). Then climb the stairs to the Scottish baronial Banff Springs Hotel for afternoon tea. A fine evening stroll, if you still have energy, is the short Fenland Nature Trail (Walk 4), an excellent spot to view animals before sunset. (Avoid the Fenland in prime mosquito season, however.)

Lake Louise:

Day 1: Drive to Lake Louise, admire the view, and stroll down the beautiful Lakeshore Trail (Walk 34). Go for tea in the famous Chateau. Later, take the short, scenic drive to Moraine Lake, which many prefer to world-famous Lake Louise. In warm, calm weather, it's delightful to rent a boat or canoe on this magnificent little lake, formerly pictured on the back of the $20 bill. Alternatively, take a short stroll to Moraine Lake Viewpoint at the end of the lake (Walk 28). The view is classic. In the afternoon, the Post Hotel in Lake Louise Village is a good place for tea.

Day 2: If visibility is good, take the Lake Louise Gondola east of Lake Louise Village. It whisks you up to the 2034-m (6672-ft) level of Mt. Whitehorn. There's a stunning overview of Lake Louise and glacier-clad peaks along the Continental Divide. Another option is brunch at the Post Hotel, and then a walk to Lake Agnes teahouse (Walk 38) for late lunch or, if you're up to it, a walk up the Big Beehive (Walk 39). Book dinner at the Lake Louise Station before you leave, or get picnic fixings at Laggans in Samson Mall.

The Icefields Parkway (Hwy. 93) (1 day):

When driving the Icefields Parkway (Hwy. 93), stop at stunning Bow Lake, 34 km (21 mi) north of Lake Louise. Take a short walk along the lakeshore past rustic Num-ti-jah Lodge (Walk 42). After your stroll, the lodge is a good place to stop for tea, home-made muffins and cakes. Continuing up the parkway, pull in at Bow Summit and take the short, paved nature trail to Peyto Lake Viewpoint (Walk 43), among the most stunning views anywhere in the mountains. Another short stroll leads down to Mistaya Canyon Gorge (Walk 44) from a parking area on the west side of the parkway, 71 km (44 mi) north of Lake Louise.

Bow Lake

Bow Valley and Kootenay National Park (1 day):

Outside Banff, the best drive is along the Bow Valley Parkway (Hwy. 1A), rather than the hectic Trans-Canada. This parkway is an interpretive drive, with frequent pulloffs at areas of geological or historical interest and a good chance to see large mammals, especially in the morning or early evening. Be sure to stop at Johnston Canyon (Walk 22) for a stroll up the paved trail past numerous waterfalls and cascades, cut deep in the limestone walls. At Castle Mountain Junction, turn up the Banff-Windermere Highway (Hwy. 93) to Vermilion Pass. Right at the top on the Continental Divide is the short, surprisingly

interesting Fireweed Trail (Walk 48), which goes through the burn of 1968. Drive 7 km (4.3 mi) more to the deep gorges of Marble Canyon (Walk 50). If you still have time and a little energy to spare, carry on to the Paint Pots (Walk 51), a fascinating area of ochre springs, a sacred place to native peoples.

Yoho National Park (1 day):

From Lake Louise, take Hwy. 1A to the Great Divide, a picnic area where a creek divides in two, one part flowing to the Pacific Ocean, the other to the Atlantic. Continue to the Trans-Canada Highway and turn west into Yoho. Drive down the steep grade to the historic spiral tunnels of the Canadian Pacific

Railway (CPR), where a short trail leads to a fine viewpoint. At the bottom of the grade on the right is the turnoff to Yoho Valley. Drive this steep-walled road for 16 km (10 mi) to Takakkaw Falls, one of the highest in North America (Walk 52). If you have any time and energy left, drive west for a short distance past Field and take the Emerald Lake turnoff. You could stroll around the lake (Walk 54) or head to the day lodge for a snack and a chance to admire the stunning blue-green of the lake and the great walls beyond.

Jasper National Park

Columbia Icefield (3 hours):

Stop first at the lavish new Glacier Gallery where interactive displays and videos tell you about the origins of the vast Columbia Icefield and all the lore of a river of ice. Many visitors take the 'Snocoach' tour up onto the glacier itself. If you'd rather head out on your own, take the short stroll through rocky desolation to the glacier toe (Walk 61).

Icefields Parkway—Jasper (half to 1 day):

Sunwapta Falls, 55 km (34 mi) south of Jasper townsite, is an impressive stop and you can stroll down to the lower falls (Walk 63) if you're energetic. Athabasca Falls (Walk 64) is right by the road at the junction of 93 and 93A, also a good spot for a picnic. The most scenic

route north from there is 93A, which leads to the turnoff for Mt. Edith Cavell. Don't miss the awesome walk along an old moraine and through the glacial rubble below rumbling Angel Glacier (Walk 69).

Jasper Townsite Area (1 day):

If the weather's reasonable, a morning trip up the Jasper Tramway to the top of The Whistlers (Walk 70) provides a stunning overview of the Athabasca Valley and a glimpse at the barren alpine tundra. Take a warm jacket. In the afternoon, visit luxurious Jasper Park Lodge and stroll at least partway around elegant Lac Beauvert (Walk 72). Finish with a soak in the Miette Hot Springs, if you have the energy, and don't mind the drive. There are restaurants and an outdoor barbecue at the hot springs.

Maligne Lake (half to 1 day):

Stop first at Maligne Canyon, 11 km (7 mi) from Jasper townsite, a deep gorge with an outstanding interpretive trail above it (Walk 82). Continue up the scenic Maligne Lake Road past disappearing Medicine Lake, where the water drains underground into the river below Maligne Canyon. The road ends at Maligne Lake, largest in the Canadian Rockies. Many visitors take the two-hour boat tours past famous little Spirit Island, much loved by photographers. After a snack at the chalet, consider the

Upper Kananaskis Lake

short lakeside trail (Walk 84), which really gives you a feel for this splendid area.

Kananaskis Country

Day 1: You'll need a vehicle to tour Kananaskis. If the weather's good, start at the top and stroll through the alpine at Ptarmigan Cirque (Walk 89) on Highwood Pass. Bring a picnic lunch and relax along the shores of Upper Kananaskis Lake in the afternoon. A late afternoon stroll by the lake (Walk 92) will cap the day nicely.

Day 2: Once you get past the noise of the Baymag plant, you'll enjoy the soaring rock walls and the ambitious climbers in Grotto Creek (Walk 95). If you can't stand the thought of starting a mountain walk beside a huge processing plant, explore exquisite Grassi Lakes (Walk 96). Finish your day in Canmore, which resembles Banff before it became an international tourist destination. If you have the energy, stroll along the Historic Walking Tour in the evening. See 'Outdoor Adventures' in chapter 5 for information on the brochure you'll need.

Best of the Rockies on a Splurge

Banff National Park

Banff Townsite:

Stay at the Banff Springs Hotel, (403) 762-211, and golf on its world-famous course. For $1500 a night, you can book the Presidential Suite with a canopied king bed, two-storey living room with grand piano, plus a library, indoor lap pool, jacuzzi and sauna. If you get tired of sampling the hotel's restaurants, try Le Beaujolais, (403) 762-2712, on Banff Avenue for traditional French dining or Ristorante Classico, (403) 762-3356, in the Rimrock Resort Hotel for northern Italian food and great views.

Lake Louise:

Stay at the Chateau Lake Louise, (403) 522-3511, and arrange for a private alpine guide through Yamnuska, (403) 678-4164. Dine at the Post Hotel, (403) 522-3989, in the valley.

Yoho National Park

Book a cabin at Lake O'Hara Lodge, (250) 343-6418—years in advance, if possible—and spend your days wandering in an alpine paradise and your evenings fuelling up in the dining room. Landscape painting lessons can be arranged through the lodge. Emerald Lake Lodge is also a luxurious choice, (205) 343-6321.

Jasper National Park

A lakeside cabin at Jasper Park Lodge, (403) 852-3301, will do nicely thank you, with dining in the huge Beauvert Room. Try Becker's, (403) 852-3535, for that intimate dinner. Work it off with golfing and horseback riding at the lodge.

Jasper Park Lodge

Emerald Lake Lodge

Best of the Rockies on a Budget

Banff National Park

Banff:

The well-appointed Banff International Hostel puts you up in rooms with four bunks each or in family rooms, and you can cook your own meals right there. The hiking's all free and you won't break your wallet with dinner at Guido's. Call (403) 762-4122 or direct from Calgary, (403) 237-8282. Half-way between Banff and Lake Louise, stay at one of the smaller cabins at Castle Mountain Village resort, (403) 762-3868, on the Bow Valley Parkway (Hwy. 1A) and cook your own meals. (The resort has one of the best little grocery stores in the mountains.) Another option is the B & B route. See 'Sources.'

Lake Louise:

The new Lake Louise International Hostel, (403) 522-2200, has better facilities than many hotels and the price is right. There's also a licensed cafe, reading room and spacious upper lounge. Stock up on muffins and banana bread down the road at Laggan's, (403) 522-2017.

Yoho National Park

Contact the Yoho information centre, (250) 343-6783, for a list of bed and breakfast accommodations in Field, which has a charming small-town feel and is still unblemished by the glitz of international tourism.

SOURCES

Note that area codes for some Alberta numbers will change January 25, 1999. See page 12.

Travel Information

Province of Alberta
Travel Alberta
P.O. Box 2500
Edmonton, AB T5J 2Z4
(403) 427-4321
1-800-661-8888 (Canada/U.S.)
Fax: (403) 427-0867
web site: www.discoveralberta.com

Toll-free information available on travel conditions, campgrounds, accommodation, ski reports, attractions and special events. Travel Alberta also books trips with some adventure travel companies and bed & breakfast operators, through its Advance Alberta program. Some discount tickets are available for popular visitor sites in Edmonton, Calgary and the Rocky Mountains. An *Alberta Accommodation and Visitors' Guide*, published by the Alberta Hotel Association, is available free from Travel Alberta. This guide can also be viewed on the Internet at www.AlbertaHotels.ab.ca.
(Note that some organizational changes were underway at Travel Alberta as this book went to press.)

Province of British Columbia
Super Natural British Columbia
Box 9830
Stn. Prov. Gov't.
Victoria, BC V8W 9W5
In North America: 1-800-663-6000
Overseas: (250) 387-1642
web site: www.travel.bc.ca

Information and booking service for accommodation and activities throughout British Columbia.

Canadian Parks Service
Canadian Heritage Parks Canada
220 4th Avenue S.E.
Calgary, AB T2P 3H8
1-800-651-7959
(403) 292-4401
Fax: (403) 292-6004
web site: www.tch.gc.ca

Information on western Canada's Rocky Mountain national parks.

Parks Canada National Office
25 Eddy Street
Hull, QC K1A 0M5
(819) 997-0055

Information on all parks within Canada's national park system.

Banff National Park
Banff Information Centre
224 Banff Avenue
Banff, AB T0L 0C0
(403) 762-1550
web site: www.worldweb.com/ParksCanada-Banff

The centre is designed to provide 'one-window' access for all the information you may require about Banff National Park. It provides park information, maps, brochures, permits, passes and backcountry reservations. The Banff/Lake Louise Tourism Bureau also operates a booth in the same building, where you can obtain information about commercial activities, including accommodation, bed & breakfast listings and dining.

Banff/Lake Louise Tourism Bureau
3rd Floor, 317 Banff Avenue
Banff, AB T0L 0C0
(403) 762-0270

Information on commercial activities and accommodation, including bed & breakfast listings and dining. The bureau operates a booth at the Banff Information Centre. See above listing.

Lake Louise Visitor Centre
(by Samson Mall)
Box 213
Lake Louise, AB T0L 1E0
(403) 522-3833

An interpretive centre and also an information centre that provides park information, maps, brochures, permits, passes and backcountry reservations. In July and August, the Banff/Lake Louise Tourism Bureau also operates a booth in the same building.

Jasper National Park
Jasper Information Centre
500 Connaught Drive
Jasper, AB T0E 1E0
(403) 852-6176
web site: www.worldweb.com/ParksCanada-Jasper

The centre is designed as a 'one-window' access point for all the information you may require about Jasper National Park. It provides park information, maps, brochures, permits, passes and backcountry reservations. Jasper Tourism and Commerce also has a booth where you can obtain information about commercial activities. The centre itself was built in 1914 and is a National Historic Site.

Jasper Tourism and Commerce
P.O. Box 98
Jasper, AB T0E 1E0
(403) 852-3858
Fax: (403) 852-4932

Information on commercial activities and accommodation. It operates out of the Jasper Information Centre listed above.

Kootenay National Park
West Gate Information Centre
Radium Hot Springs Pools complex
3 km (2 mi) from Radium
(250) 347-9505
Closed November through April. Call (250) 347-9615 in winter.
web site: www.worldweb.com/ParksCanada-Kootenay

Comprehensive information on the park, including maps and brochures. You can also obtain passes, permits and backcountry reservations.

Radium Hot Springs Chamber of Commerce
Box 225
Radium Hot Springs, BC V0A 1M0
(250) 347-9331
Fax: (250) 347-9127

Information on commercial activities and accommodation in the area.

Yoho National Park
Field Visitor Centre
Field, BC V0A 1G0
(250) 343-6783
web site: www.worldweb.com.ParksCanada-Yoho

Comprehensive information on the park, including maps and brochures.
You can also obtain passes, permits and backcountry reservations.

Golden Chamber of Commerce
Box 677
Golden, BC V0A 1H0
(250) 344-7125

Information on commercial activities and accommodation in the area.

Kananaskis Country
Kananaskis Country
Head Office
Box 280
Canmore, AB T0L 0M0
(403) 678-5508
Weekdays, Calgary Information Office: (403) 297-3362
Barrier Lake Visitor Centre: (403) 673-3985

Comprehensive information on Kananaskis Country, permits and backcountry reservations.

Peter Lougheed Visitor Centre
Box 130
Kananaskis Village
Kananaskis Country, AB T0L 2H0
(403) 591-6344
e-mail: ptrlougv@inv.gov.ab.ca

Comprehensive information on Kananaskis Country, permits and backcountry reservations.

Sources

Canmore/Kananaskis Chamber of Commerce
#12, 801 8th Street
Canmore, AB T1W 2B3
(403) 678-4094
Fax: (403) 678-3455
e-mail: canmore@telusplanet.net

Information on commercial activities and accommodation in the area.

Mt. Assiniboine
Mt. Assiniboine Provincial Park
c/o British Columbia Parks
Box 118
Wasa, BC V0B 2K0
(250) 422-4200

Park information.

Waterton Lakes National Park
Visitor Reception Centre
(north side of main Waterton road, opposite Prince of Wales Hotel)
Waterton Lakes National Park
Waterton Park, AB T0K 2M0
(403) 859-5133

Comprehensive information on the park, as well as permits and back-country reservations.

Waterton Park Chamber of Commerce & Visitors Association
Waterton, AB T0K 2M0
May through October: (403) 859-2203
November through April: (403) 859-2224

Information on commercial activities and accommodation in the area.

Accommodation

The Alberta Hotel Association offers a CD-ROM to help visitors to Alberta make their travel plans. The multimedia package provides, among other things, the opportunity to view accommodation before you make travel plans. The 1997 charge was $39.95 plus $9.91 shipping and handling.

'Hidden Treasures' CD-ROM
c/o Alberta Hotel Association
#401 Centre 104, 5241 Calgary Trail
Edmonton, AB T6H 5G8
(403) 436-6112
Fax: (403) 436-5404
web site: www.AlbertaHotels.ab.ca

Bed & Breakfast Accommodation

The *Alberta Accommodation and Visitors' Guide*, available free from Travel Alberta, lists several bed & breakfast agencies and dozens of bed & breakfast operators under its 'alternate accommodations' listings. If you want to do advance planning through Internet, you may also want to consult CAN*travel*, 'Western Canada's travel directory,' a good source of B & B accommodation. In Banff, the Banff/Lake Louise Tourism Bureau publishes a Bed & Breakfast Directory. See 'Sources' listing under Banff. If you are already in Banff, visit or call the Banff/Lake Louise Tourism Bureau at the Banff Information Centre. In summer, the bureau posts a list of available B & B accommodation at its booth in the centre.

In Jasper, a pamphlet is available listing B & B accommodation in the park. For information or to receive the pamphlet, write to Box 758, Jasper, AB T0E 1E0 or inquire at Jasper Tourism and Commerce, (403) 852-3858. For information on B & B accommodation in Kootenay, Yoho, Waterton and Kananaskis Country, ask at the visitor information centres and/or chambers of commerce.

Hostels

Hostelling International-Alberta and British Columbia operates a chain of hostels in the Canadian Rockies. Open to all; reduced overnight fees available through annual membership. Reservations advised in summer and holiday weekends; essential for groups. Not all hostels are open year-round; inquire.

In recent years, this not-for-profit organization has also teamed up with local resources to offer educational travel packages for groups at reasonable rates. These packages range from wildlife studies to avalanche awareness programs. Customized packages are also available on request. For more information about these programs in Banff and Kananaskis Country, call the Southern Alberta office (403) 283-5551; for Jasper call (403) 852-3215.

Sources

Banff National Park and Area Hostels

For hostel reservations for Banff National Park and area, except Lake Louise International Hostel, book through Banff International Hostel:

P.O. Box 1358
Banff, AB T0L 0C0
(403) 762-4122
Fax: (403) 762-3441
direct from Calgary: (403) 237-8282
e-mail: banff@mail.agt.net

Ribbon Creek Hostel
24 km (15 mi) south of the Trans-Canada Highway along Kananaskis Trail (Hwy. 40). Accommodates 47; family rooms available.

Banff International Hostel
(403) 762-4122
3 km (2 mi) from Banff townsite on Tunnel Mountain Road. New building accommodates 154; family rooms available, cafeteria, cooking and laundry; accessible to the disabled.

Castle Mountain Hostel
On Hwy. 1A, 1.5 km (1 mi) east of junction of Trans-Canada and Hwy. 93; 36 beds. Meals and groceries available.

Hilda Creek Hostel
8.5 km (5.3 mi) south of the Columbia Icefield Centre on the Icefields Parkway (Hwy. 93). Accommodates 21; meals and limited groceries.

Lake Louise International Hostel (Canadian Alpine Centre)
On Village Road in Lake Louise; accommodates 150; family rooms, licensed cafeteria, fireplace, mountaineering resource library. Reserve by calling (403) 522-2200; fax (403) 522-2253; e-mail: llouise@telusplanet.net

Mosquito Creek Hostel
26 km (16 mi) north of Lake Louise on the Icefields Parkway (Hwy. 93). Newly renovated. Accommodates 38; wood-heated sauna available; four cabins.

Rampart Creek Hostel
On the Icefields Parkway (Hwy. 93), 20 km (12.4 mi) north of junction with Hwy. 11. Accommodates 30; wood-heated sauna available.

Whisky Jack Hostel
27 km (17 mi) west of Lake Louise in Yoho National Park; 27 beds.

Jasper National Park Hostels

For hostel reservations for Jasper National Park, book through Jasper International Hostel:

P.O. Box 387
Jasper, AB T0E 1E0
(403) 852-3215
Fax: (403) 852-5560
e-mail: jihostel@telusplant.net

Beauty Creek Hostel
86.5 km (53.6 mi) south of Jasper townsite on Hwy. 93A. Accommodates 24 in two cabins.

Athabasca Falls Hostel
32 km (20 mi) south of Jasper townsite on Hwy. 93A. Accommodates 40.

Mt. Edith Cavell Hostel
13 km (8 mi) off Hwy. 93A along steep Mt. Edith Cavell Road. Accommodates 32.

Maligne Canyon Hostel
15 km (9.3 mi) east of Jasper townsite on Maligne Lake Road. Accommodates 24.

Huts

Alpine Club of Canada
Box 8040
Canmore, AB T1W 2T8
(403) 678-3200
Fax: (403) 678-3224
e-mail: ACC@mail.culturenet.ca
web site: www.culturenet.ca/acc

See backcountry huts, page 330.

Sources

Outdoor Activity Clubs

Alpine Club of Canada

The Alpine Club of Canada offers a wide range of hiking, mountaineering and climbing adventures, from hut-based hiking camps to icefield traverses. See listing on page 393.

The Skyline Hikers of the Canadian Rockies
Cambrian P.O. Box 75055
Calgary, AB T2K 6J8
(403) 282-2752

The Skyline Hikers of the Canadian Rockies is a non-profit group established in 1933 to encourage hiking in the Canadian Rockies. Each year the organization arranges and sponsors five six-day camps in Banff National Park. Each day hikers have their choice of several different hikes.

These camps, which are very reasonably priced, are hugely popular. The best strategy is to become a member and to apply as soon as the new brochures come out early in the new year.

The Trail Riders of the Canadian Rockies
Box 6742, Station D
Calgary, AB T2P 2E6

Elbow Valley Cycle Club
111 Memorial Drive N.W.
Calgary, AB T2N 3E4
(403) 295-1261
Road Schedule Hotline: (403) 283-2453
web site: www.cadvision.com/evcc

Promotes the enjoyment of on- and off-road cycling in the Calgary area. The club organizes several multi-day, van-supported bike trips in the Canadian Rockies each year. These include the Golden Triangle (see page 349) and the Banff-to-Jasper Icefields Parkway route.

Handy Web Sites

Banff park information: www.worldweb.com/ParksCanada-Banff
Kootenay park information: www.worldweb.com/ParksCanada-Kootenay
Yoho park information: www.worldweb.com.ParksCanada-Yoho
Jasper park information: www.worldweb.com/ParksCanada-Jasper
Canmore and Kananaskis information: www.discovercanmore.com
Waterton park information: www.worldweb.com/ParksCanada-Waterton

www.AlbertaHotels.ab.ca—on-line guide to over 700 inspected and approved accommodation, compiled by the Alberta Hotel Association.
www.HostellingIntl.ca/Alberta—information on Alberta hostels.
www.banffcentre.ab.ca—links to programs and facilities at the Banff Centre.
www.cadvision.com/evcc—information on the Elbow Valley Cycle Club's classic Golden Triangle bicycle trip.
www.Canadianrockies.net/kanpark.html—Kananaskis area information
www.cantravel.ab.ca—'Western Canada's travel directory'; on-line reservations for adventure travel and bed & breakfast accommodation.
www.culturenet.ca/acc—information on the Alpine Club of Canada.
www.discoveralberta.com—community events, Alberta attractions, adventure operators, tourism hints and more tourism links.

Magazines

Explore
#420, 301 14 Street N.W.
Calgary, AB T2N 2A1
1-800-567-1372
e-mail: explore@cadvision.com

Explore, Canada's outdoor adventure magazine, doesn't confine itself to the Canadian Rockies, but is one of the best sources around for knowledgeable, non-glitzy information on mountain activities ranging from ice climbing to wildflower identification. If you're not a subscriber, you may want to request a copy of *Explore's* back-issue list to help you at the trip-planning stage.

Suggested Reading

Canadian Rocky Mountain Fiction

Beneath the Faceless Mountain, by Roberta Rees (Red Deer College Press)
Drowning in Darkness, by Peter Oliva (Cormorant Books)
Fracture Patterns, by Gail Helgason (Coteau Books)
Icefields, by Thomas Wharton (NeWest Press)
Tay John, by Howard O'Hagan (McClelland & Stewart)
The Woman Who Got on at Jasper Station and Other Stories, by Howard O'Hagan (Talon Books)

Non-Fiction

Adventures with Wild Animals, by Andy Russell (Douglas & McIntyre)
Alberta-Montana Discovery Guide: Museums, Parks & Historic Sites, by the Alberta-Montana Heritage Partnership
Alpine Huts: A Guide to the Facilities of the Alpine Club of Canada, by Keith Haberl (Alpine Club of Canada)
Avalanche Safety for Skiers & Climbers, by Tony Daffern (Rocky Mountain Books)
Backcountry Biking in the Canadian Rockies, by Don Eastcott (Rocky Mountain Books)
Bear Attacks: Their Causes and Avoidance, by Stephen Herrero (Nick Lyons Books/Winchester Press)
Birds of the Rocky Mountains, by Chris C. Fisher (Lone Pine Publishing)
The Book of Banff, by Robert W. Sandford (Pronghorn Books)
The Canadian Alps, by Robert W. Sandford (Altitude Publishing)
The Canadian Rockies Trail Guide, by Brian Patton & Bart Robinson (Summerthought)
Canmore & Kananaskis Country, by Gillean Daffern (Rocky Mountain Books)
Field Guide to Hoofed Animals in Banff and Jasper National Parks, by Brian Stelfox, Shawn Wasel and Laurie Hunt (Parks for People, Jasper)
Ghost Stories of Alberta, by Barbara Smith (Hounslow Press)
Grizzly Country, by Andy Russell (Douglas & McIntyre)
Handbook of the Canadian Rockies, by Ben Gadd (Corax Press)
A Hiker's Guide to Art of the Canadian Rockies, by Lisa Christensen (Glenbow-Alberta Institute)
Hiking the Rockies with Kids, by Celia McLean (Orca Books)
Horns in the High Country, by Andy Russell (Douglas & McIntyre)
Kananaskis Country Trail Guide, by Gillean Daffern (Rocky Mountain Books)
Landscape and Memory, by Simon Schama (Random House of Canada)
The Magic of Lake O'Hara, by Don Beers (Rocky Mountain Books)
Men for the Mountains, by Sid Marty (McClelland & Stewart)
Plants of the Rocky Mountains, by Linda Kershaw, Andy MacKinnon & Jim Pojar (Lone Pine Publishing)
The Power of Place, by Winefred Gallagher (Poseidon Press)
Rest in the Peaks, by E.J. Hart and Hélène Deziel-Letnick (The Whyte Museum of the Canadian Rockies)
Scrambles in the Canadian Rockies, by Alan Kane (Rocky Mountain Books)
Ski Trails of the Canadian Rockies, by Chic Scott (Rocky Mountain Books)
Tommy and Lawrence, The Ways and Trails of Lake O'Hara, by Jon Whyte (The Lake O'Hara Trails Club)
Trees and Shrubs of Alberta, by Kathleen Wilkinson (Lone Pine Publishing)
The Valley of Rumours…the Kananaskis, by Ruth Oltmann (Ribbon Creek Publishing)
Wonderful Life, by Stephen Jay Gould (Penguin Books)

Index

Alberta area code change, 12
Along the Athabasca River 1, 236
Along the Athabasca River 2, 237
Along the Athabasca River 3, 238
Angel Glacier–Cavell Meadows
   Loop, 226–228
Athabasca Falls, 218–219
Athabasca Glacier, 211–213

Backpacking, 334–339
Bald Hills, 264–265
Banff Springs Hotel, 43, 45, 384
Banff to the Hoodoos, 77–79
Bankhead Historical Loop, 86–87
Bear's Hump, 316
Bears, 58, 246
Bicycling
   mountain biking, 274, 304, 351–356
   rentals, 304, 356–357
   road biking, 150, 167, 274, 304,
      348–351, 394
Big Beehive Loop, 131–132
Black Prince Cirque, 288–289
Boating, 28, 151, 167, 304–305,
   340–341
Boom Lake Trail, 106
Bourgeau Lake, 98–99
Bow Falls Trail, 82–83
Bow Lake Trail, 136–137
Brewster family history, 35
Burgess Shale Beds, 165, 167, 170
Burstall Pass, 299

Camping, 341–344
Canoeing
   river, 151, 344–348
   lake. See boating
Caribou, 265

Cascade Amphitheatre, 92–93
Castle Mountain, 105
Castle Mountain Lookout, 104–105
Cave and Basin Marsh Trail, 60–61
Cavell, Edith, 225
Central Park East, 80
Central Park West, 81
Chateau Lake Louise, 47, 384
Chester Lake, 297–298
Chickadees, 308
Children's programs, 29, 33, 47, 193,
   203, 274, 277, 305, 310, 357–358
Chipmunks, 367
Cliff swallows, 80
Columbia Icefield, 29, 192, 204, 213,
   378, 382
Consolation Lakes, 113
Cory Pass, 94–95
Coyotes, 222
Crandell Campground to Lake
   Crandell, 321
Crypt Lake Trail, 322–323

Day hike gear, 17, 18
Deer
   mule, 326
   white-tailed, 326
Discovery Trail, 62–63
Dolomite Pass, 135

Eagles
   bald, 336
   golden, 336
Eiffel Lake, 114–115
Elk. See wapiti
Emerald Lake Circuit, 177

Fairview Mountain Lookout, 125–126

Fenland Nature Trail, 66–67
Fireweed Trail, 156–157
Fishing, 358–363
Goat Lake, 327–329
Grassi Lakes, 294–296
Grassi, Lawrence, 296
Grotto Canyon, 292–293

Hamilton Lake, 178–179
Hector, James, 187, 219
Horseshoe Lake, 220
Hostels, 26, 51, 273, 385, 392–393
Hot springs, 24, 36, 51, 64, 150, 153,
    199, 204
Huts, backcountry, 330–332, 393

Information/visitor centres, 24, 27, 150,
    166, 192, 199, 273, 304, 387–390

Jasper Park Lodge, 204, 384
Jasper–Pyramid Lake Trail, 247–249
Jays, 321 , ⁊ɪ۹
Johnston Canyon, 100–101

Kain, Conrad, 252

Lac Beauvert Loop, 234–235
Lake Agnes, 129–130
Lake Annette Loop, 239–241
Lake Edith Loop, 242–243
Lake McArthur, 182–183
Lake O'Hara access, 184
Lake O'Hara Circuit, 180–181
Lake Oesa, 185
Lakeshore Trail, 120–122
Larch Valley, 116–117
Little Beehive, 133–134
Lodges, backcountry, 332–334
Lower Bertha Falls, 314–315
Lower Sunwapta Falls, 216–217

Maligne Canyon and Sixth Bridge,
    255–256
Maligne Canyon Loop, 253–254
Maligne Lakeside Loop, 259–261
Many Springs, 290–291
Marble Canyon, 160–161
Marmots, 333
Miette Hot Springs Trail, 266–267
Mistaya Canyon, 141
Moose, 249, 306
Moraine Lake Shoreline, 111–112
Moraine Lake Viewpoint, 110
Mountain goats, 339
Mt. Indefatigable, 284–285
Museums/galleries, 41, 48, 52, 53, 54,
    152, 194, 195, 203, 205, 278, 279,
    308, 309, 310

Native peoples, 70, 163, 296
Nigel Pass, 144–145
1982 Cdn. Mt. Everest Expedition
    Trail, 286

Old Fort Point, 232–233
Opal Hills Loop, 262–263
Overlander Trail, 244–246

Paint Pots, 162–163
Panther Falls and Bridal Veil
    Falls, 142–143
Park fees, 16, 335
Parker Ridge, 146–147
Path of the Angel Glacier
    Trail, 224–225
Patricia Lake Loop, 250–252
Peyto, Bill, 140
Peyto Lake Viewpoint, 138–140
Pikas, 333
Plain of Six Glaciers, 123–124
Prince of Wales Hotel, 311, 312

Ptarmigan, 283
Ptarmigan Cirque, 282–283

Rafting, 153, 276, 372–374
Red Rock Canyon Loop, 324–326
Rock Isle Lake, 96–97
Rowe Lake, 319–320

Saddle Pass, 127–128
Schäffer, Mary, 260–261, 264
Scrambling, 374–376
Sentinel Pass and Paradise
    Valley, 118–119
Silverton Falls, 102–103
Skiing
    cross-country, 169, 276, 363–370
    downhill, 169, 276, 370–372
Spray River Loop, 84–85
Squirrels, 367
Stanley Falls, 214–215
Stanley Glacier, 158–159
Stewart Canyon, 89–90
Stoney Squaw Lookout, 91
Sulphur Mountain Vista Trail, 71–72
Sulphur Summit, 268–269
Summit Lakes, 257–258
Summit Lake–Carthew
    Summit, 317–318
Sundance Canyon, 65

Takakkaw Falls, 172–173
Taylor Lake, 109
Teahouses/tea rooms, 47, 54, 56, 123,
    129, 206, 255, 259, 280, 380
Tramway to Whistlers
    Summit, 229–231
Trees
    larch, 117
    limber pine, 79
Tufa, 267
Tunnel Mountain, 73–74
Tunnel Mountain Drive, 75–76

Upper Bankhead, 88
Upper Kananaskis Lake, 287

Valley of the Five Lakes, 223
Vermilion Lakes, 68–70
Vista Lake, 107–108

Wabasso Lake, 221–222
Wapiti, 31
Wapta Falls, 186–187
Wilcox Pass, 208–210
Wolverines, 371

Yoho Valley and Iceline, 174–176

The Authors

John Dodd and Gail Helgason have hiked, cycled, backpacked, canoed, climbed, cross-country skied and kayaked in the Canadian Rockies for more than 25 years.

Both former outdoors columnists for the *Edmonton Journal*, John and Gail are also the authors of *Bicycle Alberta* and *The Canadian Rockies Bicycling Guide*. They have written about the outdoors for a variety of publications, including *Outside, Nature Canada* and *Bicycling*.

Gail is also the author of *Fracture Patterns* (Coteau Books), a collection of literary short stories about urban dwellers seeking wilderness adventure in the Canadian Rockies.

John Dodd

Fracture Patterns was short-listed for Best First Book Award 1995 by the Writers Guild of Alberta, and short-listed for the City of Edmonton Book Prize 1995.

Gail Helgason

Gail and John are partners in Helgason and Dodd Ltd., a professional writing and editorial consulting firm that provides speechwriting and publication services to a variety of businesses and associations. They live in Edmonton.